Chambers

BOOK OF INDIAN ELECTION FACTS

Kingshuk Chatterjee is a Professor of History at Calcutta University. He has previously served as a Founding Professor in the Department of History, School of Humanities and Social Sciences at Shiv Nadar University and as a Fulbright Scholar-in-Residence at the United States Naval Academy in Annapolis, Maryland.

Surbek Biswas is Special Correspondent at *Ei Samay*, the Bengali daily from the Times of India Group. Previously he has worked for *Anandabazar Patrika* and *Hindustan Times*. He has been covering elections since 1999. Surbek covers crime, terrorism and politics, and he frequently writes political columns in the editorial page. He runs a food blog in the digital wing of *Ei Samay*.

Chambers

BOOK OF INDIAN ELECTION FACTS

KINGSHUK CHATTERJEE

SURBEK BISWAS

First published in 2024 by Hachette India
(Registered name: Hachette Book Publishing India Pvt. Ltd)
An Hachette UK company
www.hachetteindia.com

1

Old place names (such as Madras, Calcutta and Bombay) may have been used to retain the historicity of the information as well as avoid confusion with earlier presidencies and provinces of the same name.

All efforts have been made to verify the copyright ownership of photographs as well as the correctness of the information included in this edition. Any omissions are unintentional and regretted, and, following written communication, will be rectified in the next edition.

The views and opinions expressed in this book are the authors' own and the facts are as reported by them and have been verified to the extent possible. The publishers are not in any way liable for the same.

All Wikimedia Commons photographs and those from similar sources have been accessed between 1 February and 1 March 2024 and their copyright status at the time. Any later additional notifications relating to such photographs or changes made in the copyright status of such photographs after this date cannot be considered legally valid or applicable for this book in all versions, and are not legally binding.

All information has been updated till 15 March 2024 unless stated otherwise.

Subsequent edition/reprint specifications may be subject to change, including but not limited to cover or inside finishes, paper, text colour, and/or colour sections.

ISBN 978-93-5731-838-9

Hachette Book Publishing India Pvt. Ltd
4th & 5th Floors, Corporate Centre
Plot No. 94, Sector 44, Gurugram – 122003, India

Typeset by Manmohan Kumar, Delhi

Printed and bound in India
by Thomson Press India Ltd.

CONTENTS

PREFACE

India is widely recognized to be one of the rare success stories of the representative form of government in the developing world. Indeed, the political journey of the representative form of government of India has not always been very smooth, and puritans highlight many features of the Indian polity that was patently at variance with the liberal democratic archetype that is often peddled as the benchmark. However, the Indian polity was quick to adapt to the key benchmark of the representative form of government – the idea of popular sovereignty operating through the institution of a government chosen by and accountable to the people. Despite the twists and turns in the annals of Indian politics and periodic tendencies of fraying of the principle of accountability, that the Indian polity resoundingly manages to qualify as a democracy is largely because of the unwavering regularity with which elections have been held in India, except for a brief period during the Emergency.

Chambers Book of Indian Election Facts is essentially an attempt to document this achievement of the Indian people. The book is slightly different from most other books that are there in the market, in the sense that while there are hundreds of books on Indian politics, there are very few that specifically focus on elections in India within the larger template of a fact-book. It purports to be a collection of all sorts of facts pertaining to elections in India, the world's largest democracy – right from the embryonic beginning in the second half of the nineteenth century, flowering into the most stable democratic system in the decolonized world, to present-day India which comprises the largest electorate constituting a representative government.

While the book purports to be a collection of *all sorts* of facts, it does not even come close to being a collection of *all* facts about elections in India. For every fact that you will find between these two covers, there would remain numerous others that could easily have made it here. When the authors set out with this book, they made a conscious decision to confine themselves only to direct elections – such as the elections for the Lok Sabha and the Vidhan Sabha i.e., the lower houses respectively of the Indian Parliament and the state legislatures (in most cases the only house of the state legislature) – where the people of territorial constituencies directly elect their representatives on the basis of first-past-the-(winning)-post. This book thus leaves out the highly complicated mode of elections associated with the selection of the president and the vice president – a system no less fascinating than that of the first-past-the-post. The book also leaves out the election of members to the Rajya Sabha and the many provincial assemblies or the Legislative Councils (in the many provinces where they exist), because they are organized on the principle of indirect representation, viz. proportional representation through single transferable vote.

Even in terms of direct elections, this book does not even come close to being a compilation of facts about *all sorts* of direct elections in India. Thus, while fully mindful of the tremendous significance of the municipal, village and district level elections dating back to the colonial times right down to the Panchayati Raj closer to our times, the authors had to take a conscious decision to stay away from representative politics at the level of the *locality* because such a compilation involving the whole country of India would not be possible in a single book, it would have required a multi-volume encyclopaedia.

The authors decided to confine themselves, therefore, to direct elections only at the level of the province/state and the nation/union, leaving the domain of representative politics in the locality for another volume, another time.

Having decided early on what this book would *not* have was only a part of the task. Next they had to decide on how to classify the facts that would be compiled between the two covers. Would it be all data and statistics (who won? by how many votes? defeating whom) at the constituency level – opening up the frightful prospect of yet another type of encyclopaedic compilation? Or would it be a collection of simply the data set of the various general and assembly elections arranged in terms of the party-political character i.e., which party won the election? which was the main party of the Opposition? who were the various leaders of the political parties? and so on. But then such a dry compilation of statistics would not be able to bring out the flavour that makes the study of politics such a fascinating subject. Also, if the innumerable anecdotes that circulate freely in this highly politicized country was completely left out, how could dry facts and statistical data capture the highly colourful world of Indian politics?

Accordingly, the authors decided to follow a simple template of sequential treatment of Indian politics using direct elections as the register of our study in this book, in the order they were held in the various component parts of India. The book thus begins with a very brief treatment of the flirtation with representative politics that started under colonial rule and helped Indian politics navigate its transition from the colonial to the post-colonial era. The book then divides into three parts – the period of almost hegemonic domination of the Indian political landscape by the Congress party (roughly 1952–77);

the period of political fragmentation (1977–99) when the Congress became incrementally weaker without any single party being able to replace it at the union level; and finally the age of ascendancy of the BJP (roughly 1999 onwards), when the BJP acquired the hegemonic status previously characterizing the Congress.

Most studies of Indian politics (and of politics in general) are characterized by a basic tension in terms of what constitutes the motive force. Do some certain towering personalities singlehandedly direct the course of things, and leave their stamp on the face of time (the 'great man' view of history)? Or do individuals account not for much, and are little more than playthings in the hands of the social forces and movements that shape the form, content and direction of politics? Most accounts of Indian politics since 1947 tend to fall into one or the other of these two categories. The authors of this book consciously decided to not fall for this binary and adopt features of both these strategies into a conjuncturalist kind of approach (kind of 'cometh the hour, cometh the man'), where the individuals are given their due significance, but only upon being situated in the larger landscape of politics within which they operate.

Accordingly, within each of the three parts, we begin with a treatment of the various general elections, the party-wise break-up of the Lok Sabha from one general election to the next, (both in terms of seats won and votes received), as also state-wise break-up of the performance of each political party. The next few chapters have then gone on to study the performance of the political parties (again in terms of seats and vote share) at each of the state assemblies for which elections were held, highlighting in particular the performance of the regional parties and the manner in which they have engaged with the power at the federal centre. The last chapter of each of the three parts deals with some of the more colourful events and protagonists who populated the preceding chapters – the authors call these 'Beyond the Ballot' because these chapters cast greater light on the larger world of Indian elections beyond the realm of the ballot itself.

Being a fact-book, the authors have consciously tried to keep analysis at a minimum – partly because there are literally hundreds of books where detailed analyses could be found. However, while plotting the electoral journey of how the Congress began with a nation-wide presence and then began to progressively shrink and even wither in different parts of India (yet never get wiped out totally except in certain pockets), then plodding through the era of political fragmentation and then coming to the story of the BJP's ascendancy, it is important to highlight the dynamics that influenced such developments. This is largely owing to the fact that if you take a closer look at the election results, it becomes clear that neither the Congress nor the BJP (so far) has really dominated *all* the states at even one time, let alone all the times. All the component states/ regions of India do not pulsate in tandem – there are regions in the country that Congress never really controlled even at the height of its power (and the same holds for the BJP), there are other regions where a large chunk of the votes invariably went to the Congress, no matter what (and the same for the BJP and its ideological antecedents like the Jan Sangh, the Ram Rajya Parishad and the Hindu Mahasabha). There are other regions where smaller national (such as the Janata family, the Communists and their fellow-travellers) and regional parties have always mounted strong challenge to both these hegemonic organisations. In other words, India truly lives in its regions, and no amount of electoral data would make sense unless the regional dynamics are also studied to make sense of why the ballot was cast in the manner in which it was. Hence, the authors have tried to introduce a degree of analysis at a subcutaneous level, in a bid to contextualize developments in the component regions of the country – the manner of its entry into the Indian union, the context in which it obtained the shape and structure it did and some of the more significant issues that shaped such regional dynamics.

If the readers get even a little bit of the fun we had in putting the book together, we would think of our endeavour as having been worth its while.

Chapter 1

ELECTIONS IN INDIA

The Backstory – Elections under the Raj

Elections in India date back to the second half of the nineteenth century, by way of a ripple effect from being under British rule. In the nineteenth century, as the social and economic landscape of Britain was transformed by the rise of a more urban and industrialized society, British politics undertook 2 major reforms of its system of political representation – the Great Reforms of 1832 and the Reform Act of 1867 – which broadened the electorate to include not only those paying certain direct and/or municipal taxes, but also virtually all adult male population paying any kind of direct and/or municipal taxes at all. Influential people in India, living under the rule first of the East India Company and then of the British crown, were intrigued by this mechanism of choosing a country's rulers, and were intrigued and inspired by the notion of the politics of representation.

By the middle of the nineteenth century, a segment of the educated Indian middle class began setting up political associations – the Bengal British Indian Society, Madras Native Association, Bombay Presidency Association, among others – that aspired to a kind of representative politics after the passage of the Indian Councils Act of 1861. Asserting that the needs and expectations of the Indian subjects should inform the British government of India's policy, these proto-political associations of Indians began to seek introduction of the representative principle. They vied to choose the membership of the councils set up to advice the viceroy of India and the provincial governors on legislation for the administration. This demand gained greater focus after the reforms of 1867 in Britain, when a very large section of the population in Britain was given the right to vote. A kind of restricted franchise was introduced in British India with the creation of some municipalities with elected functionaries (such as commissioners) as early as 1872, even though very often locally influential people successfully undermined that representative function. In the 1880s, 48 of Calcutta (now Kolkata) municipality's commissioners were elected by a very small number of voters; in Madras (now Chennai), of the 9 municipalities that had

The idea of Home Rule as a way of constitutional devolution comes from Ireland. The island of Ireland used to have its own parliament before it was abolished in 1801, when Ireland was brought under the direct rule of Westminster with elected representatives in the British parliament. By the second half of the nineteenth century, the principal demand of the Irish people revolved around revival of the parliament at Dublin, and responsible government by delegates in 'Home', i.e. Ireland. This came to be known as the Home Rule Movement. It became successful in 1911, when the House of Commons first passed the Home Rule Bill, which became law in 1914 despite resistance from the House of Lords. With the Irish precedent before them, Indian politicians began to talk of similar devolution on the basis of the principle of representative government. This took shape through the Home Rule movement, or the Home Rule Leagues, led by Annie Besant (Madras), Bal Gangadhar Tilak (Bombay) and Muhammad Ali Jinnah (Bombay).

been given the right to elect their members, only 4 actually bothered to exercise it. Bombay (now Mumbai) municipality alone seemed to have taken the early introduction of the elective principle seriously and seemed to have bred similar aspirations among their counterparts in Poona (now Pune) and Ahmedabad.

Introduction of the elective principle as clear official policy began with Lord Ripon's Resolution on Local Self-Government (18 May 1882), which proclaimed that municipal and local rural boards (village boards, union boards - anticipating what would be later known as the Panchayati Raj) should be established wherever possible, with a large preponderance of elected non-official members. Rural boards were gradually to be given control of all local rates and taxes and were eventually to be allowed to initiate and direct the construction of local works. Although this policy ran into rough weather both in London and among colonial officials in India and was effectively stone-walled, changes crept in incrementally. By 1888, with the Bombay Municipal Corporation Act, the idea of elected municipal councilors finally came into life in Bombay.

Encouraged by this major change in the policy of British government of India, the Indian National Congress (INC) began to ask for the introduction of the elective principle for choosing Indian members of the provincial and central legislative councils as well. After nearly 2 decades of the INC agitation, the elective principle was introduced in the constitution of the provincial and central legislative councils under the Indian Councils Act (aka Morley–Minto Act) of 1909. While the introduction of the elective principle galvanised Indian politics at the municipal level, resistance from within the Government of India ensured that elections were held neither at the level of the provincial nor central legislative councils before the First World War broke out.

By the time the Great War ended, the British empire was severely weakened and impaired, and the Raj decided upon some devolution of power in India under the Government of India Act of 1919 (also known as the Montagu-Chelmsford Act), albeit not the Home Rule that Indian politicians were demanding. Indian politicians were now to be elected to the provincial and central legislative assemblies on a restricted franchise. Some members of the provincial government were to be drawn from among the elected members of provincial legislative assembly.

The first elections under the provisions of the Government of India Act were held in 1920, which were boycotted by the largest Indian political party at that date, the Indian National Congress. In the central legislative assembly, there were 104 elected seats, of which 34 were reserved for European members (representing the various chambers of commerce) and 66 were open to Indians to contest. All the provincial assemblies together had 440 out of 637 seats up for election, with 38 seats reserved for Europeans; 188 of the seats designated for Indians had only 1 candidate contesting and thus were elected unopposed.

The 4 elections that followed under the Government of India Act of 1919 were held in 1923, 1926, 1930 and 1934. The Indian National Congress (represented by the Swarajya Party in 1923) constituted the largest bloc of Indian members in all elections (except 1930, which the party had boycotted) – winning 38 seats in 1923 and 1926 (under Motilal Nehru) and 42 seats in 1934 (under Bhulabhai Desai). A splinter group from the INC, the Nationalist Party (later known as the Congress Nationalist Party led by Madan Mohan Malviya) won 22 seats in 1926, 40 in 1930 and 12 seats in 1934, thus becoming a steady second. At this stage, the elected Muslim members were mostly listed under independents, with the League being nowhere in the picture.

The next round of devolution of powers took place under the Government of India Act of 1935, which expanded the number of people with the vote to about 30 million, the responsibilities of Indian politicians elected under the expanded franchise. While the provisions pertaining to the central government never came into effect except partially before 1945, the complete devolution of powers at the provincial level in the hands of elected Indian politicians constituted the first major experience of fully responsible representative government in Indian history. Only 2 elections were held under the provisions of the Government of India Act (1935) - these were held in 1937 and 1945.

In the 1937 elections to the various provincial assemblies, the Indian National Congress won in 7 states - Bihar (98 of 152 seats), Bombay (86 of 175), Central Provinces (70 of 112), Madras (159 of 215), North-West Frontier Province (NWFP) (19 of 50, rest being independents), Orissa (36 of 60) and United Provinces (133 of 228). Additionally, the INC was the single largest party in Assam (33 of 108 seats) and Bengal (54 of 250 seats). Of the total of 1,585 seats all over British India, the INC won 711 seats - easily the largest political entity, but not one that was able to win even half of all the seats that were contested. Its principal political adversary, the Muslim League, was not much successful. Of the total 468 seats designated for Muslims, the League could take only 116 (less than 1 in 4), while the INC managed to have less than 30 of its Muslim members elected. The only province it came to power in was Bengal, forming a coalition with the Krishak Praja Party (36 seats) in its capacity as a senior partner (43 seats). It could win only 2 seats in Punjab, and drew blanks in Sind, NWFP and Bihar.

This picture changed a lot in 1945–46. In the 1945 elections to the central legislative assembly, the INC won 57 of the 102 seats, while the Muslim League won 37 and the Akalis 2 seats. But more importantly, the provincial assembly elections of 1946 showed a crystallisation of the political polarisation between the INC and the League. Of the 1,585 seats that were contested for all the 11 provinces, the INC won 923 seats and the League won 425. In 8 of the provinces, the INC was in a position to form the government - Assam (58 of 108), Bihar (98 of 152), Bombay (125 of 175), Central Provinces (92 of 112),

Madras (163 of 215), NWFP (30 of 50), Orissa (47 of 60) and United Provinces (153 of 228). In the remaining 3 provinces, the Muslim League was able to form governments on its own – Bengal (113 of 250, with 12 seats taken by others and 14 independents, while the INC finished at 86), Punjab (73 seats of 175, with the Unionist party 20, Akalis 22 and the INC 51) and Sind (28 of 60, 4 independents and the INC at 18).

It was in this background of the electoral landscape of the subcontinent, 2 of the 3 provinces won by the Muslim League were constituted into Pakistan along with 1 province that had voted for the INC and another that had never voted (Balochistan). Of the provinces that voted the INC to power, only NWFP was made over to Pakistan. The remaining 10 provinces constituted the landmass that came to be the core of the Republic of India.

> The first election in independent India took place from 25 October 1951 to 21 February 1952.

Elections in Independent India

From the time India became a republic in 1950, its political life has rested on universal adult franchise. Initially, this meant anyone above the age of 21 was entitled to cast their vote in the Lok Sabha, Vidhan Sabha and local body elections. In 1988, the Sixty-first Amendment to the Constitution reduced the voting age to 18 years.

Lok Sabha and Vidhan Sabha: Franchise and Constituencies

The country is divided into a number of Lok Sabha and Vidhan Sabha constituencies. This was arrived at by dividing the total population of the various provinces of the country into electoral constituencies of roughly equal demographic value. Constituencies tend to have roughly the same number of people, even though the territory covered could be very small in densely populated regions and very big in sparsely populated regions.

THIS IS THE REASON WHY MORE POPULOUS PROVINCES SUCH AS UTTAR PRADESH (TERRITORIALLY FOURTH LARGEST STATE) AND BIHAR (TWELFTH LARGEST) HAVE MUCH GREATER NUMBER OF ELECTORAL CONSTITUENCIES THAN LESS POPULOUS ONES, SUCH AS RAJASTHAN (LARGEST STATE) AND MADHYA PRADESH (SECOND LARGEST).

Delimitation and Delimitation Commission

The requirement of roughly equal demographic value of each constituency has made periodic exercises of 'delimitation' and readjustment of constituencies, in the light of periodic changes in the population as reflected in the census. Given the dramatic rise in Indian population in over 7 decades since independence, the corresponding increase in size of the electorate has periodically been followed by increase in the number of constituencies – from 489 (1952) through 494 (1957 and 1962), 522 (1967), 542 (1977) to 543 (1987). Similarly, through periodic changes, the total number of Vidhan Sabha constituencies have increased from 3,280 (1952) through 4,061 (1988) to the present strength of 4,123 (2022).

The task of delimitation is meant to be the preserve of delimitation/boundary commissions, set up by the Government of India under Delimitation Acts passed by the Houses of Parliament. These commissions are generally headed by retired judges of the Supreme Court, and they work with the mandate of redrawing the boundaries, and if required, of increasing the size of constituencies for both the state legislative assemblies and the Lok Sabha in the light of the most recent census report available. Upon completion of their task, the commission submits its report before Parliament for discussion (but not modification) before it is presented to the president. The government can delay implementation of the commission's recommendation, but it cannot do so selectively.

Four such Delimitation Commissions have been constituted so far. The first Delimitation Commission was set up in 1952, headed by N. Chandrasekhar Aiyyar (ex-Supreme Court judge), which submitted its report in 1953 based on the Census of 1951. On the basis of its report, the number of Lok Sabha constituencies was settled at 494, which came into force by 1957.

The second Delimitation Commission was set up in 1963, to redraw and delimit assembly and parliamentary constituencies on the basis of the Census of 1961. This was the first delimitation exercise after the States Reorganization Act that divided the Indian territory into linguistically homogenous provinces. As per the recommendations of this commission, the number of Lok Sabha constituencies was revised upwards to 522, and the number of assembly constituencies was at 3,771.

The third Delimitation Commission was in 1973, based on the Census of 1971. Headed by retired justice K.L. Kapur, the commission increased the number of Lok Sabha constituencies from 522 to 542 (later increased by 1 to 543 with the induction of Sikkim), and the number of assembly constituencies from 3,771 to 3,997 – this of course included the 32 seats that were added for the legislative assembly of Sikkim.

After the third Delimitation Commission, the Forty-second Amendment Act to the Constitution froze assembly and parliamentary seats in each state till after the next delimitation exercise, which it was ordained could not be held before 2001. This was to not let delimitation become a reward for failure in birth control for states with a burgeoning population while others get punished for successfully slowing down population growth.

The fourth Delimitation Commission was appointed, thus, in 2002 under the retired justice Kuldip Singh, to accommodate the findings of the Census of 2001. The commission interestingly left the Lok Sabha landscape undisturbed, but it increased the number of assembly constituencies from 3,997 to 4,123.

In accordance with the Eighty-fourth Amendment to the Indian Constitution (yet again to not end up rewarding failure in birth control), the next Delimitation Commission could be held only after the first census that is held after the year 2026.

The Election Commission of India

Elections in India are organized and supervised by the Election Commission of India (ECI), set up by the Representation of the People Act 1950. Till 1994, the Election Commission used to be presided over by the chief election commissioner (CEC), the first one having been Sukumar Sen, ICS. He presided over the first 2 general elections (1951–52 and 1957). The CEC used to enjoy a broad range of powers in deciding the timing and manner in which elections were to be held in the country. In 1989, for the first time prime minister Rajiv Gandhi created 2 more election commissioners, but both of them were sacked by his successor V.P. Singh in 1990, who restored the CEC as the sole head of the ECI. The tenure of T.N. Seshan (December 1990–1996) as the CEC brought the full potential of the office into light, virtually for the first time. Seshan caused much consternation among the political class because of a number of reforms that were associated with him (including the election photo identity card, or EPIC), purportedly to reduce fraudulent and illegitimate electoral practices that had become almost routine by then. This made the government of P.V. Narsimha Rao to revive the office of the 2 ECs in December 1991. This was formalized in 1993, through the Election Commission (Conditions of Service of Election Commissioner and Transaction of Business) Act, creating 2 more election commissioners in addition to the CEC with co-equal powers and making all decisions subject to majority opinion among the 3 ECs. This was initially disputed by CEC Seshan, who managed to win a Supreme Court verdict in his favour. It was finally overturned by a five-member bench of the Supreme Court upholding the validity of the 1993 Act.

First CEC: Sukumar Sen

About two and a half years after India got independence in August 1947, the election commission was set up on 25 January 1950. On 21 March 1950, Sukumar Sen was appointed the first chief election commissioner (CEC). Assigned with the Herculean task of conducting the first general election in independent India, Sen turned out to be 'an unsung hero of Indian democracy'.

Born in 1898, Sukumar Sen went to Presidency College, Calcutta, and then the London University (where he was awarded a gold medal in mathematics) for his higher education. He joined the Indian Civil Service (ICS) in 1921 and served in various districts. After independence, Sen was serving as chief secretary of West Bengal, from where he was sent on deputation as the first CEC of India.

According to the provisions for election in the Constitution, any Indian citizen 21 years or above of age residing in a particular constituency for more than 180 days was considered eligible to vote from that constituency. Per Census 1951, India's population (excluding Jammu and Kashmir) stood at 356.6 million. The total number of registered voters, as per the electoral roll, was 179 million. Of this, women voters constituted nearly 45% of the electorate.

Sukumar Sen

About 85% of the total voters could not read or write. Each voter had to be identified, named and registered.

Given the range and scale of the task ahead of him, Sen had to start virtually from zero.

Shyam Saran Negi, a schoolteacher in Kalpa of Himachal Pradesh, was declared by the Election Commission in 2012 to have been the first to cast his vote in the first general elections of independent India.

Many women, especially in northern India, wished to register themselves as 'the mother of someone' or 'the wife of someone'. This was a social problem, wherein women were not used to being called by their own names. Sukumar Sen was firm in rejecting voter registration without a definite name. As a result, 2.8 million women out of 80 million potential women voters could not make it to the electoral rolls.

Allotment of symbols of the contesting parties were drawn from daily life so that these were easily recognizable - a pair of bullocks, a hut, an elephant, an earthenware lamp, and so on. Multiple ballot boxes were used lest the (mostly illiterate) Indian elector (often voting for the first time) cast their vote wrongly. Each party, thus, had a ballot box with its symbol marked in each polling station, so that voters could simply drop their paper in it.

CEC Sukumar Sen visited every state to check its preparedness before the elections. He attended at least polling rehearsals in most states. Sukumar Sen also conducted India's second general elections in 1957. Given his

FIRST USE OF INDELIBLE INK

Indelible ink is generally believed to have been used for the first time in the third Lok Sabha elections in 1962. Mysore Paints and Varnish Ltd, based in Mysore (now Mysuru), Karnataka, was authorized to manufacture the ink. The company continues to supply this ink to this date. However, there are sources that mention similar use of ink in 1952 as well.

exemplary conduct as the CEC and the success of the 1952 elections, Sen was given the responsibility of holding the first election in Sudan in 1953. There he created a template which was followed by the Sudanese Election Commission when it was set up in 1957. Sen passed away on 13 May 1963.

Electronic Voting Machines

Among the many changes introduced by the ECI in the 1990s, probably the most important has been the introduction of the electronic voting machines (EVM). When elections began in independent India, it was done with ballot papers, detailing the names of the candidates, their parties and their electoral symbols (for the benefit of those among the electorate who could not read). Over the years, electoral malpractices – such as, party-workers denying access to genuine voters and stuffing ballot-papers into the ballot-boxes – were indulged in by virtually all major parties to such an extent that electoral irregularities had become a regular feature of Indian elections.

In a bid to stop such malpractices, the ECI came up with the idea of introducing EVMs. A pilot-run of indigenously manufactured battery-operated EVMs were carried out in 1982 at some polling stations of the Parur assembly constituency in Kerala. Pilot-run being satisfactory, the machines were used in 10 other contests. However, when the Parur contest was challenged by the losing side in the courts, the Supreme Court annulled the elections on account of the use of EVMs, saying the Representation of Peoples' Act 1951 clearly laid out that votes were to be cast by ballots, not voting machines.

Persisting with its recommendation for EVMs, the ECI recommended an amendment to the said law, which came through in 1989 – even though a general consensus about their use came about nearly a decade later in 1998. A pilot-run was this time carried out in 25 assembly constituencies in Delhi,

Madhya Pradesh and Rajasthan in 1998. The first assembly elections to have EVMs operationalized in all constituencies were held in 2001 in Kerala, Pondicherry (now Puducherry), Tamil Nadu and West Bengal. The first general elections to see EVMs deployed (more than a million) in all 543 Lok Sabha constituencies was that of 2004. Machines with voter-verified paper audit trail (VVPAT, where the voter gets to see if his vote has been properly recorded or not) were introduced first in 2014. By virtue of a Supreme Court judgement of 2019, the Election Commission has to randomly check at least 5 VVPAT machines in every assembly constituency.

Independents – a Quick Look

An independent candidate is one who contests polls without being affiliated to any political party. In normal circumstances, independents have roles of little significance to play except for being in contention. However, in the event a party falls short of majority, independents play a crucial role in government formation – viz. state governments in Kerala and Meghalaya have repeatedly been made as much as broken by independents either joining or leaving a political combination. In such cases, independents often support policies that are similar with those of major political parties. Also, in many cases, like-minded politicians in pursuit of a common agenda have run for election first as independents, and only upon being elected have gone on to successfully register as regional parties and have even come to power at the regional level – good examples of this were the Dravida Munnetra Kazhagam (DMK) and the Asom Gana Parishad (AGP). Even in the Lok Sabha, owing to delay in registration of political parties, candidates affiliated with a platform or an agenda may run as independents – viz. Vishwanath Pratap Singh won the Allahabad bypoll of 1988, representing the entire political opposition to the Congress, running as an independent candidate.

The number of independent candidates vying for a seat has been on a steep rise since the first general elections of 1951–52, but the number of winners has been dwindling. In the 17 parliamentary elections that have taken place in India, the second general elections in 1957 marked the best performance of independent candidates. In that parliamentary poll, total 42 independent candidates had gone to the Lok Sabha.

In terms of both the number of seats won by the independent candidates and the vote share they grabbed, they were in second position, as the Indian National Congress once again attained a thumping majority. The independent candidates, in total, bagged 23,284,249 votes and they got the vote share of 19.32%. If we consider the performance of political parties, then regarding the number of seats, the Communist Party of India (CPI) got second position (27) and concerning the vote share, the Praja Socialist Party (PSP) became number two. Therefore, independents surpassed both the CPI and PSP regarding the number of seats and the vote share respectively.

> India is a multi-party democracy, where the principal exercise of elections is configured along the lines of political parties. However, in each and every election – parliamentary or assembly – a large number of independent candidates have always been among the contenders, clearly revealing the fragmented nature of the electoral landscape. The more polarized an electorate gets along agenda or ideological lines, fewer the possibilities of independents getting past the winning post.

The second-best performance of the independent candidates was seen in the first general election in 1952, when they won 37 seats, followed by 35 in 1967. Besides these, independents won 20 seats in 1962, 14 seats in 1971 and 12 seats in 1989 parliamentary polls. In the remaining general elections that took place till 2019, independents were not able to cross into double digits.

The Law Commission of India in March 2015 submitted its Report No. 255 on 'Electoral Reforms', where it sparked a debate by recommending that independent candidates should be disqualified from contesting elections as 'they are either not serious or contest elections just to confuse the voters' - a curious observation by a government body. However, no final decision on this issue has been taken yet.

Funding Elections in India

Election funding has remained a thorny question in India right from the very beginning, and especially the manner in which incumbent political parties are supposed to have taken advantage of their incumbency in harnessing resources to meet the cost of fighting elections. In India, before 1947, proximity of M.K. Gandhi and many of the top leadership of the Indian National Congress with capitalists like the house of Birla had always excited comment, but such connections have seldom been conclusively attributed to funds required for contesting elections. Right from the first elections in 1952, accordingly, there has not been a single government in power - either at the Centre or in the states - that has not been charged with corruption and financial impropriety ('money power') in the manner in which elections have been fought.

Such persistent narrative about financial impropriety has periodically occasioned attempts at 'cleaning up' the system. In the Representation of People's Act (1951) itself, limits were placed on expenditure that could be incurred in contesting an election - the ceiling being periodically revised in the light of movement of prices. In course of the 1960s and '70s, the infiltration of the political system by people with 'black money' exercising undue influence on governments had been flagged by the Santhanam Committee on the Prevention of Corruption

(1964) and Wanchoo Direct Taxes Enquiry Committee (1971). Prime Minister Mrs Gandhi had even outlawed corporate donations to political parties in a bid to 'cleanse the system'– her critics argued this was more to reduce the financial wherewithal of the Opposition parties (especially the Swatantra Party). Corporate funding of political parties was allowed once again by the Companies Act of 1985, but not before political parties were exempted from paying income and wealth taxes subject to regular filing of tax returns (1979). These were coupled with a number of amendments of the Representation of People Act in course of the 1990s, including allowing free air-time on nationalized TV and Radio for recognized national and regional parties, and also ensuring that privately owned media houses remained balanced in their treatments of political parties. The Election and Other Related Laws (Amendment) Act of 1999, passed by the Vajpayee government, made financial contributions to political parties 100% tax deductible. The same government also made declaration of assets mandatory in 2003, in the light of the recommendations of the ECI.

Among the more notable of efforts to streamline funding of political parties and elections in India was the Finance Bill, 2017 that introduced anonymous electoral bonds that could be purchased by any citizen or corporate organisation in the country in order to contribute to a designated political party (national or regional) in denominations ranging from one thousand to one crore rupees. This was touted by the government of the day as a major step in cleaning the system of financial impropriety. However, in 2024, a five-judge bench of the Supreme Court has come down on this practice as unconstitutional, and questions are being raised on the modus operandi of the system of electoral bonds. Clearly, cleaning the process of electoral funding would seem to require a lot more sincere efforts than have been the case in the past.

BOOK I

THE AGE OF CONGRESS DOMINANCE 1952–77

Chapter 2

FROM HOPE TO HUBRIS: CONGRESS DOMINANCE IN THE LOK SABHA 1952–77

Since independence, India has had 17 general elections (i.e. nationwide elections), each electing members of the Lok Sabha – with 1952 being the first and 2019 being the seventeenth – whose tenure is meant to last for a period of not exceeding 5 years, or as long as a government could be formed that enjoyed the confidence of the House, whichever is less. In other words, if a government can be formed that enjoys the confidence of the majority members of the Lok Sabha, it can work only as long as it enjoys the confidence on the floor of the House. However, even if it enjoys the confidence of the House, it cannot be in power for period longer than 5 years.

Of the 17 such Lok Sabhas so far, 6 Lok Sabhas have had their terms truncated, of which 2 were dissolved a year (in 1971 and 1984) before their time in anticipation of better electoral prospects of the incumbent party (viz. Indian National Congress, or INC, hereafter to be used interchangeably with Congress); the remaining 11 have lasted the full term. This means that for well over 58 years India has enjoyed considerable political stability – a far better record on the democratic path than in any other country in the Indian subcontinent, or indeed in most of the decolonized world.

Among the Lok Sabha terms that were much shorter than usual, the first was the sixth Lok Sabha, formed after the 1977 general election. It failed to throw up a stable government and lasted about 3 years (1977–80). The second of the truncated Lok Sabha terms was the ninth Lok Sabha (1989–91), resulting from the 1989 general election. The next Lok Sabha with a truncated term was the eleventh one (1996–1998). The briefest Lok Sabha yet was the thirteen-month long twelfth Lok Sabha (1998–1999), which was coterminous with the thirteen-month long government of Atal Bihari Vajpayee.

The longest time between 2 general elections was of over 6 years, between 1971 and 1977, with a caesura caused by the imposition of the Emergency (1975–77). The caesura was caused by the political turmoil that began when the Allahabad High Court set aside the election victory of Prime Minister Indira Gandhi in the contest for the Raebareli seat in 1971, upon the charge of illegal use of the machinery of the government for her own political advantage. In the wake of a nationwide agitation led by Jayaprakash Narayan demanding her immediate removal, instead of stepping aside in favour of some pro-tem prime minister pending the ruling of the Supreme Court on her appeal, Indira Gandhi invoked provisions of National Emergency (Article 352) of the Indian Constitution, forcing the animated suspension of the fifth Lok Sabha without dissolving it altogether.

A stamp commemorating Jayaprakash Narayan

The end of the Emergency effectively marked the end of Congress's virtually unchallenged dominance of the Indian political landscape. The INC has not since enjoyed that kind of political and electoral dominance and looks unlikely to do so ever again. In the

2 decades that followed – despite pulling off 3 electoral victories in 1980, 1984 and 1991 – the electoral dominance of the party has been circumscribed by its progressive weakening all across north India, and periodic dips in the fortunes of the party in some parts of the country, and almost terminal decline in some other parts (West Bengal, Tamil Nadu, Uttar Pradesh etc.). So much so, that by the time of the general election of 1991 it was being confidently predicted that India had ushered in an era of coalition politics, since no other party had appeared to be strong enough to dominate the political landscape like the Congress.

The thirteenth general election, which brought the NDA government led by Atal Bihari Vajpayee to power (1999–2004, his only government to complete the full term), was considered by many to be the dawn of an era of stable coalitions. This assessment was further reinforced by the fourteenth and fifteenth general elections that were won by the United Progressive Alliance (UPA) led by the INC with Dr Manmohan Singh as prime minister.

Throughout this so-called period of coalition politics, however, the progressive strengthening of the organization of the Bharatiya Janata Party (BJP) and its persistent improvement in electoral performance made complete political fragmentation a possibility. By the time of the sixteenth general election in 2014, it was clear that the BJP had become strong enough to dislodge the INC from the dominant position in Indian politics that it had hitherto enjoyed – winning 31% of the votes in 2014 and improving it further to win 37.3% of the votes in 2019. But in the decade that has elapsed since 2014, the severely weakened INC has refused to be expunged from the political landscape, easily remaining the second-largest party in terms of its vote share (19.49% in 2019) – emerging as a natural rallying point for the anti-BJP forces in the forthcoming general election of 2024.

An interesting feature of India's general elections is that operating under first-past-the-post system, parties have seldom won more than 50% of the total votes in any elections, even though they have often carried more than half the seats of the various legislative assemblies, of both the union and the states.

1951–52: the Feel Good Election

The first general elections were held between 25 October 1951 and 21 February 1952, in 68 phases. The scheduled time for the elections was February, but predicting adverse climatic conditions in the territory of Himachal Pradesh (that then constituted a chief commissioner's province), the polls there were held in the month of October 1951. No elections were held in Jammu and Kashmir. A total number of 1,949 candidates entered the fray to contest over 489 seats, of which 314 were single-member constituencies, and 86 were two-member constituencies, electing 1 general and 1 scheduled caste candidate each. The total number of eligible voters was 173 million, making India the largest electorate in the world. Voter turnout in the first general election was an impressive 45.7%.

The election was contested by 53 political parties and 533 independent candidates. Many members of the interim government resigned their posts to enter into the contest for the Lok Sabha. B.R. Ambedkar, law minister in the interim government, left the cabinet to revive his Scheduled Castes Federation (later, the Republican Party); Shyama Prasad Mukherjee left the cabinet to set up the Bharatiya Jana Sangh. Even former Congress politicians like Acharya Kripalani had left the party to set up the Kisan Mazdoor Praja Party (KMPP); the Socialist Party was set up by Ram Manohar Lohia and Jayaprakash Narayan.

The results were declared on 10 February 1952. The election was won by the Indian National Congress with over 44% of the votes, which helped them carry away more than 75% of the seats (364 out of 489); the second-largest party was the Communist

Party of India (CPI), which won 16 seats with only 3.3% of the vote share. The Socialist Party (SP) took 12 seats with 10.59% vote share and the Kisan Mazdoor Praja Party (KMPP) 9 seats; the Shiromani Akali Dal, the All India Hindu Mahasabha (AIHM) and Tamil Nadu Toilers' Party won 4 seats each; the Bharatiya Jan Sangh (BJS), Akhil Bharatiya Ram Rajya Parishad (ABRRP), the Commonweal Party, the Revolutionary Socialist Party (RSP) and the Jharkhand Party won 3 seats each; the Scheduled Castes Federation (SCF), the Peasants and Workers' Party of India (PWPI) and the Lok Sewak Sangh won 2 seats each; the Krishikar Lok Party, Forward Bloc (Marxist), Chota Nagpur Santhal Parganas Janata Party (CNSPJP), Travancore Tamil Nadu Congress (TTNC) and Indian Union Muslim League won 1 seat each. Thirty-one parties failed to win any seats at all. Independent candidates won 37 seats with about 16% of the vote share. The law minister, B.R. Ambedkar of the Scheduled Castes Federation, lost his election to the Congress candidate, Narayan Sadoba Kajrolkar, his former associate in the constituent assembly.

In regional terms, deadening preponderance of the INC included all the constituent states of the country with a crushing majority in most of the states (except for Tripura and Bilaspur, where it failed to win any seats,). Among the smaller states, it took all the 6 seats from Saurashtra, all 3 seats from (the then) Himachal Pradesh, and both the seats from Ajmer, Bhopal and Kutch, and the only seat from Coorg. In Bihar, the INC took 45 of the 55 seats, the SP 3, others 6 and 1 seat went to an independent candidate. In Bombay, the INC took 40 out of 45 seats, 1 with the SCF, PWPI 1 seat each and independents 3. In Delhi, the INC took 3 of the 4 seats, while the KMPP took 1. In Hyderabad, the INC took 14 of the 25 seats, People's Democratic Front (PDF, mass front of the CPI) won 7 seats, while a seat each were taken by the SP, SCF, an independent and others. In Madhya Bharat, the INC took 9 of the 11 seats (others taking 2); in Madhya Pradesh, the INC took 27 of the 29 seats (2 taken by independents); in Vindhya

Pradesh, the INC took 4 of the 6 seats, the SP and KMPP taking the remaining 2. In Mysore, the INC took 10 of the 11 seats, while the KMPP took 1. Madras was the only state where the opposition/ non-Congress parties won a plurality of seats: while the INC took 35 of the 75 seats, the CPI won 8 seats, the KMPP 6 and the SPI 2 seats, 4 seats were taken by the Tamil Nadu Toiler's Party, 5 seats were taken by others and 15 seats were taken by independents. In Travancore-Cochin, the INC won 6 of the 12 seats, with others taking 2 and independents 4. In Orissa, the INC won 11 out of 20 seats, followed by the All India Ganatantra Parishad (AIGP, or simply GP) with 6, and the CPI, SPI and an independent with 1 seat each. In the then state of Punjab, the INC took 16 out of the 18 seats, and the then Patiala and East Punjab States Union (PEPSU), the INC took 2 of the 5 seats; the Shiromani Akali Dal won 2 seats each in both Punjab and PEPSU. In the then state of Rajasthan, the INC won 9 of the 20 seats, with the Akhil Bharatiya Ram Rajya Parishad (ABRRP) winning 3 seats, and the Bharatiya Jana Sangh (BJS) and the Krishikar Lok Party (KLP) winning a seat each. In Uttar Pradesh, the INC won its most decisive victory, winning 81 of 86 seats, with the SP and independents winning 2 seats each. In West Bengal, the INC won 21 of the 34 seats from the state, while the CPI won 5 seats and other smaller parties won 3 seats. The Bharatiya Jana Sangh (BJS) won 2 seats. Among the states of the north-east of India, of the 13 seats from Assam, the INC took 11 seats and the Socialist Party 1 (1 MP was appointed). The only 2 other stand-alone entities of the region were Manipur and Tripura. In Manipur the INC and the SP won a seat each, while in Tripura, both the seats went to the CPI.

1957: Still Feeling Good?

The second general elections were held between 24 February and 9 June 1957. In the second Lok Sabha, 5 more seats came into being, taking the full strength to 505. These were divided into 403 constituencies, of which 312 were single-member and 91 were two-member constituencies.

The landscape of the Lok Sabha after the second general elections (1957) was much the same: while the vote share of the INC remained nearly the same, their seat tally improved to stand at 371 out of 494 (up 7); the CPI remained the second-largest party improving its tally with 27 seats (more than doubling its vote share to over 8%), while the newly formed Praja Socialist Party (PSP, the result of merger between Jayaprakash Narayan's SP and KMPP of Sucheta Kripalani) came third with 19 seats (albeit with over 10.4% of the total number of votes, i.e. more than the CPI); the BJS emerged the fourth largest group in terms of vote share (8%), although with only 4 seats, same as the Bombay based PWPI. The AIGP won 7 seats, the SCF and the Jharkhand Party won 6 seats each. The Chhota Nagpur Santhal Paraganas Janata Party (CNSPJP) increased its seats tally to 3; the PDF and Marxist Forward Bloc (MFB) won 2 seats each while the Hindu Maha Sabha (HMS) managed to win only 1 seat.

The Lok Sabha also had 11 appointed members – 6 representing Jammu and Kashmir, 1 representing the tribal areas of Assam, 1 representing Amindive, Laccadive and Minicoy Islands and 1 representing Andaman and Nicobar Islands, and 2 representing Anglo-Indians.

In terms of regional domination of the Lok Sabha seats, in the new layout of the states, the INC's hegemony over most states of the country remained in place, although it got a bit dented. Of the 41 seats in Madras, the INC won 31, independents won 8 seats and the CPI 2. In Kerala, the first state that the INC lost dominance in, the INC won 6 of its 18 Lok Sabha seats, while the CPI won 9, the PSP 1 and independents 2. Of the 43 seats of Andhra Pradesh, the INC won 37, the CPI 2, the PDF 2 and independents 2. In Mysore, of the 26 Lok Sabha seats, the INC won 23, the PSP, SCF and an independent won 1 seat each. The other state that saw the strength of the opposition increasing significantly from the second general election itself was Bombay, where the INC won 38 of the 66 Lok Sabha seats; the PSP and SCF won 5 seats each; the CPI and PWPI won 4 seats each, the BJS 2 and independents won 8. In newly created state of Madhya Pradesh, the INC domination was near total, winning 35 of the 36 seats. In the newly created state of Rajasthan the INC won 19 of the 22 seats, while independents took the remaining seats. In Himachal Pradesh, the INC won all 4 seats; in Delhi it won all 5; and in Punjab 21 of 22, the CPI taking 1. In Orissa, the INC hegemony saw an early challenge from the GP, both of whom won 7 seats each; the CPI won 1 seat, the PSP 2 and 3 seats for the independents. In Uttar Pradesh, the INC won 70 seats out of 84, while the PSP won 4, the BJS 2, the CPI 1 and independents 9. In Bihar, the INC won 43 of the 51 Lok Sabha seats, 2 seats were taken by the PSP and 6 seats by the Jharkhand Party. Three seats were taken by others, and 1 seat went to an independent candidate. In West Bengal, the INC won 23 of the 36 Lok Sabha seats; 6 seats were taken by the CPI; the PSP 2; others took 2. Three went to independents. In Assam, the INC won 9 of the 12 seats and 2 seats were taken by the PSP. An independent won a seat there. In Manipur, the INC and an independent candidate won a seat each. In Tripura, the INC and the CPI won a seat each.

The 1957 general elections were also believed to have witnessed the first instance of booth capturing in India, in the Begusarai constituency in Bihar – a myth that is now largely debunked.

1962: Nehru's Last Bow

The third general elections were held between 19 and 25 February 1962. The total number of Lok Sabha seats increased to 508.

General elections of 1962 saw the INC's electoral performance take a dip as its vote share fell below 45% for the first time.

ITS SEATS TALLY FELL TO 361 OUT OF 508, WHICH WAS 371 OUT OF 494 IN 1957.

The CPI remained the second-largest party in the Lok Sabha with 29 seats (and 9.9% vote share) but the PSP fell to fifth place with 12 seats (vote share fell to 6.8%). The third slot was taken instead by the Swatantra Party, formed in 1959, and made up of economic liberals from the INC (C. Rajagopalachari, Minoo Masani, N.G. Ranga, and so on). The Swatantra Party won 18 seats on the strength of a 7.9% share of the total votes. This was also the first election when the Bharatiya Jana Sangh (BJS) came up with a double-digit tally (14 seats with 6.44% vote share). The new Socialist Party (Lohia), which broke away from the PSP in 1956, also had a decent showing with 6 seats (although on the back of a paltry 2.69% vote share); another outfit with a concentrated vote share of 2.01% winning plurality of seats (7) to make an entry into the Lok Sabha was the Dravida Munnetra Kazagham (DMK), led by C.N. Annadurai. The Ganatantra Parishad (GP) of Orissa saw its tally come down to 4 seats; the Republican Party of India (RPI), Shiromani Akali Dal (SAD) and the Jharkhand Party (JP) each won 3 seats; the AIFB, AIRRP, RSP, Lok Sewak Sangh and the debutant Indian Union Muslim League (IUML) won 2 seats each. The Hindu Mahasabha (AIHM), Nutan Maha Gujarat Janata Parishad, Haryana Lok Samiti and All Party Hill Leaders

A stamp commemorating C. Rajagopalachari

Conference (APHLC) won 1 seat each. The PWPI was reduced to 0 seats, while the debutant Tamil National Party, the We Tamil party, the Gorkha League and the Eastern Indian Tribal Union contested but failed to win any seats. The number of appointed members was increased to 14 – adding a member for Dadra and Nagar Haveli, 1 for Goa, Daman and Diu, 1 for North East Frontier Agency (NEFA) and 1 for Tuentseng and Naga Hills District, 6 for Jammu and Kashmir, 2 for Anglo-Indians, 1 for Amindive, Minicoy and Laccadive, 1 for Andaman and Nicobar Islands.

At the regional level, the INC hegemony remained, but continued to weaken. In Madras, the INC won 31 seats, followed by DMK's 6, the CPI and independents at 1 each. In Kerala, the INC and CPI were tied at 6 Lok Sabha seats each, with the IUML taking 2 seats and the RSP 1, and independents clinched 3. In Andhra Pradesh, the INC won 34 seats, while the CPI got 7, the debutant Swatantra Party got 1 and independents 1. In Mysore, the INC took 25 of the 26 seats, and the Lok Sewak Sangh took 1. Of the 44 seats meant for the new state of Maharashtra, the INC won 41 seats; the PSP and independents took 1 each. In the new state of Gujarat, the INC took 12 seats out of the 18, the Swatantra Party won 4, the Nutan Maha Gujarat Janata Parishad and independents won 1 seat each. In Madhya Pradesh, the INC led the tally with 24 seats, followed by 3 seats each of Jana Sangh and the PSP, 1 each of the Socialist Party and the Ram Rajya Parishad, plus 1 independent. In Rajasthan, the INC continued to dominate winning 14 Lok Sabha seats, but this time round the Swatantra Party won 3 seats, the AIRRP and BJS won 1 seat each with 3 being won by the independents. In the then Punjab state, the INC won 14 of the 21 seats, the SAD won 3, the BJS won 3 and the Haryana Lok Samiti, socialists and an independent won 1 seat each. The INC carried all 5 seats of Delhi and all 4 of Himachal Pradesh. In Uttar Pradesh, the INC lost quite a few seats to finish with 62 seats, with the BJS winning 7, the Swatantra Party 3, the

PSP and CPI winning 2 seats each and the AIHM and the SP winning 1 seat each. Independents bagged 3. In Bihar too, the INC domination continued with 39 seats, but the Swatantra Party managed to win 7, the Janata Party won 3, the PSP 2, and the CPI and the SP won 1 seat each. In Orissa, the INC finally beat the GP handsomely, winning 14 seats to GP's 4, whereas the PSP and the SP won 1 seat each. In West Bengal, the INC ran the show with 29 seats, followed by 9 of the CPI and 1 seat each for the AIFB, RSP and Lok Sewak Sangh. In Assam, the INC won 9 of the 12 Lok Sabha seats, while the PSP won 2 seats and the APHLC won 1. In Manipur the INC and the SP won 1 seat each, while in Tripura, once again the CPI won both the seats.

The 1962 general elections were the first instance when it was conducted in a week, unlike the previous 2 elections, which spanned over months. It was also the first time that each constituency elected only a single member. And it was also the first time that there was a downward swing of votes for the Congress. In terms of seat numbers, the Congress got the lowest compared to its tally in 1952 and 1957 parliamentary polls. Although hairline, it was nevertheless a crack in the Congress's electoral performance.

Congress parliamentary representation from the states of Bombay, Gujarat, West Bengal, Orissa and Madras had risen from 100 to 124. But in the Hindi heartland, often referred to as the cow belt, the Congress fared badly – in Madhya Pradesh, Rajasthan, Uttar Pradesh, Bihar and Punjab, the Congress parliamentary representation has dropped from 186 to 150. A section of top Congress leaders began to lose their grounds. Although the Congress improved its position in Gujarat, Balwantrai Mehta, who was the projected chief minister, was defeated in the state assembly elections. Siddavanahalli Nijalingappa, the Mysore state congress committee president, who was to become chief minister, was also defeated in the assembly polls. In Madhya Pradesh, where the Congress failed to get absolute majority in the assembly election, Kailash Nath Katju, the incumbent chief minister, was defeated.

It seemed that Nehru had started losing his grip to some extent over the party and the central government. The Mundhra Scandal, independent India's first big financial scam and the first sign of serious corruption in government, surfaced in 1958. The government-owned Life Insurance Corporation (LIC) invested over ₹1.25 crores into companies owned by Haridas Mundhra, which came under scrutiny. Feroze Gandhi, Nehru's son-in-law and the then Congress MP from Raebareli constituency, was instrumental in exposing the Mundhra Scam when he raised a question in this regard in Parliament demanding an explanation. Gandhi charged the principal secretary of finance, H.M. Patel, and Finance Minister Tiruvellore Thattai Krishnamachari for bringing pressure to bear on LIC to make that investment, claiming that he had possession of confidential letters that were exchanged between Krishnamachari and Patel on this matter. Facing such serious allegations, Prime Minister Nehru appointed Mohammadali Carim Chagla, who had then just retired from the post of chief justice of Bombay High Court, as a one-man commission to enquire into the matter. Justice Chagla submitted his report in 24 days. Several leading stockbrokers associated with the LIC stated that had the LIC consulted the Investment Committee, they would have pointed out the episode of Mundhra's forged shares that began in 1956. Justice Chagla's report eventually led to the resignation of the Finance Minister T.T. Krishnamachari in February 1958. Haridas Mundhra was sentenced to 22 years in prison. The scam was quite an embarrassment to Nehru and his government.

Again, the way the first communist government was dismissed in Kerala on 31 July 1959 also generated apathy and, to some extent, fear among a section of people. The episode raised finger at the whims and fancies of the central government that hurt the core of electoral democracy. The incident also for the first time displayed the tendency of dominance of the Centre in the politics of federal structure and clearly portrayed the possibilities of abuse of Article 356 of the Indian constitution. The Congress, as a party, had to pay the price in the election of 1962.

The death of Nehru on 27 May 1964 from a heart attack at the age of 75 years was considered by many to be the beginning of a new era in Indian politics. The INC finally looked like losing its advantage of being the premier political formation in India's freedom struggle. The opposition parties, on the other hand, tried to form political coalitions to prevent split in the anti-Congress votes. Ram Manohar Lohia of the Socialist Party (Lohia faction) voiced the hope that the inexperience of Mrs Indira Gandhi, daughter of Nehru and the successor of Prime Minister Lal Bahadur Shastri, gave the opposition a good opportunity to topple the Congress before the general election of 1967.

1967: Anti-Congress Mood and Attempts at Consolidation of Votes

Elections to the fourth Lok Sabha were held between 17 and 21 February 1967 – the reduced number of days indicating growing proficiency in conducting the elections. The number of seats increased from 508 to 523, of which 520 went to the polls – because only Anglo-Indians and the people of NEFA continued to be represented by appointed members; Jammu and Kashmir, Andaman and Nicobar, Goa, Daman and Diu, Laccadives and Minicoy Islands all sent their elected representatives for the first time.

The general elections of 1967 saw the INC's seats in the Lok Sabha reduced considerably to 283 out of 523 (from 361 out of 508 in 1962), even though the vote share dropped by a comparatively smaller margin (40.78%). The elections in 1967 witnessed till then the lowest ever tally of seats and the share of votes of the Congress since 1952. The BJS broke past the CPI, and the Socialist Party became the third-largest party in Parliament, having won 35 seats (albeit with a marginally better vote share of 9.31%); the Swatantra Party made it to the second slot with 44 seats (but an even smaller share of 8.67% of vote share). The CPI came fifth along with the newly formed Samyukta Socialist Party, (formed first as the result of a split from the PSP in 1964, with the split faction uniting with the Socialist Party [Lohia] faction to create the SSP) with 23 seats each. Yet another part of the leftist votes were consolidated and won by the Communist Party of India (Marxist), or CPI(M), which split from the CPI in 1964 and put up a decent show with 19 seats (with 4.28% of the votes cast). The DMK however increased its tally from Tamil Nadu and took the fourth slot in the Lok Sabha with 25 seats (but only with 3.79% of vote share). The PSP won 13 seats, and the Bangla Congress (led by Ajoy Mukherjee), which broke away from the INC, won 5 seats. The SAD (Fateh Singh faction) managed to win 3 seats; the PWPI, AIFB, and AIML won 2 seats each. The debutant Jammu and Kashmir National Conference (JKNC), Jana Kranti Dal, APHLC, United Goans Party (Seqveria) and Nagaland Nationalist Organisation won 1 seat each. Independents accounted for 35 seats.

In the 1967 elections, the Congress appeared to fade before its antagonists and inner-party dissidents. In the Madras state, the split in the INC between Rajagopalachari and Kamaraj fuelled the rising power of the DMK which grew rapidly, winning 24 of the 39 seats. The INC could win only 3, Rajagopalachari's Swatantra Party won 6, the CPI(M) 4 and independents 2. In Kerala, the CPI(M) won 9 of the 19 seats, the CPI and the SSP won 3 seats each, the IUML won 2 seats, and the Congress was reduced to 1 seat, along with an independent candidate. In

Mysore, the INC's standing was somewhat salvaged, winning 18 of 27 seats, with the Swatantra Party a distant second with 5 seats; the PSP won 2 seats, the SSP won 1 seat and 1 seat went to an independent candidate. The 1 Congress bastion that survived 1967 intact was Andhra Pradesh, with the INC winning 35 of the 41 seats, while the Swatantra Party could win only 3 seats, independents 2 and the CPI 1. The other Congress bastion that survived intact was Maharashtra, with the INC winning 37 of the 45 seats, with the PWP, SSP and CPI winning 2 seats each. One seat went to an independent candidate. Even in Madhya Pradesh, the INC did not fare altogether badly, winning 25 out of 37 seats, with the BJS winning 10 seats, and the Swatantra Party and an independent contestant winning 1 seat each. In Goa, Daman and Diu, the INC took 1 seat while the United Goans took the other. Dadra and Nagar Haveli seat was also taken by the INC.

In some states, the INC got a severe drubbing. In Gujarat, the INC won only 11 seats while the Swatantra Party won 12, with 1 seat being won by an independent. In Rajasthan, the INC scraped in with 10 seats, while the Swatantra Party won 8 and the BJS won 3 seats, with 2 seats being won by the independents. In the newly created Punjab, the INC had a clear victory in 9 out of 13 seats, while the SAD took 3 seats and the BJS took 1. In Haryana the INC won 7 seats, and the BJS and an independent won 1 seat each. In Himachal Pradesh the INC took all 6 seats, but in Delhi the BJS claimed 6 while the INC could claim only 1. In the first ever Lok Sabha elections in Jammu and Kashmir, the INC won 6 seats while the JKNC won only 1. The Lok Sabha seat of the UT of Chandigarh was taken by the BJS. The INC's most significant drubbing came from Uttar Pradesh, where the INC won 47 of the 85 seats, the BJS won 12 seats, SSP 8, CPI 5, BJS and PSP won 2 seats each, while the CPI(M), RPI and Swatantra Party won 1 seat each. In Orissa, the Swatantra Party won 8 seats, ahead of the INC, which won only 6; the PSP won 4, the SSP 1 and 1 went to an independent.

In Bihar, the INC held out somewhat, winning 34 out of 53 seats; the SSP won 7 seats, the CPI 5, PSP, BJS and Jharkhand Party won 1 seat each while 4 seats went to independents. In West Bengal, while the INC won 14 seats, the CPI, CPI(M) and Bangla Congress won 5 seats each, the AIFB won 2 and independents won 7 seats. In the North-East, Assam remained an INC bastion, winning 10 of the 14 seats, with the PSP winning 2 seats, and the CPI and the APHLC 1 seat each. In Tripura the INC managed to win both the seats, while in Manipur the CPI and an independent candidate successfully won the 2 seats (denying the INC even 1). In the newly constituted Nagaland the sole Lok Sabha seat was taken by the Naga National Organisation.

The INC's poor performance in 1967 brought the Congress to a breaking point. Earlier, towards the closing years of Nehru's premiership, and more particularly after India's defeat in the war with China that left the prime minister badly shaken, a group of leaders had begun to attempt at developing a collective leadership – the prototype of what has come to be known as Congress's high command culture. The prototype comprised then party president Kumaraswamy Kamaraj (party's supreme leader in Tamil Nadu), Atulya Ghosh of West Bengal, Neelam Sanjiva Reddy of Andhra Pradesh, Siddavanahalli Nijalingappa of Karnataka, Sadashiv Kanoji Patil of Maharashtra, Krishna Ballabh Sahay of Bihar and Biju Patnaik of Orissa. These leaders later came to be known by the moniker *Syndicate*.

The Syndicate's first lunge for power was the Kamaraj Plan of 1963, suggesting that senior leaders of the party should give up their positions in the administration and return to party work. By the time of Nehru's death in 1964, they were powerful enough within the INC to first install Lal Bahadur Shastri as prime minister, and then Mrs Indira Gandhi as Shastri's successor (upon his untimely demise at Tashkent in 1965, which remains open to conspiracy theories as the Indian government has not declassified the documents related to his death). They had a decisive role to play in Mrs Gandhi's first cabinet and policies formulated there till 1967.

The hammering the INC received in 1967 resulted in the defeat of a number of Congress stalwarts and half the members of Mrs Gandhi's cabinet, including all the 4 top leaders of the Syndicate: Kamaraj in Tamil Nadu, Patil in Maharashtra, Sahay in Bihar and Ghosh in West Bengal. As we would see later, this also resulted in Congress's loss of power at the state level all across north India and the deep south. In north India and West Bengal, however, while the Congress lost hugely, no single party was strong enough to replace it. At the state level, coalitions were formed by non-Congress legislators to constitute what came to be known as Samyukt Vidhayak Dal. No similar force emerged at the Lok Sabha level, allowing the INC to stay in power, but only just. The result of the 1967 general elections in India is termed as a 'political earthquake' by a section of political observers and politicians. The Congress for the first time received a solid jolt; the hairline crack that was seen in 1962 poll results developed into a clear fracture in Congress hegemony.

The 1967 election saw a major political awakening with a turnout of 61.1% among eligible voters, the highest witnessed till then (as compared with 45% in the first general elections, 46.6% in the second, and 55.4% in the third). Such a high turnout augured a milieu for change. The 'Pro-Incumbency Era' (1952–1977) began coming to an end in 1967 – a veritable 'watershed in Indian politics'.

While the Congress had a narrow escape when its Lok Sabha seat share slumped from 73.1% of the seats in 1962 to just about 54.5% of the seats in 1967, coming dangerously close to losing its majority for the first time since independence somehow. The Congress's losses were not just reflected at the Centre; of the 16 state assemblies, the Congress could retain only 8. The 8 seats returned the Congress to power with absolute majorities in the state legislatures.

The Congress's review of the 1967 general elections had observed: 'The anti-Congress vote did not exactly represent opposition to the Congress ideology ... There were certainly sections among voters for those opposition parties who supported the ideologies which these parties preached but there were those among their supporters who just wished to express their resentment against the Congress for the hardships they suffered and for other reasons'.

This resentment was largely occasioned by economic factors. Between 1962 and 1967, India had fought 2 wars – the Indo– China conflict (October–November 1962) and Indo–Pakistan war (August–September 1965) – which significantly dented the Indian economy. In addition, the country was struggling with chronic food shortage and rising prices of goods. After a steep devaluation of the rupee by 57%, the effective value of the rupee went from ₹4.76 against the dollar to ₹7.50 per US dollar – almost halving the purchasing power parity of the Indian currency. The impression was gaining ground that the Congress was losing its grip over the situation and the country was hopelessly drifting towards chaos and economic stagnation. The devaluation of the rupee did little to improve matters, and it began to be said openly that the government had succumbed to Western pressure in agreeing to do it.

In 1967, about half of the electorate was under 35 years of age, thus representing a post-Gandhi and post-independence generation, and the failure of the Congress to reach the younger voters was a costly one. Even more costly was its declining influence in rural India. It was observed that in the campaign 'grievances, not issues' were 'to the fore'. A report in the *Times of India* on the eve of the voting observed, 'In the general election this time, there are no all-India issues as such – there are only all-India grievances. The people are more concerned about food shortage, inflation, parochialism, indiscipline and the general atmosphere of violence which has created vaguely negative atmosphere in the country.'

To a large section of the electorate, these concerns were genuine, and the Congress was held to be mostly responsible for the gloomy situation. Critics said that the Congress gave little evidence of a capacity, or even willingness, to tackle grave national problems vigorously, to put its own house in order, or to identify itself more realistically with the felt needs and aspirations of an increasingly conscious and increasingly demanding electorate. Furthermore, factionalism weakened the party from inside. Thousands of party members left the Congress before the elections; over 1,000 of them stood for election against Congress candidates, either as independents, or as members of dissident Congress groups, or as new recruits to various opposition parties.

Prime Minister Indira Gandhi was held responsible by the Syndicate for the drubbing the party got in 1967. She anticipated such criticism and saw it as an attempt by the Syndicate to marginalize her. She embarked on a bold strategy to outmanoeuvre her opponents within the INC and in the larger political opposition by veering her government's policies into a more leftward direction, which was purportedly to deal with the dire economic situation. The Ten Point Programme she had the Congress Party adopt in May 1967 spoke of social control of banks, nationalisation of General Insurance, ceiling on urban property and income, public distribution of food grains, land reforms and housing to the rural poor among others in a bid to regain lost ground electorally. The result of this leftward thrust was that, as her father had done before her, Mrs Gandhi effectively hijacked traditional socialist agenda on the Indian political spectrum, without allowing the left to benefit from it.

By 1968, the benefits of the Green Revolution (which made India self-sufficient in wheat, maize and rice) began to deliver bumper crops. On 19 July 1969, Indira Gandhi nationalized 14 large private commercial banks, each with reserves of more than ₹50 crore. These banks, according to the government, were only upholding the interest of the rich and they did not provide credit to the poor. This step was aimed at winning the hearts of the poor and vanquishing the Syndicate (which represented the pro-business section of the party) and the Opposition camp.

The Syndicate was outmanoeuvred into accepting this, and they resented this leftward turn away from the political centre. In 1969, when the Syndicate nominated its leader and the Speaker of the Lok Sabha N.S. Reddy for the post of the president of India, Mrs Gandhi quietly encouraged V.V. Giri to run as an independent candidate, and went on to ask for a 'conscience vote' as against the official whip to vote for Reddy that was issued on Congress MPs and MLAs. The victory of V.V. Giri at the expense of N.S. Reddy resulted in the expulsion of the prime minister from the Congress on account of 'anti-party activities', occasioning the biggest split in the INC ever.

Congress party-men who supported Mrs Gandhi had 'requisitioned' for a meeting of the All India Congress Committee (AICC) when the whip was issued in favour of N.S. Reddy. They gathered around Mrs Gandhi and claimed to now constitute the real Congress, thus implying the expulsion itself an infructuous act. The Election Commission of India, however, recognized Mrs Gandhi's faction as the successor to the old party, which was now to be called Congress (Requisitionists)* or Congress(R);

* After the 'requisition' that was sought to discuss the matter of the whip during the presidential elections. The Congress(R) continued to be the official name of the party till the Congress(O) merged into the Janata fold. Congress(R) was then split into Congress(I) and Congress(Urs). While Congress(Urs) was later interchangeably referred to as Congress(S). By the time of January 1978, INC, Congress and Congress(I) began to be used interchangeably with each other.

the INC old guard, reconstituted itself as the Congress (Organisation) or Congress(O) [the Old Congress]. Since most of the MPs remained with Mrs Gandhi, presumably because she was the incumbent prime minister, she remained in office despite being reduced to a minority (221 seats out of 523), with issue-based support being extended to the government by the CPI (23 seats) and the DMK (26 seats).

After the nationalization of banks, Indira Gandhi's government moved to discontinue special privileges for India's hereditary princes by abolishing privy purses, or payment, which hereditary princes received from the government. However, a Constitution Amendment Bill for the abolition of privy purses, which was placed before Parliament in September 1970, was defeated in Rajya Sabha. Mrs Gandhi obtained a presidential proclamation to make it a law, but it was challenged successfully by the princes in the Supreme Court. Before that, the Supreme Court also nullified the compensation provisions for nationalized banks. This made Mrs Gandhi consider the idea of a fresh and categorical mandate in the name of her agenda. Her government steered firmly leftward by aggressively pushing for land reforms and projecting its socialist disposition.

By December 1970, Mrs Gandhi became confident enough to go to the country seeking a fresh mandatc, and recommended dissolution of the Lok Sabha a full year before it was required (i.e. February 1972), bringing the election forward to March 1971 – the first such instance in the history of electoral democracy of India. Being advised by P.N. Haksar or 'Babboo' Haksar (a Kashmiri pundit, London School of Economics Graduate and a friend of Indira's husband Feroze Gandhi), who was the prime minister's principal secretary (1971–73), Mrs Gandhi had gone for an early election looking for a mandate for her pro-poor and populist policies.

The fear 1967 put paid to the idea that Congress was to stay forever. However, the voters did not give any clear indication of their alternate preferences, except in certain local and state situations. As a leading Indian newspaper observed, the elections 'have produced a mixed bag altogether. It is amply clear that the electorate does not want the Congress. It is not very clear what it does want'. Certainly, except in 2 or 3 States, the elections did not produce a viable alternative to the Congress, nor did they produce a clear polarization of forces. Mrs Gandhi thus hoped in 1971 that her populist measures would help the Congress regain its political dominance, and thus help her marginalize her opponents inside the party.

1971: Mrs Gandhi and the Onset of Hubris

The fifth general elections were held between 1 and 10 March 1971, in 518 constituencies, each with a single seat.

In the general election of 1971, Congress(R) won a landslide victory, powered by an electoral alliance with the CPI. The combination won 48.1% of the votes, and 375 seats out of a total of 521: the Congress(R) on its own won 352 seats (43.68% of the votes), while the CPI led by S.A. Dange won 23 seats (4.73% of vote share). The Congress(O) suffered a stunning defeat, winning only 16 seats (albeit drawing on a vote share of 10.43%, the second-largest). The CPI(M), fighting on its own, secured 25 seats on a vote share of 5.12% to become the second-largest party in the parliament. Many of the major non-Congress and non-Communist parties – such as the SSP and the PSP from the left, the BJS, the Swatantra Party, the Bharatiya Kranti Dal (BKD, founded in 1967 by Chaudhry Charan Singh, who became chief minister of Uttar Pradesh) – had formed a

Grand Alliance to prevent splitting non-Congress votes.* The alliance, the first major one of this nature, ended up with only 40 seats, of which the BJS alone won 22 (on a vote share of only 7.22%) – the fourth largest party in the Lok Sabha; the Swatantra Party won 8 seats, the SSP won only 3 seats and the PSP 2, the Bharatiya Kranti Dal 1. The DMK secured the third-highest tally of 23 seats along with the CPI with its vote share of 3.84% in the Tamil country. The Telangana Praja Samithi, led by Mari Chenna Reddy, voicing the demand for the creation of a separate Telangana won 10 seats. The Kerala Congress and the RSP won 3 seats each; the AIFB and IUML won 2 seats each; the SAD, Utkal Congress, Bangla Congress, Vishal Haryana Party, All India Jharkhand Party, RPI, UG(S), APHLC and United Front of Nagaland won 1 seat each. More than 30 parties, some new (such as the Shiv Sena and the Soshit Dal) some old (the AIRRP, PWPI, etc) failed to win any seats at all.

The INC(R) did spectacularly well in north India. It won 73 of the 85 seats in Uttar Pradesh, with the CPI and the BJS winning 4 seats each, the Bharatiya Kranti Dal and the INC(O) winning 1 seat each and independents winning 2 seats. In Punjab, the INC(R) won 10 of the 13 seats, the CPI winning 2 and independents 1. In Haryana, the INC(R) won 7 of the 9 seats, the BJS won 1, and the Vishal Haryana Party 1. In Rajasthan, the INC(R) won 14 of the 23 seats, 1 was won by the BJS and 3 by the Swatantra Party, with 2 successful independent candidates. In Jammu and

* The high priest of such a strategy of forming an anti-Congress alliance was Ram Manohar Lohia, the charismatic socialist leader and founder of the SSP. He devoted himself to the mission of destroying the Congress monopoly of power by uniting all anti-Congress forces in the country. As political scientist Rajni Kothari observed, 'Lohia was fairly successful in his mission, polarized the country along Congress versus anti-Congress lines, and in the process took on whoever was prepared to oppose the Congress.' Lohia died on 12 October 1967, when he was just 57. But his dream to some extent would come true in 1971 elections with the formation of the Grand Alliance.

Kashmir, the INC(R) won 5 of 6 seats, with independents winning 1. In Madhya Pradesh, the INC(R) won 21 of the 37 Lok Sabha seats from the state, followed by the BJS with 11 and 1 of SSP and 4 independents. In Maharashtra, the INC(R) won 42 of the 45 seats, with 1 PSP and 2 others. In Orissa, the INC(R) won 15 of 20 seats, with the Swatantra Party winning 3, and the CPI and Utkal Congress winning 1 seat each. In Bihar, the INC(R) won 39 seats out of 53, followed by the CPI with 5 seats, INC(O) with 3 seats, the BJS and SSP with 2 seats each and 1 seat won by an independent candidate. The INC(R)'s best result at the state-level, however, was 27 out of 27 seats from Mysore. In the North-East, Assam saw the INC(R) 13 of the 14 Lok Sabha seats from the state, with APHLC picking up the remaining one.

The INC(R) did not do so well in some states. In Gujarat, the INC(R) and INC(O) won 11 seats each, with the 2 remaining seats being taken by the Swatantra Party. In Andhra Pradesh, the INC(R) won 28 of the 41 seats, followed by 10 seats for the TPS, and the CPI, CPI(M) and independents claiming 1 seat each. In Tamil Nadu, the DMK led with 23 seats out of 39, followed by the INC(R) with 9 seats, the CPI with 4 and the INC(O) with 1. In Kerala, the INC(R) won 6 of the 19 seats, with the CPI winning 2 seats, the CPI(M) 3 and smaller state-level parties winning 7. In West Bengal, INC(R) won 13 seats out of 40, with the CPI(M) winning 20 seats, the CPI winning 3 seats, the PSP and Bangla Congress 1 each.

In the then Himachal Pradesh, the INC won 4 out of 4 seats and in Delhi 7 out of 7. The lone seat of Chandigarh was also taken by the INC, as was that of Laccadives, Minicoy and Amindivi Islands and that of Dadra and Nagar Haveli; the INC won 1 of the 2 seats of Goa, Daman and Diu and the solitary seat of both Pondicherry and Andaman and Nicobar Islands.

The people of India had made it clear in 1967 that they were fed up with the Congress, which had been in power since independence, and they wanted an alternative. Mrs Gandhi packaged her splitting of the party in 1969 well, saying she was providing them the alternative to the old Congress party – the Congress(R). A reporter of *Newsweek* (American news magazine) asked Mrs Gandhi what the main issues were in the 1971 election. She answered, 'I am the issue.' As Mrs Gandhi once said, while her adversaries ran their campaigns on the one-point campaign of *Indira hatao* (Remove Indira), she ran her campaign on the more meaningful slogan of *Garibi hatao* (Remove poverty). Her campaign was calculated to develop an appeal for the Congress among the disadvantaged sections of the Indian population, especially among the landless labourers, dalits and adivasis, minorities, women and the unemployed youth.

In a month and a half, Mrs Gandhi travelled over 58,000 kilometres, addressed over 300 meetings, and was heard or seen by an estimated 20 million people. She toured India extensively, addressing 3 or 4 meetings a day and received handsome returns. The newly born party got two-third majority with 352 seats just 17 months after its birth. It was a personal victory for Mrs Gandhi.

> In the words of eminent journalist and writer Vir Sanghvi, 'This was the election that proved that the importance of the party organization was over-rated. Indira Gandhi's candidates were younger, under-financed... What they did have behind them however was the charisma of their leader.'

The Coming of Hubris

Fortuitously the election victory was followed by the crisis in east Pakistan in 1971, in which Mrs Gandhi successfully intervened, winning the war with Pakistan and bringing about the liberation of Bangladesh. Riding high on the nationalist wave (in course of which even opposition leaders like Atal Bihari Vajpayee adulated her as the Goddess Durga incarnate), Mrs

Gandhi swept the provincial assembly polls of 1972, restoring the Congress to power wherever they had lost office in 1967.

By 1974, Mrs Gandhi was at the height of power. Yet that period also marked the onset of her encounter with hubris. Back-to-back harvest failures in 1972, 1973 and 1974 were pushing food prices up already. The oil price shock of 1973 after the Yom Kippur War pushed prices still higher, just as the economy was beginning to slow down. The youth were not ready to weather the economic crisis in silence. They held the system responsible, which came to be personified by Mrs Gandhi. Even within the Congress, there were men such as Chandra Shekhar and Mohan Dharia, young Turks who had earlier fought against the Syndicate, who now began to oppose her just as violently as they had once opposed the old guard of the old party. Across the country, the new icons were the men who fought the system, who lived by their own rules. Bollywood, the film industry of Bombay (now Mumbai), read the pulse right and mirrored the mood in movies, having the angry young man archetype (epitomised by films like *Zanjeer* and *Deewaar*, both starring Amitabh Bachchan) replace the romantic and tragic heroes of earlier generations.

Protests, gheraos and strikes roiled the country. Food riots erupted in Bombay (now Mumbai), Mysore, Nagpur and some parts of Kerala. More than 12,000 strikes took place in Bombay alone in 1972 and 1973. Factories were closed down as unemployment assumed epidemic proportions. Mrs Gandhi portrayed all this as the handiwork of opposition parties. She said, 'Anti-Congress parties were obstructing development... their aim was to paralyse the government and walk to power over the body of the nation'.

Perhaps the fiercest protest and the most brutal state response were seen in West Bengal in connection with the Naxal movement, an ultra-left armed movement that had started in Bengal from 1967. Armed peasants started a violent uprising in the Naxalbari block of Siliguri sub-division in Darjeeling district. The Naxalites, followers of Chairman Mao Zedong of China and his idea of armed struggle to acquire state-power, began to gain support in many parts of rural Bengal and among a section of Calcutta's urban and educated youth. How the Naxalite movement in Bengal was dealt with by the police and paramilitary forces first under president's rule and the Congress government of Siddhartha Shankar Ray (chief minister from 1972 to 1977) remains a recurring theme in Bengali popular culture.

The government received a deadly blow from the judiciary. In April 1973 in the Kesavananda Bharati case, depicted as the case that saved Indian democracy, 7 judges on a 13-judge bench of Supreme Court gave the verdict that Parliament did not have unlimited power to amend the Constitution and if Parliament would make changes to the basic structure of the Constitution, then the courts could dismiss it. The judgement was a serious setback to the Indira government. The day after the verdict, Chief Justice of India S.M. Sikri retired. Prime Minister Indira Gandhi bypassed 3 senior justices to appoint A.N. Ray, who earlier had announced a judgment in favour of her government, as the new chief justice of India. It created a furore. The 3 justices who were bypassed resigned. The judiciary struck back, signing a statement protesting the government's attempt to undermine the independence of the courts.

Meanwhile, unrest continued to spread. In May 1973, Uttar Pradesh Provincial Armed Constabulary (PAC), an armed police force of Uttar Pradesh, broke out in revolt. They demanded availability of basic commodities and better pay and working conditions. They seized armouries and attacked government properties. The army was called in. They shot dead 30 rioting policemen. UP Chief Minister Kamalapati Tripathi resigned.

In December 1973, students gathered on the roads in Gujarat to protest against high prices, which by January 1974 snowballed into the *Nav Nirman Andolan* (a movement for political regeneration), where students, lawyers, teachers and factory-workers voiced their disaffection with the economic crisis and the alleged corruption of Congress Chief Minister Chimanbhai Patel. Buses were burnt, shops looted and anarchy loomed large. In 1 month, at least 100 people were killed, almost 3,000 were injured and 8,000 were arrested. Chimanbhai Patel had to resign on 9 February 1974. President's Rule was imposed even though the Congress had 140 out of 167 MLAs in the state assembly. *Nav Nirman Andolan* is probably the only successful agitation in the history of independent India that dismissed an elected government of a state.

Mrs Gandhi's hubris and the incremental weakening of the Congress was neither confined to, nor manifested in, at the level of the union government of India. To understand the full complexity of the phenomenon, it is necessary to factor into consideration the developments in the constituent states and their assemblies, and how electoral politics evolved in the states in parallel with the Centre.

Chapter 3

ASSEMBLING LEGISLATURES 1952–56

The Lok Sabha looks at the representation of the Indian people on a national matrix, and elections to the Lok Sabha are generally seen in terms of party-political strengths and agenda. However, the story of the formation and mutation of the provincial/state assemblies – which came to be known under the generic Vidhan Sabha (legislative assemblies) – brings out the complexities of the Indian political landscape in ways which the Lok Sabha do not always manage to.

When India gained independence in 1947, there were 17 provinces and 565 princely states. Of these, 3 provinces – NWFP, Baluchistan and Sind went to Pakistan in their entirety; 3 provinces – Bengal, Punjab and Assam – were partitioned; and the remaining 11 provinces – Ajmer-Merwara, Andaman and Nicobar Islands, Bihar, Bombay, Central Provinces and Berar, Coorg, Delhi, Madras, Orissa, Panth-Piploda, and United Provinces – joined India. Of the 565 princely states, 552 had joined, or were made to join, the Indian Republic. By 1950, the 14 provinces and 552 princely states were reconstituted into 28 states classified into four categories – Parts A, B, C, and D. There were 9 Part A states – Assam, Bombay, Bihar, Patiala and Madras, Madhya Pradesh, Orissa, Uttar Pradesh, West Bengal; 8 Part B States – Hyderabad, Saurashtra, Mysore, Rajasthan,

Travancore-Cochin, Jammu and Kashmir, Madhya Bharat (Central India Agency) and East Punjab States Union (PEPSU); 10 Part C states – Ajmer, Bhopal, Vindhya Pradesh, Tripura, Himachal Pradesh, Bilaspur, Coorg, Delhi, Kutch and Manipur; and 1 Part D state – Andaman and Nicobar Islands.

In 1952, legislative assembly elections were held in 22 states. These were Ajmer (formerly Ajmer-Merwara), Assam, Bhopal, Bihar, Bombay, Coorg, Delhi, Himachal Pradesh, Hyderabad, Madhya Bharat, Madhya Pradesh, Madras, Mysore, Orissa, PEPSU, Saurashtra, Travancore-Cochin, Uttar Pradesh, Vindhya Pradesh, Punjab, Rajasthan and West Bengal. Some of these states, such as Bihar, Uttar Pradesh and West Bengal by and large remained for a long time as they had been in 1952; many of these states – mostly those of Part C – totally disappeared during the states reorganization in 1956, merging into or merging with other entities; some (such as Delhi and Himachal Pradesh) ceased to exist as states and became union territories for the time being (only to be revived as states later).

Those that Lasted

Bihar

The province of Bihar had come into being under the Government of Act of 1935, separating from Orissa and was given a bicameral legislature, constituting of a 30 member Vidhan Parishad (set up in 1936) and a fully elected Vidhan Sabha (set up in 1946, during the interim government). Shri Krishna Sinha was appointed premier of Bihar, with its own legislative assembly for which the first elections were held in 1937. Afterwards Sinha was elected as the prime minister of Bihar, after a short 3-month stint by Muhammad Yunus of the Muslim Independent Party. That government stepped down in 1939, along with other Congress governments of the provinces, under protest for not being consulted by the Government of India before declaring war against Germany in September 1939. Sinha led the party back to power in the 1946 elections, the last under the Government of India Act.

In 1952, when the first elections were held to the G. B. Bihar Vidhan Sabha, it had 226 single-member constituencies and 50 two-member constituencies, i.e. 326 seats in all. The INC won 239 seats (41.38% vote share), while the Socialist Party won only 23 seats (with its 18.11% of votes). The Jharkhand Party, founded in 1949 by Marang Gomake Jaipal Singh Munda with the demand for a separate Jharkhand state, came second in seats tally with 32 seats (8.01% vote share), while Chota Nagpur Santhal Parganas Janata Party (CNSPJP, set up by Maharaja of Ramgarh, Kamakhya Narayan Singh) came fourth in seats tally with 11 seats. The Lok Sewak Sangh (later known as Manbhum Lok Sewak Sangh) set up by Nibaranchandra Dasgupta and Bibhuti Dasgupta, and operating in the Purulia district was the only other party to win a plurality of seats – 7 (vote share or 1.56%) – and was instrumental in the transfer of the predominantly Bengali speaking regions of Bihar to West Bengal in 1956. The Kisan Mazdoor Praja Party (KMPP), the Forward Bloc (Marxists), often referred as MFB, Akhil Bharatiya Ram Rajya Parishad (ABRRP estd 1948) of Swami Karpatri won 1 seat each.

INC victory allowed for the party to return to power under Shri Krishna Sinha (who served as the premier previously during 1937–39, and again 1946–62) as the first chief minister of Bihar.

Orissa

Orissa was created as an independent state in 1936 with its own legislative assembly, which was constituted first in 1937;

the second assembly was elected in 1946. Its first premier, Krushna Chandra Gajapati (a scion of the Eastern Ganga family) was nominated to the post of premier, who was replaced by the first elected PM of Orissa, Bishwanath Das of the INC. Gajapati resumed the office of PM in 1941 (after Das resigned in 1939 along with other INC premiers) and held it till he was replaced by Harekrushna Mahtab of the INC in 1946. Harekrushna Mahtab then took the Orissa assembly into its first Vidhan Sabha elections in 1952.

The first elections were fought over 140 seats in 107 constituencies. The INC won 67 seats (with 37.87% of the votes) to emerge at the top of the pile; the All India Ganatantra Parishad (a party founded by the Singh Deo clan of Sambhalpur and comprised of ruling class of the princely states and big landlords of the region) came second with 31 seats (20.5% of votes). The Socialist Party won 10 seats (11.77% of vote share), the CPI won 7 seats (5.62% of vote share) and the Forward Bloc (Marxist) won 1 seat.

The INC, despite being the single largest party, fell short of a majority. Nabakrushna Chaudhury of the INC went on to form the first elected government of Orissa after independence with support of 6 independent MLAs, and served as chief minister from 1952 to 1956, when he was replaced by Harekrushna Mahtab once again.

Uttar Pradesh

The United Provinces of Agra and Awadh, which came to be known as the United Provinces under the Government of India Act in 1935, had its first legislative assembly with 228 seats. The first elected prime minister of United Province was Govind Ballav Pant (1937–39) of the INC, who resumed office in 1946 and presided over the period of transition when in 1950 it became Uttar Pradesh. Then he became its interim chief minister. G.B. Pant took UP into its first assembly elections in 1952, where the electoral contest was for 430 seats, of which 264 were single-member constituencies and 83 two-member constituencies.

The INC won the first assembly elections convincingly with a tally of 388 seats (47.93 vote share), way ahead of the Socialist Party that won 20 seats (12.03%). The BJS won only two seats and the KMPP, ABRRP and ABHM only 1 seat each.

G.B. Pant, thus, became the first elected CM of UP as well, an office he held for only 2 years, before joining the Union cabinet as home minister. He was succeeded by Sampurnanand, who held the office for the rest of the term (1954–57), and led the party to the next elections.

West Bengal

Bengal was technically one of the only 3 British provinces to be actually partitioned in 1947. The province had come into being in 1912, when the 5 Bengali speaking divisions (Presidency, Burdwan, Dacca, Chittagong, Rajshahi) of what used to be the Bengal Presidency were constituted into the state of Bengal, separating it from the regions that came to constitute Bihar and Orissa state (which survived till 1936), and the state of Assam.

The legislative council of Bengal was turned into the legislative assembly of Bengal by the Government of India Act of 1935, which had its first elections in 1937 returning a hung assembly. The coalition government (between the Krishak Praja Party and the Muslim League) that was formed in 1937 under Fazlul Haque made Bengal one of the two major provinces where the ministry was not formed by the INC. By 1946, the junior partner in that coalition, the Muslim League, had overwhelmed Haque's Krishak Praja Party, and was able to form a League-led government in Bengal, and was working towards taking the whole province into Pakistan. In 1947, while the League and other members of eastern Bengal wanted the state to remain united and be claimed by Pakistan, the Congress and other Hindu members of the assembly favoured a partition of the province along the religious lines, with full support of the INC top brass in Delhi. Accordingly, the assembly was dissolved at the time of independence, and as the Radcliffe Award declared the partition of Bengal, the eastern part went to Pakistan, and the western part was reconstituted into the state of West Bengal. The princely state of Cooch Bihar was merged into the state in 1950.

The legislative assembly of West Bengal was constituted on 21 November 1947, with Prafulla Ghosh as the interim CM before handing over to Bidhan Chandra Roy. In West Bengal, the first elections under the Indian Constitution were eventually held in 1952. The assembly had 238 seats from contests in 189 constituencies of which 140 were single-member and 49 were two-member constituencies. The Congress won a clear victory with 150 seats (vote share being 38.82%); the CPI came second with 28 seats (10.76% vote share), and the KMPP came third with 15 seats (8.97% vote share). The Forward Bloc (Marxist), an electoral ally of the CPI won 11 seats (5.29%). The other socialist electoral combination of SP, Forward Bloc (Ruikar) and RSP fared quite badly, with only the FB(R) winning a seat between them. Among the right-wing outfits, the BJS won 9 seats and ABHM won only 4.

Bidhan Chandra Roy went on to form the government as the first elected CM of West Bengal, an office he held on to till 1962 elections. He presided over the absorption of both the French enclave of Chandannagar in 1955 and then of the Bengali-speaking Manbhum region under the States Reorganisation Act of 1956.

States in Transition

Ajmer and Rajasthan

In Ajmer state, which was a Part C state, the only election ever to its legislative assembly was held in 1952. In the 30 member assembly, the INC won 20 of the 30 seats (with a vote share of 44.47%), with the Bharatiya Jana Sangh (BJS) and the Pursharathi Panchayat winning 3 seats each (with 11.95% and 7.72% of vote share), and independents winning the remaining 4.

Ajmer was geographically contiguous to the 19 princely states and 3 chiefships of the Rajput Agency which joined the Indian Union in 5 phases and were merged to create the single state of Rajasthan in 1949, with Heera Lal Shastri as the first chief minister. In 1951 he was replaced by Jai Narayan Vyas, who led the state into its first assembly elections.

In 1952, Rajasthan had its first legislative assembly elections, where the contest was for 160 seats – the INC emerged as the largest party with 82 seats (with a vote share of 39.46%); Akhil Bharatiya Ram Rajya Parishad (ABRRP, which eventually merged with the Bharatiya Jana Sangh after 1962) won 24 seats (with 12.46% vote share); the BJS won 8 seats, and 7 seats were won by Krishikar Lok Party (led by N.G. Ranga, an ex-Congressman who broke from the Congress in 1951 to first to join Hyderabad State Praja Party, and then to set up KLP. He later went on to become the founder-president of the Swatantra Party). 2 seats were won by the Akhil Bharatiya Hindu Mahasabha (ABHM), and 1 each by the Socialist Party and Kisan Mazdoor Praja Party (KMPP). Soon after the election of 1952, the latter 2 merged to form the Praja Socialist Party (PSP).

In Rajasthan, the INC formed a government under Tika Ram Paliwal for a brief period, before Jai Narayan Vyas returned as the chief minister (1952–54). Vyas eventually persuaded 22 MLAs from ABRRP to join the Congress, which resulted in some rancour in the party because they, being landlords with vested interests, were suspected to be inclined to oppose prospective land reforms. The discontent acquired such a pitch that Vyas was directed to seek a vote of confidence within the Congress Legislature party. In the contest that followed, Vyas was defeated by his own cabinet colleague Mohan Lal Sukhadia, who now became the chief minister for the rest of the term (1954–57), a position he went on to occupy for the next 17 years.

In 1956, Ajmer State was merged into Rajasthan, where the legislative assembly ended up with 190 seats.

Punjab and PEPSU

The lands west of the Sutlej River, which comprised the heartland of the Khalsa state in the nineteenth century, constituted the province of Punjab after 1849. In British Punjab, Muslims constituted the single largest group but not the majority of the population. Hence, after the partition of the subcontinent was decided upon, Muslim and non-Muslim members of the legislative assembly decided on partitioning the province in July 1947; the assembly members also began to sit separately since then.

In the Punjab State after independence, the INC nominated Bhim Sen Sachar to serve as the first chief minister of the state, but he had to resign in the face of bitter factionalism in 1949. This was followed by the first instance of imposition of President's Rule under Act 356, even as Punjab went to the polls in 1952.

Elections to the first legislative assembly in Indian province of Punjab took place in 1952 for 126 seats in 105 constituencies (84 single-member and 21 two-member constituencies). As in most other states, here too the INC emerged the clear winner, winning 96 seats (with 36.69% of vote share); the Shiromani Akali Dal (SAD) came second with 13 seats (12.44% vote share) and the CPI won 4 seats (3.89%), and the Zamindar's Party (the rump left behind after the Unionist coalition from before partition broke up) won 2 seats.

Bhim Sen Sachar of the INC was sworn in as chief minister of Punjab (1952–56), and held office till he was replaced by Partap Singh Kairon in 1956.

On the East bank of the Sutlej, 8 princely states of Patiala, Kapurthala, Jind, Nabha, Faridkot, Malerkotla, Kalsia and Nabhagarh were constituted into the Patiala and East Punjab States Union (PEPSU) in 1948, which lasted for 8 years – with the last Raja of Patiala, Maharaja Yadavindra Singh becoming the *rajpramukh*.

Elections to the 60 seats of PEPSU legislative assembly were fought in 40 single-member constituencies and 10 two-member constituencies. The INC managed to win only 26 seats (with 28.66% vote share, the lowest of all states); the Akali Dal won 19 seats, the CPI 2, the KMPP 1, Lal Communist Party Hind Union (which merged into the CPI in 1952) won 1.

In 1956, under the States Reorganisation Act, the PEPSU was merged into the Punjab state, increasing constituencies from 105 to 126, and seats from 121 to 154 seats.

GIAN SINGH RAREWALA, A VICTORIOUS INDEPENDENT CANDIDATE FORMED A UNITED FRONT COALITION OF ALL NON-CONGRESS ELEMENTS (MINUS THE 2 SEATS OF JANA SANGH) TO BECOME THE CHIEF MINISTER OF THE STATE, THE FIRST NON-CONGRESS CHIEF MINISTER TO RULE ANY STATE IN INDIA.

Bombay and Saurashtra

The Bombay state was created in 1950 by merging the Bombay Presidency (comprising much of what is now Maharashtra, excluding southern Maharashtra and Vidarbha regions) with Baroda, Western India and Gujarat States Agency (a collection of princely states that were constituted into an Agency in three stages in 1937, 1944 and 1947). The Bombay state was ruled by Balasaheb Gangadhar Kher from 1946–52, presiding over the creation of the state.

Because of the complexity of the stages in the emergence of the state, of the 268 constituencies of the Bombay state, there was 1 three-member constituency, 47 two-member constituency and 220 single member constituency – thus the assembly had 317 seats in all. When the elections were held, the INC won 270 of 315 seats (vote share of 49.95%), with the Peasants and Workers Party of India (a Marxist party set up in 1948, concentrated primarily in the districts of Satara, Kolapur and Solhapur) coming second with 14 seats (vote share of 6.45%) and the Socialist Party came third with 9 seats (11.96% vote share). The Scheduled Castes Federation (of B.R. Ambedkar) and CPI ended with 1 seat each; the ABRRP, ABHM, BJS and the Forward Bloc drew blanks.

Courtesy the overwhelming victory, the home minister of the Kher government and a prominent freedom fighter Morarji Desai became the first chief minister of the Bombay state where he held office till October 1956. Desai's period in office was marred by escalating disturbances led by demands of bifurcation of the Bombay state into 2 states – 1 for the Gujarati speaking people and 1 for the Marathi speakers. Desai, himself a Gujarati-speaking Brahmin from Valsad region of Gujarat, was opposed to the demand for the creation of a separate state of Gujarat, led by Indulal Kanaiyalal Yagnik of the All India Kisan Sabha, and the life force of the Mahagujarat Movement. He also came into conflict with the Samyukta Maharashtra Samiti (led by Pandurang Mahadev Bapat), whose protests at the Flora Fountain demanding separate state for the Marathi-speaking regions of western and central India were subjected to brutal police firing that left more than a hundred people dead. The unfortunate incident caused Desai's removal from Bombay and his induction into the Union cabinet. Flora Fountain was renamed Hutatma Chowk (Martyrs' Square) in memory of those who lost their lives that day. Partly in acknowledgement of the demands of the Samyukta Maharashtra Samiti, the States Reorganisation Act of 1956 added the Marathi-speaking Berar and Nagpur divisions of the Central Provinces and Berar, and the Aurungabad Division of the Hyderabad state. However, the Gujarati-speaking Saurashtra and Kutch states were also inducted into the Bombay state, enlarging not only the state itself, but also the Gujarati-speaking component of the unit. However, the southern-most regions of the Bombay state were taken away and merged into the Mysore state, and the Abu Road taluka was given to the newly created state of Rajasthan. As a consequence of all this reorganization, the assembly constituencies of the state increased in number from 315 to 391 by the end of 1956. At this stage, Morarji Desai was replaced by Yashwantrao Balwantrao Chavan, who took the Congress into the assembly elections of 1957.

By contrast with the Bombay state, the Saurashtra state constituted of what used to be the 200 odd princely states of Baroda, Western India and Gujarat States Agency of colonial era, which were merged after 1947 to form the United State of Kathiawar, and later the United State of Saurashtra in 1948, into which the princely state of Junagadh was merged in 1949. Before elected assemblies came into being, the last rulers of Bhavnagar and then that of Nawanagar functioned as the *rajpramukh*, while INC activist Uchchhrangarai Nawalshankar Dhebar functioned as the chief minister during 1948–54.

In the only election that was held for the Vidhan Sabha of Saurasthra State, contests were held for 60 seats in 50 single-member constituencies and 5 two-member constituencies. The INC swept the polls, winning 55 seats on a vote share of 63.79%; the Socialist Party won 2 seats and a farmers' outfit, Saurashtra Khedut Sangh, 1 seat. The ABHM, the ABRRP, BJS, CPI, Kisan Mazdoor Sabha and the Scheduled Castes Federation - each drew a blank.

The Saurashtra state, of course, had a very brief life. Headed by Nawalshankar Dhebar (1952–54) and then Rasiklal Umedchand Parikh (1954–56) as the two INC chief ministers, the state was merged into Bombay by the States Reorganisation Act of 1956.

Madhya Pradesh, Bhopal, Vindhya Pradesh, Madhya Bharat

The core of what came to constitute the central Indian state of Madhya Pradesh was what used to be the Central Provinces and Berar during British rule, which had an elected legislative agency of its own since 1937. After 1947, it was merged with a number of small princely states to constitute the state of Madhya Pradesh which in 1952 went on to elect its Vidhan Sabha of 184 constituencies, of which 136 were single-member constituencies and 48 were dual-member constituencies.

The INC won an emphatic victory with a tally of 194 seats and vote share of 49.07%; the Kisan Mazdoor Praja Party (KMPP) came second with 8 seats (5.22% share of votes) and the Socialist Party came fourth with 2 seats (but 9.46% of the votes) while the ABRRP won 3 seats (2.51% vote share).

Pt Ravi Shankar Shukla, a veteran Congressman who had entered the cabinet of Central Provinces and Berar (1937–39) and then became its chief minister in 1946, and continued as the chief minister of Madhya Pradesh in 1940, was the natural choice for chief minister in the elected government of MP. He was a pivotal factor in the integration of the princely states of Central India into the Indian Union and became the architect of the state of Madhya Pradesh under the Reorganisation Act of 1956 – which he was to administer only briefly before his death in 1956 itself.*

At the time of India's independence, the Nawab of the princely state of Bhopal intended to remain outside the Indian Union, in the teeth of opposition from his subjects, led by Shankar Dayal Sharma. Although popular demonstrations were cracked down upon and Sharma was sent to jail, eventually under public pressure the Nawab acceded to India in 1949, whereupon it was constituted as a Part C state under a chief commissioner.

The only election to the legislative assembly was held in 1952. The assembly had 30 seats that were made up of 16 single-member and 7 two-member constituencies. The INC formed the government with 25 seats and the Hindu Mahasabha won 1 seat. The elected government of the state was formed under the leadership of Shankar Dayal Sharma, which lasted till the state of Bhopal was merged into the state of Madhya Pradesh under the States Reorganisation Act of 1956. Sharma went on to serve in the newly constituted government of Madhya Pradesh, and later as its chief minister.

The 25 princely states of the Central India Agency that acceded to the Indian Union comprised the state of Madhya Bharat, which came into being in 1948. The state was headed by

* One of his sons Shyama Charan Shukla went on to become the chief minister of the province, while another of his sons Vidya Charan Shukla had a long political career – beginning with the Congress, then going through Jan Morcha (founder member along-with Arif Muhammad Khan and Arun Nehru), Janata Dal (where he served in both VP Singh and Chandra Sekhar government), then returned to Congress and held a ministerial berth in Narasimha Rao government), left it again for first NCP and then BJP before a final return to the Congress, where he stayed till his death in 2013.

Jivaji Rao Sindhia as the *rajpramukh* (1948–56), while Liladhar Joshi, G.K. Vijayvargiya and Takhatmal Jalori served as chief ministers of Madhya Bharat till the first legislative assembly elections in 1952.

The Vidhan Sabha of Madhya Bharat had 99 seats for its 79 constituencies, of which 59 were single-member and 20 two-member constituencies. The INC emerged as the clear winner with a tally of 75 seats (vote share of 47.24%). The ABHM came second with 11 seats (11.92%), while Socialist Party and the BJS won 4 seats each and the ABRRP won 2. The government was formed under Mishirlal Gangwal, who led the state till 1955, before he was briefly succeeded again by Takhatmal Jain Jalori who held the office till the merger of the state under the Reorganisation in 1956.

The 37 states to the eastern part of the Central India Agency that came to constitute the Baghelkhand and Bundelkhand states after their accession in 1948 were merged to create the Vindhya Pradesh in 1950. The 60-seat legislative assembly that came into being in 1952 was made up of 36 single-member and 12 two-member constituencies. The INC won 40 of these seats (with a vote share 39.60% of the votes), while the Socialist Party came second with 11 seats (18.82% vote share) and the KMPP with 3 seats (16.2% vote share). The BJS and the ABRRP won 2 seats each cornering 14% of the votes between themselves.

The government of Vindhya Pradesh that was sworn in after the polls was headed by Sambhu Nath Shukla from 1952 to the time the state was merged into that of Madhya Pradesh in 1956.

Assam and the North-East

The province of Assam had been reconstituted and was given its own legislative assembly under the Government of India Act of 1935. Apart from the present state of Assam, the territories of the present states of Meghalaya, Nagaland, Mizoram and

Arunachal Pradesh were also included in it. Later at the time of partition Sylhet was taken from the state of Assam and made over to Pakistan.

In 1947, upon being constituted as a state in the Indian Union, Gopinath Bordoloi, a veteran Congressman became the first chief minister of Assam. Upon his death in 1950, Bishnuram Medhi, the finance minister of the Bordoloi cabinet, became the second CM of Assam, who took the state into the first elections after independence.

In 1952, elections to the legislative assembly for the state were held in 81 single-member and 13 two-member constituencies. 9 national parties and 10 unregistered parties from the region contested the elections. The INC contested in 92 constituencies and ended up with a tally of 76 seats (vote share of 43.48%) – being the only party to end up with a double-digit tally. The Socialist Party with 4 seats (13.3%) came second, while Garo National Council with 3 seats (0.6% of vote share) tied for the third spot with Mizo Union (1.19% vote share). The CPI, Khasi Jaintia Durbar, and Khasi Jaintia Federated State National Conference won 1 seat each. Independents won 14 seats with a 28.34% share of the votes.

Bishnu Ram Medhi became the first elected CM of Assam, an office he held on to till 1957. He became known for his hard line against the Naga insurgency and illegal migration while in office.

Madras

The Madras Presidency was constituted into the Madras State in 1937, comprising much of what are the present-day states of Tamil Nadu, Andhra Pradesh and parts of Kerala and Karnataka. Chakravarti Rajagopalachari of the INC became its first premier till INC provincial ministries resigned in 1939.

In 1946, INC regained power but was plagued by factionalism with Telugu-speaking T. Prakasam becoming the chief minister of the Madras state. He was soon replaced by O.P. Ramaswamy Reddiyar, who was in turn replaced by P.S. Kumaraswamy Raja – all as a result of machinations of Kumaraswamy Kamaraj. In 1951, the Andhra faction of Tanguturu Prakasam broke away to join Jivatram Kripalani to form the Kisan Mazdoor Praja Party (and eventually broke away from the KMPP also to form the Hyderabad Krishak Praja Party). Thus, the Congress went to the 1952 elections to the Madras legislative assembly as a divided house with clusters representing multiple factions – particularly the Tamil Brahmin (Rajagopalachari) faction and the Tamil non-Brahmin (Kamaraj) faction.

In 1952 the Madras legislative assembly was delimited to have 375 seats, divided between 243 single member constituencies and 66 were two-member constituencies. The INC emerged as the single largest party, winning 152 seats (34.88% vote share), but well short of majority – which included 96 of the 190 Tamil constituencies, and 9 of the 11 in the Kannada speaking areas, but only 4 of the 29 seats from the Malabar region and only 43 of 143 Telugu-speaking areas. The incumbent chief minister PSK Raja lost the election.

The CPI won 62 seats and the KMPP won 35 seats, the Socialist Party 13, the Krishak Lok Party (of NG Ranga) another 15, Tamil Nadu Toilers' Party 19, and the score of Commonweal Party 6 and independents stood at 62. This encouraged all the non-Congress parties to attempt to form a coalition government, with T. Prakasam actually staking claim. While Kamaraj maintained that a non-Congress coalition should be allowed to form only to prove itself untenable, others such as T.T. Krishnamachari and Ramnath Goenka persuaded the Congress to stake claim, bringing Rajagopalachari in as a consensus candidate. Rajaji's refusal to run for a bypoll made it necessary for him to be sent through the Legislative Council, making him the first unelected head of a state government of any province in independent India. Also, Rajaji became the first Indian head of government to stand a floor test in the assembly to prove the confidence of the house. The floor test was won by 206 votes to 162, by engineering defections from the KLP, and making independent legislators to join the Congress; the Commonweal Party was won over with promise of a cabinet post, and Tamil Nadu Toilers' Party was rewarded with subsequent induction in the cabinet – first instance of what now passes for horse-trading in the history of Indian politics above the municipal level.

In the months that followed, the demand for separating the Telugu-speaking regions of the Madras state accelerated, resulting in the bifurcation of the province by the end of the next year. In October 1953, a separate Andhra state was constituted by removing all the Telugu-speaking districts of Madras, and the Kannada-speaking area of Bellary district was merged into the Mysore state – reducing the size of the Madras assembly to 230, with 140 seats going to Andhra and five to Karnataka, resulting in resignation of ministers who were representing the affected constituencies. More crucially for the Madras government, in the 230-strong rump assembly, the Congress had 118 seats which gave it an outright majority. Kamaraj used this crisis to topple Rajagopalachari (who was left weakened by the departure of his allies within the party), and formed the next government (1954–57) offering cabinet berths to Tamil Nadu Toilers' Party and the Commonweal Party – marking the end of the prolonged Brahmin domination of the politics of the Madras state.

Madras underwent another round of reorganization in 1956. Under the States Reorganisation Act, the Malabar district was taken out of Madras and clubbed with Travancore-Cochin to create the state of Kerala, while the Tamil-speaking regions of Travancore-Cochin was merged into Madras – the regions of Kanyakumari and Shenkottah. The archipelago of 36 islands off the Malabar coast was taken from the Madras state and reconstituted as the Union Territory of Laccadives, Minicoy and Amindivi Islands (which later became the UT of Lakshwadeep in 1973). As a result of all these territorial reorganization and delimitation of constituencies, the Madras assembly came to have 205 seats when it went to the elections in 1957.

From Hyderabad to Andhra Pradesh

Hyderabad was one of the largest princely states of British India, embracing large parts of the Deccan, ruled by the Nizam based in the city of Hyderabad. When British rule came to an end, Hyderabad wanted to either remain independent or sign the instrument of accession in favour of Pakistan. By 1948, Hyderabad was beginning to unravel with the Telangana uprising on the one hand, and the violent Razakar movement on the other. Thus, India seized the initiative and took over Hyderabad in a police action in September 1948, and incorporated the princely state into the Indian Union in January 1950 as the state of Hyderabad. The last Nizam, Asaf Jah VI, Mir Osman Ali Khan was made the *rajpramukh*, an office he held till the dissolution of the state in 1956.

In 1952, elections were held for the 175 seats of the Hyderabad legislative assembly in 109 single-member constituencies and 33 two-member constituencies. The INC won a clear majority with 93 seats (vote share being 41.86%). The People's Democratic Front, which was a front organization of the CPI (which was banned in the Hyderabad state), won 42 seats (20.76%) to come second, the Socialist Party won 11 seats, the Peasants and Workers's Party of India won 10 seats and the Scheduled Caste Federation won 5 seats (with less than 5% of the vote share).

The state of Hyderabad had gone to the polls in 1952 under the ICS officer M.K. Vellodi, but after the elections, Burgula Ramakrishna Rao became the first and only elected chief minister of the state.

The Andhra state that came into being in 1953 as a result of the agitation demanding a state for the Telugu-speaking people of Seemandhra region of Madras state (after the death of Potti Sreeramalu in December 1952), with the popular leader of Hyderabad State Praja Party, Tanguturi Prakasam Panthulu becoming the first chief minister of the Andhra state. However, allegations of corruption led to the fall of the Prakasam government in 1955. In the polls that followed in the Andhra state, the assembly came to be constituted of 167 constituencies (of which 138 were single-member and 29 two-member constituencies) with 196 seats. Of these, the INC won 119 seats (39.35% of the vote share), thus forming a government with a comfortable majority. The Krishikar Lok Party (of N.G. Ranga, and ex-Congressman) emerged the second-largest party with 22 seats (vote share of 7.26%), the CPI following with 15 seats and the PSP with 13 seats, and the Praja Party (a breakaway faction of KMPP after it decided to merge with SP) won 5 seats.

B.G. Reddy of the INC went on to become the only elected chief minister of the Andhra State in 1955, and remained in office till in 1956 the Telugu-speaking regions of Hyderabad state were merged with the Andhra State, creating Andhra Pradesh. Since the Kannada speaking regions of Hyderabad state – Raichur, Bidar and Gulbarga – were merged into the Mysore state, and the Marathi-speaking region of Marathwada was given to Maharashtra, Andhra Pradesh became a largely homogenoeus Telugu-speaking province, which went to the polls for the first time in 1957.

Coorg and Mysore

The princely state of Kodagu, which was annexed by the British in 1834, became a Commissioners' province of Coorg (the smallest province), which upon independence in 1947 became the state of Coorg. The first elections to the Coorg assembly took place in 1952. The INC went to the polls led by C.M. Poonacha, with the demand for Coorg to be merged with the state of Mysore; the principal opposition Takkadi party led by Pandyanda Belliappa resisted the idea of the merger.

The Coorg legislative assembly was made up of 18 constituencies (12 single member and 6 two-member constituencies) with 24 seats. The INC won 15 of the seats (with 55.54% vote share), with independents (opposing merger, affiliated to the Takkadi party) winning 9 seats. The CPI, which was the only other major party to contest in Coorg, drew a blank.

The Poonacha government subsequently worked to bring about the merger with Mysore state, an agenda that was accomplished in 1956.

The Mysore state was one of the largest princely states of British India, whose ruler Jayachamarajendra Wadiyar signed the Instrument of Accession in favour of India in August 1947 itself, with the maharaja continuing to be addressed as the maharaja of Mysore state. In 1950, when the state officially became a state of the Indian Union, the maharaja was made the *rajpramukh* (1950–56) of the Mysore state, and then its governor (1956–64). During the period of the interim government, the Vokkaliga activist for representative government in Mysore state, the Congress leader Kyasamballi Chengaluraya Reddy, was made the chief minister (1947–52).

In the first ever elections held in Mysore state in 1952, the legislative assembly saw contest over 99 seats (of which 19 were two-member constituencies, and 61 single-member). The INC won 74 seats (with a vote share of 46.35%), with the KMPP emerging the second-largest party with 8 seats (14.22% vote share), the Socialist Party 3 seats (8.73%), the Scheduled Caste Federation (SCF) 2 seats (1.74%) and CPI 1 seat (vote share of 0.91%).

Kengal Hanumanthaiah, a Vokkaliga leader of the INC, became the first elected chief minister (1952–56) of the Mysore state.

In November 1956, the Coorg state was merged into the Mysore state. Further, Kollagal taluk of Coimbatore and south

Kanara region (minus Kasaragod) of the Madras state, the districts of Raichur and Gulbarga from Hyderabad state, and the Kannada speaking regions of Dharwar, Bujapur, North Kanara and Belgaum from Bombay state was also clubbed with the Mysore state. As a result of this reorganization, the Mysore legislative assembly came to have 179 constituencies (150 single-member and 29 two-member constituencies), with 208 seats.

Travancore–Cochin

The state of Travancore–Cochin came into being in 1949, when the princely states of Travancore and Cochin were merged to form one single state. The kingdom of Cochin was one of the oldest princely states on the Indian subcontinent to have survived (dating back to at least the fourteenth century). By the nineteenth century, though, the kingdom of Travancore (Thiruvithamkoor) gained greater significance. At the time of India's independence, the kingdom of Travancore actually toyed with the idea of staying independent, which was firmly opposed by a burgeoning group of communists who mounted a violent resistance. The communists were believed to have been behind the assassination bid on the Diwan, C.P. Ramaswamy Iyer, which presumably hastened the accession of Travancore to thc Indian Union. The maharaja of Travancore was made the *rajpramukh* of Travancore–Cochin when the state came into being; the ruler of Cochin declined any titles or roles after accession.

At the time when the states of Travancore and Cochin entered into the Indian Union, political leaders in the two states were made the prime minister of people's governments – Pattom A. Thanu Pillai, succeeded in 1948 by Parur T.K. Narayana Pillai, as the PM of Travancore; Panampilly Govinda Menon, Thozhur Krishnan Nair and then finally E. Ikkanda Warrier as the PM of Cochin. Upon merger, P.T.K. Narayana Pillai became the first chief minister of Travancore–Cochin, but was soon replaced by Congressman and social activist C. Kesavan, who led the state into the polls of 1952.

The state of Travancore–Cochin had 86 single-member and 11 two-member constituencies, which returned the 108 seats of the legislative assembly. The polls were contested by 3 national parties – INC, SP, and the RSP – and 4 state parties; namely, the Cochin Party (CP), Travancore-Cochin Republican Praja Party (TCRPP), Travancore Tamil Nadu Congress (TTNC), Tamil Nadu Toilers' Party (TNTP), Kerala Socialist Party (KSP) and Tamil Nadu Peoples' Front (TNPF). The CPI was banned in the state by then, hence its candidates ran as independents, who later went on to form the United Left Front after the elections. The INC emerged as the single largest party with 44 seats (vote share of 35.44%), which was well short of the majority mark. It therefore went on to form a coalition with the TTNC which won 8 seats, the KSP with its 1 seat and a nominated member. The Socialist Party with its 11 seats (14.28% vote share), the RSP with its 6 seats (3.48% vote share) and a good many of the 37 independents (who were actually from the CPI) posed a powerful opposition.

Anaparambil Joseph John of the Congress became the first elected chief minister of Travancore–Cochin, but when in 1953 Kanyakumari was taken from Travancore–Cochin and given to Madras state, TTNC withdrew its support from the Congress government and led to its fall, and dissolution of the assembly – the first case of dissolution for want of majority on the floor of the House anywhere in India.

In the elections that followed in the spring of 1954, the assembly came to have the reduced strength of 106 constituencies (95 single-member and 11 two-member constituencies) with 117 seats. The INC emerged as the single largest party with 45 seats (with a vote share of 45.32%), the CPI winning 23 seats (16.78% of vote share) came second; the Praja Socialist Party (PSP, formed by the merger of the Socialist Party and the KMPP) fighting its first elections won a tally of 19 seats; the TTNC won 12 seats and the RSP won 9 seats. The CPI, RSP and KSP had formed an alliance called the United Front of Leftists (UFL) in 1952, who thus had a tally of 32 seats. When the PSP, now led by former Congressman and former PM of Travancore, Pattom Thanu Pillai joined hands with the INC, the coalition came to have 64 seats and was able to form a majority government, with Pillai becoming the fourth chief minister of Travancore-Cochin. He was succeeded by Panampilli Govinda Menon in 1955, who continued in office till 1956, when President's Rule was imposed in the state.

In November 1956, under the States Reorganisation Act, the Tamil speaking regions of southern Travancore were given to the Madras State, and the Malabar district, Kasaragod taluk and south Kanara of Madras were merged with Travancore–Cochin to form the state of Kerala.

States With a Brief Spurt of Life

Delhi

In 1952, the Delhi Vidhan Sabha came into being for a brief period of around 4 years when the territory was constituted into a Part-C state, governed by a Chief Commissioner, with a council of Ministers in an advisory capacity drawn from the Delhi Vidhan Sabha.

The assembly had 48 members – with 36 constituencies being one-member and 6 being two-member constituencies. The Congress effortlessly won 39 seats in the assembly (with 52.09% of the vote share). The ABJS with five seats came second (with 21.89% vote share). The Socialist Party won 2 seats, and the ABHM one. The council of ministers was headed by Chaudhary Brahm Prakash Yadav (who later joined the JD and finally landed up with Charan Singh).

However, the States Reorganisation Act 1956 turned Delhi into a Union Territory under the direct control of the central government. It was only in 1991 that the National Capital Territory of Delhi was reconstituted as a state by the Sixty-ninth Amendment to the Constitution.

Himachal Pradesh

In 1948, 30 princely states of the Western Himalayas were merged to create the Chief Commissioner's Province of Himachal Pradesh. In 1950, it became a Part C state under the aegis of a Lt Governor.

The legislative assembly came into being after the election of 1952. Of the 36 seats that were up for grabs, the INC won 24 (with 47.25% of the votes), while the Kisan Mazdoor Sabha came second with 3 seats (14.67% vote share) and the Scheduled Castes Federation came third with 1 seat (5.77% vote share).

However, existence of that assembly was quite brief. The state was turned into a Union Territory under the States Reorganisation Act of 1956, and was dissolved forthwith. The territory was reconstituted into a state once again at the time of Punjab Reorganisation Act, 1966.

The One that Stood Out

The election that stood out was the one in Jammu and Kashmir, for very curious reasons. The Dogra King of Jammu and Kashmir, Hari Singh, wanted to remain independent like many other princely states, and routinely rebuffed overtures by both Indian and Pakistan to join either of the two unions. In the face of incursion by tribals from Pakistan which led to a brief war, Hari Singh signed the treaty of accession in favour of India - which was the precondition of Indian intervention to save his kingdom.

The leader of the opposition in the kingdom, Shekih Abdullah, was appointed the head of the Emergency Administration for the duration of the 1948 war with Pakistan. After the ceasefire was signed, Sheikh Abdullah was appointed the prime minister of the state of J&K in March 1948. When the J&K government declared its intent in October 1950 of setting up a Constituent assembly, a lot of diplomatic tussle ensued between India and Pakistan upon the latter's protest against attempts at formalizing Indian control over the princely state. In April 1951, the prince regent Karan Singh announced elections that were scheduled to be held in September–October 1951.

The Constituent assembly was meant to have 100 seats, of which 25 were earmarked for the region under Pakistani occupation. Of the remaining 75, 43 were to be allocated to the Kashmir valley, 30 went to Jammu and 2 to Ladakh.

In 1951, elections were held for the 75 seats in the Jammu and Kashmir Constituent assembly, with a 6-year term and a mandate for the drafting of a constitution for the state. The Jammu & Kashmir National Conference was elected unopposed in all 75 seats. This was largely because nominations of all 13 candidates of Jammu Praja Parishad were rejected. The 2 seats of Ladakh, including that of the Kushak Bakula (the head Lama), were in the capacity of nominal members of the National Conference.

Sheikh Abdullah continued as the prime minister of J&K, with Bakshi Ghulam Mohammad, serving as deputy prime minister. Frictions began between Abdullah and the Jammu Praja Parishad, as well as Kushak Bakula, in addition to conflicts with the Union government. Accordingly, in August 1953, Sheikh Abdullah was dismissed from the position of prime minister in August 1953 (and subsequently arrested) and was replaced by Bakshi Ghulam Mohammad, who completed the process of drafting of the constitution, which was adopted in November 1956 and came into effect in January 1957.

Chapter 4

REORGANISATION AND AFTER 1957–67

1957

Elections were held in 1957 for 13 legislative assemblies all over the country. Eight states were voting for the assembly for the second time, viz. Assam, Bihar, Bombay, Madras, Mysore, Orissa, Uttar Pradesh, West Bengal; 5 others were voting for the first time: Andhra Pradesh, Kerala, Madhya Pradesh, Punjab and Rajasthan. Delhi, which was deprived of its statehood by the States Reorganisation Act of 1956, was reduced to a municipal administration.

Assam

In 1957, 94 constituencies (80 single member and 14 two-member) of the Assam legislative assembly went to the polls for 108 seats. The INC continued its domination of the state's politics and largely held on to its support base, winning 71 seats (5 less than 1952) with 52.35% of the vote share. The PSP came to the second slot, winning 8 seats (12.74% vote share), while the CPI improved its tally to 4 seats (8.10% vote share), and independents ended up with 25 seats.

Despite winning the polls, the incumbent chief minister Bishnuram Medhi was removed, presumably because of his growing unpopularity in the Naga hills. He was replaced by another veteran freedom fighter, Bimala Prasad Chaliha, who held the office for 3 consecutive terms from 1957 to 1970.

Bihar

By the time of the 1957 elections, Bihar had seen the removal of the Manbhum-Purulia region, which was given to West Bengal by the States Reorganisation Act, 1956. Accordingly, the number of assembly seats came down from 330 to 318, which were distributed over 264 assembly constituencies (210 single-member and 54 two-member constituencies). Of the 318 seats up for grabs, the INC won a comfortable majority with 210 seats (29 seats less than in 1952), with a vote share of 42%. The new entry made up of old parties, the PSP won 31 seats (vote share 16.01%) to share the second slot with the Jharkhand Party (7.08%). The Chota Nagpur Santhal Parganas Janata Party (of Maharaja Kamakhya Narain Singh) improved its tally to win 23 seats (7.83%), while the CPI won made its entry into the Bihar assembly with seven seats (5.15%).

Despite losing a few seats, Chief Minister Sri Krishna Sinha was perceived to have performed sufficiently well to continue in office, which he held till his death in 1961.

Bombay

The Bombay state was considerably transformed by the States Reorganisation Act, 1956 – losing territory to Mysore state to the south and Rajasthan to the north, but gaining the Kutch and Saurashtra states by merger, as also the Marathi speaking regions of erstwhile Madhya Pradesh and Hyderabad. Accordingly, the assembly strength increased from 315 to

396 seats, distributed over 339 assembly constituencies (282 single-member and 57 two-member constituencies).

The INC won by a comfortable but considerably reduced margin of 234 seats (36 seats less than the previous one, constituency by constituency) with a marginally lower vote share of 48.66%. The PSP came second with 36 seats (vote share of 8.97%); the Peasants and Workers' Party came third with 31 seats (vote share of 6.6%), while the Scheduled Caste Federation and the CPI drew level with each other at 13 seats each (gain of 12 seats for both). The BJS and ABHM entered the state assembly with 4 and 1 seats respectively; independents won 64 seats, 45 more than the last time.

Y.B. Chavan, who took the bilingual Bombay state into the assembly polls, was elected leader of the Legislature party and sworn in as (what turned out to be) the last chief minister of the Bombay state (1957–60). The INC had performed badly in the Marathi-speaking areas, having lost 101 seats out of 133 to members of the Samyukta Rashtra Samiti (running as members of some local parties as well as independents) – it held on to power only with support of Gujarati-speaking regions, Vidarbha and Marathwada. In a payback to the Gujarati-speaking constituency of the Bombay state, Chavan, thus, though not personally a supporter of bifurcation of Bombay state, recommended creation of Marathi-speaking Maharashtra and a new state of Gujarat as two separate states – which came into being in May 1960. Chavan continued in office, now as the chief minister of the new state of Maharashtra.

Madras

The 1957 assembly elections were the first since reorganization of the Madras state, effectively along linguistic lines. K. Kamaraj, who had toppled C. Rajagopalachari over his pro-Hindi education reforms to become the chief minister of the state in 1954, led the INC as a party now dominated by Tamil non-Brahmins. Rajagopalachari left the INC to float his own party, called Congress Reform Committee (CRC). Also at these elections, the Dravida nationalist movement - Dravida Kazhagam (DK, foundeds in 1944 by Periyar Ramaswamy) made its entry in the electoral field. While the DK was not a political party, rather a movement, it split in 1949 when C.N. Annadurai split from it to create Dravida Munnetra Kazhagam (Dravidian Progressive Federation) in 1949, with the demand to create a Dravida Nadu (Dravidian state), which grew into a powerful movement. The creation of linguistic Madras state encouraged the DMK to enter the electoral field, but not being a registered party yet, its members ran mostly as independents. With Periyar at the head of the rump, DK decided to support Tamil non-Brahmin Kamaraj as chief minister.

The strength of the Madras assembly when it went to the polls was 205, split over 129 single-member and 38 two-member constituencies. The INC swept the polls, winning 151 seats (vote share of 45.34%); the CRC won 13 seats (with 4 more seats to its ally AIFB); among registered parties the CPI won 4 seats (losing 58 seats as a result of the break-up of the state), and the PSP won 2 seats; independents won 48 seats (of which 16 seats were won by the DMK politicians, who won 14% of the vote share.).

K. Kamaraj returned as the chief minister and lasted in office for the full term, leading his party to the polls in 1962. The CRC was soon joined by 5 more independents, and the party was reconstituted as the Indian National Democratic Congress - which emerged as the official party of the opposition in the state. In 1959, the INDC merged into the Swatantra Party.

Mysore

After the States Reorganisation Act of 1956, Mysore assembly came to have 208 seats for which elections were held in 1957 across 179 constituencies (150 single-member and 29 two-member constituencies).

Riding high presumably on the euphoria of reorganization of the state, the INC won 150 seats in the assembly (winning 52.08% of the popular vote), a crushing majority. The PSP came second with 18 seats; the CPI and Scheduled Castes Federation failed to win a single seat. The independents came with a decent tally of 35 seats.

S. Nijalingappa, who held the chief minister's office since 1956 and led the Congress into the polls, continued in the office till 1958, when he was made to step down, and was succeeded by Basappa Danappa Jatti (1958–62) – hailing from the region of the Mysore state that came in from Bombay state. Jatti was later to steer the committee on land reforms that helped abolish tenancy system and landlordism in the state in 1961.

Orissa

Elections to the second Orissa legislative assembly in 1957 took place in 140 seats of 101 constituencies (69 single-member constituencies and 39 two-member constituencies). The INC fared poorly in these elections, winning only 56 seats (38.26% vote share), 11 seats less than the last time. It faced a tough competition from the All Indian Ganatantra Parishad (AIGP) that won 51 seats (vote share 28.74%), 20 more than the last time. The PSP finished with 11 seats and the CPI with 9 seats.

Harekrushna Mahtab, who had been the first chief minister of Orissa (1946–50) before he was succeeded by Nabakrushna Chowdhury, and then had resumed the office in 1956, became the head of a minority government; Rajendra Narayan Singh Deo of the AIGP became the leader of the opposition. The government eventually collapsed in 1959, and a mid-term poll was avoided only with the formation of a INC-AIGP coalition with Harekrushna Mahtab as the chief minister and R.N. Singh

Deo as the finance minister. The coalition eventually collapsed in 1961, and President's Rule was imposed in Orissa.

Uttar Pradesh

In 1957, the UP went to assembly polls for the second time since independence, without any change in the make-up of the state. The contest was for 430 seats in 252 single-member and 89 two-member constituencies.

The INC went to the polls led by Chief Minister Sampurnanand (1954–60), and won a comfortable but much reduced majority, winning 286 seats (102 seats less than in 1952) with a vote share of 42.42%. The PSP, contesting for the first time in its new avatar, won 44 seats (14.47% in terms of vote share); the BJS won 17 seats (9.84% vote share) and the CPI won 9. Seventy-four candidates running as independents also made it to the assembly.

Sampurnanand continued comfortably into his second time and held office till 1960, when an internal political squabble had him shunted out of the office, and Chandra Bhanu Gupta became the chief minister for the remaining term of the assembly (1960–62).

West Bengal

West Bengal saw minor territorial changes as a part of the Purnea district and the Purulia sub-district of the Manbhum district was added to the state, which increased the number of assembly constituencies from 187 to 195, and seats from 238 to 252.

The INC, led by Dr Bidhan Chandra Roy won a comfortable majority with 152 seats (vote share of 46.14%), but did not manage to add much to its tally of seats. The Congress had to face down three major electoral alliances in this election. The United Left Election Committee – an electoral alliance comprising the CPI,

PSP, AIFB, MFB and RSP – managed to win 75 seats (as against 39 seats in 1952, with a vote share of 33.6%), with the CPI winning 46 seats, the PSP 21, the RSP 8; the United Democratic Peoples' Front (UPDF), which comprised the BJS, AIHM, Revolutionary Communist Party of India (RCPI), and another left-wing alliance the United Left Front – made up of the SUCI, BPI (Bolshevik Party of India) and Democratic Vanguard in India (DV) – failed to win any seats. The CPI, with 46 seats and a vote share of 17.81% became the second-largest party in the assembly.

Dr Bidhan Chandra Roy remained in office for the full second term (1957–62).

Andhra Pradesh

In 1957, the newly constituted state of Andhra Pradesh went to the polls in 85 constituencies (65 single-member and 20 double-member constituencies) for 105 seats for the region of Telengana alone. The members of the assembly who won the 1955 elections (in what used to be the Andhra state) were given a 7-year term so that the assembly could go to polls for all its constituencies at the same time.

The INC won 68 of the 105 seats up for grabs in what would later become Telangana, with a vote share of 47.38%. The Peoples' Democratic Party (PDP), a front for the CPI (which was still banned in the region), won 22 seats (25.73% in terms of vote share); the PSP and the People's Party (PP) won a seat each.

In the INC Legislature Party of the whole of Andhra Pradesh after the 1957 elections, Neelam Sanjeeva Reddy was chosen the chief minister (1957–60).

Kerala

The state of Kerala came into being after the States Reorganisation Act of 1956, with the merger of Travancore-Cochin with the

Malabar district. The state assembly had 114 constituencies (102 single-member and 12 two-member constituencies) with 126 seats.

The CPI emerged as the single largest party with 60 seats (with 35.28% of the vote share), beating the INC in number of seats for the first time. The INC won 43 seats (with a larger share of the popular vote at 37.85%), emerging as the second-largest party in the legislature. The PSP won 9 seats and the independents 14.

E.M.S. NAMBOODIRIPAD OF THE CPI BECAME THE FIRST CHIEF MINISTER OF KERALA, THE SECOND MAN TO HOLD THE CM'S OFFICE WITHOUT EITHER BEING A CONGRESSMAN OR IN ALLIANCE WITH THE CONGRESS – THE FIRST ONE BEING GIAN SINGH RAREWALA OF THE PEPSU.

Madhya Pradesh

In 1956, the states of Bhopal, Madhya Bharat and Vindhya Pradesh were merged into the state of Madhya Pradesh (with some adjustments of territories that were given to Rajasthan an Bombay state). Elections to the assembly of the new state were held in 1957 in 218 constituencies (149 single-member and 69 two-member constituencies) for 287 seats.

The INC won a comfortable majority with 232 seats (and 49.83% of the vote share), thus forming a majority government. The PSP with 12 seats (vote share of 13.17%), the BJS with 10 seats (9.9%), the ABHM with 7 and the CPI with 2 seats made up the Opposition.

Kailash Nath Katju, a former Union Cabinet minister was made the first chief minister of Madhya Pradesh, an office he occupied till the assembly term ended in 1962.

Punjab

In 1956, under the States Reorganisation Act, the PEPSU was merged into the state of Punjab. The newly reconstituted assembly of Punjab now had 121 constituencies (88 single-member and 33 two-member constituencies) for 154 seats.

In the elections that were held in 1957, the INC won a thumping majority with 120 seats (with a vote share of 47.51%). The BJS came second with 9 seats (8.61% of votes), the CPI with 6 and the Scheduled Castes Federation won 5 seats with 13 seats going to independent candidates.

Pratap Singh Kairon of the INC, who had led the INC into the polls as the chief minister of Punjab since 1956 continued in office for the full term (1957–62), leading his party into the next polls in 1962.

Rajasthan

The state of Rajasthan witnessed its final territorial adjustment after integration of the numerous princely states in 1956, when Ajmer was merged into Rajasthan, and other territories were acquired from Bombay state and Punjab, while some others were made over to Madhya Pradesh. The reconstituted legislative assembly increased in size to 136 constituencies (96 single-member and 40 two-member constituencies) with 176 seats.

The INC won a clear majority in the assembly, with 119 seats (45.13% vote share), way ahead of the remaining political parties. The ABRRP came second with 17 seats, the BJS third with 6 seats, the PSP and the CPI winning 1 seat each.

Mohan Lal Sukhadia, who had become the chief minister of Rajasthan in 1954, remained in that office for the full second term of the assembly (1957–62).

The Curious Case of Jammu and Kashmir

The Constituent assembly of Jammu and Kashmir having completed its task of drafting a constitution for the state dissolved itself in 1957, elections were to follow for the election to the legislative assembly. By then the political landscape in J&K was considerably different from what obtained in 1951. The first prime minister of J&K and the original leader of the National Conference, Sheikh Abdullah, along with his associate Mirza Afzal Beg and 33 other leaders of the party, had been imprisoned. Upon being released, Beg along with G.M. Hamdani formed the All Jammu and Kashmir Plebiscite Front (AJKPF), demanding the plebiscite that they had been promised in 1947–48. Other minor local outfits – like the Kashmir Political Conference and the Kashmir Democratic Front – aligned with the AJKPF.

The electoral irregularities of the Constituent assembly period continued into the first legislative assembly as well. Of the 43 seats in the Kashmir valley, the JKNC was elected unopposed in 30 seats, and 10 more seats in Jammu had a similar outcome after nomination papers by the Opposition were rejected on various flimsy grounds – thus giving the party a majority in the assembly before even a single vote was cast. Of the 30 seats that went to the polls, 20 were in Jammu and 8 in the Valley. The only seat in the Valley that the JKNC failed to win was won by a dissident JKNC candidate who won on his own reckoning. In the Jammu Division, the JKNC won 13 of the 20 seats contested; the Praja Parishad 6 and the Harijan Mandal 1 seat. The AJKPF had boycotted the election.

Finishing with a tally of 62 seats, Bakshi Ghulam Mohammad continued in the office of the prime minister, after excluding the left-wing faction led by G.M. Sadiq, Girdhari Lal Dogra and D.P. Dhar from ministerial office that they had enjoyed previously.

1960

Kerala

In Kerala, the Namboodiripad government embarked on a number of its signature policy reforms soon after coming to power which met with severe resistance from sections of the Kerala society. This resulted in a series of agitations against the Communist government which brought all the major political parties (INC, PSP, RSP, KSP and the reconstituted Indian Union Muslim LEAGUE [IUML] as also social organizations of the Syrian Catholics and the Nair Service Society.

After a brief period of President's Rule, Kerala went to the polls yet again in 1960, in 114 constituencies (102 single-member and 12 two-member constituencies) with 126 seats – as before. In this election the INC went into an electoral alliance with the PSP and IUML. The INC emerged as the single largest party with 63 seats (with a vote share of 34.42%), barely reaching the halfway mark by itself. The performance of its electoral allies, the PSP (20 seats, and vote share of 14.14%) and the debutant IUML (11 seats with 4.96%) gave the alliance the numbers to have a comfortable majority (94 seats in an assembly of 126). The CPI sat in the opposition

WHEN THE GOVERNMENT RESORTED TO A VIOLENT CRACKDOWN, THE NAMBOODIRIPAD GOVERNMENT WAS DISMISSED BY THE UNION GOVERNMENT IN JULY 1959, AND PRESIDENT'S RULE WAS IMPOSED UNDER ARTICLE 356, DESPITE ENJOYING MAJORITY ON THE FLOOR OF THE ASSEMBLY – FOR THE FIRST TIME IN THE HISTORY OF THE COUNTRY.

with a much reduced strength of 29 seats (even though with 39.34% of the votes cast it turned out to have the largest share of votes).

Having failed to obtain sufficient seats by itself, the Congress had to forego the chief ministership to Pattom Thanu Pillai of the PSP, who became the chief minister of Kerala in 1960, with Raman Sankar of the Congress as his deputy. When Pillai was made the governor of Punjab in 1962, Sankar became the chief minister (1962–64) and served till he lost a vote of no-confidence against his government in 1964.

1961

Orissa

Harekrushna Mahtab, the chief minister of Orissa had formed a minority government after the polls of 1957. By late 1960, irreconcilable differences appeared within the ruling Congress government, causing Mahtab to resign. In absence of any other party or combination that could stake claim, President's Rule was imposed in Orissa in February 1961, which was followed by a fresh assembly election – the first one to be held after abolition of two-member constituencies.

In the elections that were held in 1961, 140 constituencies went to the polls for 140 seats in the assembly. The INC won 82 seats (with 43.28% vote share), thus obtaining a comfortable majority. The party of the princely states of the region, Ganatantra Parishad, emerged as the second-largest party with 37 seats (27.23%). The PSP won 10 seats, and the CPI 4.

After the elections, the president of the state unit of the INC, Biju Patnaik became the chief minister of the state government, but resigned in 1963 – long before the end of his term in office – under the Kamaraj Plan, to revitalize the party. His successor

Biren Mitra continued in office till 1965, when he was replaced by Sadashiva Tripathy who remained in office for the rest of the assembly term, till 1967 - pointing to inner-party factionalism and resulting political destabilisation.

1962

The year 1962 saw a string of legislative assemblies going to the polls, most of which had gone to the polls in 1957.

Andhra Pradesh

Andhra Pradesh legislative assembly had a full term from 1957, even though the incumbent chief minister, N.S. Reddy left his post upon becoming the president of the INC in 1960. He was replaced by the provincial Congress president, Damodaram Sanjivayya. He happens to have been the first Dalit chief minister (1960–62) of any Indian state.

CM Sanjivayya led the INC to yet another convincing victory at the assembly polls. The INC won 177 seats out (down 10) of the 300 seats that were up for grabs, with a vote share of 47.25%. The CPI with 51 seats (increasing its tally by 14), and a vote share of 19.53% came second. The newly formed Swatantra Party entered the assembly with 19 seats while the SP were left with only 2 seats (losing 14). The PSP, BJS and the Republican Party of India (with its roots in Ambedkar's Scheduled Castes Federation) failed to win any seats at all, and had less than 1% of the popular vote.

N.S. Reddy came back to Andhra Pradesh to be its chief minister for a second time (1962–64), but did not stay to complete a full term. He resigned in 1964 after the Supreme Court made some adverse comments over nationalization of bus routes. He was succeeded by Kasu Brahmananda Reddy, who held office right to the end of the term of the assembly and led his party into the polls in 1967.

Assam

Assam went to the polls in 1962 for the 105 seats of the assembly (77 general seats, 23 reserved for Scheduled Caste candidates and 5 seats for the Scheduled Tribes),

The incumbent chief minister of Assam, B.P. Chaliha led the INC into another convincing assembly election victory, as the party finished with 79 seats (vote share of 48.25%). The second position was taken by the All Party Hill Leaders' Conference (APHLC) led by Williamson A. Sangma, concentrated in the Hill districts that in 1972 would go on to constitute the state of Meghalaya. The APHLC won 11 seats (out of the 15 seats for autonomous Hill districts of the Assam legislative assembly), with a vote share of 5.51%. The PSP won only 6 seats, the RCP 1 seat; both the CPI and the BJS failed to win any seats.

The convincing victory and the lack of any opposition allowed the incumbent chief minister B.P. Chaliha another full term at the helm, as he went on to lead his party into the 1967 elections as well.

Bihar

Upon the death of the incumbent chief minister of Bihar Shri Krishna Sinha in 1961, the party appointed the veteran INC leader and a member of the Constituent assembly, Binodanand Jha, who went on to lead the party to the polls in 1962.

The INC won a neat victory and ended up with a simple majority – with 189 seats out of the 318 seats of the assembly. The Swatantra Party won 50 seats, the PSP 29, the Jharkhand Party 20 and the CPI won 12 seats and the Jan Sangh won only 3.

Binodanand Jha was sworn in as the CM in 1962, but within a year he became one of the 8 chief ministers to be removed under the Kamaraj Plan to leave the government in order to concentrate on party activities. In the wake of his resignation, Krishna Ballabh Sahay became chief minister (1963–67) with the support of the influential Satyendra Narayan Sinha, the minister for education.

Gujarat

The year 1962 saw Gujarat hold its first assembly election after being cleaved out of Bombay state, alongside the creation of the state of Maharashtra in 1960.

Out of the 154 seats in the Gujarat assembly, the INC won 113 seats (with 50.84% of the vote share). The Swatantra Party came second with 26 seats (24.44%) and the PSP third with 7 seats (vote share of 7.74%).

The former Diwan of the Baroda state and a seasoned Congressman, Jivaraj Narayan Mehta became the first chief minister of Gujarat, an office he held till 1964, when he was succeeded by Balwantrai Mehta (1963–65). B. Mehta became the first chief minister to die in a mishap – his death came when his civilian commuter aircraft was shot down by mistake during the Indo-Pak war of 1965 by a Pakistani fighter plane. He was succeeded by Hitendra Kanhaiyalal Desai who held office during the rest of the assembly term (1965–67) and led his party into the next assembly elections in 1967.

Jammu and Kashmir

When Bakshi Ghulam Mohammad formed his government after the 1957 election, he excluded the faction of the JKNC led by G.M. Sadiq from public offices. Sadiq, in response left the JKNC and set up the Democratic National Conference. As the incumbent faction began to lose popularity, the central government brought about a reconciliation of the two groups, reuniting the JKNC, even though some of those who had joined the DNC remained outside. It was in this disheveled condition of the JKNC that J&K went to polls in 1962.

The 1962 elections to the J&K assembly was the first one organized under the aegis of the Election Commission of India, not the State's Franchise Commissioner. And yet, 32 of the 43 constituencies of the valley went unopposed to the JKNC. In the valley, 41 of the 43 seats were taken by the JKNC, remaining 2 being taken by independents. In the Jammu Division, 27 of the 30 seats were taken by the NC (of which 2 were unopposed). The remaining 3 seats were taken by the Praja Parishad.

The stranglehold that the 70 out of 75 legislators gave the JKNC in the assembly continued to be disputed on allegations of electoral malpractice that were difficult to dispute. Bakshi Ghulam Mohammad began to prove an embarrassment for the union government, who forced him to be replaced by Khwaja Shamsuddin in 1963, ostensibly in accordance with the Kamaraj plan. However, Shamsuddin's stint as the prime minister proved short-lived. Faced with public outrage in the valley over the disappearance of the Prophet's hair from the Hazratbal Mosque in Srinagar, Shamsuddin had to resign in 1965 (despite the recovery of the relic), and Ghulam Mohammad Sadiq, who had been hitherto kept out of the government, was now made the chief minister who held the office for the rest of the term (1965–67).

Madhya Pradesh

The assembly elections of 1962 in Madhya Pradesh took place for 288 constituencies.

The INC took a massive hit, winning only 142 seats (90 less than what it had in the previous assembly), with 38.54% of the vote share. The BJS with 41 seats (a gain of 31) and a vote share of 16.66% was the principal beneficiary; the PSP with 33 seats (a gain of 21) and the Socialist Party with 14 and Akhil Bharatiya Ram Rajya Parishad with 10 seats were the other beneficiaries of the disenchantment with the Congress. The debutant Swatantra Party won 2 seats while the CPI took 1.

Bhagwantrao Annabhau Mandloi became the Congress chief minister in 1962, and remained in office for a year and a half. He was then succeeded by Dwarka Prasad Mishra, who remained in office till the elections of 1967.

Madras

The 1962 assembly Elections might be said to have marked a turning point in politics of the Madras state. Since 1957 elections, C.S. Annadurai, having broken away from Perriyar Ramaswamy's Dravida Kazhagam, built up his party the DMK in the urban areas of northern districts of north and south Arcot, and even won municipal elections in 5 cities – Madras, Coimbatore, Madurai, Salem and Tiruchirappalli – in alliance with the CPI. This caused a four-way split in the heart of politics in the Madras state. The Dravid movement had begun with Perriyar Ramaswamy's twin agenda of resisting 'northern' (Delhi) domination by establishing primacy of Tamils and resisting upper-caste domination in Madras politics by establishing primacy of the Dravid agenda. Sensing the rising resentment towards the INC and also because of his own turf war with the Brahmin leader Rajagopalachari, the incumbent chief minister Kamaraj had been playing the Tamil card. When Annadurai split the DK to set up the DMK, Perriyar threw in his support behind Kamaraj in the 1962 elections. Mindful of the

DMK's weakness in the southern and central parts of Madras state, Annadurai wanted to team up with Rajagopalachari and his Swatantra Party. Hence he chose to soften DMK's agenda of autonomous Tamil province in order to reduce domination by the Union government. This irked E.V.K. Sampath, another stalwart of the DMK, who wanted no truck with Rajagopalachari and sought alignment with the CPI instead (to which Rajaji was opposed). Thus Sampath left the DMK and set up his own Tamil Nationalist Party, with the goal of setting up an autonomous Tamil state.

At the elections, the INC finished with a tally of 139 seats (down 12) out of a total of 206, with a vote share of 46.14%. The DMK, powered by not only Annadurai but also the movie star M.G. Ramachandran, made a major official debut with 50 seats (37 more than its unofficial debut in 1957), with 27% vote share. Rajagopalachari's Swatantra Party finished with a paltry 6 seats on debut, with the Forward Bloc 3 and the CPI 2. Sampath's Tamil National Party not only failed to win a seat, but also to win even 1% of the popular vote, despite being supported by movie stalwarts like Sivaji Ganshen. At the Kancheepuram seat, ironically, Annadurai himself failed to win.

Chief minister of Tamil Nadu K. Kamaraj was sobered by steady diminution of INC's popularity, came up with what came to be known as the Kamaraj Plan, which required senior Congress ministers to leave their governmental responsibility and return to party work. Kamaraj, despite being returned to power, himself resigned his office as a part of this plan on 2 October 1963, whereupon he was taken to Delhi. There he became president of AICC. By then, Kamaraj was also successful in bringing about a merger of E.V.K. Sampath's TNP into the INC. Upon Kamaraj's resignation, the home minister in his cabinet, Minjur Bhaktavatsalam was made chief minister (1963–67). He went on to preside over attempts to introduce Hindi in 1965, which resulted in violent agitations that rocked the Congress in the state.

Maharashtra

The Maharashtra assembly went to the polls in 1962 for 264 seats with the incumbent Yashwantrao Balwantrao Chavan at the helm of the Congress government.

The Congress won a definitive victory, with 215 seats and vote share of 51.22%. The PWPI was reduced to 15 seats, and the PSP to 9 seats; the CPI won 6 seats and the RPI won 3. The Swatantra Party, the ABHM and the BJS failed to win any seats.

After the elections, Y.B. Chavan was called on to join the Union cabinet, and came to be succeeded by Marotrao Shambshio Kannamwar in 1962, who held the office of the chief minister briefly till his death in 1963. Kannamwar was succeeded by interim CM Parashuram Krishnaji Sawant for just 9 days before Vasantrao Naik took over and held office for the rest of the term (1963–67).

Mysore

The Mysore assembly went to the polls in 1962, a year after tenancy and land reforms. The architect of the land reforms, the incumbent chief minister, Basappa Danappa Jatti led the INC to a decisive victory in the elections.

In the 208-seat assembly, the INC won 138 seats (with vote share of 50.22%) – nearly two-thirds majority. The PSP with 20 seats (vote share of 14.08%) came second; the Swatantra Party won 9 seats; the Maharshtra Ekikaran Samiti (seeking the merger of the Belgavi district into Maharashtra) won 6 seats and CPI won 3 seats.

Despite such a convincing victory, CM Jatti failed to win the support of his Legislature Party and was forced to step down, and was succeeded by the assembly Speaker Shivalingappa Rudrappa Kanthi for just 96 days, before making way for Siddavanahalli Nijalingappa (1962–68).

Punjab

Elections to the third Punjab legislative assembly were held in 1962 for 154 seats.

The INC was led to the polls by the incumbent chief minister Partap Singh Kairon, and finished with the tally of 90 seats (with vote share of 43.72%). The Shiromani Akali Dal finished second with 16 seats (and vote share of 11.87%), while the CPI came third with 12 seats (7.1% of popular vote). The BJS won 8 seats (9.72% of votes), the rump Socialist Party with 4 seats (1.39% vote share) and the Swatantra Party and Haryana Lok Samiti won 3 seats each.

Having won the elections decisively, the incumbent chief minister Kairon began his third term in the office on a high, only to be accused of corruption and abuse of power. Kairon remained in office till the inquiry exonerated him, and then resigned mid-term in 1964. Thereupon, after a brief term as caretaker by Gopi Chand Bhargav, Ram Kishan took over (1964–66) witnessing a spell of agitation that was to culminate in the bifurcation of Punjab and Haryana, and imposition of President's Rule in 1966.

Rajasthan

The Rajasthan assembly went to the polls in 1962 for all 176 seats.

The incumbent chief minister, Mohan Lal Sukhadia took the INC into the polls, with the party finishing with 88 seats (down 31, with vote share of 39.98%), just enough to touch the halfway mark. The debutant Swatantra Party finished with an impressive tally of 36 (17.11% of vote share) in the second place. The BJS won 15 seats, the CPI and the Socialist Party won 5 seats each, the ABRRP won 3 and PSP 2 seats.

Sukhadia continued in office till the end of his term.

Uttar Pradesh

All 430 seats of the UP assembly went to polls in 1962.

The incumbent chief minister Chandra Bhanu Gupta led the INC to yet another victory, but one with a majority that had shrunk considerably. The INC won 249 seats (down 37), with popular vote standing at 36.45%. The BJS had its best show till that date in 1967, winning 49 seats (up 32) with only 16.46% vote share, and the PSP won 38 seats (down 6) with 11.05% vote share. The Socialist Party won 24 seats, the Swatantra Party won 15 and the CPI won 14 seats. The Republican Party of India finished with 8 seats, and the Hindu Mahasabha with 2 seats.

Chandra Bhanu Gupta became chief minister for the third time, but unlike previous terms he could not last a full term of five years. Gupta had to resign in 1963 under the Kamaraj plan, and was succeeded by the minister of labour in his cabinet, Sucheta Kripalini, who held the office for the rest of the term (1963–67).

West Bengal

The West Bengal assembly went to polls in 1962 for all its 252 seats.

The state was rocked by a long-enduring food crisis, which finally brought the two leftist political coalitions together as the United Left Front, constituting of the CPI, AIFB, Marxist Forward Bloc (MFB), Revolutionary Communist Party of India (RCPI), BPI, and the RSP. The INC was led into the polls by the incumbent chief minister Bidhan Chandra Roy.

The INC finished with a tally of 157 seats (vote share of 47.29%), almost the same as the previous time. The CPI with 50 seats finished in the second place; the AIFB with 13 seats, the RSP with 9 and the RCPI with 2 seats helped the ULF with a combined tally of 74 seats. The PSP won 5 seats. The Lok

Sewak Sangh of the Purulia-Manbhum region won 2 seats. The Swatantra Party, the BJS and ABHM failed to win any seats. In a new turn, the Akhil Bharatiya Gorkha League (set up by Damber Singh Gurung as early as 1943, seeking the creation of Gorkhaland) won 2 seats from Darjeeling and Kalimpong.

Within 2 months of the polls, Bidhan Chandra Roy passed away, and was replaced by the veteran congressman Prafulla Chandra Sen (1962–67).

1963

Goa, Daman and Diu

Of all the European colonial outposts, the Portuguese based in Goa, and in Daman and Diu, had been the most intransigent. While India had remained very patient, the resistance to Portuguese rule in Goa by outfits like the Goa Congress (founded and led by Tristão de Bragança Cunha), the Gomantak Praja Mandal (founded by Juliao Menezes) and Azad Gomatak Dal (speaking of armed resistance to the Portuguese) made the liberation of Goa and its merger with India only a matter of time. In 1954, Indian operatives, RSS, the CPI, United front of Goans and other outfits entered into the enclave of Dadra and Nagar Haveli and forced the Portuguese police there to surrender. Since this was a landlocked enclave, the Portuguese sought permission from India to be able to venture for the colony's defence, which was declined. Lisbon took New Delhi to the International Court of Justice, where in 1960 the verdict upheld the sovereign claims of the Portuguese over Dadra and Nagar Haveli, but also upheld India's right to deny the Portuguese through their realm. A simultaneous blockade of the outpost of Goa, and Portuguese military reinforcements of Goa, made chances of any diplomatic solution to the status of the colony recede. This prompted a military action, which resulted in the liberation of Goa, Daman and Diu in December 1961. Shortly thereafter Goa, Daman and Diu were made into a Union Territory under the administration of a Lieutenant Governor, and was accorded its own legislative assembly with 30 seats, to which the first elections were held in 1963.

In the elections, the Maharashtrawadi Gomantak Party won the highest tally of 14 seats (with a vote share of 40.13%); the United Goan Party came second with 12 seats (and a vote share of 29.19%). The INC won only 1 seat, and independents won 3 seats, of whom 2 actually belonged to the PSP.

The leader of the Maharashtrawadi Gomantak Party, Dayanand Bandodkar, was sworn in as chief minister.

1964

The year 1964 saw assembly elections take place for the first time in 2 entities, 1 newly constituted state and 1 Union Territory – Nagaland and Pondicherry.

Nagaland

The Naga Hills and its adjoining territory came within the scope of British suzerainty of the Indian subcontinent after the Burma Wars, which after some time was brought within the administrative realms of the province of Assam. The Nagas sought severance from Assam at least from the time of the Simon Commission, but it never quite worked out that way. After 1947, the area remained a part of the province of Assam, but the Nagas refused to take it lying down. The Naga National Council resorted to violence looking for a political union of the Naga lands, to subdue which the central government sent the military in 1955. In 1957, Naga leaders and the Indian government reached an agreement, and they created a single separate region of the Naga Hills. The Tuensang frontier was merged with this region, forming a Union Territory with significant autonomy that came to be known as the Naga Hills Tuensang Area (NHTA). This, nonetheless, could not put an end to disturbances. In July 1960, Nehru and the leaders of the Naga People's Convention (NPC) thrashed out a 16-point agreement forming Nagaland as a state within the Union of India. The Nagaland Transitional Provisions Regulation, 1961, provided for an interim body of 45 members, who were to be elected by the local tribes. Nagaland officially became a state in 1962 and was formally inaugurated on 1 December 1963.

FIRST ASSEMBLY ELECTIONS WERE HELD IN NAGALAND IN JANUARY 1964 FOR ALL THE 40 SEATS EARMARKED FOR THE STATE'S LEGISLATURE. NO POLITICAL PARTIES WERE REGISTERED FOR THE ELECTION, HENCE ALL CANDIDATES RAN AS INDEPENDENTS.

The man who headed the Interim body between 1961–63, P. Shilu Ao, led a loose formation called the Naga Nationalist Organisation (NNO), which won 30 seats in the assembly. People associated with the National Democratic Party (NDP, later the Naga National Democratic Party or NNDP) won the rest.

After the elections, P. Shilu Ao was returned to the office of the chief minister, in which capacity he was involved with the negotiation of a ceasefire (even though the insurgent groups refused to accept his government in Kohima as an interlocutor) in September 1966. Shortly before that ceasefire was announced. However, Ao lost a vote no-confidence on the floor of the house and had to step down in August 1966. He was succeeded by Thepfulo-Ü Nakhro Angami as chief minister (1966–69).

Pondicherry

Pondicherry on the Coromandel coast had been a French colony and the principal seat of French empire in South Asia from 1674. After India gained independence, the Government of India negotiated a peaceful transfer of the colony back to India, which was eventually accomplished on 1 November 1954, even though formal jurisdiction was relinquished by the French only in August 1964, and Pondicherry became a Union Territory, with erstwhile French colonies of Karaikal, Mahe and Yanam remaining under its jurisdiction.

After the 1954 agreement for the transfer of Pondicherry, the first elections to the Pondicherry Representative assembly took place in 1955, but did not produce any stable administration. Eventually the territory had to be handed over to the Chief Commissioner for administration. The second election to the Representative assembly took place in 1959, when the INC won 21 (41.1% vote share) out of the 39 seats, while the CPI-affiliate People's Front won 13 (34.3% vote share). But not being a legislative assembly, they had little means of conducting serious business during the interim administration.

Elections were held in 1964 to all the 30 seats in the legislative assembly for the UT of Pondicherry – 21 for Pondicherry, 6 for Karaikal, 2 for Mahe and 1 for Yanam. The INC won a convincing victory with 22 seats (54.3% vote share), with the CPI-affiliated People's Front winning 4 seats (18.2% vote share) and 4 seats being taken by the independents.

The polls cleared the air somewhat. The first chief minister of Pondicherry, Edouard Goubert (1963–64) had at one time sought Pondicherry to remain an autonomous French colony, and when that appeared an impossibility he switched sides to join the INC advocating quick and complete merger. Before the elections, Goubert pitched himself as the chief minister of the UT, arguing he would manage to keep the communists out of power. But V. Venkatasubah Reddiar, the minister for planning in the Pondicherry since 1954, solicited and received support of K. Kamaraj, the president of the Madras PCC. When the results came through, 17 of the 22 successful Congress candidates were from the Reddiar group, while 5 were with Goubert (and also 3 others whom he put up as independent candidates were successfully returned to the assembly). Given the relative strength of the 2 factions, V.V. Reddiar was sworn in as chief minister (1964–67) at the head of a 4-member cabinet.

1965

Kerala

The 1965 elections to the Kerala assembly was one of the few to eventually prove completely abortive even if replete with significance. Both the leading parties in the state had split before the elections, leaving 4 major players in the field, instead of 2.

A section of the INC split in 1964 to form the Kerala Congress in October 1964 at Kottayam. The trouble began with the resignation of the home minister Pulloli Thomas Chacko from the Raman Sankar government. Chacko then abortively tried to win the leadership of the PCC. Shortly after that, his death prompted some 15 MLAs under K.M. George and R Balakrishna Pillai to break away from the INC, topple the Raman Sankar government with a no-confidence motion, and to form the Kerala Congress.

Around the same time, trouble began to brew within the CPI among supporters of a less violent revolutionary path (purportedly following Moscow) and those that favoured a more radical politics and revolutionary path (purportedly following Beijing). The protagonists of the more radical wing – EMS Namboodiripad in Kerala (and Jyoti Basu in West

Bengal) found their differences with other faction becoming irreconcilable, precisely at a time when the more revolutionary wing of the CPI came under major crackdowns all over India. In October-November 1964, simultaneously two conventions of the party were called. The Calcutta Convention was attended by those who eventually came to be called the Communist Party of India (Marxist), which denounced the increasing collaboration between the Indian bourgeoisie and the forces of imperialism; the Bombay Convention was attended by those that continued to be called the CPI.

In this backdrop of the split among both the INC and the CPI, elections were held for all the 133 seats of the Kerala assembly. The INC won 36 seats (down 27) with a vote share of 33.55%; the debutant Kerala Congress, dominating the central regions of the state, finished up with 23 seats (with a vote share of 12.58%). The CPI was reduced to 3 seats (with a vote share of 8.3%), the debutant CPI(M) emerged the single largest party with 40 seats (with 19.87% of the votes). The Samyukta Socialist Party (product of merger between a split section of the PSP with the Socialist Party [Lohia]) won 13 seats and the IUML 6 seats.

Given the highly fragmented assembly, with no party in a position to even cobble together a coalition, President's Rule remained in place in Kerala (September 1964–March 1967).

Chapter 5

BRINGING CONGRESS DOWN A PEG OR TWO

A whole range of provincial elections that were held in the years beginning in 1967 began to show signs of the INC slowing down as it continued to battle with its internal strife. The reason that Congress dominance continued in some good measure right up to 1975 was largely because the Opposition remained in disarray all along. Thus, while some provinces continued to be Congress bastions for a while, others began to show signs of the party weakening from 1967, if not earlier.

1967

Andhra Pradesh

Andhra Pradesh was one of the few states to remain completely impervious to the larger trend of the weakening of the INC. Elections to the Andhra Pradesh assembly took place in 1967 for all the 287 seats.

The INC, led by Kasu Brahmananda Reddy, won a convincing victory with 165 seats (with over 45.42% of the vote share) to retain power. The Swatantra Party with 29 seats (9.84%) beat the CPI to second place. The CPI was pushed down to the third place with 11 seats, presumably because many of its voters went with the debutant, the CPI(M), winning 9 seats, splitting the communist vote share to 7% each. The BJS won only 3 seats and the PSP and the SSP won just 1 seat each. Curiously, independents won as many as 68 seats, showing a large section of the people no longer found either the INC or the other parties being adequately representative, leaving the electorate badly fragmented.

K. Brahmananda Reddy was sworn in to the office of the CM for the second time, but he did not last the full term, being taken to Delhi largely as a response to the Telangana agitation of 1969, which he failed to handle.

From the time of the States Reorganisation Commission of the 1950s, when it was decided to merge the Marathi-speaking regions of Hyderabad with Bombay state, opinion was divided on the merger of the Telugu-speaking regions of Hyderabad state (i.e. Telangana) with the Andhra state. Many voiced their suspicions that the more educationally-backward regions of Telangana would fall further behind in competition with the more advanced coastal Andhra. Against the advice of a large number of members of the SRC, Union Home Minister Govind Ballav Pant favoured the merger of the two regions into the state of Andhra Pradesh. However, the problems of educational backwardness and employment opportunities were realized soon enough, which resulted in the inception of the agitation for a separate Telangana. In 1969, when this movement took a violent turn, CM K.B. Reddy resorted to the heavy hand of police repression, resulting allegedly in over 300 fatalities. While the Congress High Command remained against splitting up the state, the prime minister herself was seized of the nature of the problem, and urged the state leadership to be sensitive towards it. Since the Union or State Congress did not prove sympathetic, many Congress functionaries broke rank at the local level. Chief among them was M. Chenna Reddy, who set up the Telangana Praja Samiti. The TPS won 10 out of the 14 parliamentary seats from Telangana, which made Prime Minister Indira Gandhi intervene personally. On the demands of the TPS, CM K.B. Reddy was replaced in 1971 by P.V. Narasimha Rao (1971–73) – the first chief minister of Andhra Pradesh from the Telangana region as a palliative for the TPS to stem down the agitation for a separate Telangana. Rao's appointment helped secure the merger of the TPS into the Congress.

Assam

The elections to the 126 seats of the Assam assembly in 1967 took place in 2 phases.

The incumbent INC went to the polls under its chief minister, Bimala Prasad Chaliha, and ended up winning 73 seats (a vote share of 43.60%). The APHLC finished as the second-largest party with 9 seats (3.49% of total vote share); the CPI won 7 seats, PSP 5, SSP 4 and Swatantra Party 2 seats. Independents finished with a high tally of 26.

Following the elections, Bimala Prasad Chaliha remained in office till his death in 1970, after a long tenure of 13 years. He was succeeded by Mahendra Mohan Choudhury (1970–72).

CM Chaliha was a great proponent of keeping Assam intact in the shape and form he had found it when he entered the CM's office – which made him resist the separation of the Naga Hills from Assam in 1963. But it was another of his policies (imposition of the Assamese language across the state) which had led to the rise of the APHLC, and its demand for the separate state of Meghalaya, which materialized in 1972, 2 years after his death.

Bihar

Bihar was one of the first states in north India which the Congress lost after years in power. In the 1967 elections, 318 constituencies went to the polls for the state assembly.

The INC was led into the polls by Chief Minister Krishna Ballav Sahay, but it ended up with huge losses, finishing with 128 seats (down 57) with more than 33% of the popular vote. The debutant, SSP, powered by Ram Manohar Lohia, finished with 68 seats (albeit with only 17.62% of the vote share). The Jan Sangh won 26 seats, the CPI 24; the rump PSP, led by Jaiprakash Narayan, won 18, the Jan Kranti Dal won 13, and independents won 33 seats.

In the absence of numbers, the INC was unable to stake claim, being certain of a steadfast and hostile majority on the floor of the assembly. The SSP went on to form a minority government where it had to concede the chief minister's post to Mahamaya Prasad Sinha, a former Congressman who had left the party to join the Jan Kranti Dal, which had been set up by Maharaja Kamakhya Narain Singh. Sinha was the first non-Congress chief minister of Bihar (March 1967–January 1968), but lasted in office only briefly. Upon the fall of Sinha's government, the INC supported, from the outside, another minority government, led by a new party that emerged after a split in the Samyukt Socialist Party – the Soshit Dal. Since the proposed chief minister from the latter, Bindheswari Prasad Mandal, was a member of Parliament at that time, another member from the Soshit Dal, Satish Prasad Singh became the chief minister for five days while Mandal resigned his seat in the Lok Sabha. Thereupon, B.P. Mandal was sworn in, but he resigned after only 30 days in office (February–March 1968), officially in protest against the Congress (whose support he relied on) attempts at suppressing evidence of corruption. The brief tenure of the ministry was characterized by the domination of Other Backward Classes in the Bihar cabinet (even if for only 47 days). Mandal was succeeded by Bhola Paswan Shastri of the Congress, who went on to occupy the office as the first Dalit chief minister of Bihar. Paswan held the office for 100 days in 3 stints during the period of 1968–72, alternating with Harihar Singh and then Karpuri Thakur as Bihar came in and out of President's Rule.

Gujarat

The first term of the Gujarat assembly had seen as many as 3 chief ministers, largely because of internal squabbles (leading to the replacement of Jivraj Mehta) and the unfortunate death of the second chief minister Balwantrai Mehta, (when his aircraft was mistakenly shot down by a Pakistani air force pilot) – leading to the elevation of Hitendralal Kanhaiyalal Desai as chief minister in 1965. Desai led a shaky INC into the assembly elections of 1971.

The polls were held for all 168 seats of the Gujarat assembly. The INC won the elections with 93 seats (and 45.96% of the vote share), but the tally was 20 seats less than in 1962. The Swatantra Party finished with a handsome tally of 66 seats (a vote share of 38.19%) – 40 more than the last election; PSP won 3 seats and the BJS won 1.

The incumbent H.K. Desai remained in office through most of the second assembly term. He became part of that section of the old guard that held Mrs Gandhi responsible for the woes of the Congress and voted for her expulsion from the party in 1969, splitting the provincial unit up in the process. By 1971, as more and more of the party members switched over to Mrs Gandhi, Desai lost the confidence of the assembly and had to step down, as Gujarat went under President's Rule (May 1971–March 1972).

Jammu and Kashmir

Jammu and Kashmir, since the assembly elections of 1962, had shown some signs of change, most indicating that cross-currents of national politics were beginning to affect political life in the province. In 1963, the Jammu Praja Parishad had already merged itself with the BJS, in a bid to consolidate the

Hindu vote in Jammu. The appointment of Ghulam Mohammed Sadiq as the last prime minister of J&K (February 1964–March 1965) marked a process of the steady swallowing up of the political space in the state by the INC. In 1965, the faction of J&K National Conference under Sadiq decided to merge with the INC, and became its front in the valley. Around the same time, the post of the prime minister of J&K was abolished, and replaced by that of the chief minister – with G.M. Sadiq being installed in that office. A rival faction led by Bakshi Ghulam Mohammad refused to merge with the Congress and continued to operate under the banner of the JKNC. The political landscape in 1967 was thus going to be a triangular one, with a much depleted JKNC being the only regional outfit, since the All Jammu & Kashmir Plebiscite Front (led by Mirza Afzal Beg, a close associate of Sheikh Abdullah) decided to boycott the elections (as it had been doing since its founding in 1958).

Of the 75 seats in the J&K assembly, the Valley had 42 seats, Jammu 31 and Ladakh 2. The BJS contested only in Jammu, and many leaders of the Plebiscite Front ran as independent candidates. More than a hundred nominations were rejected on technicalities, of which 52 was on account of candidates refusing to swear the oath of allegiance to the Indian Constitution – as a result no less than 22 seats in the Valley went unopposed to the INC.

The INC finished with a final tally of 61 seats (53.02% of the vote share in the Valley) in its political 'debut' in the state's assembly. Bakshi Ghulam Mohammed's JKNC finished with only 8 seats (down 62), with only 17.16% of the popular vote; the BJS won 3 seats but polled 16.45% of the popular vote. Independents took 3, of whom at least 1 was from the Plebiscite Front.

The results being what they were, G.M. Sadiq continued in the office of the chief minister, which he held till his death in 1971.

Kerala

For two years after the 1965 assembly elections, Kerala had been under President's Rule. In 1967, when the Kerala assembly went to polls again, the opposition to the INC was better organized. The CPI(M) and the CPI closed ranks and formed a Seven Party Alliance (Sapthaka Kakshi Munnani), also known as the United Front, along with the SSP, Kerala Socialist Party (founded by Mathai Majooran, part of the first Namboodiripad government,) Indian Union Muslim League and the Karshaka Thozilali Party (founded by Fr. Joseph Vadakkan and B. Wellington). The INC went to the polls by itself.

In the 133 seats that went to the polls, the INC managed to win only 9 (down 27 seats, and vote share standing at 35.43%). The CPI(M) won 52 seats (with 23.51% of the vote share) of the 59 it contested; the CPI won 19 of the 22 seats it fought for (with a vote share of 8.57%), the SSP won 19 of the 21 it contested (with 8.4% of its vote share), and the IUML won the 14 of the 15 seats it fought for. The Swatantra Party and the BJS drew a blank, while the breakaway Kerala Congress won only 5 seats.

The pre-poll alliance of SKM/UF having won 104 seats, and having being supported by 13 of the 15 independents, E.M.S. Namboodiripad (now leader of the CPI(M)) went on to form the government as its chief minister. However, due to internal bickering and factionalism, the Namboodiripad government collapsed after 32 months in 1969. He was succeeded by the CPI leader C. Achutha Menon, whose first tenure as chief minister (with outside support from the INC) lasted only between November 1969 and July 1970 (followed by 2 months of President's Rule).

Madhya Pradesh

The INC went to the polls in Madhya Pradesh in 1967 under the incumbent chief minister Dwarka Prasad Mishra.

In the elections, the INC won with a clear majority of 167 seats (a vote share of 40.6%) in an assembly with 296 seats. The BJS finished second with 76 seats (28.28%), the SSP third with 10 seats and the PSP fourth with 9; the Swatantra Party won 7 seats and the CPI 1.

The incumbent CM Dwarka Prasad Mishra was sworn in again as the chief minister, and played a crucial role in brokering a truce between Indira Gandhi and Morarji Desai over the position of the PM. However, Mishra was unable to save his own government. Govind Narayan Singh, a Congress MLA, soon got into rebellion mode and resigned from the party with a number of MLAs to set up the Lok Sewak Dal, which then went on to form a coalition with the Samyukt Vidhayak Dal (a combination of a number of non-Congress political parties) which chose Govind Narayan Singh as the chief minister. He served as the chief minister from July 1967 to March 1969 – whereupon he returned to the Congress. He was succeeded for a period of 10 days by another former Congressman (Minister of Tribal Welfare from 1957), Raja Naresh Chandra Singh whose brief stint as chief minister (March 1969) came to an end when the SVD coalition broke down and the Congress returned to power with Shyama Charan Shukla, son of the first CM of Madhya Pradesh, Ravi Shankar Shukla, forming a minority government which somehow survived for nearly the rest of the term of the assembly, i.e. 1972.

Madras (becomes Tamil Nadu)

The 1962 elections resulted in the INC government under K. Kamaraj, who however seems to have accurately read the tea leaves. The Kamaraj Plan he produced for consideration by the party was followed by Kamaraj's own resignation from the office of the chief minister in order to move to New Delhi to assume the presidency of the INC. His successor as chief minister of

Madras, M. Bhakthavatsalam, presided over the terminal decline of the party in the state.

The INC lost its electoral support in Madras over two major issues, one national and one regional. The steady and occasionally sharp rise in food prices began from the Kamaraj era, culminating in massive agitations after the assembly elections of 1962 by the DMK. The agitations were handled roughly, with 6,000 arrested, including DMK legislators (such as Annadurai himself) and parliamentarians. English was replaced by Hindi as the official language (while assigning associate status to English), in January 1965, and this generated further agitation by the DMK which accused the incumbent INC government of complicity with the Union government's policy of imposition of Hindi. The agitation degenerated into large-scale violence and had an impact on the polarization of votes against the INC.

But the real reason for Congress's defeat was possibly the successful consolidation of the non-Congress vote by the alliance that was led by the DMK but forged by Rajagopalachari, purportedly with the sole objective of undermining K. Kamaraj. The DMK-led alliance consisted of the Swatantra Party, the CPI(M), PSP, SSP, RPI, Tamil Nadu Toilers' Party (party of the Vanniyar community) and the IUML. Further, the Tamil Arasu Kazhagam (founded by M.P. Sivanagam to pressurize the INC to increase the use of Tamil in Madras state) and the outfit, We Tamils, also campaigned for their organizations under the banner of the DMK. Film stars like Sivaji Ganeshan and M.G. Ramachamdran campaigned full time – Sivaji Ganeshan for the INC, MGR for the DMK. A major point of sensation was when MGR was shot at by another film actor, M.R. Radha – which is believed to have caused a sympathy wave in favour of the DMK.

In the elections that followed in 1967, the DMK-led coalition won 179 seats (and a cumulative vote share of 52.58%) out of the 234 that went for the polls. The DMK won 137 seats by itself (up 87), with a vote share of 40.69%; the Swatantra Party won 20 seats (up 12), with a vote share of 5.3%; the CPI(M) won 11 seats (with a vote share of 4.07%); the PSP won all the 4 seats (a vote share of 0.89%) and the IUML all the 3 seats they contested, while the SSP and DMK-backed independents won 2 seats each. The INC, backed by Perriyar Ramaswamy of the DK, won only 51 seats (but with the single largest vote share of 41.1%), 84 less than the last time. The CPI fighting by itself won 2 seats. Former chief minister K. Kamaraj and the incumbent chief minister M. Bhakthavatsalam were both defeated. In fact all the ministers of the outgoing government, except one, G. Bhuvaraghan, lost their assembly seats.

The DMK government that was sworn in was led by Conjeevaram Natarajan Annadurai, who became the fourth and the last chief minister of the Madras state, which in 1969 was renamed Tamil Nadu. Annadurai served as the first chief minister of Tamil Nadu for only 20 days (January–February 1969). After his death, V.R. Neduncheziyan – a founder-member of the DMK – officiated as the chief minister for a week before the baton passed on to another close associate of Annadurai, Muthuvel Karunandhi, who held the office for the rest of the assembly term (1969–72). Neduncheziyan was to serve twice more as the officiating chief minister of Tamil Nadu – thus being the only person to have done so three times in Indian politics.

Maharashtra

The elections for the third term of the Maharashtra assembly was held in 1967 for 270 seats.

The INC was led into the polls by the incumbent chief minister Vasantrao Naik (1963–67) to another emphatic victory. The INC won 203 (down 12) of the 270 seats, with a vote share of 47.03%. The Maharashtra-based Peasants and Workers' Party, with 19 seats (7.80% vote share), emerged as the second-largest party; the CPI with 10, PSP with 8 and RPI with 5 seats; the BJS and the SSP won 4 seats each. The CPI(M) won only 1 seat; the Swatantra Party failed to win any.

Vasantrao Naik remained in office as the chief minister for the full term of the assembly (1967–72), and led his party into the next one.

Mysore

The state of Mysore witnessed discontent against the INC as seen elsewhere, but the incumbent Chief Minister Siddhavanahalli Nijalingappa managed to stem the tide.

In the 1967 assembly elections in Mysore, of the 216 seats in the assembly, the INC finished with 128 (down 12) with a vote share of 48.43%. The PSP finished with 20 seats, the Swatantra Party with 16, the SSP with 6 and the BJS with 4. The CPI, CPI(M) and RPI won 1 seat each, while the tally for the independents was as high as 41.

While S. Nijalingappa returned to the office, he did so for only a brief time (1967–68). In 1968, he resigned from his office to take up the presidency of the INC, as he locked horns with Mrs Gandhi. In Bangalore, Nijalingappa had groomed his 2 protégés – 1 from the Lingayat community (Veerendra Patil) the other a Brahmin (Ramakrishna Hegde) for quite some years. In 1968, Veerendra Patil succeeded him to the office of the chief minister for the rest of the term (1968–71).

Orissa

In the 1967 elections to the Orissa assembly, the INC was delivered a resounding defeat, even though the elections did not really throw up a clear winner.

Out of the 140 seats contested, the INC led by the incumbent chief minister Sadashiv Tripathy won only 31 seats (down 51), with a vote share of 30.66%. The debutant Swatantra Party had its best showing ever with 49 seats (a vote share of 34.78%); the Orissa Jana Congress (aka Jana Congress), founded in 1966 by former Congress chief minister Harekrushna Mahtab, won a surprising tally of 26 seats (a vote share of 37.17%), eating heavily into the INC votes. The PSP won 21 seats, the CPI won 7 and the CPI(M) only 1 – the BJS yet again drew a blank.

The Swatantra Party entered into a coalition with the Jana Congress to form a coalition government under Rajendra Narayan Singh Deo (originally of the Ganatantra Parishad before he joined the Swatantra Party). The Singh Deo government lasted nearly the full term till its collapse in 1971, when the ruling coalition broke down, and President's Rule was imposed.

Rajasthan

Elections to the Rajasthan assembly in 1967 had Mohan Lal Sukhadia leading the INC into his fourth term as chief minister.

Of the 184 seats in the assembly, the INC managed to hold on to its majority, winning 89 seats (with a vote share of 41.42%) – by and large the same as the previous election. However, the Swatantra Party did better than previously to win 48 seats (up 12) with a vote share of 22.1%, eroding the social constituency of the Congress. The BJS also improved its tally to finish with 22 seats, and independents finished with a tally of 16 seats – indicating that, if the Opposition managed to consolidate its votes, defeating the INC would not be a far-fetched possibility.

Uttar Pradesh

The assembly elections of 1967 constituted the surest sign of the beginning of the INC's decline. The incumbent chief minister, Chandra Bhanu Gupta finished his third term in office running the party down in the state that had given it the biggest lift earlier.

Out of the 425 seats that went to the polls, the INC won 199 seats – remaining the biggest party in the state. The BJS came second with 98 seats (its best performance ever); the SSP third with 44 seats; the CPI won 13 seats, the Swatantra Party 12, PSP 11, RPI 10 and the tally for the independents stood at a staggering 37 seats. Chandra Bhanu Gupta continued in office at the head of a minority government for only 19 days, when a veteran Congressman, Chaudhry Charan Singh, defected from the legislature party and joined a post-poll alliance of all the Opposition parties in north India, which came into being as the Samyukt Vidhayak Dal. Charan Singh set up his Bharatiya Kranti Dal, which was joined by the SSP, PSP and the BJS. The first non-Congress government in UP thus came into being with Charan Singh as chief minister, an office he occupied for only a year when factional squabbles with the PSP and SSP resulted in the latter pulling out, leading to Charan Singh's resignation in 1968, followed by President's Rule.

West Bengal

The 1967 elections to the West Bengal legislative assembly bore the signs of a seismic shift. The INC, which had formed all the governments in the state since 1947, was ridden with factional tensions right since the 1962 elections, and finally split in 1966. The provincial congress old guard being dominated largely by leaders like Chief Minister Prafulla Chandra Sen (1962–67) and Atulya Ghosh – who were part of the party coterie named 'the Syndicate' and of that lobby in the party Congress who opposed sweeping land reforms. The young (often Left-leaning) leaders Siddhartha Shankar Ray, Pranab Mukherjee, A.B.A. Ghani Khan Choudhury, fell out with this old guard largely on account of the government's policies in the face of the food crisis, and finally broke with the party to form the Bangla Congress in 1966 under the leadership of the veteran leader from the Midnapore region, Ajoy Mukherjee. Thus the INC went into the assembly elections in 1967 with party ranks split between the incumbent group, led by the urbane chief minister Prafulla Chandra Sen, and the splinter group, led by the provincial Ajoy Mukherjee.

In the 1967 assembly elections, the INC finished with the highest tally of seats – 127 (with a vote share of 41.13%) out of 280 – but considerably short of the halfway mark. The pre-poll electoral combination of the Peoples' United Left Front won 63 seats between themselves – the Front constituted of the Bangla Congress (34 seats, 10.16% vote share), the CPI (16 seats, 6.53% of vote share), the AIFB (13 seats, 4.43%) and the BPI. The United Left Front won 62 seats – being an alliance of the CPI(M) (43 seats, 18.11%), the SSP (7 seats, 2.13%), the RSP (6 seats, 2.14% vote share), the MFB (1 seat), the SUCI (4 seats, 0.72% vote share), the RCPI (1 seat) and the Worker's Party of India. Apart from these two non-Congress combinations, the PSP won 7 seats (a vote share of 1.88%), and the BJS and the Swatantra Party won 1 seat each, and the independents' tally stood at 31.

After the elections, the People's United Left Front and the United Left Front came together to form the United Front, which was then joined by the PSP. The Front staked its claim to form a minority government under Ajoy Mukherjee, with Jyoti Basu of the CPI(M) as its deputy chief minister. The United Front government survived from March to November 1967, with major friction emerging between the CPI(M) (with its policy of industrial militancy, its trenchant critique of the food policies of the government and its treatment of the Naxalbari uprising as a socio-economic problem) and the Bangla Congress (a section of which was opposed to industrial militancy and wanted to deal with the Naxalbari uprising as a law and order problem).

By November, the paralysis of the state machinery resulted in 16 MLAs of the Bangla Congress leaving the party under the food minister Prafulla Chandra Ghosh (of whom the CPI(M) was particularly critical). P.C. Ghosh, a former chief minister of West Bengal, floated his own outfit, the Progressive Democratic Alliance Front and professed his intention to stake claim to the government. The INC immediately voiced its support for Ghosh's effort. The governor asked Chief Minister Mukherjee to go for a floor test in the assembly in 2 weeks' time, and upon being told that this was not possible, dismissed the United Front government, controversially, without waiting for the floor test, and inviting Ghosh to form his government.

P.C. Ghosh formed his minority government in November 1967, but was hobbled by persistent protests by the United Front questioning the legitimacy of the dismissal of the government. Strikes called by labour unions, run by the UF constituents, turned violent, and as the matters progressively appeared to slip out of hand, Ghosh's government was dismissed in February 1968, and President's Rule was imposed.

Punjab and Haryana

From the time of the Partition, the (predominantly Sikh) Punjabi-speaking people had been demanding a state for themselves in what used to be East Punjab. When East Punjab and the PEPSU were merged to create the state of Punjab, of the 13 districts of the new entity, the population of the 7, mostly rural (Gurdaspur, Ambala, Hoshiarpur, Jalandhar, Ambala, Faridpur and Ludhiana) districts were predominantly Sikhs, speaking Punjabi (written in the Gurmukhi script), while 6 (Hisar, Karnal, Rohtak, Gurgaon, Kangra and Shimla) were predominantly Hindu population using the Devanagari script, clustered in urban areas. Right from 1948, the demand for a Punjabi Suba in the 7 northern districts was raised by Master Tara Singh, and then pushed in earnest by the Akali Dal (enjoying close connection with the groups that were the dominant force in the Shiromani Gurudwara Prabandhak Committee (SGPC), the federative body administering gurudwaras around the country). The Akali Dal, of course, demanded the autonomous 'Punjabi Suba' in the name of the language, not religion – and hence became particularly active around the time of the States Reorganisation Commission (1953–56).

The Congress government under Bhim Sen Sachar (1952–56) had previously developed a formula for bilingualism by which Punjabi in Gurmukhi script was to become the regional language of the 7 districts of the north, while that written in Devanagari would be that of the south. While the Sikhs, especially the Akali Dal, insisted that the former alone should be considered the official language, the Hindus led by the Arya Samaj movement (with strong representation in the Congress) with the support of the BJS and ABHM, refused to accept this – resulting in prolonged agitation by both sides. Partap Singh Kairon, the Congress chief minister of Punjab held the balance well between the Punjabi Suba demand (to which he himself was believed to be sympathetic) and the resistance to it. For the duration of the Nehru era, the matter remained at a standstill. With the coming of Mrs Gandhi to the office of the prime minister and the appointment of Gulzarilal Nanda to the Ministry of Home, the Union government took a second look at the idea of a Punjabi-speaking state. Accordingly in 1966, to the great chagrin of the protagonists of Punjabi Suba and its antagonists, Punjab was trifurcated. The predominantly Punjabi-speaking districts of the north became the new state of Punjab, the predominantly Hindi-speaking districts of the south were constituted into the state of Haryana, and the Union Territory of Himachal Pradesh was given the hill districts of Shimla and Kangra – and the capital city of Chandigarh was now declared to be shared between Punjab and Haryana, and administered as a Union Territory.

After the trifurcation, the legislative assembly of Punjab was reduced to 104 seats. The electorate was very deeply fragmented and thus returned a hung assembly in 1967. The INC, led by the Giani Gurmukh Singh Musafir, finished with 48 seats (down 42) and 37.45% of the vote share. The Shiromani Akali Dal, which had powered the movement for a Punjabi suba, had split in the early 1960s. The Shiromani Akali Dal (Sant Fateh Singh group, which was set up in 1962 to push the reorganization of Punjab along linguistic lines), finished with 24 seats (20.48% of the vote share), presumably by dint of the faction's hold over the SGPC since 1962. The Shiromani Akali Dal faction led by Master Tara Singh, which from 1948 pressed its demand for a separate state for the Sikhs, had lost its control over the SGPC to the Fateh Singh group after calling off a hunger strike in 1961 after 48 days, at the intervention of Nehru on merely an assurance of a linguistic reorganization (not a religious one). Accordingly, the SAD (Tara Singh group) finished with only 2 seats, behind even the parties that spoke for Hindu interests in Sikh-dominated Punjab – viz. the BJS (9 seats), CPI (5 seats), CPI(M) (3 seats) and RPI (3 seats).

With no party within sight of power, the SAD (FS) group took the initiative of setting up a coalition government of the United Front comprising the SAD (FS), SAD (TS), BJS, CPI, CPI(M), RPI and the Socialist Party, along with 6 independent MLAs. A coalition government was sworn in under Gurnam Singh, who held office between March and November 1967. The government collapsed yet again upon the defection after a split in the SAD government, led by Lachhman Singh Gill, at the head of 16 other MLAs. The INC, as elsewhere, gave the Gill government (November 1967–August 1968) support from outside, and then withdrew that support to impose President's Rule.

When Haryana was cleaved out of Punjab, Bhagwat Dayal Sharma, the Minister for Labour and Cooperatives of the erstwhile Punjab government and a veteran freedom fighter, was appointed chief minister of the incoming administration of Haryana.

In the first assembly elections held for the state of Haryana, the state had 81 constituencies that went to the polls. The Congress, having the advantage of an early start, won 48 seats (with 41.33% of the vote share), with the BJS being the only other party to win any seats - 12 seats with a vote share of 14.39%; the SSP, PSP, CPI, CPI(M), RPI and the Swatantra Party failed to win any seats.

After the assembly elections, Rao Birender Singh was elected the leader of the Congress legislature party, and therefore the party's nominee for chief minister. But owing to differences with party members, R.B. Singh defected from the Congress with a large number of MLAs and forming his own outfit, the Vishal Haryana Party (VHP), staked claim to form a non-Congress government. That VHP-led government, however, lasted only 6 months or so (March–November 1967) before President's Rule was imposed.

Himachal Pradesh

Himachal Pradesh had been a state in the first years of the interim government and even had a legislative assembly Election in 1952, before it was stripped of its statehood under the States Reorganisation Act of 1956. However, with the reorganization of Punjab and the creation of Haryana, the hill districts of Shimla, Kangla, Kulu and Spiti were merged with the Union Territory of Himachal Pradesh, which was now restored its statehood in 1966. The first chief minister of Himachal Pradesh, Yashwant Singh Parmar whose resistance had stopped Himachal Pradesh's merger with Punjab, was reappointed by the INC to lead the party into the polls.

The legislative assembly of the new entity of Himachal Pradesh had 60 seats. The INC finished with 34 seats (with a vote share of 42.19%). The BJS, with 7 seats, finished in the second slot; the CPI won 2 seats and the Swatantra Party won only 1, with the independents finishing with a tally of 16 seats.

Manipur and Tripura

The princely state of Manipur had been a subsidiary ally of the British since 1824. After independence, the Government of India had it merge into the Indian Union, whereupon it was classed as a Part C state, and then into a Union Territory in 1956. In 1963, it was decided that Manipur would be given a legislative assembly of its own, and upon the completion of the course of its delimitation, the first elections to the legislative assembly was held in 1967 for a total of 30 seats.

In the elections that were held in 1967, the INC ended with a tally of 16 seats (with a vote share of 32.53%), just over the majority mark. The SSP finished second with 4 seats (11.7% of votes) and the CPI 1 (5.47%), while independents finished with 9 seats. Mairembam Koireng Singh was sworn in as the first chief minister of Manipur. His government, however, collapsed after 198 days, which was then followed by a brief term with Longjam Thambou Singh of the Manipur United Front, followed in its turn by President's Rule being imposed for nearly 4 months. In February 1968, M.K. Singh was sworn in again at the head of a Congress-led minority government. The second Singh government during this assembly term lasted till October 1969, when it fell yet again, leading to a resumption of President's Rule (October 1969–March 1972).

Tripura was yet another princely state which signed its merger into the Indian Union (1949), leading to its classification as a Class C state. It was made into a Union Territory in 1956 and given an elected ministry in 1963 through the constitution of Tripura Territorial Council. This TTC was later converted to a legislative assembly in 1967.

In the assembly elections of 1967, 30 seats went to the polls. The INC won 27 of these, the CPI(M) won 2 and the CPI won 1; the BJS and SSP both drew blanks. Veteran Congressman Sachindra Lal Singh, who was elected in 1963 to be the chairman of the TTC, now became the first elected chief minister of the Union Territory of Tripura.

The Union Territory of Goa, Daman and Diu

The Union Territory of Goa, Daman and Diu had elected its first government in 1962, when the Maharashtrawadi Gomantak Party successfully installed a minority government under Dayanand Bandodkar. Relying on a social constituency made up primarily of non-Brahmin Hindu migrants from the Konkan region and beyond, Bandodkar generously opened Goa to inland migration from neighbouring Maharashtra, and pushed for Goa's merger with her larger Marathi-speaking neighbour. However, this was faced with a stiff resistance from the native Goans (a large number of whom were Christians) who were mostly Konkani-speakers. The latter merged as many as four local parties (Partido Indiano, Goancho Paksh, United Front of Goans and Goan National Union) to form the United Goan Party, under the leadership of Jack de Sequeira (earlier of Goancho Paksh). Sequeira mobilized opinion against the merger with Maharashtra lest Goa's distinctive character was lost.

De Sequeira negotiated with prime ministers Nehru and Shastri before finally being able to persuade Mrs Gandhi to take a stand.

MRS GANDHI DECIDED TO LEAVE THE MATTER TO THE GOANS, WHETHER THEY WANTED TO JOIN THE STATE OF MAHARASHTRA, OR REMAIN A UNION TERRITORY. IF THIS WAS DECIDED ON THE FLOOR OF THE FIRST LEGISLATIVE ASSEMBLY OF GOA, DAMAN AND DIU, THE VERDICT WOULD HAVE BEEN A FOREGONE CONCLUSION IN FAVOUR OF A MERGER, GIVEN THE NUMBERS THAT THE MAG ENJOYED. DE SEQUEIRA THEREFORE PERSUADED MRS GANDHI TO OFFER THE GOAN PEOPLE A REFERENDUM – THE ONLY ONE THAT HAS BEEN ALLOWED SINCE 1947. HE ALSO MANAGED TO HAVE THE MAG GOVERNMENT RESIGN BEFORE THE REFERENDUM COULD TAKE PLACE.

In the referendum that followed in December 1966, 55.48% of the voters favoured Goa to remain a Union Territory rather than merge with Maharashtra; 44.52% favoured the merger of Goa with Maharashtra and of Daman and Diu with Gujarat.

With the merger question being laid to rest, Goa, Daman and Diu went to the polls in 1967. The United Goan Party had by then split, because a faction led by Alvaro de Loyola Furtado criticized de Sequeira for having accepted the UT status for Goa instead of full statehood. Thus the MAG utilized the fragmentation of the 'remainers' and the huge influx of the Marathi-speaking people to win 16 seats in the 30-seat legislature (with 40.42% of the vote share); the United Goans Party (de Sequeira group) came second with 12 seats (37.98% of the vote share).

Accordingly Dayanand Bandodkar returned to the office of the chief minister of Goa and held it for the full term of 5 years (1967–72), despite failing to fulfil his agenda of having Goa merge into Maharashtra.

Chapter 6

THE PATHWAY TO EMERGENCY 1968–75

1968

Haryana

After a year of President's Rule, Haryana went to the polls in 1968 for all 81 seats.

The Congress, after being deprived of a victory the year before, came back on top with 48 seats (with a vote share of 43.83%). Rao Birender Singh's Vishal Haryana Party, the principal instrument by which the Congress was denied the fruit of victory, could win only 16 seats (with a 14.86% vote share). The BJS came third with 7 seats and the Swatantra Party fourth with only 2 seats. Charan Singh's Bharatiya Kranti Dal won only 1 seat, the same as the Republican Party of India.

Upon such a clear margin of victory, the INC formed its government under Bansi Lal for the full term of the assembly (1968–72), the first of his three stints in that office.

1969

Bihar

After about a year under President's Rule, Bihar went to the polls for its assembly in 1969, which saw its propensity to political fragmentation continuing.

The INC emerged as the single largest party in the assembly, winning 118 out of 318 seats (with a vote share of 30.46%) – nowhere close to the number required to form the government. The SSP won 52 seats (a vote share of 13.68%); the BJS won 34 seats (a vote share of 15.63%); the CPI won 25 seats (a vote share of 10.10%); the PSP won 18 seats (a vote share of 5.64%); and the Janata Party won 14 seats (a vote share of 3.34%). The fragmentation of seats in this assembly election however left behind a large number of other parties with a handful of seats each – the Loktantrik Congress Dal won 9 seats; the Shoshit Dal (of B.P. Mondal) and Bharatiya Kranti Dal (of Charan Singh) won 6 seats each; the Bihar Prant Hul Jharkhand (which split from the Jharkhand Party, demanding a separate state for the Santhal Parganas) won 5 seats; the Swatantra Party and the CPI(M) won 3 seats each while the AIFB won 1 seat. There were many other parties (such as the Hindu Mahasabha, SUCI, ABRRP) that failed to win any seats, but succeeded in fragmenting the electorate, leaving independents a wide field with about 24 seats.

The Loktantrik Congress Dal, PSP and SSP had fought the election as an alliance, with a seat adjustment with the CPI – this front ended up with a combined tally of around 104 seats, very close to the INC by itself. The Congress, however, managed to stitch together a post-poll combination with 5 other parties – Janata Party, Bharatiya Kranti Dal, Shoshit Dal, Swatantra Party and Bihar Prant Hul Jharkhand, with 33 seats between themselves, plus a few independents – which enabled the INC to form a minority government with Harihar Singh being sworn in as chief minister.

The Harihar Singh government, however, lasted only a few months, when the Congress split into Congress (Organisation) and Congress (Requisitionists). Also, as one of the component parties, the Shoshit Dal defected during the budget session. Bhola Paswan Shastri remained with the Congress(O) to become chief minister of Bihar for a second time, this time for 13 days only, before his government collapsed, and President's Rule was imposed once again.

Nagaland

The first Nagaland government completed its full assembly term under the second chief minister T.N. Angami of the Naga National Organisation. His efforts at ending Naga insurgency resulted in a ceasefire. The NNO thus went into the assembly elections of 1969 riding high on its success.

In the elections, the NNO won 22 seats out of the 40, securing a vote share of 38.66%. The new outfit, United Front of Nagaland, took 10 seats, and the independents took 8.

Despite being voted back to power, T.N. Angami stepped down, presumably because of his disagreement with the Union Government's unilateral creation of the North Eastern Council. He was replaced by Hokishe Sema, who served for the full term (1969–74) despite 2 no-confidence motions being brought against him.

Pondicherry

The Congress government of Chief Minister Reddiar was among the first to collapse (1967), with the split beginning between the Congress old-timers and those who supported Mrs Gandhi. A minority government was formed by one of the independent candidates, affiliated to the DMK, M.O. Hasan Farook Maricar, the youngest chief minister of any Union Territory. Farook Maricar's government lasted less than a year before V.V. Reddiar regained power briefly before losing it again to factionalism in 1968. Since the opposition did not have the numbers to form an alternative government, President's Rule was imposed on Pondicherry for the rest of the assembly term 1968–69. When elections were held next in Pondicherry, the ground had shifted substantially.

In the 1969 assembly polls, of the 30 seats that went to the polls, Congress won only 12 seats (albeit enjoying 42.62% of the vote share). The polls threw up a surprising winner in the DMK which won 15 seats (and a vote share of 33.7%) on its debut. The CPI managed to win 3 seats and independents 2.

M.O. Hasan Farook Maricar returned to power as chief minister, and this time survived for the full assembly term (1969–74) at the head of the DMK government.

Punjab

Bifurcation had left Punjab with a hung assembly, and therefore after a few attempts at government, it went under President's Rule.

Just before the assembly elections were held in 1969, the two factions of the Akalis (the Tara Singh group and the Fateh Singh group) merged into the Shiromani Akali Dal. The SAD emerged as the single largest party with 43 seats (vote share of 29.36%) out of 108; along with its pre-poll ally, the BJS, which had 8 seats (with only 8.1% of votes), the Akali Dal was already close to the halfway mark. The INC, which had a larger share of the votes (39.18%), had a much smaller tally of 38 seats. The CPI won 4 seats, the CPI(M) and the Socialist Party won 2 seats each, and the Punjab Janata Party, Swatantra Party and PSP won 1 seat each.

The second hung assembly in 2 years resulted in attempts at the formation of a minority government and the SAD–BJS combine staked claim under Gurnam Singh (1969–70), with outside support from the CPI and CPI(M). However, Gurnam Singh is supposed to have owed his victory, in a good measure, to the SGPC connection, which made the President of SGPC, Sant Chanan Singh ambitious about getting ministries for his own associates. At that point, the Punjab assembly was bicameral – so while Chanan Singh wanted to get his associates inducted into the upper chamber in order to get ministerial portfolios, Gurnam Singh considered abolishing the upper chamber in the name of 'power to the people'. On the other hand, Gurnam's attempts at fulfilment of the Akali agenda of making Punjabi the solitary official language conflicted with their coalition partner the BJS's demand for Hindi as the official language.

By 1970, Gurnam Singh was able to reduce his dependence on the BJS by poaching into the INC, bringing at least 5 INC and 1 independent legislators into the Akali Dal. When the Rajya Sabha polls took place for 2 seats from Punjab, Gurnam Singh was able to have his own candidate, Giani Bhupinder Singh, elected instead of the SGPC's preferred Jathedar Santok Singh. This prompted the SGPC to ask its protégé Finance Minister Balwant Singh, to notify the mooting of an Appropriation Bill for payment of official salaries, but then not to table it as a blackmailing tactic. When the finance minister refused to move it despite notification, it put the government into a crisis because it could no longer have paid its bills. Hearing this, Chief Minister Gurnam Singh himself moved the bill, which was defeated on the floor of the House by a margin of 22 votes (14 Akali, 3 independent, 2 SSP, 1 PSP, 1 Swatantra Party and 1 INC) to 44 (35 SAD, 7 BJS and two CPI(M), with 28 INC and 4 CPI MLAs being absent.

Once this transpired, Punjab Governor D.C. Pravate asked Gurnam Singh to step down because he had been defeated on a Money Bill. As Gurnam was footdragging, the governor actually communicated his compulsion to sack the CM if he would not relent. So, on 26 March 1971, Gurnam Singh resigned. Parkash Singh Badal, representing the SGPC component of the SAD, staked claim by saying that 54 MLAs were backing him. After initial demurring, the governor, relented and Badal was sworn in with SAD ministers and a disproportionately large number of BJS ministers (4 out of the 7 MLAs). This caused some heartburn among SAD MLAs, who began to accuse the main BJS ministerial figure, Balwant Das Tandon, of corruption. This made the Jan Sangh finally withdraw its support from the Badal government in early June. By that time, the 1971 general elections had already taken place and seemed to indicate that the Congress(I) was regaining ground in Punjab. By 15 June, before Gurnam Singh could topple the Badal government, Parkash Singh Badal already tendered his resignation. The governor then went on to dissolve the assembly and impose President's Rule in Punjab yet again.

Uttar Pradesh

After a year under President's Rule, Uttar Pradesh went back to the polls for the 425 seats of the assembly in 1969.

The INC, led by 3-time chief minister Chandra Bhanu Gupta, finished with the highest tally of 211 seats (a vote share of 33.69%), while the Bharatiya Kranti Dal, led by Charan Singh, in its first electoral contest, finished with 98 seats (21.29%). The BJS ended with a tally of 49 seats (down 49) and the SSP with 33 seats (down 11). The Swatantra Party won 5, PSP 4 and CPI 3, and the RPI, CPI(M) and AIHM won 1 seat each.

Chandra Bhanu Gupta became the chief minister of UP for one last time, at the head of a minority government. In 1969, when Mrs Gandhi was expelled by the INC old guard, the party split into the INC(O) and INC(R). In Uttar Pradesh, this resulted in a split in the party down the middle, causing the government to collapse. C.B. Gupta was replaced in office by Charan Singh in February 1970. Charan Singh's government lasted only up to October 1970, which caused yet another round of turmoil, before Tribhuvan Narayan Singh of the Congress(O) was appointed at the head of yet another minority government, in alliance with the BJS, Swatantra Party and Bharatiya Kranti Dal, which comprised the Samyukt Vidhayak Dal. At the time he was appointed chief minister, T.N. Singh was not a member of the UP assembly, so he had to stand for election at a bypoll. Upon losing the bypoll, T.N. Singh stepped down and the SVD government collapsed. Thereupon, Congress(R) staked its claim for another minority government under veteran Kamalapati Tripathi, who served as the chief minister from April 1971 till a revolt by the Provincial Armed Constabulary toppled his government, and Uttar Pradesh went under President's Rule yet again. In November 1973, another minority government was finally formed under Hemvati Nandan Bahuguna, which took UP towards the next assembly elections.

West Bengal

In West Bengal also, elections were held in 1969 after a year of President's Rule. Despite the dismissal of the government, the United Front actually became stronger and turned into a 12-party coalition.

Divisions in the Congress brought it down to its worst show till date – 55 seats out of 280 (down 72 seats), with a vote share of 41.32%. The United Front coalition won a landslide of 214 seats (and 49.7% of the vote share). Of this the CPI(M) finished on top of the pile with 80 seats (a vote share of 19.92%). The Bangla Congress, led by Ajoy Mukherjee, won 33 seats, the CPI 30, AIFB won 22, RSP 12, SUCI 7, RCPI and WPI won 2 seats each, the PSP 5 and the Lok Sewak Sangh (Manbhum) won 4, with another 9 seats going to the SSP.

Even though the CPI(M) had a much larger count of seats, in accordance with a previous agreement, Ajoy Mukherjee was made chief minister again. The CPI(M) got the largest number of ministerial portfolios, including Home, for Deputy CM Jyoti Basu. The SSP didn't join the cabinet but supported it from outside. The CPI(M) was trying to gain maximum mileage from this situation, helping accelerate the levels of political violence, which reached a still higher pitch because of both industrial action and strikes, as of inter-party struggles within the ruling front. This was further aggravated when the Naxalites led by Charu Majumdar and Kanu Sanyal set up their own outfit CPI(ML). By March 1970, Ajoy Mukherjee found it necessary to resign and have the assembly dissolved in July 1970. West Bengal went on to have another stretch of President's Rule.

1970

Kerala

The collapse of the brief period of the Achutha Menon government was largely owing to the internal bickering of the Congress and the splits within the Socialist Party, which had propped it up. Sobered by 2 months of President's Rule, Kerala returned for mid-term polls in 1970.

In the elections to the assembly held in 1970, 3 main alliance formations contested the elections. These were the Aikya Munnani (United Front) – with the CPI, IUML, RSP and PSP, in electoral understanding with the INC; the second combination comprised the CPI(M), the SSP, Karshaka Thozilali Party (KTP of Fr Joseph Vadakkan), Indian Socialist Party (a breakaway faction of the SSP) and Kerala Socialist Party; the third combination comprised the Kerala Democratic Congress and the INC(O).

The United Front won 66 seats out of 133 – the INC was at the top of the pile with 30 seats; the CPI won 16 seats, IUML – 11, RSP – 6, PSP – 3. The Opposition comprised the CPI(M) with 29 seats, the Janata Party 6, the rebel Kerala Congress 12, the rebel IUML – 2.

The United Front government was sworn in under C. Achutha Menon for the second time, but this time for a full term. The Congress, despite being a part of the United Front, initially extended outside support, but subsequently joined the government in 1971. The government also received outside support from the Kerala Congress (12) and NDP (5), with the former actually joining the government in 1975. Although the legal term of the Menon government ended in 1975, it was extended for 3 periods of 6 months each during the Emergency and went to elections only in 1977.

Achutha Menon became the first chief minister of Kerala to finish a full assembly term.

1971

Orissa

Orissa had its first full-term, non-Congress government under Chief Minister R.N. Singh Deo, before a brief period of President's Rule. When the next elections took place in 1971, the political landscape of the state was opened even wider. After the electoral defeat of most of the Congress leaders in the state in 1967, the party went through a turmoil which crystallised to form a split between the Congress(O) and the Congress(R). At that stage, the rising Congress star in Orissa, Biju Patnaik, remained with Congress(R). However, when the central and state leadership party failed to agree on a Rajya Sabha candidate from the state, Biju Patnaik – who eyed the seat – broke with the party in 1970 and floated a new outfit, the Utkal Congress with the support of two former non-Congress chief ministers, H.K. Mahtab and R.N Singh Deo. Eventually, when the SSP dissolved itself in 1972, the state unit of the SSP also went to merge with the Utkal Congress.

In the elections that took place in 1971 to the 140 seats of the Orissa assembly, a hung assembly was returned as before. The Congress faction, led by Mrs Gandhi, now called Congress(I), emerged with the highest tally of 51 seats and a vote share of 28.18% capturing virtually the whole of the Congress support base – the Congress(O) won only 1 seat with only 1.81% of vote share. The Swatantra Party, with 36 seats, came second, with a vote share of 17.44%, and the debutant Utkal Congress came third with 33 seats and 23.99% of the vote share. The performance of the Utkal Congress reduced all the other parties to the level of non-entities. The PSP, CPI and the debutant, All India Jharkhand Party (in the tribal belt of north-western Orissa), won 4 seats each; the CPI(M) won only 2 seats and the Orissa Jana Congress (led by H.K. Mahatab, who failed to win his own seat) won only 1 seat. The ABJS, SSP, AIFB and SUCI failed to win any seat at all.

Given the fractured verdict, a United Front coalition was put together between the Swatantra Party, the Utkal Congress and the Jharkhand Party, who invited a former chief minister of Orissa (1937–39) and a member of the Constituent assembly, Bishwanath Das, an independent candidate, to become the chief minister. Das remained in office from April 1971 to June 1972, when his government collapsed after a section of the Utkal Congress decided to return to a newly invigorated Congress(I). On the strength of the MLAs returning to the Congress, a minority government was formed under Nandini Satpathy, which lasted only between June 1972 and March 1973, whereupon President's Rule was imposed yet again.

Tamil Nadu

The DMK government of C. Annadurai and then M. Karunanidhi had it somewhat easy in its first term of office (1967–71) because the principal opposition party, the INC, was cracking up during this period. Because of K. Kamaraj's domination over the provincial Congress for a long time, when the INC split, it was the Congress(O), led by Kamaraj, that was the dominant faction in Tamil Nadu. Mrs Gandhi managed to continue as the prime minister with the support of the CPI and the DMK, and thus they decided to turn this alliance to mutual advantage. Both the Lok Sabha and the Tamil Nadu assembly were dissolved a year before their term ended. In the elections that were held in 1971, Congress(I) contested only 9 of the 39 Lok Sabha constituencies from the state, and none of the assembly seats – veritably writing off her party in Tamil Nadu – in return for continued DMK support in Parliament.

In the 1971 assembly election, the DMK led a 7-party coalition, the Progressive Front, which constituted of the DMK, the Congress(I) (which did not field any candidates in the assembly elections), the CPI, PSP, AIFB, the Muslim League and the Tamil National Party. On the other hand were ranged the Congress(O), led by Kamaraj, the Swatantra Party, led by Kamaraj's sworn adversary, Rajagopalachari, the SSP, the Tamil Nadu Toilers' Party, the RPI and the Coimbatore District Agrarian Association.

The DMK swept the 1971 assembly polls, winning 184 seats (up 47) out of 234, with a vote share of 48.58%; its allies, the CPI won 8 seats, the Forward Bloc won 7, PSP 4, and the Muslim League 2 – giving 205 seats to the Progressive Front. The opposition Democratic Front won merely 21 seats – the Congress(O) won 15 seats, and the Swatantra Party won only 6.

Accordingly, M. Karunanidhi returned to the office of the chief minister and held it for the full term (1971–76), virtually without any threat to his government at any time.

West Bengal

After the fall of the second Ajoy Mukherjee government and a second stretch of President's Rule, West Bengal went to the assembly polls in 1971 with a set of political combinations different from the previous election. The United Front had collapsed, with the government and the component parts choosing to go their separate ways. The United Left Front constituted of 6 parties – CPI(M), RCPI(Sudhindranath Kumar group), Biplabi Bangla Congress (a breakaway faction of the Bangla Congress, led by Sukumar Roy), Bolshevik Party of India (Nepal Bhattacharya group), Workers' Party of India and Marxist Forward Bloc. The United Left Democratic Front was now a combination of eight parties – the CPI, AIFB, SUCI, All India Gorkha League, Bolshevik Party of India (Barada Muktamoni group), RCPI (Anadi Das group), SSP and RSP (Rebel). They tried, in vain, to reach a kind of seat arrangement with the Bangla Congress, but managed to accomplish that with Congress(R). The Congress(R) declined attempts at seat-sharing with the Bangla Congress.

The elections resulted in a hung assembly yet again. The CPI(M) emerged as the largest party with 113 seats, increasing its tally by 33 since the previous election. Congress(R) secured 105 (up 50) to come second and the CPI won 13 seats (down 17). The SUCI and the Muslim League won 7 seats each; the Bangla Congress was reduced to 5 seats (down 28); the AIFB, RSP, PSP and RCPI (SK) won 4 seats each; Congress(O), Jharkhand Party, Workers' Party, MFB and AIGL won 2 seats each, while the BJS, SSP (rebel) and Biplabi Bangla Congress got 1 seat each.

After the election, Congress(R) and Bangla Congress came together to form a minority government with outside support from the ULDF (minus SUCI, which pulled out from the coalition). Two components of the ULDF, the AIGL and the SSP, joined the government. Ajoy Mukherjee thus had his third stint as chief minister, which turned out to be briefer than before (February–June 1971), before West Bengal saw President's Rule being imposed yet again (June 1971–March 1972).

After this, Ajoy Mukherjee split from the Bangla Congress with some of his associates and merged back with the Congress, which by then was under the control of Mrs Gandhi. Ajoy Mukherjee was offered a ministry in the Union Cabinet, but excusing himself over his age, he put forward Pranab Mukherjee (who had earned Mrs Gandhi's trust as an intermediary between Congress(I) and Bangla Congress) for the ministerial portfolio – marking the beginning of a long journey during which Mukherjee became a veritably constant feature of the Union Cabinet of all governments headed by Mrs Gandhi and most other Congress Prime Ministers as well.

1972

Assam

Assam was reduced in size by the separation of its western Hills region, which was to become the separate state of Meghalaya. Elections were then held for the assembly of Assam, with a reduced strength of 114 seats, i.e. excluding the 12 seats of the Hills region.

The incumbent chief minister Mahendra Mohan Choudhury, was replaced by Sarat Chandra Singha, who led the Congress to an emphatic victory in the assembly elections in 1972, where the party won 95 seats out of 114, with a vote share of 53.20%. The SSP came second with 4 seats and the CPI third with 3. The Plain Tribals Council of Assam (which was set up after 1967 with the demand of a separate state of Udayachal comprising the territory dominated by the Bodo people of the plains) won 1 seat, as did the Swatantra Party.

Sarat Chandra Singha remained in office for the full term (1972–78) through the Emergency years. He presided over the shifting of the capital from Shillong to Dispur once the separate state of Meghalaya actually came into being.

Andhra Pradesh

Rocked by the Telangana agitation, Andhra Pradesh had its first chief minister from the Telangana region in Pamulaparthi Venkata Narasimha Rao.

Rao led the Congress(R) to an emphatic victory in 1972, winning 219 of the 287 seats, 52.27% of the vote share. The CPI finished with 7 seats, the Swatantra Party with 2 and the CPI(M) with 1. Fifty-seven seats were taken by the independents, largely as a result of factional differences within the Congress.

P.V. Narasimha Rao went on to assume his second term in office, but he could only hold it very briefly. Given the landslide, he felt confident enough to push through serious land reforms, but while this benefitted many in the Telangana region and made him popular, in coastal Andhra, this caused a lot of annoyance.

AS THE LAW AND ORDER SITUATION IN THE STATE RAPIDLY BROKE DOWN, PRESIDENT'S RULE HAD TO BE IMPOSED IN ANDHRA PRADESH IN JANUARY 1973, WHICH LASTED ONLY TILL DECEMBER OF THAT YEAR – PROBABLY THE ONLY CASE OF PRESIDENT'S RULE IN INDIAN POLITICS TO SAVE AN ELECTED GOVERNMENT FROM THE WRATH OF ITS OWN PEOPLE.

Finally when in October 1972, a Supreme Court judgement upheld the legality of Mulki rules (giving preference to locals/ regionals in government employment), it resulted in the 'Jai Andhra' agitation asking for a separate Andhra state. Even the Congress ministers were divided as the agitation gained in strength and vehemence.

When things settled down, the assembly was restored, and the erstwhile home minister, Jalagam Vengala Rao, was sworn in as chief minister of Andhra Pradesh, representing the segment of the Congress (led by former chief minister K.B. Reddy) that was opposed to Mrs Gandhi. J.V. Rao remained in office for the rest of the assembly term with 3 extensions during the Emergency up to 1978. It was his disastrous handling of a devastating cyclone in 1977 that was later believed to have prompted N.T. Rama Rao to enter into the political arena to challenge the domination of the Congress.

Bihar

After a period of political instability, with multiple minority governments and President's Rule, Bihar went to assembly polls in 1972.

The elections that were held saw Congress re-emerge as the single largest party with a simple majority, winning 167 seats out of 318. The CPI finished second with 35 seats and the Samyukta Socialist Party (SSP) finished third with 33 seats. The Congress(O) won 30 seats, while the Jan Sangh won 25 seats. The Hindustani Soshit Dal of B.P. Mondal and the All India Jharkhand Party won 3 seats each, the Bihar Prant Hul Jharkhand Party won 2 and the Progressive Hull Jharkhand Party (Shibu group) and the Swatantra Party won 1 seat each.

Veteran Congressman and one of the original young turks of the Bihar Congress, Kedar Pandey, was sworn in as the chief minister (March 1972–July 1973). He was succeeded by one of the other young turks, Abdul Ghafoor, who held the office for 2 years of the 5-year term (July 1973–April 1975) before remitting the office to Jagannath Mishra (April 1975–April 1977) – a patent sign of the bane of Congress politics where internecine rivalry drained the strength of the party.

Goa, Daman and Diu

In 1972, Chief Minister Bhausaheb Bandodkar led his Maharashtravadi Gomantak Party into the elections 10 years after winning the first assembly elections in the UT. The MAG won 18 of the 30 seats of the assembly; the United Goans Party (Sequeira group) came down 2 seats to finish at 10 seats, while the Congress gained a toehold with 1 seat.

Bhausaheb Bhandodkar resumed his position as the chief minister of the UT, but died in office the very next year. He was succeeded by his daughter and the health minister of the UT, Shashikala Kakodkar. Despite initially favouring Marathi over Konkani in pursuit of a kind of divisive politics in Goa, CM Kakodkar gradually ended up favouring parity between the two languages. Over time, she also gained a reputation for both administrative efficiency and nepotism in awarding official contracts to her family members (including her husband) – which helped her stay in office, while also progressively weakened her hold over her own party.

Gujarat

Gujarat had been a Congress stronghold for so long that even when the party split down the middle between the old-timers and the Requisitionists, no alternative government could be formed and the state had to go for around 10 months under President's Rule before the assembly elections in 1972.

By 1972, Mrs Gandhi had more or less established her control over the state unit of the party. Thus, in the elections that followed, the Congress(R) won 140 out of the 168 seats of the assembly, with a vote share of 50.93%. The Congress(O) emerged as the second-largest party with 16 seats; The BJS finished third with 3 seats and the CPI fourth with 1. All other parties failed to win any seats; the BJS and Swatantra Party had their deposits forfeited in 69 and 42 seats respectively.

Ghanshyam Chhotalal Ozha, a Union cabinet minister, was sent to the state to become the chief minister, who held that office for just 16 months (March 1972–July 1973). He was then replaced by Deputy Chief Minister Chimanbhai Patel (July 1973–February 1974), who was forced out of office in less than a year on charges of corruption, faced with a mass movement called Nav Nirman movement. This remains the only instance of the dismissal of an elected government and dissolution of assembly to assuage public grievances about corruption. President's Rule was imposed in February 1974, which remained in place for the next 16 months or so.

Haryana

The Haryana assembly went to polls for its second term in 1972. The ruling Congress(I) won 52 of the 89 seats, with a vote share of 46.91%. The Congress(O) won 12 seats, with a vote share of 10.80%; Vishal Haryana Party of Rao Birender Singh finished with 3 seats (with a vote share of 6.94%); and the BJS won 2 seats. Parties like the CPI, CPI(M), SUCI, AIHM, SP, SUCI among others. failed to win any seats at all.

Bansi Lal Legha returned to the office of the chief minister, which he held on to till 1975 when he was inducted into the Union cabinet as the defense minister. Bansi Lal was replaced by Banarsi Das Gupta as chief minister of Haryana (1975–77).

Himachal Pradesh

Himachal Pradesh was returned its status of a full-fledged state in 1971, and the incumbent chief minister Yashwant Singh Parmar took the Congress to the polls in 1972. The Congress remained the largest party with 53 (up 19) out of the 68 seats, with 53.24% of the vote share. The BJS came second with 5 seats and the newly-constituted Lok Raj Party Himachal Pradesh (set up in 1967 by Thakur Sen Negi and Jai Bihari Lal Khachi) won 2; the CPI finished with 1 seat.

Yashwant Singh Parmar was sworn in for his second term which he mostly completed, before resigning (upon having major disagreements with Sanjay Gandhi over the Emergency) his office in January 1977.

Jammu and Kashmir

After the death of ex-JKNC leader and Congress chief minister Ghulam Muhammad Sadiq, Syed Mir Qasim – who is believed to have been the founder of the Congress in the Kashmir valley – was appointed chief minister in 1971 for the rest of the assembly term. Chief Minister Qasim took the J&K assembly to the polls in 1972.

In the 1972 elections, the INC won 58 of the 75 seats, with 55.44% of the vote share. The BJS won 3 seats and Jamaat-e Islami Kashmir 5. The National Conference did not contest.

Syed Mir Qasim resumed the office of the chief minister, which he eventually demitted, in 1975, for Sheikh Abdullah to return after he and the Government of India signed an accord.

Madhya Pradesh

A couple of months before the 1972 assembly elections in Madhya Pradesh, the chief minister Shyama Charan Shukla was replaced by an old Gandhian leader, Prakash Chandra Sethi, who led the INC into the polls.

The INC returned to power with a convincing victory, winning 220 (up 53) out of 296 seats, with a vote share of 47.93%. The Jana Sangh retained its second position with 48 seats (down 30) with a vote share of 28.64%; the SSP came third with 7 seats, while the CPI finished with 3 seats.

Prakash Chandra Sethi was sworn in for his first proper term in March 1972 and continued to hold office till 1975, when, because of differences with the Congress High Command, he relinquished his position, and was once again succeeded by Shyama Charan Shukla, who remained in office for the rest of the term of the assembly (1975–77).

Maharashtra

Vasantrao Naik, the incumbent INC chief minister of Maharashtra led the state into the polls in 1972.

The Congress emerged the largest party with 222 seats of the 290, with 56.36% of the vote share. No other party even won seats in double digits, with the PWPI finishing second with 7 seats, the BJS third with 5 and the SSP fourth with 3 seats. The RPI, CPI, and AIFB won 2 seats each. In a noticeable first, debutant Shiv Sena (founded in 1966 by Balasaheb Thackeray with a Marathi nationalist agenda) won 1 seat, drawing level with the CPI(M) and Bharatiya Kranti Dal. The INC(O) was one of the parties that failed to draw a single seat.

Vasantrao Naik was sworn back in as chief minister, for what was to be his third and last term in that office (1972–75), presiding over the steady rise of the Shiv Sena, which he effectively manipulated, to break industrial strikes in urban Maharashtra organized by the parties of the Left.

Manipur

In 1971, Manipur, while still under President's Rule, was made into a full-fledged state. The state of Manipur thus went for its first assembly elections in 1972.

In the first state assembly elections in Manipur, the INC remained the single largest party with 17 seats out of 60, with a vote share of 30.02%. The debutant, Manipur People's Party (set up in 1968 by a group of INC dissidents), won 15 seats (with 20.17% of the vote share); the CPI won 5 seats and the Socialist Party won 3. The INC(O), CPIM and BJS failed to win any seats.

Mohammed Alimuddin, a leader from the Manipur People's Party, staked claim for a minority government with outside support from the socialists and independents, and when sworn in became the first elected chief minister of the state, albeit for only a year (March 1972–March 1973), whereupon President's Rule was imposed (March 1973–March 1974).

Meghalaya

In 1960, the Assam assembly passed the Assam Official Language Act 1960, which made Assamese the sole official language of the state. This led to a major backlash among the tribal peoples – such as those in the Mizo Hills and those in the Garo and Khasi hills as well, whose languages were being effectively derecognized for official purposes. The APHLC repeatedly tried to negotiate for a separate state, only to settle for a degree of autonomy at the intervention of Nehru (twice) and Mrs Gandhi (once). Its persistent electoral victories made it difficult to spurn its demands, but cross-party resistance within Assam made it difficult for Chief Minister Chaliha to give the Garo, Khasi and Jainitia Hills the parity of status they were promised by Mrs Gandhi in 1968. Once the proposed bill (1968) on reorganizing the Assam state, with a fully autonomous hill state within Assam, was scuttled, a hardline faction left the APHLC, and set up the Hill States' Peoples' Democratic Party (HSPDP). To prevent further unrest in the hills, the APHLC pressurized the central government to concede on the demand for a separate state, that was to be called Meghalaya. The process was completed in January 1972, when Meghalaya came into being as a full-fledged state.

In the first state assembly elections held in 1972, the APHLC, led by Williamson Sangma, won 32 of the 60 seats (with a vote share of 35.67%). The INC came second with 9 seats with a vote share of 9.89%; 8 states were won by Hill State People's Democratic Party (led by Hopingstone Lyngdoh) and another 10 seats were taken by independent candidates.

Given the simple majority his party enjoyed in the assembly, Williamson Sangma became the first elected chief minister of the state of Meghalaya.

Mizoram

Mizoram was constituted into a Union Territory out of the territories of the Mizo Hills, taking them out of Assam under the North-Eastern Areas (Reorganisation) Act 1971.

The first elections to the Mizoram legislative assembly took place in 1972, with 30 seats being at stake. The INC finished with 6 seats (a vote share of 30.91%) and while officially independents won 24 seats (a vote share of 67.55%), the Mizo Union members made up a large number of them. C. Chhunga of the Mizo Union had been instrumental in the creation of Mizoram as a separate entity, and his interactions with the Congress central leadership had resulted in mutual appreciation of their respective political worth. Thus, talks were opened towards the formation of a coalition under C. Chhunga, which eventually resulted in a merger of the state unit of the Congress with the Mizo Union. Hence the government that was formed under C. Chhunga lasted almost its full term quite easily (1972–77), before the cabinet resigned in May 1977, to facilitate the conclusion of the Mizo Accord to bring to an end the insurgency that had kept the region restive till then.

Mysore

The state of Mysore survived a minor political instability in 1971 when President's Rule was imposed after Veerendra Patil's government fell having lost their majority.

In 1972, when the Mysore assembly went to the polls again, Congress(R) had virtually overcome its internal squabbles under the leadership of Devraj Urs, winning 165 seats out of 216 seats in the assembly, with a vote share of 52.17%. The INC(O) won 24 seats on a vote share of 26.22%; the CPI and the SSP won 3 seats each and the independents won 20 more.

Devaraj Urs, who had declined to join the Congress(O) under Neejalingappa, Veerendra Patil and R.K. Hegde in 1969, staked claim for the Congress(R) to form a government in 1972, which lasted its full term (1972–77).

Punjab

Punjab had come under President's Rule in 1971, and thus went for its next assembly elections in 1972 after a full term of political instability.

In the 1972 assembly elections, the INC(R) won 66 of the 104 seats (42.84% of the vote share); the Shiromani Akali Dal, which had reunited by then, won 24 seats (27.64%), the CPI won 10 seats and the CPI(M) only 1.

Giani Zail Singh was sworn in as the chief minister of the state, in which capacity he served the full term till 1977.

Rajasthan

Rajasthan had been very stable under Chief Minister Sukhadia. His death in 1971 brought Barkatullah Khan to the office of the chief minister, who then led the Congress to the assembly elections next year.

In the 1972 assembly elections, of the 184 seats of the assembly, the INC actually improved its tally by winning 145 seats (up 56) with a vote share of 51.13%; the Swatantra Party came second with 11 seats, and the BJS with 8. The Socialist Party and the CPI won 4 seats each and the Congress(O) got just 1 seat. The tally of the independents fell sharply to 11.

A victorious Congress(R) had Barkatullah Khan returned to office, who held it briefly till his death in 1973. He was succeeded by Hari Dev Joshi who was made chief minister, which he remained for the rest of the assembly term (1973–77).

Tripura

Tripura was recognized as a full state in January 1972, and in March that year, Tripura had its first state assembly polls.

In the elections to the 60 constituencies of the Tripura assembly, thc INC won 41 seats, with 44.83% of the popular vote; the CPI(M) came second with 16 seats (37.82% of the vote share), and the CPI finished with 1 seat. The BJS and AIFB drew a blank in terms of seats, and even though they did not win any seats, the Tripura Upajati Juba Samiti managed to win more votes than the AIFB and the BJS individually.

Sukhamoy Sen Gupta was elected as the legislative party leader, and thus appointed as the first elected chief minister of the state of Tripura, in which capacity he served the nearly the full term of the assembly (1972–77).

West Bengal

The period of political instability in West Bengal since 1967 had been unprecedented, having already had 3 elections within a space of 5 years, with President's Rule becoming almost the default mode. The elections of 1972 became the last in which the INC came up on top.

The political landscape changed a little in 1972. On the one hand stood the Congress(R) and the CPI, who constituted the Progressive Democratic Alliance, on the other hand stood the CPI(M)-led alliance, which brought in the RSP, SUCI, RCPI, MFB, WPI and the Biplabi Bangla Congress (breakaway faction of Bangla Congress). Just before the elections, this alliance came to an electoral understanding with the AIFB. A third front also came up comprising the Congress(O), Bangla Congress (Sushil Dhara faction) and SSP.

In the elections that were held, the INC finished with 216 seats out of 280, and a vote share of 49.06%, its best result ever in the province. The CPI won 35 seats (a vote share of 8.33%); the CPI(M) won 14 seats, the RSP 3. The Congress(O) and the All India Gorkha League won 2 seats each, the SUCI, WPI and Muslim League won 1 seat each, and independents won 5.

With 251 seats out of 280, the Congress(R)-led government was going to be a juggernaut. The elections were widely believed to have been heavily rigged, with the margin of victory being improbable enough to lend credence to the allegations. Siddhartha Shankar Roy, a grandson of the veteran Congressman Chittaranjan Das, was sworn in as the fifth chief minister of West Bengal (1972–77), who, while in office was faced with, and brutally crushed, a major Naxalite insurgency. Roy also gained the trust of Prime Minister Indira Gandhi over the years sufficiently to be involved in the darkest stain on the reputation of the Indian National Congress as an organization – it was Roy's legal advice that is believed to have given the final legal shape to the decree of Emergency in 1975.

1974

Manipur

After a brief period of President's Rule on account of having a hung assembly, Manipur went to polls yet again in 1974.

As the political fragmentation remained constant, the Manipur People's Party was able to increase its tally by 5 seats to reach 20 seats (out of 60) with a vote share of 27.62%. The INC(R) came second with 13 seats (down 4), albeit with a higher vote share (27.62%). The Manipur Hills Union won 12 seats (vote share 9.37%), the CPI 6 seats, and the Socialist Party and the Kuki National assembly won 2 seats each. The INC(O) and the CPI(M) failed to win any seats.

Mohammed Alimuddin was able to cobble together another MPP-led minority government in March 1974 only for it to collapse in July 1974. Once the MPP-led coalition broke down, Yangmaso Schaiza, an independent MLA who had set up a new party, the Manipur Hills Union (dominated by Kuki people), staked a claim for the government. He was sworn in as chief minister, but the government collapsed after only 148 days. At this stage, the INC, as the single largest party staked its own claim to form government, resulting in the formation of yet another minority government under Rajkumar Dorendra Singh (December 1974–March 1977).

Nagaland

Since its elections to the assembly in 1969, Nagaland's government had remained more-or-less stable. By the time the state went for its next assembly polls, the number of seats in the assembly had been increased from 40 to 60.

After years in power, the ruling Naga Nationalist Organisation fell short of a majority, winning 23 seats out of 60. The debutant,

United Democratic Front (a party formed with a breakaway faction of the NNO, led by S.C. Jamir at its core) finished with 25 seats, with the independent candidates taking up the remaining 12 seats.

Upon the declaration of results, Vizol Vitso-n Koso, an Angami Naga leader who had worked towards bringing to heel the Naga insurgency, was elected chief minister. The government (February 1974–March 1975) collapsed with a string of defections. Those defectors went and merged into the Naga National Democratic Front whose leader, John Bosco Jasokie, became the fifth chief minister of Nagaland at the head of the NNO/NNDP government, albeit for only 10 days in March 1975, before President's Rule was imposed (March 1975–November 1977).

Orissa

After a year under President's Rule on account of having a hung assembly, Orissa went to the polls yet again in 1974.

In the 1974 assembly elections, the INC(R) won 69 of the 146 seats that were contested, with a vote share of 37.44%. Biju Patnaik's Utkal Congress came second with 35 seats (a vote share of 26.45%), while the Swatantra Party won 21 seats. The CPI won 7 seats, CPI(M) 3 and the Socialist Party 2 seats. The Jana Congress and the Jharkhand Party won only 1 seat each. The Congress(O), SUCI, AIFB, BJS and RCPI failed to win any seats.

Being the single largest party, INC yet again staked claim for government formation under Nandini Satpathy, who became chief minister yet again and remained in office through most of the Emergency period before being forced to step down in December 1976 by her own party members.

Pondicherry

In 1972, a section of the DMK, under M.G. Ramachandran, fell out with M. Karunanidhi over the use of party funds, and set out to create a new party, the All India Anna Dravida Munnetra Kazhagam (AIADMK). By December 1973, the new party was joined by many DMK politicians across Tamil Nadu and Pondicherry, resulting in the collapse of the government in the latter, whereupon President's Rule was imposed for just over 2 months (January–March 1974) before elections were held.

In the assembly elections of 1974, AIADMK emerged as the largest party with 12 seats out of 30 (27.83% of the vote share). The INC(R) came second with 7 seats; the INC(O) won 5 seats, while the ruling DMK was reduced to 2 seats. The CPI won 2 seats and the CPI(M) won 1 seat.

The AIADMK formed an alliance with the CPI with Subrahmanyam Ramaswamy as the chief minister of a minority government. It lasted just 3 weeks (6–28 March 1974). Thereupon President's Rule was imposed in Pondicherry, which remained in place till July 1977.

Uttar Pradesh

After a tumultuous 5-year period, in and out of President's Rule, Uttar Pradesh went to the assembly polls in 1974 under CM Hemvati Nandan Bahuguna.

The INC(R) ended up winning 215 of 424 seats of the assembly, with a vote share of 32.29%. The Bharatiya Kranti Dal won 106 seats (27.22%) to come second; the BJS, with 61 seats (17.62%), came third; the CPI won 16 seats, and a much diminished Congress(O) only 10. The CPI(M) won only 2 seats, and the AIHM, Soshit Samaj Dal, Muslim League and Swatantra Party managed to win 1 seat each.

Hemvati Nandan Bahuguna was sworn in for a fresh term in March 1974 only to step down in November 1975, confronted with considerable infighting, and President's Rule was imposed yet again for a period of 52 days before another government was sworn in under Narayan Dutt Tiwari. The N.D. Tiwari government remained in office for the rest of the Emergency years till it was toppled in April 1977 despite having a majority in the assembly.

1975

Gujarat

The resignation of the Chimanbhai Patel government in 1974, in the face of anti-corruption protests, was followed by President's Rule for more than a year.

The only assembly election to take place in 1975, thus, was in Gujarat. The INC(R) won 75 of the 182 seats of the assembly, winning 40.7% of the popular vote. The INC(O) came second with 56 seats; the BJS won 18 seats, while the debutant, Kisan Mazdoor Lok Paksha, won 12 seats. The other debutant, Bharatiya Lok Dal, formed in December 1974 by the union of the 7 parties opposed to Mrs Gandhi – Bharatiya Kranti Dal, Swatantra Party, SSP, Utkal Congress, Rashtriya Loktantrik Dal, Kisan Mazdoor Party and Punjabi Khetibari Zamindari Union – under Chaudhary Charan Singh, managed to win a paltry 2 seats, with the socialists chalking up a similar tally.

1975 saw the first ever non-Congress government being sworn in under Babubhai Jashbhai Patel at the head of what came to be known as the Janata Morcha – constituting of the Congress(O), BJS, SSP and BLD. One week after the

Gujarat government was sworn in, Mrs Gandhi declared the Emergency. The government however continued in office and was eventually toppled only in March 1976 and after a period of 8 months a minority Congress government was sworn in under Madhav Singh Solanki (December 1976–March 1977). With the Janata Party gaining power in the Centre, Babubhai Patel was sworn in yet again in the revived assembly, and continued to hold office till his government was toppled yet again in 1980, and President's Rule was imposed once more.

Chapter 7

BEYOND THE BALLOT 1952–77

The Prime Minister Sets the Example

In a way, Jawaharlal Nehru had tried to set the standards of electoral politics in India in the 1950s. When the first general elections took place in 1951–52, Nehru already had been prime minister of India for 5 years. The government and the Congress party were almost synonymous with him. Nehru was the party's main vote-catcher and orator. However, between 1947 and 1952, the government was not directly voted to power. Therefore, during the 1951–52 election campaign, Nehru had gone to the people and asked for their votes to bring his party to power and to *make* him PM, in his capacity of the president of the Indian National Congress (1951–54).

Before the first general elections took place, Nehru's multi-party cabinet included such men of distinction as Sardar Vallabhbhai Patel, Chakravarti Rajagopalachari and Bhimrao Ramji Ambedkar. Sardar Patel, the first deputy prime minister of independent India, died in 1950. Chakravarti Rajagopalachari, popularly known as Rajaji, resigned from the cabinet in 1951 because of his differences with Nehru on several issues. Ambedkar resigned in the same year expressing his frustration and dissatisfaction. But Nehru wouldn't give in to such discomforting changes.

While campaigning for the election, Nehru crisscrossed the country travelling over 25,000 miles: approximately 18,000 miles by air, 5,200 by car, 1,600 by train, and at least 90 by boat. It is said that during the course of the campaign, Nehru travelled more than he slept and talked more than he travelled. Congress people used to say he must have addressed close to 20 million people directly, while an equal number only managed to get *darshan*, flanking the roads to see him as his car whizzed past.

NEHRU'S CAMPAIGN BEGAN IN LUDHIANA, WHERE HE DECLARED 'AN ALL-OUT WAR AGAINST COMMUNALISM'. ON 2 OCTOBER, NEHRU SAID IN NEW DELHI, 'IF ANY PERSON RAISES HIS HAND TO STRIKE DOWN ANOTHER ON THE GROUND OF RELIGION, I SHALL FIGHT HIM TILL THE LAST BREATH OF MY LIFE, BOTH AT THE HEAD OF THE GOVERNMENT AND FROM OUTSIDE.'

In 1952, Nehru was elected from Phulpur parliamentary constituency of Uttar Pradesh with a margin of more than 1 lakh votes. He had also stood for election at Allahabad East.

Father of the Constitution Loses the Election

Bhimrao Ramji Ambedkar, popularly known as Babasaheb contested from Bombay North Central Parliamentary Constituency (reserved for Scheduled Caste candidates) as a candidate of the Scheduled Caste Federation Party (later the Republican Party of India). His main contender was Narayan Sadoba Kajrolkar, a relatively unknown Congress candidate, who himself had been an assistant to Ambedkar in the Constituent Assembly. Eventually, Kajrolkar secured 1,38,137 votes, defeating

Ambedkar (1,23,576 votes) by a margin of 14,561 votes.

Ambedkar was later to enter Parliament as a member of the Rajya Sabha, the upper house of Indian Parliament, representing Bombay as a candidate of the Scheduled Caste Federation Party.

He lost again when he stood from erstwhile Bhandara constituency of Maharashtra in a by-election in 1954. The Bhandara by-election was won by Asoka Mehta, the then general secretary of the Praja Socialist Party.

Dr Ambedkar chaired the Constituent Assembly drafting committee, which was formed on 29 August 1947. Dr Rajendra Prasad was president of the Constituent Assembly. On 21 February 1948, Dr Rajendra Prasad received the draft constitution, which was formally approved on 26 November 1949. The Indian constitution came into effect on 26 January 1950.

IRONICALLY, AMBEDKAR, FATHER OF THE INDIAN CONSTITUTION, HIMSELF FAILED TO WIN IN HIS OWN SEAT IN THE LOK SABHA.

After the poll results came out, Ambedkar himself attributed his defeat to the vicious campaign against him led by Shripad Amrut Dange, one of the founder members of the Communist Party of India and a trade union leader. It is often believed that during the poll campaign in the Bombay North Central parliamentary seat, Dange asked the voters to even spoil their ballots if required, rather than casting their votes for Ambedkar.

The communists were simply reciprocating the strong antipathy Ambedkar had towards them. Ambedkar opposed the communists in India for their subscribing to the theory of the dictatorship of the proletariat. He considered the Communist Party of India as being under the control of a Brahmin leadership (P.C. Joshi, Dange and B.T. Ranadive being the main leaders at the time) and believed that the upper caste would be the real dictators in the name of the proletariat. He believed that if communism succeeded as a political alternative, the exploited and oppressed castes would continue to be under the thrall of Brahminism.

According to the communists, Ambedkar was dividing the working class and misleading the downtrodden along caste lines. They went on to denounce him as 'a stooge of imperialists'. The CPI Central Committee adopted a special resolution in March 1952 against the Scheduled Castes Federation (which Ambedkar founded in 1942).

From 'Jhuti Azadi' to Second-largest Party

An interesting detail about the 1952 elections was that while the INC won the elections by a huge margin, the second-largest – albeit a distant second – party was the Communist Party of India. This was a curious turn for a party that carried out processions in August 1947 saying 'Yeh Azadi Jhuti Hai'. The CPI, which had once also opposed the Quit India Movement of 1942 (saying it would hamper the war effort during World War II, which the CPI labelled a 'people's war' after Hitler attacked the Soviet Union), maintained that the independence of India obtained in 1947 was not the real independence from economic hardship that the people demanded. And yet, the CPI participated in the first general elections to be held in the country like any other political party.

> The slogan of 'Yeh Azadi Jhuti Hai', raised during the CPI's 1948 Congress in Kolkata, was discarded long ago, in 1951, when the party adopted a new programme and entered electoral politics in 1951–52.

During the first few years of independence, the communist movement attempted mass mobilisation of peasants against the exploitation of landlords that ran from (what were to become) Andhra region, Telangana, Tamil Nadu, Kerala, and Maharashtra to West Bengal, Assam, Tripura and Kashmir. The CPI worked against all kinds of of economic and social oppression that had roiled the country for ages. This mass mobilisation occasionally turned into armed revolts. However, as the limitations of armed resistance movement became obvious, the party lost its appeal among the tribes, and the intensity of the resistance dulled. Hence the CPI decided to withdraw from armed resistance in 1951. So doing, the government's strict stance against the party softened to the extent of releasing CPI's political prisoners and withdrawal of arrest warrants. The draft programme of the Communist Party, first published in April 1951, subsequently amended and adopted by the All-India Party Conference, Calcutta, (held in October 1951) clearly stated its position: 'India's path of revolution cannot be the Russian path or the Chinese path, but a path of Leninism applied to Indian conditions.' This became the changed party line that allowed the CPI's entry in parliamentary politics. The politburo was reconstituted with Ajoy Kumar Ghosh elected the party's new general secretary.

In this background of revamping of the party line, the CPI contested the 1952 elections. Party documents show that immediately after the conclusion of its All-India Conference, although hampered by severe limitations, the CPI began preparations for the forthcoming elections. At that time, the party was banned in parts of the country, as a result of the peasant uprising against the princely state of Hyderabad in the region of Telangana in the mid-1940s – organizationally, it was in a bad state. Most of the members of the central committee of the party could not campaign as the repressive measures of the military and police forces in the communist strongholds continued. With thousands of leaders jailed, and thousands wounded in police action in the first 3 years of rule, the Communist Party of India contested the first general elections virtually in a state of siege.

The election manifesto of the Communist Party called for the defeat of the Congress. The party campaigned for electing 'people's candidates' to establish a 'people's government'. The CPI attacked the Nehru-led Congress government as a government of landlords and monopolists. The manifesto announced that the people's government would ensure a complete break with the British Empire and ruin the feudal elements. Further, the manifesto of the CPI promised adequate wages for agricultural labourers besides providing them with land, living wage for industrial workers and recognition of their right of organize, collective bargaining and strike. The manifesto also promised to end caste oppression, penalize untouchability, penalize communal hatred and discrimination, and guarantee women's full freedom and equality. Two options were given by the CPI to the Election Commission by way of its election symbol that symbolised the nature of its political agenda – the hammer and sickle, and ears of corn with a sickle. Eventually, the CPI was allotted the latter.

Ravi Narayana Reddy, contesting from the Nalgonda constituency (Hyderabad) as a candidate of the People's Democratic Front, or PDF, (a pseudonym or cover for the CPI which was banned in Andhra Pradesh) got the highest number of votes (3,09,162) in any individual constituency in the first general election. Reddy polled more votes than Jawaharlal Nehru did (2,33,571) in his home base of Allahabad East in Uttar Pradesh.

World's First Elected Communist Government and Its Undemocratic Dismissal

The exercise of reorganisation of states on the basis of language in independent India caused the Travancore–Cochin State and the Malabar district of Madras along with the Kasargod *taluk* of the South Canara district to be merged to form the state of Kerala. The people in these regions spoke Malayalam. These regions had a strong communist base from pre-independence times. The peasants and the working class were influenced by communist thoughts and their approach to nationalism. The communists, in fact, had spearheaded the whole agitation about having a linguistic state for the speakers of Malayalam.

The new state, Kerala, came into being on 1 November 1956. The Election Commission of India conducted elections in the newly created state between 28 February and 11 March 1957. Elections were held in 126 seats (114 constituencies) including 12 two-member constituencies. The Communist Party of India (CPI), with 60 seats, emerged as the single largest party as it got 60 seats, though no party got absolute majority. The Congress finished second with 43 seats. However, in terms of the vote share, Congress (37.85%) was ahead of the CPI (35.28%).

Elamkulam Manakkal Sankaran Namboodiripad, popularly known as EMS, approached the Governor B. Ramakrishna Rao to stake its claim to form the new government in Kerala. The CPI politburo appealed in vain to the Praja Socialist Party (PSP), which had 9 seats, to support them. Supported by some independents (taking the assembly tally up to 65), the 11-member communist government led by EMS Namboodiripad was sworn in Kerala on 5 April in 1957 – the first ever communist government to gain power through democratic election anywhere in the world.

The Namboodiripad government introduced many new policies in the sphere of industry, agriculture, education, public health, public distribution system (PDS), social security measures, decentralization of power, police policy and administrative reforms – many of which were quite revolutionary. The most significant contribution by India's first communist government was in the field of agrarian reforms, aiming at improving the condition of the peasantry. Among these steps, Kerala Agrarian Relations bill was decisive in imposing limits to the private land holdings of the landlords in Kerala, aiming at ending socio-cultural domination of a mass of rural poor by a small minority of the upper-caste landlords.

In the realm of police reforms, the Namboodiripad government strictly prohibited third-degree torture during interrogation. It also forbade the use of the police by landlords and the bourgeoisie to suppress strikes and struggles of the peasantry and the other working people.

Probably the most provocative measure of the Namboodiripad government was the Education Bill, trying to curb privately managed institutions in the field of education, which accounted for nearly four-fifths of the over 10,000 schools in the state. Most of these schools were privately run. Either the Church or caste associations like the Nairs dominated the scene. These private schools received finances from the government. Quite like the Agrarian Relations Bill and the Police Policy, which aroused the anger of the bourgeois-landlord ruling classes in general, the Education Bill also annoyed a section of the same classes belonging to the Christian community, being connected with the ownership and management of community educational institutions. Opposition to the bill was mobilized among the Christians by saying that their religion was under attack.

The CPI government did not to seek to abolish private management of educational institutions altogether. Rather, the Namboodiripad government wanted to ensure that the teachers in private educational institutions would receive the same salaries as their counterparts in government institutions without any deductions by private managements. But a large section of Christian churches and the Nair Service Society (NSS), the 2 major bodies that used to manage private educational institutions, successfully unleashed an extensive propaganda that the bill was an attack on their right to property and a measure to nationalize educational institutions.

The bill caused a furore when it was introduced in the state assembly on 13 July 1957, and was carried in September 1957 despite opposition from the Congress and the IUML. In light of the public protests against the bill, the governor sent it to Delhi 'for consideration of the president', instead of giving his assent and thus rendering it into a law. The president of India referred the matter to the apex court for consideration. On 22 May 1958, the Supreme Court pointed out certain discrepancies in some provisions, but found nothing unconstitutional with the bill as passed by the state assembly. The state government amended the bill in accordance with the opinion of the Supreme Court and passed it again by the state assembly on 28 November 1958.

Despite not being much involved with the initial protests against the bill, political parties began to find opportunities for political mobilization against the Namboodiripad government. On 4 September 1958, the Socialist MP Asoka Mehta raised a debate in the Lok Sabha and called for intervention by the Union government. By 18 September 1958, the Congress Working Committee resolution echoed concerns similar to Mehta's. Thus, an anti-communist front was formed consisting of representatives of the Congress, Muslim League, Praja Socialist Party, the Catholic Church and the Nair Service Society. This front launched a violent Vimochana Samaram (Liberation Struggle) during which government offices and police stations were ransacked, which the government denounced as 'a conspiracy of the imperialists, Congress and the Catholic Church, to sabotage the progressive government of the working class.'

The Education Bill became law on 19 January 1959. The opposition forces joined hands to rally together. They had a clear plan to start direct action against the government. The newly elected Congress president Indira Gandhi visited Kerala on 28 April 1959 and expressed her concerns over the deteriorating law and order condition in the state. On 1 May 1959, a conference of all the community organizations took place, and a Vimochana

Samara Samiti was constituted. On 3 May 1959 a convention of private schools run by religious institutions vowed to 'end the communist rule in Kerala'. Within a few days, the Congress Working Committee extended their support to this campaign.

During the 6 weeks of agitation and mass rallies by the Samiti, more than 1,50,000 people were arrested and 15 were killed in police firing. The agitators included workers, peasants, teachers, students, religious men, political and community leaders. It also registered massive participation for women. Prime Minister Jawaharlal Nehru described the agitation as a 'mass upsurge' against the communist regime.

Chief Minister E.M.S. Namboodiripad declared that he was ready to meet the agitators to discuss the Education Bill. However, on 21 June 1959, Congress President Indira Gandhi announced that her party did not intend to negotiate on the bill and that the agitation was independent of any compromise on it. On 10 July 1959, in a memorandum to the president the Congress Party accused the Kerala government of subverting democracy, denying people their fundamental rights, reducing the bureaucracy and the police to impotence, institutionalizing corruption and jeopardizing the security of life and property of the majority of the people.

Prime Minister Nehru, however, seemed to be at variance with his party, saying as late as June 1959 that central intervention was an extreme and last step. In July, Nehru and EMS met in Shimla. Nehru requested EMS to resign and hold mid-term elections under his caretaker government. The top leadership of the CPI realised that the call for fresh elections was 'nothing but giving a democratic garb to a discriminatory demand which the opposition parties sought to enforce through illegal means'.

Namboodiripad was reneging on the issue of resignation, when the prime minister advised President Rajendra Prasad to dissolve the government. On 31 July 1959, Dr Rajendra Prasad, issued a proclamation dismissing the government of Kerala. Invoking article 356 of the provisions of the Indian constitution, President's Rule was imposed. Thus, the first democratically elected communist government in the world survived for only 28 months.

The First Booth Capturing: A Myth Debunked

Booth capturing typically refers to incidents where members or workers or supporters of a party forcefully occupy a polling booth and cast fake votes on behalf of those registered as voters. Allegations about this practice used to plague the electoral process when the standard voting system was conducted by means of paper ballot. 'EVMs are the major contribution in reducing the incidents leading to tampering of votes,' Navin Chawla, the sixteenth chief election commissioner was quoted in a 2009 *Business Standard* article called 'Booth capturing is history now, thanks to EVMs'.

In 2005, several media reports were floated that booths were captured in Indian elections for the first time in Rachiyahi village of Begusarai district in 1957 election. Some analysts claim that it happened in Rachiyahi village of Matihani assembly constituency (even though the Matihani assembly seat did not exist before 1977).

Contrary to media reports, Kachhari Tola of Rachiyahi village may not have witnessed booth capturing in true sense in 1957. Reports indicate that the incident took place 1 km away on the eastern side of the booth at Rachiyahi, where the people of 4 villages had to travel to vote. It is alleged that one such group of villagers, believed to be supporters of CPI leader Chandra Shekhar Singh (in tactical alliance with the PSP candidate for the constituency), coming from the neighbouring Rajapur village on a bullock cart, were stopped by the rival Congress leader Saryu Prasad Singh. The Congress activists tried to desist the CPI supporters from casting their votes, which resulted in a scuffle. The members of both the groups got injured in the clash, and those who got hurt seriously were taken for medical treatment. Eyewitnesses indicate except for those who were sent for medical treatment, everyone else from the various villages were able to cast their votes.

The records of the Election Commission of India state that Mathura Prasad Mishra was elected from Begusarai parliamentary constituency defeating his nearest candidate, Brahmadeo Prasad Singh of the Praja Socialist Party (with which the CPI was in tactical understanding), by a margin of 9,220 votes. Thus, any conclusive evidence on the first booth to be 'captured' in the history of the country is yet to emerge.

The Brief Life of the Swatantra Party

In the general elections of 1962, the Swatantra (meaning 'independent') Party emerged as a considerable political force, as well as controversial.

The Swatantra party was born on 4 June 1959. It dared to be the voice of a liberal-democratic order in Indian political firmament, which was arguably overwhelmingly of a socialist disposition. Polling almost 8% of the popular vote and bagging 18 seats, it secured the third-largest contingent in the 1962 elections.

The Swatantra Party was the first economically liberal but socially conservative political party of India, ideologically. Chakravarti Rajagopalachari, popularly known as Rajaji, was the founder of the Swatantra Party. An Indian statesman, writer, lawyer, a veteran leader of India's freedom struggle and a follower of Mohandas Karamchand Gandhi, Rajagopalachari was the last governor-general of India (and the only Indian to occupy that office) before the office was abolished as India became a republic in 1950.

It was said that Rajaji felt that there was no one to challenge Jawaharlal Nehru after the death of Sardar Vallabhbhai Patel and that it was imperative to create a political platform to raise questions against Congress rule. Rajagopalachari declared that the Swatantra Party is 'against social justice and welfare being brought about by violence and compulsion but is in favour of the doctrine of trusteeship adumbrated by Gandhiji'. The party took a firm stand against what it considered was an ever-increasing trespassing by the state. Rajaji, at the party's inaugural address, saw the State transforming into a Leviathan that was 'menacingly poised against the citizen, interfering with his life at all points... hypnotizing the people with slogans that are mistaken for thought and wisdom, a scheme of government in which it is taken for granted that the citizen is ignorant of what is his own interest...' Micro-managing the economy was an anathema to him. The party manifesto for the 1962 elections, *To Prosperity through Freedom*, clearly stated, 'The business of government is government, not business.' The government's focus, it held, should be in developing physical and social infrastructure; and not managing trade and manufacturing directly.

It was with these objectives that Rajagopalachari joined hands with leaders like N.G. Ranga (president of the party who was an Oxford-educated economist, a 'veteran anti-communist ideologuc'), Minoo Masani (party's general secretary, an economist educated at the London School of Economics, a management consultant, and a highly anglicized Parsi from Bombay) and Sir Homy Mody (party's treasurer, another anglicized Parsi from Bombay and one of India's preeminent businessmen and financiers), and others. The Congress and the Leftists, in response, tagged the Swatantra Party as a 'feudalist-capitalist' group of ex-Congressmen who were who didn't about the plight of the poor and the marginalized of India.

An additional dimension is often overlooked. Founders of the party were mostly people that had been elbowed out by new social groups and new agenda that had come to dominate the INC in course of the 1950s. The veteran Rajaji, a representative of Sanskritic and Brahminical values, was himself systematically marginalized by the rising wave of Tamil politics represented by Kumaraswami Kamaraj and later by the DMK. Similarly, Gujarati-speaking and heavily Anglicised Masani and Mody became marginalized in Bombay/Maharashtra politics as the demand for the creation of Gujarat left Bombay/Maharashtra into the hands of Marathi-speaking people.

In its brief life, the Swatantra party had attracted enough people to give the INC a jolt in 1962, and a bigger jolt in 1967, when a large number of disgruntled members of the Congress rallied behind the Swatantra Party, in conjunction with other forces of the opposition. After Rajaji's death on 25 December 1972, the party lost its momentum and virtually ceased to exist by 1974. Those people who had joined it gradually moved out to join and vote for the INC (Organisation) and later for the Janata Party.

The First of 'Ugly and Dirty' Election Campaigns

In 1966–67 the poll campaign was carried out under nation-wide frustration and insecurity. India's economy was deteriorating, the price of the essential commodities was skyrocketing and the shortage of food posed threat to a famine-like situation mostly in Bihar and some other states. The law and order situation was also worsening. There were frequent bandhs, gheraos, strikes and some violent forms of public protests and mass agitations, which resulted in damage of properties and even loss of lives. Assessing this situation, *The Times* (London) even predicted an end to the democratic process in India, which many Indian political analysts, however, would not agree with.

Nonetheless, the election campaign of 1967 was, according to many of the analysts, 'the ugliest and dirtiest' till then. During a period of just over one month of 1967, almost 80 poll meetings were disturbed (73 of those were of the Congress, and almost half of the disturbances took place in Uttar Pradesh and Bihar). What is most important, there was a violent attack even on the prime minister. It happened in Bhubaneswar, the capital of Orissa, in February 1967. A stone was pelted at Mrs Gandhi's face, damaged her nose and plastic surgery had to be done. Mrs Gandhi had to stop her campaign for a couple of days.

Aandhi (The Storm), a Bollywood film of 1975 which was often believed to be based on a part of the life of Indira Gandhi and her relationship with her estranged husband, Feroze Gandhi, had a similar scene in it. This film was banned on the alleged grounds of violation of the Model Election Code of Conduct, claiming it can cause damage to the reputation of the Congress party. The Election Commission of India stopped the film from releasing. After 2 years, the ban was withdrawn.

In 1967, Madhu Limaye, leader of the Samyukta Socialist Party (SSP), was stopped and beaten. That made him unable to take part in the campaign even in his own constituency. Albeit, he won by a considerable margin.

On 7 November 1966, a crowd of thousands people, led by naked sadhus carrying tridents, spears, and other symbolic instruments or weapons, marched down Parliament Street towards Parliament House when the Parliament was in session. They were protesting against cow slaughter. Suddenly a group of youths began to torch vehicles and buildings. They surrounded the residence of Kumaraswami Kamaraj, then president of the Congress. Kamraj somehow managed to escape but the incidence caused loss of lives. The matter became worse because of the prolonged 'fast unto death' of the Shankaracharya of Puri.

Sant Fateh Singh, leader of the dominant wing of the Akali Dal in Punjab, also went on a 'fast unto death' on a totally different subject. He was disgruntled with the government's concessions on the Punjabi Suba issue. Sant Fateh Singh was swayed to end his fast shortly before the time he had set for his self-immolation. The election campaign of 1967 polls witnessed too many acts of violence and extra-constitutional methods of protest. Till then such conduct was unprecedented in India – later it became almost a routine.

The Interim Prime Minister

India had 3 prime ministers during the period 1962–67 – Jawaharlal Nehru, Lal Bahadur Shastri and Indira Gandhi. Nehru died in 1964 and he was succeeded by Shastri. On 11 January in 1966, Shastri suddenly died at Tashkent in Uzbekistan of erstwhile Soviet Union the day after signing a the Tashkent Declaration to end the 1965 Indo–Pakistan War. Then Indira Gandhi was sworn in as PM. However, there were 5 swearing-in ceremonies of prime ministers held in that same 5-year period. Because before the appointments of both Shastri and Gandhi to the prime minister's office, Gulzarilal Nanda had taken oath as the interim PM, serving for 13 days on both occasions. Since Nanda was the home minister of India during both these periods, he was chosen as prime minister for an interim period, being the second in the cabinet hierarchy. He was the only interim prime minister in the history of electoral democracy of India.

The Rise of the Matriarch: Indira Gandhi and the Syndicate

One the eve of the seventeenth general elections in 2024, Nehru continues to be the longest serving prime minister of India, having served over 17 years, of which the first 5 (1947–52) was as the leader of the largest political party in the interim government, without having stood for direct election. The longest serving elected prime minister of independent India to date is his daughter Indira Gandhi, having won 3 full terms and serving for 14 years and 10 months – first phase being from March 1967 to March 1977, and the second phase being January 1980 to October 1984.

Indira Gandhi was sworn in as prime minister of India for the first time on 24 January in 1966 after Shastri's demise. From January 1966 to March 1967, Mrs Gandhi served as prime minister in her capacity of the successor to Shastri as the leader of the Legislature Party. Her spell as an elected prime minister began on 13 March in 1967, the day she was sworn in after getting the victory in general elections that year – the only 'matriarch' so far in Indian electoral and political history.

After Shastri's death, Mrs Gandhi, however, was not an automatic choice of the party leadership, dominated by the Syndicate. The Syndicate's choice of Nehru's daughter in the chair of prime minister was only a calculated move. The Syndicate's favourite candidate was the party president and the group leader Kamaraj. But at the last moment Kamaraj backed out by saying 'No Hindi, No English [I do not speak in these languages] – how (can I be PM)?' At this situation, the group had to stop the other contender Morarji Desai by any means. Morarji was considered a threat all along by the Syndicate. Even after Nehru's death, the Syndicate threw its weight behind Shastri mainly because they wanted to keep out Desai, though a significant section within the party and bureaucrats agreed on Desai's capability and administrative acumen. Mrs Gandhi also disliked Desai and was always suspicious of the latter's right-wing leanings. The Syndicatc, cmpowered with this knowledge, swung in favour of Mrs Gandhi. The Syndicate recognized her as a national figure not only because she was Nehru's daughter, but also because of Indira's pro-active performance during Shastri's regime, in her capacity as the Information and Broadcasting Minister (I&B) – first during the language related disturbances in Madras, and then flying to the frontier during the 1965 war.

Shastri included Mrs Gandhi in his cabinet because he wanted to bridge the gap between his government and the loyalists of Nehru. After being sworn in as minister in June 1964, Mrs Gandhi became a member of Parliament in August

1964 but from the Rajya Sabha, upper house of the Indian parliament, where the members are not directly elected by the electorate, but by the Members of legislative assemblies (MLAs) of different states. Mrs Gandhi chose not to contest the by-election in Phulpur Lok Sabha constituency that year, from where Nehru had won 3 times in a row. Nehru's sister Vijaya Lakshmi Pandit won from Phulpur. Thus, when Mrs Gandhi became the country's third prime minister, she was a member of Rajya Sabha (from Uttar Pradesh).

Initially, the Syndicate identified Mrs Gandhi as Shastri's successor, because the 48-year-old woman was promising to be the vote-catcher that her father used to be. The general election of 1967 was supposed to take place only after 13 months. The Syndicate didn't perceive Nehru's daughter as a threat. The group was sure they could rule from behind the curtains by manipulating her.

Desai, however, did not give up. The staunch Gandhian openly declared his intention to become prime minister by projecting himself as the most competent and capable. Mrs Gandhi modestly said that she would be guided by the wishes of the Congress and party president Kamaraj. Desai demanded an open election between himself and Mrs Gandhi. What followed was the only incident when an election was held within a ruling party or coalition to decide on the office of the prime minister of India. All MPs of Congress voted by secret ballot. Because of her personal popularity and certainly because of the Syndicate's conviction to keep Desai at bay, Indira won 355 votes to Desai's 169. In the words of eminent journalist Inder Malhotra (*The Statesman, The Guardian, The Times of India*), 'The joke at that time was: There may be no unanimity for Indiraji, but there certainly is "unanimosity" against Morarji.' On 24 January in 1966, Mrs Gandhi was sworn in as prime minister. To date, she remains the only female prime minister of India. But Indira said, 'I do not see myself as a woman in regard to this task... I am no feminist, I'm a human being.' During Shastri's short tenure of 19 months, Indira was described as 'The only man in a cabinet of old women', as reported in a *New York Times* article published in 1971 called 'Woman in the News'.

Immediately after becoming prime minister, Mrs remained quite shaky. She was not so vocal at the time while facing scathing attacks from the stalwart opposition leaders in parliament viz. Minoo Masani (a founder-leader of the Swatantra Party), Nath Bapu Pai (barrister, eloquent orator and prominent leader of the Praja Socialist Party), Hiren Mukherjee (communist, Oxford-educated barrister and Nehru's favourite parliamentarian), Ram Manohar Lohia (articulate socialist leader, known for lifelong opposition to Nehru and his daughter). At one point Lohia even taunted the prime minister that 'she is nothing but a *Goongi Gudiya* (dumb doll)'.

At that time, India was running out food stocks and there was dearth of foreign exchange to import food. In March 1966, Mrs Gandhi went to America to persuade US President Lyndon Johnson to give India food and foreign exchange. Johnson assured 3 million tonnes of food and aid of $9 million. In return, the International Monetary Fund (IMF) and the US administration placed the most important demand, along with other claims, for substantially devaluing the Indian rupee. Consequently, on 6 June in 1966, just 4 months after becoming prime minister, the Indian rupee was devalued by 36.5%. The perception gained strength that India, tarnishing its own image, was begging before the US and that the Indian prime minister had become an American stooge.

Even the Syndicate-dominated Congress Working Committee (CWC) passed a resolution condemning the decision. How could their protégée dare to decide, without even consulting party president Kamaraj before the devaluation of Indian currency? The Syndicate wanted to be all-powerful in decision-making on the policies of the government. Mrs Gandhi, on the other hand, soon after settling in the chair, started asserting herself as the prime minister – making a conflict inevitable.

As the elections approached in 1967, the Syndicate tried to ensure that party members loyal to Mrs Gandhi would not get the party ticket. When they could not stop the loyalists from contesting, those candidates were given a very little amount as election expenses from the party funds.

Mrs Gandhi, however, started election campaign with energy and enthusiasm. She travelled tirelessly across the country to make the people feel that no other leader cared for them as much as she did. She contested from Raebareli constituency, from where her husband Feroze Gandhi was elected in 1952 and 1957, and won by a huge margin of more than 91,000 votes.

However, the electorate delivered Congress party a heavy blow. Congress somehow managed to get the majority. But the Syndicate was decimated. K. Kamaraj, S.K. Patil, Atulya Ghosh and Biju Patnaik had to face disastrous defeats. Only N. Sanjeeva Reddy emerged victorious, albeit to a lower margin compared to Indira's. Hence, despite the party's electoral setback, with the Syndicate cut down to size, Mrs Gandhi became stronger.

On 13 March in 1967, Indira Gandhi was sworn in for the second time as prime minister of India. Though she had to compromise with Kamaraj and had to accept Morarji Desai, who had also won the election, as deputy prime minister and finance minister.

A fresh battle broke out between Mrs Gandhi and the Syndicate in April 1967 on who should be India's third president. The Syndicate, already resenting Indira's leftward turn from the political centre, pushed for a second term for the incumbent Sarvepalli Radhakrishnan, but Mrs Gandhi wanted someone of lower stature than Radhakrishnan so that the person would not be a threat for her. In May 1967, Mrs Gandhi prevailed upon all concerned to have Zakir Husaain as the third president of India in the face of the Syndicate's determination. But when Zakir Hussain died on 3 May in 1969, another conflict of interests began.

The party's (Syndicate's) official candidate to succeed Hussain was Neelam Sanjiva Reddy, who was then the speaker of Lok Sabha. Reddy, the Syndicate-man from Andhra Pradesh, himself won and was able to hold the fortress of Andhra Pradesh, even when the party was decimated in many other parts in the country. However, Mrs Gandhi openly announced that forcing a presidential candidate on a prime minister was tantamount to an assault on her office and therefore, she fielded her nominee Varahagiri Venkata Giri.

The presidential election took place in August 1969. Giri fought the election as an independent candidate. Without naming anyone, Mrs Gandhi appealed to the party MPs and MLAs to vote on the 'voice of conscience', against the official whip to vote for Reddy that was issued on Congress MPs and MLAs. Giri won the election defeating Reddy by 1.79% margin of the votes. The victory of Mrs Gandhi's nominee Giri and the defeat of party's official candidate Reddy made the split in the Congress all the more inevitable.

In October 1969, Siddavanahalli Nijalingappa, who replaced Kamaraj as Congress president in 1968, wrote an open letter to Indira Gandhi accusing her of creating a personality cult and making loyalty to her synonymous with loyalty to the Congress and to India. On 1 November 1969, two Congress Working Committee meetings took place simultaneously; one at the Congress headquarters on Jantar Mantar Road, convened by the old guards and the other at the PM's residence at 1, Safdarjung Road. Nijalingappa expelled Mrs Gandhi from the primary membership of the Congress on account of 'anti-party activities', occasioning the biggest split in the INC ever. Mrs Gandhi, undaunted, asked Congressmen to make a choice. She got support from 310 MPs out of a total number of 429

MPs in both Houses of Parliament. The Congress party's men and women who supported Mrs Gandhi now claimed to constitute the real Congress, thus implying the expulsion itself an infructuous act. The Election Commission of India also recognised Mrs Gandhi's faction as the successor to the old party, which was now to be called Congress (Requisitionists)* or Congress(R); the INC old guard, reconstituted itself as the Congress (Organisation) or Congress(O). Since most of the MPs remained with Mrs Gandhi, presumably because she was the incumbent prime minister, she remained in office despite being reduced to a minority (221 seats out of 523), with issue-based support being extended to the government by the CPI (23 seats) and the DMK (26 seats).

Jayaprakash Narayan and His Sampoorna Kranti

In 1974, Jayaprakash Narayan was 72 years of age. JP had been a freedom fighter, and once an admirer and friend of Jawaharlal Nehru, whom Mrs Gandhi grew up calling *chachaji*, and his wife had been the best friend Kamala Nehru ever had. JP represented a strange combination of Marxism and Gandhian philosophy. Born in Sitab Diara of Bihar in a rustic lower-middle-class home, JP was educated at Berkeley, California. His Gandhian background and his refusal to accept any office in the government of independent India, even when offered by his friend Nehru, had given JP the halo of adoration and acceptability. He was not a member of parliament and stayed mostly in Patna, but whenever JP spoke people took notice of him.

JP stepped forth to assume leadership of the anti-Indira movement saying that he could no longer be a 'silent spectator to misgovernment'. The point of departure for JP's movement was

* After the 'requisition' that was sought to discuss the matter of the Whip during the Presidential elections.

a meeting, organized by the Patna University Students' Union, which took place in the Senate Hall of Patna University in 1973. Lalu Prasad Yadav, who later became chief minister of Bihar and the railway minister of the country, was then the president of Patna University Students' Union. The meeting addressed the hardship faced by the common people, and it charged the Congress government in the centre. JP was overwhelmed by the public response. The hall was full, with many more standing outside on the road. Veteran journalist Kuldip Nayar claims that the idea of the moniker 'Janata' was conceived during that meeting in 1973, even before JP launched his movement. The next day, at a rally in Gandhi Maidan of Patna, JP gave the public the slogan of *Parivartan* (the change).

In February 1974, Jayaprakash Narayan went to Gujarat, where the *Nav Nirman Andolan* had already toppled the Congress government, to lend his support. The movement, initiated by students, clearly showed that public rage could overthrow an elected government even though it had a thumping majority in the legislative house. The success of *Nav Nirman Andolan* gave impetus to the anti-Indira movement, and JP decided that the agitated students of Bihar could also carry out a movement inspired by the experience of Gujarat.

The student protests had already begun in Bihar. On 18 February in 1974, just a week after JP's visit to Ahmedabad, Patna University Students' Union organized a convention, where the student leaders from across the state were invited. They formed *Bihar Chhatra Sangharsh Samiti* (BCSS), where political student outfits like Akhil Bharatiya Vidyarthi Parishad (ABVP) connected with the Jana Sangh, Samajwadi Yuva Jana Sabha (SYJS) connected with the Samajwadi Party, and the All-India Students' Federation (AISF) connected with the CPI joined hands and Lalu Prasad Yadav was chosen as president. Other important students' leaders were Sushil Kumar Modi (who later became the deputy chief minister of Bihar and is currently a member of Parliament in Rajya Sabha backed by the BJP) and Ram Vilas Paswan (who later became a central minister). The protest of the students was against the misrule, corruption and the excess of the Abdul Ghafoor-led Congress government.

The BCSS *gheraoed* the Bihar legislative assembly when the budget session was going on, on 18 March 1974. This metastasized into road blockades and destruction of government property. The protesters set the telephone exchange and former education minister Ramanand Singh's residence on fire. The police retaliated with force, making, in effect, killing 3 students in Patna.

As Sushil Modi, former deputy CM of Bihar, would later recall, JP was drawn into the movement on request of a group of students. He agreed to lead but on conditions of absolute leadership for him and total non-violence.

This changed the pattern of the movement. On 30 March in 1974, JP led a silent march in Patna, where a group youth was holding a banner with a slogan *Hamla chahe jaisa hoga, hath hamara nahi uthega* (however you may attack, we shall not fight). Eight more students were killed in police firing on 12 April, which reinforced JP's protests and a stronger demand for electoral reforms and integrity in public life.

Elsewhere, unrest was brewing among railway workers over demands for pay revision and 8-hour shifts – an agitation that brought forth George Fernandes, who became leader of the All-India Railwaymen's Federation. The all-India strike Fernandes called on 8 May had him and other leaders arrested but brought the country to a standstill. The retribution was swift, with the Centre resorting to brutal repression through paramilitary forces. Laws such as the Maintenance of Internal Security Act (MISA) were used against protesters. On 28 May, the strike was called off and most leaders were jailed.

On 5 June in 1974, Jayaprakash Narayan called for *Sampoorna Kranti* (total revolution) at a rally in Patna. A Satyagraha on the state assembly premises was held every day. With more than 1,500 protesters in jail and many detained under MISA, students began to to boycott classes and join the movement. JP's movement reached the full-blown texture with his call for Sampoorna Kranti. The central government felt the tremor.

After the call for Sampoorna Kranti, JP, Morarji Desai of Congress(O), the Jana Sangha, and the Socialists along with other anti-Congress parties formed the Janata Morcha or Janata Front, which later became the Janata Party. Its first successful electoral venture was with the victory of Sharad Yadav in the by-election in Jabalpur parliamentary constituency in Madhya Pradesh, a Congress bastion. Yadav, who then represented Bharatiya Lok Dal, won the by-election as a candidate of Janata Front despite being an unknown engineering student contesting from behind bars, having been arrested during his participation in the students' movement. Yadav, at 27, became the youngest member of the Indian Parliament. The experiment of Janata Front got the first electoral success. It was, as the *Times of India* wrote, 'a veritable tornado' against the Congress. After Jabalpur, the Janata Front won more bypolls.

The Fateful Verdict: June 1975

In Indian Politics, 12 June 1975 was a fateful day. First, came the verdict from Gujarat assembly election, where the Congress was trounced by the Janata Morcha (a combined force of the Congress(O), Jan Sangh, PSP and Lok Dal). The Chimanbhai Patel government was already dismissed in early 1974 as a result of the *Nav Nirman Andolan*. On that same day, the Allahabad High Court declared Indira Gandhi's election to the Lok Sabha from Raebareli in 1971 invalid. Justice Jagmohan Lal Sinha of the Allahabad High Court delivered a judgement holding Indira Gandhi guilty of electoral malpractice and disqualified her from holding public office for 6 years.

The case had been filed by Raj Narain, the candidate of the Samyukta Socialist Party (SSP) whom Mrs Gandhi had defeated by a margin of 110,000 votes. It was the same Raj Narain who started the slogan *Indira Hatao*. Prime Minister Gandhi had been summoned for questioning by Raj Narain's lawyer – the first time an incumbent prime minister was summoned to appear and testify in court in a case of this kind.

Mrs Gandhi's election was invalidated on two important findings. First, her election agent Yashpal Kapur, the district magistrate of Raebareli, along with the SP of Raebareli and the home secretary of Uttar Pradesh government, arranged for barricades to be set up and for members of the police force to be posted in connection with her election tour on 1 February and 25 February 1971. This, the Allahabad High Court held, amounted to a corrupt practice under Section 123(7) of the Representation of the People Act.

Second, Yashpal Kapur was a gazetted officer of Government of India. He was in the post of officer on special duty (OSD) in the prime minister's secretariat. Kapur resigned from the post and he was made the election agent of Mrs Gandhi. The question that rose was whether his resignation became effective on the day after his resignation, from 14 January 1971, or from the date of its notification issued by the PM's secretariat on 25 January 1971. Kapur took charge as the election agent of Indira Gandhi on 4 February 1971, the date on which his signed form about such appointment was submitted to the returning officer. The high court took the position that Mrs Gandhi had been projected as a candidate for the election since 29 December 1970. According to the high court, though Kapur's resignation was submitted on 13 January 1971, it did not become effective until 25 January 1971, the date when the notification had been issued in this regard. The high court said that Kapur delivered two election speeches in favour of Mrs Gandhi on 7 January 1971 and on 19 January 1971. Therefore, in the high court's view, Kapur violated of Section 123(7) of the RP Act, as he was at that time serving as a gazetted officer of the Government of India.

Even after the Allahabad high court's verdict, Mrs Gandhi did not leave her throne. It was believed that Sanjay Gandhi, her younger son, and a few loyalists such as then West Bengal Chief Minister Siddhartha Shankar Ray, then Congress president Dev Kant Barooah, and Krishna Chandra Pant (son of the freedom fighter Govind Ballabh Pant, later to become a central minister) advised Indira to continue as the PM. Some sources indicate that Mrs Gandhi was considering to step down after the verdict and she was thinking for Babu Jagjivan Ram (then defence minister) to be in the prime minister's chair for the time being. But her cronies and loyalists influenced her in a different manner. D.K. Barooah, then party president, even at that time dramatically said, 'Indira is India and India is Indira, the two are inseparable.'

The Proclamation of Emergency

The Allahabad High Court on 12 June allowed 20 days to the Government of India to find a successor to Mrs Gandhi. On 23 June, Indira made an appeal before the Supreme Court seeking for an unconditional stay on the verdict of Allahabad High Court. On 24 June, a vacation bench of the apex court allowed a partial stay on Allahabad High Court's judgment. The vacation bench of Justice V. R. Krishna Iyer said that Mrs Gandhi could continue as a member in the Lok Sabha and could attend the Lower House of Parliament but she could not participate in its proceedings or cast her vote as an MP, or draw any remuneration as a Member of Parliament. Most importantly, the Supreme Court in that order allowed Indira Gandhi to continue as the prime minister of India and permitted her to speak and participate in the proceedings of the Lok Sabha and to draw salary in her capacity as the prime minister. The order of the SC did not satisfy

Mrs Gandhi, as it reduced her to a non-functioning figurehead prime minister. Smelling blood, the opposition, led by JP, was not ready to wait and to see what the court would ultimately say, and called for her immediate resignation.

> The stage was actually set for the imposition of National Emergency much earlier. An initiative started for mass arrests of political opponents and suspension of fundamental rights about 6 months before. Coomi Kapoor, a senior journalist, in her book *The Emergency: A Personal History* (published in 2015), showed that Siddhartha Shankar Ray, had sent a confidential handwritten note to Indira Gandhi as early as 8 January 1975. In the note, Ray wrote, 'A secret telex message should go at once to every chief minister (Congress) directing him to prepare a list of all prominent Anand Marg and RSS members in his state. He need not be told of any [Emergency] ordinance but he should have the list ready. The idea is to swing into action immediately after the ordinance is ready – and it has to be ready in 24 hours' time from now.'

On the morning of 25 June, Indira Gandhi told her trusted associate Siddhartha Shankar Ray, the well-known barrister, and the West Bengal chief minister, that democracy would come to a 'grinding halt' and therefore, some drastic action was needed. Ray advised her to use Article 352 of the Indian Constitution, which would allow the government to impose a state of National Emergency to counter external aggression or internal disturbance.

The note was prepared and was sent probably in the wake of the assassination of the union railway minister and the main fund collector of the Congress party, Lalit Narayan Mishra, from a bomb blast in January 1975, on a platform in Samastipur, Bihar, while making a speech – the first Indian cabinet member to be assassinated. Gujarat was also roiled by the political turn of events. However, Mrs Gandhi did not care much about Ray's note at that time. But on 25 June, Ray was the first man Mrs Gandhi turned to for political advice after the huge rally of the Opposition parties took place at Ram Lila Maidan in Delhi. At the Ram Lila Maidan that evening, cheers and applause broke out when JP said, '*Singhasan khaali karo, ki janta aati hai*' (Vacate the throne, the people are coming). JP even gave a call that police and armed forces must not obey 'illegal and unconstitutional orders'.

Mrs Gandhi and her close aides felt that the danger had finally arrived at their doorstep. From the Prime Minister's point of view, JP was asking the armed forces to carry out mutiny. The rally provided Mrs Gandhi the ultimate trigger.

It was certain that the architect of the Emergency Proclamation was S.S. Ray. He drafted the ordinance of the Emergency and then took it to the Rashtrapati Bhavan and met President Fakhruddin Ali Ahmed, who was essentially Mrs Gandhi's nominee. Then the prime minister along with her confidant Rajinder Kumar Dhawan (popularly known as R.K. Dhawan) went to Rashtrapati Bhavan, where the President and the Prime Minister had a tête-à-tête. On her return, Mrs Gandhi asked Ray whether she was constitutionally obliged to call a cabinet meeting before sending the ordinance to Rashtrapati Bhavan. Ray, a highly esteemed legal expert, opined that there was no need to do so. Even K. Brahmananda Reddy, the then central home minister, was kept in the dark. Dhawan took the ordinance to Rashtrapati Bhavan. Just a few minutes before midnight of 25 June, the president of India signed the ordinance, suspending the institutions of Indian democracy. The Union cabinet ratified the ordinance only the next morning. It is still in debate whether it was unconstitutional to get a post-dated cabinet approval because usually, the president acts on the cabinet's advice, not just the prime minister's.

On the morning of 26 June 1975, the Republic of India woke up to the Emergency. Mrs Gandhi tried to justify her decision in her speech on All India Radio. She said, '...a climate of violence and hatred had been created... One of them (the Opposition leaders) went to the extent of saying that armed forces should not carry out orders which they consider wrong... I trust it will be possible to lift the Emergency soon...we actually saved democracy.' Later, Mrs Gandhi said, 'If a person is ill you have to give a medicine which the person may not like but is essential for him.'

The declaration of Emergency was the darkest stain in India's record as a democracy. The arrests began late from the night of 25 June. Jayaprakash Narayan and Morarji Desai were rudely woken up and placed under arrest; this was followed by arrest of most of the other opposition leaders. Even dissident Congress leaders such as Chandra Shekhar, Mohan Dharia (Shekhar and Dharia being known sympathizers of JP), Ram Dhan and Krishna Kant were not spared. On the night that the Emergency was declared, the authorities cut off electricity to newspaper offices on Delhi's Bahadur Shah Zafar Marg. From the next day, the editors were told to submit their articles for pre-censorship. Some journalists were also arrested, the first of whom was Kuldip Nayar, one of the senior-most editors of the *Indian Express*. Even ministers such as Inder Kumar Gujral (later PM of India, April 1997 to March 1998) and Sardar Swaran Singh were removed from the ministry because of their alleged lack of obedience. Across India, fundamental rights were suspended; strikes were banned; prohibition was imposed on unions; protests were cracked down upon. MISA, enacted in 1971, was put in effect to jail almost every dissident for two years without trial. The RSS, CPI(M) and CPI (ML) were among the 26 anti-Congress outfits that were banned. According to Amnesty International, more than 1,10,000 were either arrested or detained without trial in the first year of the Emergency. At least 22 Emergency prisoners died in prison.

Democracy Restored

Many suspected that Congress would lose the 1977 elections. But even they could not imagine the quantum of defeat. Congress was knocked down to its lowest tally till then. Finally, democracy was restored in India.

The meetings of Janata Party attracted huge crowds. Whether it was at the Ram Lila Maidan in Delhi or at the Marina Beach in erstwhile Madras (now Chennai) or the Maidan aka Brigade Parade Ground in Calcutta (now Kolkata), the picture was the same. Apart from the large venues, the same was applicable for many public grounds in cities, towns and villages across the country. Crowds often were staying awake up to 2 or 3 a.m. to hear the speeches of the leaders of the Janata Party. In the northern part of India, the students of college and university campaigned in urban and rural seats for Janata candidates. A large number of members of the bar associations, whose network extended from metro cities to small towns, wholeheartedly supported Janata candidates. Mrs Gandhi announced that she was relaxing the Emergency and therefore, many people, for whom the Emergency was a nightmare, apprehended that it might be restored if she would win the election again.

Two months before the general elections, the campaign began. The public attendance in her rally was small, the crowd seemed to be unresponsive and indifferent to her. There was a change in the direction of the winds. Congress candidates, who had won getting 40% of the votes or more in the 1971 general elections, were reduced to margins of 20%. Some of them were decreased to even 15% of the vote. As many political analysts said, it was obvious that the reason of the victory of the Janata Party was not only the result of a consolidation of the opposition votes, but also a shift of sizeable voters away from the Congress.

Another striking feature of the election, which restored democracy in India, was the absence of any political divide between rural and urban India. The rural and urban people responded in much the same way to the emergency. The impact of the emergency was felt mainly by the urban people. A section of leadership in the Congress was hopeful that their vote bank in rural India would remain intact. However, the parts of the country where the candidates of the Janata Party won, they were elected in both urban and rural constituencies.

Mrs Gandhi conceded defeat. However, she stuck to her position that the imposition of the National Emergency was an absolutely right decision which had saved India. Indira Gandhi even maintained that if elections were held in 1976, and not 1977, her party would have won.

The Soothing Balm of the South: 1977

South India emerged as a face-saver for Indira Gandhi in 1977 elections. The election results of the year, not for the first time, depicted a sharp division between north and south India. Only 2 of the 154 Members of Parliament in the Congress were from the Hindi belt in the north, and 92 of them were from Andhra Pradesh, Karnataka, Kerala, and Tamil Nadu. While north India voted vehemently in their outright rejection of Congress, the South stood by Mrs Gandhi and her party. North of the Narmada River there was a Janata wave. But south of it, there was a defiant show of strength by the Congress. It indicated a strange dichotomy in Indian politics.

A section of observers and analysts were of the view that the excess of the emergency had not reached the southern side of India. But this was partly true. The epicentre of the National Emergency earthquake was definitely the national capital New Delhi, where the common people had to face the excesses and the wrath was felt in most of the northern states of India. The

South, however, was not free from state oppression and human rights violation. There was the infamous Rajan case in Kerala, where a college student was 'disappeared' after being abducted in late night and tortured in police custody, or the arrest of, and tremendous torture on, activists like Lawrence Fernandes (the younger brother of George Fernandes), journalists like C.G.K. Reddy and the Film maker-actor duo of Pattabhirama Reddy and Snehalata Reddy in Bangalore (now Bengaluru). Snehalata, a close friend of George Fernandes, was considered as one of the martyrs of the Emergency. Snehalata and her husband had joined the anti-Emergency movement.

But unlike in the north, as many observers have tended to argue, these did not directly affect the common people as a whole, and thus came to be viewed more as individual cases of police atrocities than as some institutional excesses of the Emergency regime. For instance, coercion in the family planning drive is something the south rarely experienced. There has been relatively less serious grievances and therefore relatively less resentment on this particular issue. Therefore, it did not leave a strong impact on the psyche of the southern electorate and this feature was mirrored in the poll results.

However, there were local factors too. The performance of the Congress in southern India, particularly in three states – Kerala, Andhra Pradesh and Karnataka – had a major contribution from their chief ministers, who either belonged to Congress or its allies, and their policies.

It is believed that the chief minister of Karnataka D Devaraj Urs had all along maintained control over bureaucrats at the state level and became successful in preventing the kind of excess during the Emergency that had stifled the northern part of India. Furthermore, CM Urs persuaded poor voters through a number of programmes carried by his government to give them relief from the debts and to provide housing for the homeless people. Much more crucially, the Urs government developed an unusually practicable land reform law which gave local land tribunals the power to work quickly and effectively to bestow land upon tenants and the landless. All these efforts and initiatives gave confidence among the rural poor and Congress earned the support even of the dispossessed.

In Andhra Pradesh the Congress even improved its vote share by 1.63% compared to its performance in 1971. Chief Minister Jalagam Vengala Rao isolated his state from carrying out forced sterilisation programme. During the Emergency, the government carried out programmes to allocate house sites and unfarmed land, to eradicate rural debt, and to raise the minimum wage for the labourers in the agricultural sector. Again, the government funds allocated for scheduled castes and scheduled tribes had been kept by the government to release it before the polls. For these policies and their implementation, the chief minister attained credibility and could confidently and boldly claim that the Congress was the ally of the poor people of the rural part of the state. The Congress gained considerable support from SCs and STs, minorities, and the poor people from rural areas. The rural poor in many areas also supported the Congress out of fear of the rich peasants. The poor voters responded directly in a positive manner to the promises, which the several programmes of Vengala Rao's government offered to them.

Election by Miscalculation?

Immediately after the National Emergency was imposed, the Prime Minister Indira Gandhi announced that it would be possible to lift the emergency soon. Even in early 1977, it seemed like the Emergency would go on forever or even that the constitution could be rewritten (as suggested by Sanjay Gandhi and his crony Bansi Lal). On 18 January 1977, the prime minister announced that the fifth Lok Sabha was dissolved, and elections would be held after 2 months, 1 year after it was due. In course of time, several opposition leaders were released (but not all); censorship was rolled back. The Emergency officially came to an end on 21 March 1977. Sanjay Gandhi, by that time recognised as the second-in-command in both the party and government and widely held responsible for much of the worst excesses of the Emergency, told his mother, 'You are committing a horrible mistake.'

Mrs Gandhi, of course, thought she was going to win. According to R.K. Dhawan, she was cut off from the people and believed whatever her acolytes told her. They told her things were going well and her public rallies were jam-packed. The press was censored, and the reality could not surface. The Intelligence Bureau assured Mrs Gandhi that she should win 340 seats if she went to the polls shortly. It is believed an officer who was highly placed in the PMO and who was actually opposed to the emergency put pressure on the then director of IB and other officers to manufacture a report showing the imminent victory of the Congress. But take this story with a pinch of salt if you want. We would.

After the election results, Kuldip Nayar was believed to have asked Sanjay Gandhi why he called the election. Sanjay promptly replied, 'I didn't.' Even Nayar, a seasoned journalist, was startled, 'So who called it?' Sanjay pointed at his mother and said, 'Ask her. She did it.'

Prime Ministers of India

Jawahar Lal Nehru
(Tenure: 15 August
1947–27 May 1964)

Gulzarilal Nanda
(Acting, Tenure:
27 May 1964–
9 June 1964)

Lal Bahadur Shastri
(Tenure:
9 June 1964–
11 January 1966)

Gulzarilal Nanda
(Acting, Tenure:
11 January 1966–
24 January 1966)

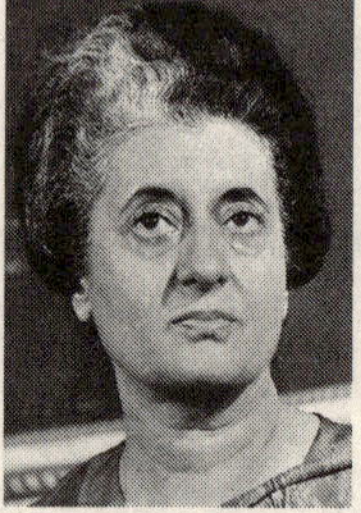

Indira Gandhi
(Tenure:
24 January 1966–
24 March 1977)

Morarji Desai
(Tenure:
24 March 1977–
28 July 1979)

Charan Singh
(Tenure:
28 July 1979–
14 January 1980)

Indira Gandhi
(Tenure:
24 January 1966–
24 March 1977)

Rajiv Gandhi
(Tenure:
31 October 1984–
2 December 1989)

V.P. Singh
(Tenure:
2 December 1989–
10 November 1990

Chandra Shekhar
(Tenure:
10 November 1990–
21 June 1991)

P. V. Narasimha Rao
(Tenure:
21 June 1991–
16 May 1996)

Atal Bihari Vajpayee
(Tenure:
16 May 1996–
1 June 1996)

H. D. Deve Gowda
(Tenure:
1 June 1996–
21 April 1997)

Inder Kumar Gujral
(Tenure:
21 April 1997–
19 March 1998)

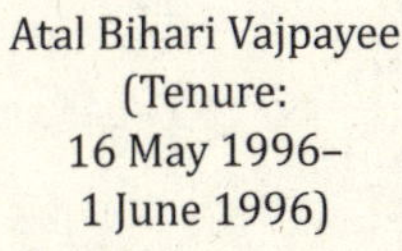

Atal Bihari Vajpayee
(Tenure:
16 May 1996–
1 June 1996)

Manmohan Singh
(Tenure:
22 May 2004–
26 May 2014

Narendra Modi
(Tenure:
26 May 2014–
Incumbent)

BOOK II

AGE OF POLITICAL FRAGMENTATION 1977–99

Chapter 8

THE AGE OF UNSTABLE COALITIONS 1977–99

1977: The First Non-Congress Government

The year 1977 was a momentous election, where the hegemonic Congress was forced out of power for the first time. Just before the elections of 1977, after a fresh round of delimitation and creation of new seats, the number of Lok Sabha seats was increased to 542 – which remained unchanged till the fourteenth general elections in 2004.

The elections were announced on 18 January 1977, even while the Emergency remained in force (25 June 1975 to 21 March 1977).

The sixth general elections were held during 16–20 March 1977. This was the first election in which the INC was actually defeated by the collective opposition. The Janata Party won 41.32% of the vote, and 295 seats – thus winning both on actual votes and in terms of seats; the INC won only 154 seats, with 34.52% of the votes cast. The CPI(M), which had previously agreed not to run candidates against the Janata Party, remained in the third position with about 22 seats. The All

ON 20 JANUARY 1977, 4 OPPOSITION OUTFITS – THE INC(O), THE BHARATIYA JANA SANGH, THE BHARATIYA LOK DAL AND THE PRAJA SOCIALIST PARTY – WHICH HAD FOUGHT AND WON THE GUJARAT VIDHAN SABHA ELECTIONS IN 1974 AS THE JANATA MORCHA – DECIDED TO FORMALLY COME TOGETHER AS THE JANATA PARTY, ADOPTING THE BLD ELECTIONS SYMBOL OF A FARMER WITH A PLOUGH. THEY WERE JOINED BY THE SOCIALIST PARTY OF RAJ NARAIN AND GEORGE FERNANDES, AND THE SWATANTRA PARTY. DESPITE THE WIDE DIVERSITY AMONG THE VARIOUS CONSTITUENTS OF THE JANATA ALLIANCE, THEY WERE ABLE TO UNITE BEHIND JAYAPRAKASH NARAYAN. CHANDRA SHEKHAR BECAME THE FIRST PRESIDENT OF THE PARTY, RAMAKRISHNA HEGDE BECAME ITS GENERAL SECRETARY AND LAL KRISHNA ADVANI, OF THE BJS, ITS FIRST SPOKESMAN.

India Anna Dravida Munnetra Kazhagam, a new party set up by M.G. Ramchandran in 1972, came fourth with 18 seats (2.90% vote share), reducing the DMK to only 2 seats. The SAD won 9 seats, the PWPI won 5, the RSP 4, AIFB and INC(O) won 3 seats each. The RPI(K), IUML, Kerala Congress and JKNC won 2 seats each, while the Jharkhand Party, United Democratic Front and MAG won 1 seat each. At least 14 parties failed to win any seat.

The INC got a major drubbing all across north India, losing every single seat in Bihar, Delhi, Haryana and Punjab, and Uttar Pradesh (including Mrs Gandhi in Raebareli and Sanjay Gandhi in Amethi). It won only 1 seat each in Rajasthan and Madhya Pradesh and got hammered out in West Bengal (where, in the assembly polls, it finally lost power to the CPI(M)-led alliance). In

Bihar, the Janata Party won 52 seats, the All India Jharkhand Party won 1 seat and an independent won 1 seat. In Uttar Pradesh, the JP won all the 85 seats – the first-ever clean sweep in the state. In Rajasthan, the JP won 24 seats to the 1 won by the INC. In Madhya Pradesh, the JP won 37, while the INC, RP(K) and independents won 1 seat each. In Haryana, the JP won all 10 seats. In Punjab, the SAD won 9 the seats, the JP won 3 and the CPI(M) won 1. In Himachal Pradesh, the JP won all 4 seats, as it did in Delhi, winning all 7, and also the solitary seat of Chandigarh. In Jammu and Kashmir, the INC managed to win 3 seats, the JKNC won 2 and independents 1. In Gujarat, the JP won 16, while the INC won 10. In West Bengal, the CPI(M) won 17 seats, the JP won 15, the AIFB, RSP and INC won 3 seats each, while 1 seat was won by an independent candidate. In Orissa, the JP won 15 seats, the INC 4, the CPI(M) and independents won 1 seat each.

INC managed to perform relatively better south of the Vindhyas – especially, Karnataka, Andhra Pradesh, Kerala and large parts of Maharashtra. In Maharashtra, the INC won 20 of the 48 seats, while the JP won 19, The PWPI won 5 and the CPI(M) 3. In Andhra Pradesh, the INC won 41 seats, leaving only 1 seat for the JP. In Karnataka, the INC won 26 seats to the JP's tally of 2. In Kerala, the INC won 11 seats, the CPI(M) won 3, the Kerala Congress and IUML won 2 seats each, while the RSP and CPI won a seat each. In Tamil Nadu, the AIADMK won 18 seats, followed by the INC with 14 seats. The INC(O) and the CPI(M) won 3 seats each, while the DMK won 2 seats. The solitary seat of Andaman and Nicobar was taken by the INC as was the 1 in Lakshwadeep and that of Dadra and Nagar Haveli. The 2 seats of Goa, Daman and Diu were split between the INC and Maharashtravadi Gomantak Party (MAG).

The INC also did relatively well in the north-east. In Assam, the INC won 10 seats, while the JP won 3 and an independent took 1. In Manipur, the INC won both the seats. In Arunachal Pradesh, the INC won the solitary Lok Sabha seat. In Meghalaya, the INC and an independent won a seat each. In Tripura, the INC and the JP won 1 seat each. In Sikkim, the solitary seat was taken by the INC. In Nagaland, the solitary seat was taken by the UDF, while that of Mizoram was taken by an independent candidate.

Veteran Congress leader, Bapu Jagjivan Ram, had left the INC just before the 1977 elections and floated his own party, Congress for Democracy. The CfD did not merge itself with the Janata Party but fought the elections together, winning 28 seats by itself, and swinging many Dalit seats for the Janata Party. The Janata government had three prime ministerial aspirants – Mrs Gandhi's long-term adversary, Morarji Desai (from the Congress(O)), Chaudhary Charan Singh and Bapu Jagjivan Ram. Desai was made prime minister at the behest of Jayaprakash Narayan. Jagjivan Ram was initially miffed, but was pacified upon being made deputy prime minister alongside the minister for defence. Ram actually went on to announce the merger of the CfD with the Janata Party. Charan Singh was also made the deputy prime minister, apart from being home minister (1977–78) and then minister of finance (1979). While the portfolio of Home was shuttled between Charan Singh, Morarji Desai and Hirubhai Patel (all ex-Congressmen), and that of Finance between Singh and Patel, the Ministry of External Affairs was held, for the entire duration of the Desai government, by Atal Bihari Vajpayee, and that of Information and Broadcasting by L.K. Advani (both from the BJS). The portfolio for Industry was held by George Fernandes (Socialist Party). This was also the first time that the Shiromani Akali Dal made its entry into the central government as part of the broad anti-Congress coalition: with 9 seats under its belt, the Akalis were given the portfolio of Agriculture, held first by Parkash Singh Badal, and then by Surjit Singh Barnala.

The momentum of victory was carried into the provinces as well, when the Desai government argued that all the 10 Congress provincial governments had lost their mandate from the people, and should seek a fresh mandate. As all 10 assemblies were dissolved and fresh elections were held, the Janata Party formed a government on its own in 7 of them – Uttar Pradesh, Bihar, Haryana, Orissa, Madhya Pradesh, Rajasthan and Himachal Pradesh. West Bengal saw the rise of the Left Front with the CPI(M) at its lead, ushering in Leftist domination for the next 3 decades, and the near-complete decimation of the Congress. The Shiromani Akali Dal formed the government, with Parkash Singh Badal, giving up his union cabinet birth, became chief minister of Punjab. Sheikh Abdullah of the National Conference, who had been dismissed from office in 1953, returned to power in Jammu and Kashmir, even as the Janata Party made its political debut in the state. The era of Congress dominance in north India seemed over.

Given the diversity of the agenda of the constituent parts of the government, not much was achieved by the Desai government except a complete revocation of all Emergency-era legislations. Vajpayee in MEA was successfully steering the government away from Mrs Gandhi's increasing policy of alignment with Moscow, pursuing a policy of 'genuine non-alignment', and reduced the confrontational posture towards Pakistan and China. His presence in the cabinet, along with Advani in Ministry of Information and Broadcasting was argued to be pushing forward the Rashtriya Swayamsevak Sangh (RSS) agenda, when Hindu–Muslim clashes began to break out in a number of places. It gave an impression that the BJS was gaining more from the government than either the BLD, PSP or Congress(O) (to the extent that they had any definite objectives to pursue). The economic policies of the government, being unable to alleviate economic hardships, caused considerable disaffection among the people. The government's insistence that foreign entrepreneurs should take on board Indian partners caused enough bad blood for Coca-Cola and IBM to leave India altogether. All of this occasioned sufficient trouble within for Morarji Desai's government to break up, first, with Vajpayee and

Advani resigning (upon being asked to choose either the RSS or the government) and, then, with a section of the Janata Party splitting away under Chaudhary Charan Singh, forming the Janata Party (Secular), expressing alarm at the steady rise of the RSS and Desai shielding corruption.

Charan Singh recommended dissolution of the Lok Sabha and had President N.S. Reddy call for general elections.

CHAUDHARY CHARAN SINGH TRIED TO FORM A MINORITY GOVERNMENT OF THE JP (S), WITH THE SUPPORT OF CONGRESS FROM OUTSIDE. BUT ONCE THE EXTENT OF PUBLIC DISAFFECTION WITH THE JANATA MOVEMENT BECAME CLEAR, MRS GANDHI PULLED THE CARPET FROM UNDER SINGH, WHO RESIGNED AFTER ONLY 23 DAYS IN THE PM'S OFFICE – THE ONLY PM WHO DEMITTED OFFICE WITHOUT FACING PARLIAMENT.

1980: The Return of the Prodigal

Elections were held on 3 and 6 January 1980 for the seventh Lok Sabha.

Mrs Gandhi and her party Congress(I) [i.e. Congress (Indira), founded in January 1978], with of the open palm as its election symbol] was handed a huge victory, bringing her back to power. The Congress won 353 seats of the 531 that went to the polls, winning 42.69% of the total votes cast; the rump Janata Party won 31 seats, with 18.97% of the votes, while the Janata Party (Secular) won 41 seats with only 9.39% of the votes. The CPI(M) had the third-highest representation in the Lok Sabha with 37 seats (on the basis of only 6.34% of the votes cast), whereas the CPI won 10 seats on the back of only 2.49% of the votes cast. The

DMK regained its strength in the Lok Sabha winning 16 seats on the basis of a 2.14% vote share, which was ironically less than 2.36% votes won by the AIADMK, who limped home with only 2 seats. Mrs Gandhi won her Lok Sabha seat from Medak in Andhra Pradesh, one of the few states in which the Congress(I) felt safe. The RSP won 4 seats; the AIFB and JKNC won 3 seats each; the AIADMK and IUML won 2 seats each, while the SAD, Kerala Congress, Jharkhand Party, MAG and Sikkim Janata Parishad won 1 seat each. Nearly 19 major local parties failed to win a single Lok Sabha seat.

The INC regained its dominance of the Lok Sabha seats from north India. In Uttar Pradesh, the INC won 51 of the 85 Lok Sabha seats, followed by the JP(S) with 29 seats and the JP with 3, the CPI and independents with 1 seat each. In Bihar, the INC took 30 seats, the JP 8, JPS 5, CPI and Congress (Urs)* 4, the Jharkhand Party and an independent taking 1 seat each. In Madhya Pradesh, the INC took 35 seats, while the JP took 4, and an independent 1. In Rajasthan, the INC won 18 seats, the JP 4, JP(S) 2 and Congress(U) 1. In Punjab, the INC won 10 seats, the CPI 2 and SAD 1. In Haryana, the INC won 5 seats, and the JP(S) 4 and JP won 1 seat. In Jammu and Kashmir, the JKNC won 4 seats, while the INC, the Congress (Urs) and an independent won 1 seat each. In Himachal Pradesh, the INC took all 4 seats, in Delhi 6, out of 7, and the solitary seats in Chandigarh and Dadra and Nagar Haveli as well. In Gujarat, the INC won 25 of the 26 seats, while the JP took the remaining seat. In Maharashtra, the INC took 39 seats, the JP 8 and Congress (Urs) 1. In Orissa, the INC won 20 seats, the JP took 1 seat. In West Bengal, the CPI(M) won 28 seats, while the INC took 4, the CPI took 3 seats, while the RSP 4 and FB took 3 seats.

* Congress (Urs) was a splinter faction of Congress(R) that broke away under Devaraj Urs, in protest at the return of Sanjay Gandhi into the party fold.

In the south, the INC prevailed in Andhra Pradesh, winning 41 seats, while the Congress (Urs) won 1 seat. In Karnataka, the INC won 27 seats, while the JP won 1. In Kerala, however, the INC tally came down to 5, the Congress(Urs) 3, CPI(M) 7, IUML 2 seats, while the CPI, Kerala Congress and independents won 1 seat each. In Tamil Nadu, the INC-DMK alliance won 37 of the 39 seats, with the DMK winning 16, INC 20, CPI 4 and AIFB 1; the AIADMK took the remaining 2 seats. The INC won the solitary seats in the constituencies of Pondicherry, Andaman and Nicobar, and Lakshwadeep. The 2 seats of Goa, Daman and Diu were split between the INC and MAG (Maharashtravadi Gomantak Party).

In the north-east, the INC took both of the 2 seats that went to the polls in Assam (which was going through a period of turmoil and thus no polls could be held in the remaining 12 constituencies). In Meghalaya, the INC took 1 seat, while polling was not held in the other constituency. The INC took both the seats from Manipur, while the CPI(M) took both the seats from Tripura. The seat from Nagaland was won by an independent candidate, as was the one from Mizoram. The seat from Sikkim was taken by the Sikkim Janata Parishad. Both seats from Arunachal Pradesh were won by the INC.

Following the Mandate Theory pushed earlier by the Desai government, the Congress now pushed for legislative assembly elections in 12 states in 1980 to regain its nationwide dominance. Mrs Gandhi plunged straight into the battle for the assemblies, helping Congress win in 10 states – Bihar, Goa Daman and Diu, Gujarat, Madhya Pradesh, Maharashtra, Manipur, Odisha, Punjab, Rajasthan and Uttar Pradesh. In most of these, its principal opposition remained the Janata Party, but the Bharatiya Janata Party – the BJS component which had broken away from the Janata Party in 1979 and reconstituted itself under a new name in April 1980 – tried to hold on to the BJS voter base and gained some more traction to emerge as a political force of some significance in the politics of north India. Curiously, the two states the Congress failed to win in 1980 were both from the south, which had saved the Congress from a washout in 1977 – Kerala was held by the Left Democratic Front, while Tamil Nadu was retained by the AIADMK-led alliance.

1984: The Sympathy Wave Election

Indira Gandhi's third government was characterized by an initial improvement in the state of the economy, but more by her machinations against political forces that stood opposed to her. While she successfully cut many down to size, her strategy in Punjab went haywire, giving rise to the Khalistan movement, culminating in Operation Blue Star, the fateful assault on the Golden Temple in Amritsar, the holiest of Sikh shrines. The resultant assassination of Mrs Gandhi at the hands of her own Sikh bodyguards in October 1984 was followed by a disconcerting Congress-led anti-Sikh backlash in large parts of India, which took the shape of a veritable carnage against innocent Sikhs. Sensing the public mood, Mrs Gandhi's eldest son, Rajiv Gandhi, who had been chosen by the Congress(I) to lead the party and the government, decided to go to the country immediately.

Elections to the eighth Lok Sabha were held on 24, 27 and 28 December 1984. They were held in only 516 Lok Sabha constituencies, since Punjab and Assam were gripped with too much disturbance for polling to be carried out. The Congress won 404 parliamentary seats with a vote share of 49.4% – the largest ever mandate won by any Indian party and government. The Janata Party was reduced to 10 seats with a 6.89% share of the total votes cast; even though the debutant BJP won a greater share of the votes (7.74%), it could win only 2 seats (Chandu Patla Janga Reddy defeating the union Home Minister

P.V. Narasimha Rao in Andhra Pradesh and A.K. Patel in Gujarat being the only victorious candidates). The CPI(M) had the third-highest tally of seats (22, with a vote share of 5.87%), while the second-highest tally of 30 (with a vote share of only 4.31%) was claimed by the new outfit of Telugu Desam, founded in 1982 by Nandamuri Tarak Rama Rao – the first ever regional party to become the main opposition party in the Lok Sabha. When elections took place in Punjab and Assam belatedly, the Congress added 10 more seats to its tally (thus, 414 out of 543), while the Shiromani Akali Dal carried all the 7 seats in Punjab (presumably as a backlash to the killing of the Sikhs in 1984). The AIADMK, in alignment with the INC, won 12 seats, while the DMK was reduced to 2. Among other parties to win multiple seats were the CPI with 6 seats, Indian Congress (Socialist) with 4; RSP and JKNC with 3 seats each; and the AIFB, IUML and Kerala Congress (Joseph) won 2 seats each. The Indian Congress (Jagjivan) and PWPI won 1 seat each. Eighteen parties failed to win any seats. Only 5 independent candidates were successful in winning a seat.

The year 1984 turned out to be a freak election in north India. In Uttar Pradesh, the INC won 83 of the 85 seats, with 2 seats being won by the Lok Dal, led by Charan Singh. In Bihar, the INC won 48 seats, with 2 seats being taken by the CPI and 1 each by the Indian Congress (Jagjivan), JP, Lok Dal and an independent candidate. In Madhya Pradesh, the INC took all 40 seats; in Rajasthan, all 25; in Delhi, all 7; in Himachal Pradesh, all 4; in Haryana, all 10. In Gujarat, the INC took 24 seats, while the BJP and JP took 1 seat each. In Jammu and Kashmir, the INC and its ally, the JKNC took 3 seats each. In Maharashtra, the INC won 43 seats, the Indian Congress (Socialist) won 2, with the PWPI, the JP and an independent winning 1 seat each. In Orissa, the INC won 21 and JP 1. In West Bengal, the INC won 16, whereas the CPI(M) won 18 seats, the CPI and RSP 3 seats each, while the AIFB won 2 seats.

In the south, the biggest surprise was the stronghold till the 1980 elections, Andhra Pradesh. There, the TDP swept the polls, with 30 seats, with the INC winning only 6 seats, and with the JP, BJP, CPI, CPM, Indian Congress (Urs) and an independent winning a seat each. In Karnataka, the INC won 24 seats, while the JP won 4. In Kerala, the INC won 13, the Kerala Congress (Joseph) and IUML won 2 seats each, while the CPI, CPI(M) and the Indian Congress (Socialist) managed to win 1 seat each. In Tamil Nadu, the INC won 25, the AIADMK won 12, while the DMK won only 2 seats. The INC also took the solitary seats of Chandigarh, Pondicherry and Lakshwadeep, and the 2 seats of Goa, Daman and Diu. However, Dadra and Nagar Haveli was taken by an independent candidate.

In the north-east, elections were to be held for Assam later. Among those states, where it was held, the INC took both the seats in Arunachal Pradesh, Meghalaya and Manipur, and the solitary seat from Nagaland. The CPI(M) won both the seats from Tripura. The INC won the seat from Mizoram, uncontested. When elections were held later in Assam, the INC won 4 seats, the Indian Congress (Urs) and Plains Tribal Council of Assam won 1 each, while 8 seats were taken by independents, most of whom were to gain affiliation with the Asom Gana Parishad at a later date.

1989: The Bofors Election

In a way, Rajiv Gandhi may be said to have squandered the landslide he had won in 1984. A virtually full-fledged insurgency in Punjab, rumblings in Jammu and Kashmir and Assam, repercussions of the LTTE insurgency in Sri Lanka and mounting economic problems stymied the Gandhi government. Rajiv Gandhi's missteps further gave fillip to the forces of Hindu communalism when he undermined the progressive verdict on the Shah Bano case (giving Muslim women similar rights to alimony as their non-Muslim counterparts) by introducing legislation that reduced Muslim women's right to alimony. The fledgling Hindu nationalist BJP played this up in a big way to undermine Rajiv Gandhi, who decided to give the soft soap to the Ram Janmabhoomi-Babri Masjid dispute by opening the lock on the premises and allowing worship – which ironically put wind in the sails of the BJP. Major differences emerged within the government with the finance minister, Vishwanath Pratap Singh, (who later also held the portfolio of Defence), becoming a vocal critic of the government's penchant for financial irregularities which culminated in the Bofors scam.

Upon being sacked from the cabinet, V.P. Singh resigned from the Congress and went on to set up the Janta Morcha with Arun Nehru and Arif Mohammad Khan. V.P. then went on to unite the disparate factions of the erstwhile Janata Party, the Lok Dal (set up in 1979 by Charan Singh, merging the JP(S), SP and Orissa Janata Party) and Indian National Congress (Jagjivan) (set up by Jagjivan Ram in 1981) in October 1988 to give birth to the Janata Dal. Singh further brought together other anti-Congress parties from outside the JP fold, such as the Telugu Desam, DMK and Asom Gana Parishad (founded after the Assam Accord of 1985) to create the National Front (NF). The NF also ensured outside support from the Left Front and the BJP – each opposed to the Congress for purely political reasons of their own.

In the elections that were held on 22 and 26 November to elect the members of the ninth Lok Sabha, the bifurcation of Goa, Daman and Diu and the addition of 1 seat to Daman and Diu increased the total number of LS seats to 543. But since insurgency-inflicted Assam never went to the polls, the total seats that went to vote was 529. The Congress emerged with the highest tally, with 197 seats (and a vote share of 39.53%) – having clearly lost the stupendous mandate it earned 5 years ago. The Janata Dal emerged the second-largest party with 143 seats (with 17.79% of the vote share), while the BJP became the third-largest party with 85 seats (but only 11.36% of the votes), and the CPI(M) had the fourth highest tally (33 seats with 6.55% vote share). The CPI followed with 12 seats and the AIADMK with 11. SAD (Simranjit Singh Mann faction) took 6 seats, while SAD (Badal) failed to win any seat. The RSP won 4 seats, the AIFB, JKNC, JMM and the Bahujan Samaj Party (BSP) won 3 seats each; the TDP (second-largest party in 1984 elections) and IUML won 2 seats; the GNLF, All India Majlis-E-Ittehadul Muslimeen (AIMIM), Shiv Sena, Indian Congress (Socialist, S.C. Sinha faction), Kerala Congress (Mani), Marxist Coordination Committee, AIHM, MAG and Sikkim Sangram Parishad won 1 seat each. Independents won 12 seats.

The ninth Lok Sabha provides a clear marker for the political fragmentation that was beginning to characterize the Indian political landscape. In 1989, the hitherto largest number of registered political parties ran for elections and polled a plurality of votes – 111 major and minor parties polled nearly 285 million votes, with independents polling another 15 million. Among the parties who entered the Lok Sabha for the first time in 1989, and went on to play important roles in Indian politics thereafter were the Bahujan Samaj Party, the Shiv Sena and the All India Majlis-E-Ittehadul Muslimeen. As many as 87 parties failed to win any seats, of which some, like the DMK, were able to win back their position in subsequent general elections, while quite a few turned out to be fly-by-the-night type.

In regional terms, the verdict was no less fractured than it was at the union level, because no single party was able to dominate the northern part of India, although both the JD and the BJP fared collectively better in the north than in the south. In Bihar, the Janata Dal won 32 seats, followed by the BJP with 8 seats, the CPI and INC with 4 seats each, the JMM with 3, the CPI(M), Marxist Coordination Committee and Indian People's Front won 1 seat each. In Uttar Pradesh, the JD won 54 seats, the INC won 15, the BJP won 8, the BSP, CPI and independents won 2 seats each, the CPI(M) and HMS won 1 seat each. In Rajasthan, the BJP won 13 seats, JD won 11 and CPI(M) won 1. In Madhya Pradesh, the BJP gained prominence for the first time with 27 seats, with the INC winning only 8 seats, JD 4, and an independent 1. In Himachal Pradesh, the BJP ate into INC domination, winning 3 seats, while the INC won only 1. In Jammu and Kashmir, the JKNC won 3 seats, INC 2 and an independent 1. In Punjab, the SAD(M) swept aside the SAD (Badal) to win 6 seats, while the INC won 2 seats, JD and BSP won 1 each and independents won 3. In Delhi, the BJP won 4 seats, the INC won 2 and the JD won 1 seat. In Haryana, the JD won 6 seats and INC 4 seats. In Gujarat, the JD won 13 seats, BJP 10 and INC 3 seats. In Maharashtra, the INC remained the dominant force winning 28 seats, followed by the BJP with 10 seats, JD 5 seats, the Shiv Sena and the CPI won 1 seat each, while the independents won 3. Orissa saw the JD winning 16 seats, the INC won 3 seats, and the CPI and CPI(M) won 1 seat each. In West Bengal, the CPI(M) won 27 seats, the INC and RSP won 4 seats each, the CPI and AIFB won 3 seats each, while the Gorkha National Liberation Front (GNLF) won 1. The seats of Dadra and Nagar Haveli and of Daman and Diu went to independents. The Chandigarh Lok Sabha seat was taken by the JD.

In the south, in Andhra Pradesh, the INC regained its foothold to win 39 seats, reducing the TDP to 2 seats, while the Hyderabad-based AIMIM won its maiden Lok Sabha seat. In Karnataka, the INC won 27 seats, while the JD won 1. In Kerala, the INC won 14 seats, IUML and CPM won 2 seats, Kerala Congress(M) and ICS (SCS) won 1 seat each. In Tamil Nadu, the INC won 27 seats and its ally, the AIADMK, won 11 seats and the CPI won 1. The INC won the solitary seats in the constituencies of Lakshwadeep, Pondicherry and Andaman and Nicobar Islands. The JD won both the Lok Sabha seats of Goa.

There being no elections in Assam, the north-eastern contingent to the seventh Lok Sabha was noticeably smaller. The INC won 2 seats each from Arunachal Pradesh, Manipur, Tripura and Meghalaya. The solitary seats from Mizoram and Nagaland also went to the INC, while the solitary seat from Sikkim went to the Sikkim Sangram Parishad (SSP).

THE FRACTURED VERDICT OF THE NINTH GENERAL ELECTIONS PLACED THE INDIAN POLITICAL SYSTEM IN AN UNPRECEDENTED SITUATION. THE INCUMBENT GOVERNMENT HAD CLEARLY LOST THE ELECTIONS, LOSING MORE THAN HALF OF ITS SEATS FROM FIVE YEARS AGO AND YET IT WAS CLEARLY THE SINGLE LARGEST PARTY – WHICH CONVENTIONALLY IS INVITED TO FORM THE GOVERNMENT. UPON PRESIDENT R. VENKATARAMAN CHOOSING TO FOLLOW CONVENTION, OUTGOING PRIME MINISTER RAJIV GANDHI DECLINED THE OFFER, SAYING THAT THE CONGRESS ACCEPTED THE MANDATE OF THE PEOPLE AND WOULD CHOOSE TO SIT IN THE OPPOSITION – THE FIRST (AND SO FAR THE ONLY) INDIAN POLITICIAN TO HAVE DONE SO, BY NOT RESORTING TO THE STRATEGY OF HORSE-TRADING.

After the elections, in the Central Hall of Parliament, Singh proposed the name of Chaudhary Devi Lal, a Haryana Jat leader, for the post of prime minister. Devi Lal declined, and suggested the name of V.P. Singh instead. This surprised Chandra Shekhar, an avowed opponent of V.P. Singh in the Janata Dal, who was led to believe and accept that Devi Lal was the unanimous choice.

Unwilling to accept V.P. as the prime minister, Chandra Shekhar refused to serve in the cabinet.

In the government that was formed, V.P. Singh retained the Defence portfolio for himself; Devi Lal became the deputy prime minister; Inder Kumar Gujral was made the minister of external affairs; George Fernandes, a veteran of the 1977 non-Congress government, entered the cabinet with the Ministry for Railways; Mufti Muhammad Sayeed from J&K was given Home; Arun Nehru was given Commerce and Industry; Arif Mohammad Khan was given Energy and Civil Aviation; Ajit Singh, the son of Charan Singh was given Industry; Ram Vilas Paswan entered the cabinet with Labour and Employment - a veritable line-up of the most successful generation of Janata politicians in Indian politics.

V.P. Singh held the office of the prime minister for less than a year (December 1989–November 1990). During that year, militancy in Punjab was brought to heel, with Singh's visit to the Golden Temple, seeking forgiveness, some say, working like a balm on Sikh sentiments. Singh also brought back Indian troops from Sri Lanka (committed by former PM Rajiv Gandhi). But insurgency in Kashmir was entering its critical phase, with Kashmiri pundits being forced out of the valley after threats from separatist militants.

As things appeared to be unravelling, V.P. Singh concentrated on caste consolidation of the social constituency that had powered the Janata Dal to power - the economically underprivileged social groups, that lay outside the matrix of scheduled castes and tribes, which had hitherto been given the benefit of caste-based reservations in educational institutions and public services. In the assembly elections of 1989–90, the plank of social justice powered an NF victory in Haryana (under Devi Lal's son Om Prakash Chautala), Gujarat (Chimanbhai Patel), Orissa (Biju Patnaik), Bihar (Lalu Prasad Yadav) and

Uttar Pradesh (Mulayam Singh Yadav). The NF allies retained power in Left-ruled West Bengal and Kerala, and gained power in Rajasthan (under BJP's Bhairon Singh Sekhawat, with NF support from the outside). Resorting to promote the cause of social justice further, the Singh government decided to implement the recommendation of the Mandal Commission (headed by B.P. Mandal of erstwhile Soshit Dal, appointed during the first Janata government, which had submitted its report in 1980), reserving 27% of seats in educational institutions and of jobs in all public sectors for Other Backward Classes (OBC).

The outcry among the upper castes, who saw the public sector opportunities for themselves shrinking, was leveraged by the BJP which tried to rally its social constituency in the name of Hinduism, by going full steam ahead for the Ram Janmabhoomi agitation. Lal Krishna Advani embarked on a Rath-yatra, mobilizing Hindu opinion in favour of a temple on a site in Ayodhya occupied by a sixteenth century mosque, claimed to be located where the legendary Lord Ramchandra was born. As communal passions began to be enflamed, the newly-elected JD chief minister of Bihar, Lalu Prasad Yadav arrested Advani at Samastipur on grounds of disturbing peace and fomenting communal riots. The BJP immediately decided to withdraw support from the NF government, leaving V.P. Singh to face a vote of no confidence in the Lok Sabha. By then, communal passions spiraled higher, with Hindu karsevaks trying to force their way into Ayodhya for the purpose of *Bhoomi-poojan* were fired upon by the UP police upon the orders of Chief Minister Mulayam Singh Yadav. While V.P. Singh assumed the moral high ground, saying he stood for a secular India, and that he would sooner save the Babri Masjid than his own government, he lost the vote of confidence by a margin of 142 to 346 – only the Left Front stood by him as he began to be deserted even by his own party members.

The Chandra Shekhar Interregnum

Chief among those of the Janata clan who pulled the rug from under V.P. Singh was his old adversary, Chandra Shekhar. Beginning his career in the PSP, he joined the Congress in 1964, where he used to be known as a Young Turk because of his implacable opposition to the party top brass. His trenchant criticism of the Emergency landed him in jail, which made him cross over to the Janata Party where he rose to the post of the president. At the time of the fall of the V.P. Singh government, he broke away from the Janata Dal, and floated his own party, the Samajwadi Janata Party (SJP), or Janata Dal Socialist - luminaries of the government who joined him included Devi Lal, O.P. Chautala, H.D. Deve Gowda, Maneka Gandhi (widow of Sanjay Gandhi), Janeshwar Mishra, Chimanbhai Patel, Yashwant Sinha, Mulayam Singh Yadav and Vidya Charan Shukla.

The SJP, enjoying the support of only 64 MPs, was able to form a minority government, courtesy the outside support provided by the Congress(I). It is said that the architect of the understanding between Chandra Shekhar and Rajiv Gandhi was Janata veteran, Subrahmanyam Swamy. While the prime minister retained the portfolios of Home and Defence, Vidya Charan Shukla (an old associate of Sanjay Gandhi) was made the minister for external affairs, Subrahmanyam Swamy became minister for commerce and for Law and Justice; Yashwant Sinha was given Finance; Maneka Gandhi was given independent charge of Environment and Forests, while Jagdeep Dhankhar (who was later to become the Vice President of India) was given the charge of Parliamentary Affairs.

Chandra Shekhar lasted just over 7 months (November 1990 June 1991) in power, during which India faced one of its gravest financial situations. While attempts at a reform of the economy began to be started upon by Rajiv Gandhi government itself, the onset of the crisis during Chandra Shekhar's tenure resulted in the drafting of a more serious reforms package by Subrahmanyam Swamy, with the assistance of the renowned economist, Manmohan Singh, and the accomplished bureaucrat, Montek Singh Ahluwalia. The slew of reforms, however, did not see the light of the day. For the second time in 10 years, the Congress was threatening to withdraw its support from a government to which it was extending support from outside, largely as a pressure tactic to get Chandra Shekhar to toe the Congress line. Chandra Shekhar called the bluff and resigned, hence fresh elections were called yet again.

1991: The Mandal-Mandir Elections and the Era of Manmohan

Elections to the tenth Lok Sabha were scheduled for three phases in May 1991, but saw a hiatus after the first phase, when Rajiv Gandhi was assassinated by a Tamil suicide bomber in Sriperumbudur, Tamil Nadu. Polling for the second and third phases were pushed back to 12 and 15 June. A clear pattern emerges upon close scrutiny: in the first phase, while Rajiv was alive, the Congress was virtually wiped out in the 211 of the 534 constituencies that went to the polls; but in the second and third phases, presumably riding a sympathy wave, the Congress staged a fightback to emerge as the single largest party in the Lok Sabha. At this stage, due to rising militant activities, no elections were held in Punjab and J&K. Upon some semblance of normalcy being restored, Punjab went to the polls in February 1992, while J&K sat out the tenth Lok Sabha.

The Congress ended the general elections with a tally of 232 seats out of 523 (plus, 12 seats from Punjab in 1992, so 535 in all), with a vote share of 36.26%; the Bharatiya Janata Party with 120 seats (and a vote share of 20.11%) came second; the

Janata Dal with 59 seats (11.84% vote share) and the CPI(M) with 35 seats (6.16%) held on to the third and fourth slots. The CPI (14), Telugu Desam (13) and AIADMK (11) turned out to be the only other parties to cross the double digits in Lok Sabha seats. The electorate was so badly fragmented that the Jharkhand Mukti Morcha, with 6, and Shiv Sena, with 4 seats, emerged as players of some significance. The Janata Party (set up by Arif Mohammad Khan and Subrahmanyam Swamy) won 5 seats; the RSP showed remarkable consistency and won its 4 seats, while the AIFB won its share of 3 seats; the BSP and IUML won 2 seats each. The AGP, Janata Dal (Gujarat), ICS(SCS), AIMIM, KC(M), Haryana Vikas Party, Nagaland People's Council, Manipur People's Party, Autonomous States Demand Committee and Sikkim Sangram Parishad won 1 seat each. With over 147 registered parties winning a plurality of votes, 275 million votes were split several ways. A total of 121 parties failed to win any seats in the Lok Sabha, of which at least 1 – the DMK – later bounced back in a big way.

In regional terms, the INC did poorly in some states and better in others in the north and was somewhat salvaged by the south. In Bihar, the JD, led by Lalu Prasad Yadav, won 31 seats, the CPI won 8 seats, the JMM 6, the BJP 5, and the INC and the CPI(M) at 1 seat each. In Uttar Pradesh, the BJP rose meteorically to win 51 seats, while the JD, led by Mulayam Singh Yadav, won 22 seats, the INC won 5 seats, the JP 4 and BSP and CPI won 1 seat each. In Delhi, the BJP won 5 seats, while the INC took 2. In Gujarat, the BJP won 20 seats, the INC won 5, and the JD (Gujarat) won 1 seat. In West Bengal, the CPI(M) won 27 seats, the INC won 5 seats, the RSP retained its 4 seats, the AIFB and CPI won 3 seats each. By contrast, in Madhya Pradesh, the INC mounted a sort of a comeback with 27 seats, while the BJP won 12 seats and the BSP 1. In Himachal Pradesh, the INC and the BJP won 2 seats each. In Rajasthan, the INC won 13 seats and the BJP 12. The Congress won 12 of the 13 seats in Punjab when elections were held in 1992, and the BSP won 1. In Haryana, the INC won 9 seats while the Haryana Vikas Party of Devi Lal and Chautala won the remaining seats. In Maharashtra, the INC remained dominant with 38 seats, followed by the BJP with 5 seats, Shiv Sena with 4 and the CPI(M) with 1 seat. In Orissa, the INC won 13 seats, the JD won 6 and the CPI and CPI(M) won a seat each. The solitary seats of Chandigarh and Dadra and Nagar Haveli were taken by the INC, while that of Daman and Diu was taken by the BJP.

In the south, the INC continued to dominate Andhra Pradesh, winning 25 seats, but the TDP regained its strength somewhat winning 13 seats, and the BJP, AIMIM and CPI won 1 seat each. In Karnataka, too, the INC won 23 seats, while the BJP won 4 and the JP only 1 seat. Kerala too returned 13 INC MPs, while the CPI(M) won 3, IUML won 2 seats, and the ICS(SCS) and KC (Mani) won 1 seat each. In Tamil Nadu, the INC won 28 seats, while the AIADMK won 11 seats. The INC won both the seats from Goa and the solitary seats from Lakshwadeep, Pondicherry as also Andaman and Nicobar Islands.

In the north-east, the INC managed to retain much of its earlier performance. In Assam, the INC won 8 seats, BJP 2, the Autonomous State Demand Committee, AGP and CPI won 1 seat each. The INC won both the seats from Arunachal Pradesh, Tripura and Meghalaya. In Manipur, the INC and the Manipur People's Party won 1 seat each. The Lok Sabha seat for Nagaland went to the Naga People's Council, while that for Mizoram went to the INC. The solitary seat for Sikkim was retained by the Sikkim Sangram Parishad.

It was largely this fragmentation of the electorate that helped the Congress(I) become the first minority government to last a full 5-year term in power, relying on issue-based support, strategic abstention and (as it became clear eventually) venality of some of the smaller parties. Given the political vacuum left behind by the death of Rajiv Gandhi, there was a lot of internal turmoil in the Congress with P.V. Narasimha Rao (former Home and Foreign Minister), Sharad Pawar (former CM of Maharashtra), Arjun Singh (former CM of Madhya Pradesh) and N.D. Tiwari (former Finance and Foreign Minister) in the running for the prime ministerial office. Eventually, Rao won out, largely because Sonia Gandhi was believed to have favoured him over his strongest contender, Sharad Pawar. As a kind of consolation, Pawar was given the Ministry of Defence. Rao, who initially did not contest the Lok Sabha elections of 1991, had to win the by-election at Nandyal, Andhra Pradesh, to enter Parliament. Curiously, Rao had the unusual distinction of representing three different states in the Lok Sabha – Andhra Pradesh, Maharashtra and Orissa – over a period of 19 years (1980–99).

Most crucially, the portfolio of Finance was given to the non-political technocrat, Dr Manmohan Singh, who was not even a Congressman. It is said that, when the offer was made, Dr Singh did not even take it seriously till the next morning, when a slightly annoyed prime minister summoned him to the Rashtrapati Bhavan for the swearing-in, Dr Singh had eventually to be elected to the Rajya Sabha from Assam to secure his place in the cabinet. Rao, along with his finance minister, began the liberalization of the Indian economy, with a series of reforms that started the dismantling of the ever-growing large state that characterized the Indian Republic for the first four decades after independence. The veteran Congressman and finance minister to Indira Gandhi, Pranab Mukherjee, who sought to regain his old charge, was instead assigned the Planning Commission before being given a short stint in the MEA; P. Chidambaram, who as finance minister, was later to push forward with reforms, was appointed for two stints in the Ministry of Commerce; Ashok Gehlot entered the union cabinet with independent charge of textiles and the firebrand leader from Bengal, Ms Mamata Banerjee, was brought in as minister of Human Resource Development. Unusual for an Indian prime minister, Rao proved remarkably technocratic in his approach, sufficiently for him to actually appoint Subrahmanyam Swamy, a Janata Party leader, to the cabinet rank position of chairman for the Commission on Labour Standards and International Trade. He also brought in Atal Bihari Vajpayee of the BJP to head the Indian delegation at the UN Human Rights Commission in Geneva.

The Rao government was known for quite a few things – apart from liberalization of the Indian economy, he was also responsible for a substantial overhauling of the country's foreign policy (including, establishing close diplomatic ties with Israel and launching the Look East Policy). But apart from the economic reforms, the other development that defined the Rao government was the demolition of Babri Masjid on 6 December 1992 and its aftermath. As the karsevaks brought the disputed structure down with alleged complicity of the Uttar Pradesh government under BJP chief minister Kalyan Singh, Rao let matters unfold. The communal riots that followed were used by hardliners in the Congress to dissolve all the BJP state governments (UP, Rajasthan, Himachal Pradesh, Madhya Pradesh) – giving a boost to the BJP's attempts at consolidation of the Hindu votes with Brahmins and other upper castes at its core. The twin issues of Mandal and Mandir virtually decimated the Congress vote among the upper castes in Uttar Pradesh and Bihar, and gave the BJP a bedrock of support. The hardships occasioned by the economic liberalization also served to severely erode the Congress vote-bank, particularly, as the government's reputation was badly hurt by a series of allegations of financial corruption and other scandals. Seven cabinet ministers resigned before the end of the term of the government, with 2 of them, Narayan Dutt Tiwari and Arjun Singh, leaving the party to float their own outfit, the All India Indira Congress (Tiwari). By the time its term ended, the Indian political scene was hit by the most damaging scandal during the life of the Lok Sabha – the Jain *Hawala* scam in which allegations of bribery were levelled at all the major political outfits of the time. Allegations of bribery in the context of a vote of confidence directly implicated the prime minister himself as being complicit with a stockbroker Harshad Mehta, reinforced the impression that the Congress remained a party cheerfully engaging in graft and corruption.

The loss of credibility of politicians across the political spectrum virtually guaranteed a fractured verdict as India went to the polls for the eleventh Lok Sabha.

1996: Politics of the Doldrums

Elections to the eleventh Lok Sabha was held in three phases – 27 April, 2 and 7 May 1996. This was the first election since 1980 when polls were held together for all the states, without leaving out any states – as had been the case for every election from 1984 onwards.

THE ELEVENTH LOK SABHA WAS THE FIRST TRULY HUNG PARLIAMENT WHERE NO SINGLE PARTY CAME ANYWHERE CLOSE TO OBTAINING EITHER A MAJORITY GOVERNMENT, OR EVEN A STABLE MINORITY GOVERNMENT. THE BJP, CAMPAIGNING ON A FOUR-POINT PROGRAMME (PROBITY IN PUBLIC LIFE, ECONOMIC SELF-RELIANCE BY REDUCING THE SIZE OF THE PUBLIC SECTOR, SOCIAL HARMONY BY REDUCING APPEASEMENT OF MINORITIES AND GREATER EMPHASIS ON NATIONAL SECURITY) EMERGED AS THE SINGLE LARGEST PARTY IN THE LOK SABHA – THE FIRST NON-CONGRESS PARTY (AS AGAINST AN ALLIANCE OR A COMBINE) TO DO SO.

The BJP won 161 seats out of total of a 545 with 20.29% of the vote share; the Congress, despite winning a larger vote share (28.8%) than the BJP, chalked up a tally of only 140 seats. The Janata Dal, with 46 seats (but only 8.08% of the votes) finished third, while the CPI(M), with 32 seats, finished fourth.

What appears remarkable about the eleventh Lok Sabha elections was the complete fragmentation of the political landscape, with a large number of previously very small, marginal or non-existent parties picking up a large number of seats (mostly at the expense of the Congress), but refusing to go with either of the top 2 parties. The Tamil Maanila Congress, led by M. Mupanar and P. Chidambaram (who broke with the Congress upon its alignment with the AIADMK in the 1996 polls), chalked up a tally of 20 seats (with only 2.19% of the votes); its election ally, the DMK (after sitting out 2 consecutive Lok Sabhas), won 17 seats, along with the SP; the Shiv Sena's tally shot up to 15 seats, jumping from its previous figure of around 5. The CPI managed to win 12 seats. The BSP, set up in the 1980s, but successfully consolidating the Dalit vote in UP and MP, chalked up a tally of 11 seats (on the strength of a 4.02% of the vote share). The SAD (Badal) regained its place in the Lok Sabha, winning 8 seats, equalling its tally with the Samata Party; the AGP too returned to the Lok Sabha with 5 seats, while the RSP increased its tally by 1 seat to finish at 5. The Tiwari Congress won 4 seats; the AIFB and the HVP won 3 seats each, and the IUML won 2 seats. The JMM, Karnataka Congress Party (led by S. Bangarappa), Kerala Congress(M), AIMIM, Autonomous State Demand Committee, MAG, Sikkim Democratic Front, and United Goans Democratic Party won 1 seat each. As many as 181 political parties failed to win a single seat in the Lok Sabha, including an outfit as heavyweight in the regional political landscape as the AIADMK.

The fragmentation of the political landscape becomes clear from one look at the regional break-up of representation in the

Lok Sabha. In Bihar, the JD won 22 seats, followed by the BJP with 18, the Samanta Party won 6 seats, the CPI won 3, the INC 2, JMM, SP and an independent won 1 seat each. In Uttar Pradesh, the BJP won handsomely with a tally of 52 seats, followed by the SP with 16 seats; the BSP won 6 seats, the INC won 5, the Tiwari Congress and the JD won 2 seats each, the Samanta Party and an independent candidate won 1 seat each. In Madhya Pradesh, the BJP won 27 seats, followed by the INC with 8 seats, the BSP 2 seats, the Tiwari Congress, the Madhya Pradesh Vikas Congress and an independent won a seat each. In Himachal Pradesh, the INC managed to win all 4 seats. In Jammu and Kashmir, the INC won 4 seats, while the BJP and JD won 1 seat each. In Punjab, the SAD(B) won 8 seats, the BSP 3 and INC 2. In Haryana, the BJP won 4 seats, the HVP won 3, the the INC 2, and an independent won 1 seat. In Delhi, the BJP took 5 seats, while the INC won the remaining 2. In Rajasthan, the INC and the BJP won 12 seats each, with the Tiwari Congress winning 1. In Gujarat, the BJP was somewhat ahead with 16 seats, while the INC chalked up a tally of 10. In Maharshtra, the BJP-Shiv Sena alliance won the polls with 18 seats to the BJP, 15 to the Shiv Sena and the INC each. While the INC took the two solitary seats of Dadra and Nagar Haveli and Daman and Diu, the BJP took that of Chandigarh. In West Bengal, the CPI(M) won 23 seats, its allies, the RSP won 4, the CPI 3 and the AIFB 3 – i.e. 33 for the Left Front and only 9 for the INC. In Orissa, the INC won 16, the JD won 4 and the Samata party won 1 seat.

In the south, on the other hand, the INC lost some of its strongholds. While the INC retained Andhra Pradesh with 22 seats, the TDP won 16, the CPI 2, and the AIMIM and CPI(M) won a seat each. In Karnataka, the INC lost its dominance as the JD won 16 seats, the BJP 6, INC 5 and Karnataka Congress Party won 1. In Kerala, the INC won 7 seats, the CPI(M) 5, the CPI and IUML 2 seats each and JD, Kerala Congress (M), IUML and an independent won a seat each. In Tamil Nadu, the INC was wiped out as the Tamil Maanila Congress (Mupanar) won 20 seats, the DMK won 17 and the CPI won 2. The solitary seats of Lakshwadeep, Pondicherry and Andaman and Nicobar Islands were all taken by the INC. The 2 seats of Goa, however, were taken by the MAG and United Goan Democratic Party.

In the north-east, the verdict was just as fragmented. In Assam, the AGP and the INC won 5 seats each, with the ASDC, BJP, CPI(M) and an independent taking a seat each. In Arunachal Pradesh, the INC lost both seats to independent candidates; in Manipur, the INC won both the seats. In Meghalaya, the INC and an independent split the 2 seats. In Nagaland and Mizoram, the INC won the solitary seats for both the states. The CPI(M) won both the seats for Tripura and the Sikkim Democratic Front won the solitary seat for Sikkim.

Mindful of such political fragmentation, both the Congress and the BJP tried to look for allies in the regions where they were not strong enough. The Congress decided to go with the AIADMK, led now by J. Jayalalithaa, and got wiped out in the process from Tamil Nadu (with the Maanila Congress taking away the residual Congress votes in alliance with the DMK).

The BJP forged its alliance with the emergent force of the Shiv Sena in Maharashtra. Atal Bihari Vajpayee was called by President Shankar Dayal Sharma in the capacity of being the parliamentary leader of the single largest party, to form the government and prove his majority on the floor of the House within a fortnight. Vajpayee formed his government with the support of 176 seats of the BJP and Shiv Sena combine (with Suresh Prabhu being the only Shiv Sena minister in the cabinet of 12 ministers), but could not gather any further support because of the divisiveness of the language of politics. After 13 days, Vajpayee resigned following a marathon televised session of the confidence motion without facing the actual vote on the floor of the House.

The third-largest party in the eleventh Lok Sabha, the Janata Dal, had begun to lose its component members – the departure of a breakaway faction of the Janata Dal, the Samajwadi Party, set up in 1992 by Mulayam Singh Yadav and Beni Prasad Verma, scooped up 17 seats (with only 3.28% of the votes), weakening the JD considerably. In Bihar, too, the one-time socialist-minded George Fernandes and Nitish Kumar had broken away from the Janata Dal in 1994, setting up the Samata Party, winning 8 seats in the eleventh Lok Sabha. Yet, chalking up a tally of 40 seats, the Janata Dal became the centre of a new attempt at putting together a coalition of non-Congress, non-BJP, smaller and regional parties to form a government at the Centre. A major initiative in this respect was taken by the Telugu Desam (16 seats), who brought in the breakaway outfit of the Samajwadi Party (17 seats), DMK (16 seats), Tamil Maanila Congress (20 seats), Asom Gana Parishad (5 seats), and CPI (12 seats). These constituted the core of what became the United Front, aka the Third Front. Even the CPI(M) was also sought to be included with its 32 seats.

At a gathering, the day after Vajpayee resigned, the Congress declined to form a government of its own, but expressed its willingness to support, from the outside, the non-BJP combine of the United Front of 13 parties with 136/178 seats in its quest to form a government. The office of the PM was offered first to V.P. Singh, leader of the Janata Dal. When V.P. Singh declined (partly because of being diagnosed with leukemia, and partly because of opposition from Mulayam Singh Yadav), it was offered to Jyoti Basu of the second-largest party of the combine, the CPI(M). When Basu was persuaded by the Kerala unit of the CPI(M) to decline the offer – which Basu went on to call a 'historic' blunder – the offer was made next to

Jyoti Basu

H.D. Deve Gowda, who then went on to become the eleventh prime minister of India.

Haradhanhalli Daddegowda Deve Gowda's government held office for a period of 324 days. Deve Gowda, who was a Janata veteran from Karnataka, became the second prime minister to come to Parliament from the Rajya Sabha (Indira Gandhi being the first during 1966–69). Deve Gowda's council of ministers had to accommodate 33 MPs from the Janata Dal, but except for Inder Kumar Gujaral, no other JD politician was given any of the top ministries. Finance was given to P. Chidambaram (TMC(M)); Defence was given to Mulayam Singh Yadav (SP), while Home was given to Indrajit Gupta (CPI) – who had been a member of the Lok Sabha continuously from 1960 to 1977, and then from 1980 till his death in 2001. Deve Gowda continued with the idea of market reforms begun by the Congress, but was never comfortable with his old adversary in provincial politics. He initiated a CBI inquiry to successfully topple P.V. Narsamiha Rao from his position as the party president of Congress. However, when he tried the same with Rao's successor in 1997 (if only in order to tame him to secure his own office), the new Congress president Sitaram Kesri withdrew the party's outside support, claiming that the BJP was not thwarted with any seriousness by Deve Gowda. Kesari himself was probably hoping to be able to form a government of his own (presumably with United Front support), hence he pitched for a change of the prime minister, not to bring the government down.

When Congress's attempts to form a government proved abortive, they decided to continue to support a new United Front government with a more acceptable leader. Accordingly, Deve Gowda was replaced by Inder Kumar Gujral, who was sworn in as the twelfth prime minister of India on 21 April 1997.

I.K. Gujral began his political career in the Congress(I), rising to the position of Minister for Information and Broadcasting before he fell out with Sanjay Gandhi, and was made to leave the government, being appointed instead as the Ambassador to the USSR. He held this position throughout Mrs Gandhi's tenure, and that of Morarji Desai and Chaudhary Charan Singh. Returning to India from his posting in Moscow, Gujral resigned from the Congress to join the Janata Dal. He remained with the Janata Dal to be appointed the minister of External Affairs first in 1989, during the V.P. Singh government, and then the Deve Gowda government – during which time he is credited with an unusually generous programme of outreach to India's neighbours, called the 'Gujral doctrine'.

Gujral's tenure as PM of India lasted just short of 11 months (April 1997–March 1998), and was dogged by the fodder scam of Bihar and one of the more colourful and (as it turned out) corrupt constituents of the JD, Lalu Prasad Yadav. Lalu was accused of such a brazen act of embezzlement that even his coalition allies agreed that the scam warranted investigation, and brought pressure to bear on their own government. After some to-and-fro, Lalu was expelled from the JD. He took 17 Lok Sabha and 8 Rajya Sabha MPs with himself to set up the Rashtriya Janta Dal in July 1997. The government survived after RJD decided to support the United Front government – allegedly, in return for a change at the helm of the CBI, whose proceedings against Lalu slowed down noticeably thereafter.

Gujral's government was eventually brought down by the Jain Commission's inquiry into Rajiv Gandhi's assassination. The report of the Commission was leaked in November 1997, coming down heavily against the DMK for being in league with the LTTE, which was directly responsible for the assassination. Gujral refused to table the report in Parliament but was willing to discuss it in a Joint parliamentary committee, but Congress's insistence that anyone named in the report would have to go from the government brought the government to a crisis. When the report was finally tabled in November 1997, the Congress immediately demanded the removal of the DMK from the cabinet. At Gujral's refusal to oblige, the Congress withdrew support from the government, which made Gujral resign without recommending dissolution of the House. The Congress volunteered to form a non-BJP government and solicited support from all anti-BJP forces, but Chandrababu Naidu of the Telugu Desam was able to hold the UF constituents together, denying both the Congress and the BJP any opportunity to form a government. At this stage, in December 1997, President K.R. Narayanan dissolved the eleventh Lok Sabha, with Gujral carrying on as the caretaker PM till March 1998, when the next government took over.

1998: Thirteen Months of Vajpayee: From Pokhran to Kargil

Elections for the twelfth Lok Sabha were held on 16, 22 and 28 February 1998, 3 years ahead of schedule. None of the parties or pre-poll alliances came anywhere close to the halfway mark, leaving a hung parliament as certain to not last its full term as the last one.

The Bharatiya Janata Party improved its tally to 182 seats and emerged as the single largest party in the Lok Sabha, claiming 25.59% of as the total vote share. The Congress with a marginally higher vote share (25.82%), finished with 141 seats in the Lok Sabha. The CPI(M) finished with the third-highest tally of 32 seats (5.16%).

The 1998 elections marked probably the highest point of the regional parties in the electoral landscape. The Janata Dal was reduced to a sideshow (6 seats, with 3.24% of votes) by its former constituent factions, especially in north India. Mulayam Singh Yadav's SP romped home with 20 seats (4.93% vote share) from Uttar Pradesh, while Lalu Yadav's RJD chalked up a tally of 17 seats from Bihar. The Samata Party, founded by George Fernandes and Nitish Kumar in 1994, had won 8 seats in the 1996 polls in alliance with the BJP; they now chalked up 12 seats, 10 of which were from Bihar. The Trinamool Congress, set up as late as 1998 by long-time Congress leader, Mamata Banerjee, on a plank of unwavering hostility to the CPI(M), won 7 Lok Sabha seats, badly eroding whatever remained of the Congress vote in West Bengal. The AIADMK won 18 seats by itself with only 1.83% of the vote share. The CPI and the debutant, Biju Janata Dal, finished with a tally of 9 seats each; the SAD scooped up 8 of the 10 seats in Punjab. The debutant, West Bengal Trinamool Congress, won 7 seats. Shiv Sena was reduced to 6 seats, same as the DMK. The ally of the DMK, the TMC(M), won only 3 seats – same as Ramkrishna Hegde's Lok Shakti Party, which broke away from the JD in Karnataka. The JKNC also won 3 seats. The RSP held on to its 5 seats; the Haryana Lok Dal, the PMK and the RPI each won 4 seats. The AIFB, Muslim League Kerala State Committee and the Arunachal Congress won 2 seats each. The AIMIM, the ASDC, Manipur State Congress Party, PWPI, United Minorities Front of Assam, Kerala Congress(M), Janata Party, All India Indira Congress (Secular), HVP – all of these won a seat each. Of the 174 parties that fielded candidates in the 1998 elections, 137 failed to win any seats at all.

In terms of the regional break-up of the twelfth Lok Sabha, it bore testimony to a political stalemate in India, even though, the BJP and now its allies continued to increase its seats across north India. In Bihar, the BJP won 19 seats, the Samata Party won 10 – thus 29 for what came to be known as the National Democratic Alliance; the RJD won 17 seats, the INC won 4, and others 4. In Uttar Pradesh, the BJP won 58 seats, the SP won 19 seats and the BSP 4, Samata Party 2, others 1 and an independent 1. In Madhya Pradesh, the BJP took 30 seats and the INC 10. In Rajasthan, the INC did marginally better winning 19 seats, while the BJP won 5 seats and the All India Indira Congress (Secular) won 1 seat. In Punjab, the SAD won 8 seats, 4 seats were won by its ally the BJP, thus making the NDA tally to be 12 seats. In Haryana, the Haryana Lok Dal won 4 seats, the INC won 3, the BJP, BSP and HVP won a seat each. In Himachal Pradesh, the BJP won 3 seats and the INC 1. In Delhi, the BJP won 6 seats to INC's 1. In Jammu and Kashmir, the JKNC won 3 seats, BJP 2, INC 1. In Gujarat, BJP won 19 seats to INC's 7. In Maharashtra, the INC took 31 seats, with 4 more seats won by its ally the RPI – taking the tally to 35. The Shiv Sena won 6 and the BJP 4 seats, making the NDA tally 10; the PWPI won a seat as well. In West Bengal, the CPI(M) won 24 seats, RSP won 4 seats, CPI won 3 seats and AIFB took 2 – making the tally of the Left Front 33 seats; the Opposition space was shared between the INC and the BJP with 1 seat each, but with BJP's new ally, Mamata Banerjee, and her Trinamool Congress (TMC) with 7 seats. In Orissa, the BJD won 9 seats, its ally, the BJP, won 7, while the INC was reduced to 5 seats. The solitary seats of Chandigarh, Dadra and Nagar Haveli and Daman and Diu were all taken by the BJP.

In south India, the INC's only decent showing was in Andhra Pradesh, where it won 22 seats, followed by the TDP with 12 seats, and its ally, the BJP, winning 4 seats; the CPI won 2 seats, while the AIMIM and the JD won a seat each. In Karnataka, the BJP won 13 seats, its ally, the Lokshakti Party, won 3 seats, the INC won only 9 seats and the JD(S) won 3 seats. In Kerala, the INC won 8 seats, the CPI(M) won 6 seats; the IUML and CPI won 2 seats each, while the Kerala Congress(M) and the RSP won a seat each. In Tamil Nadu, the INC was wiped out – the AIADMK won 18 seats, the DMK won 5, the MDMK, PMK, TMC(M) and the BJP won 3 seats each, and the CPI, JP and an independent won 1 each. The solitary seat from Pondicherry was taken by the DMK; those of Lakshwadeep and Andaman and Nicobar Islands were retained by the INC, as were both the seats of Goa.

In the north-east, victory in Assam gave the INC 10 Lok Sabha seats, with the UMFA, ASDC and the BJP winning a seat each. The two seats of Arunachal Pradesh, however, were taken by the debutant splinter-group of the INC, the Arunachal Congress. The two seats of Meghalaya, and the solitary seats of Nagaland and Mizoram were retained by the INC. The 2 seats of Manipur were won by the CPI and the Manipur State's Congress Party. The 2 seats of Tripura were taken by the CPI(M) as before. The SDF retained the Lok Sabha seat for Sikkim.

When Vajpayee was called on to form the government by President K.R. Narayanan, he had only a slightly higher number of MPs behind him than in 1996. However, while in 1996, the non-Congress, non-BJP parties could conceivably hang around a third national party (the JD), by 1998, the JD was almost irretrievably fragmented. Also, outside support from the Congress was badly discredited as a model of government formation by 1998. Thus, the third front was dismissed as a non-starter by all serious political observers. Since Congress (with its presence in each and every state of the country) was the principal adversary of virtually all the political outfits, many of them considered the Congress to be the greater of the two evils, and began to find the BJP as a viable option in government formation. Hence in addition to the post-poll allies of the BJP from 1996 – Shiv Sena, Shiromani Akali Dal and Samata Party – the BJP was able to align a sufficient number of political parties to cobble together the second Vajpayee ministry – viz. AIADMK, Patkali Makkal Katchi, Biju Janata Dal (the JD faction from Orissa which broke away under Navin Patnaik, son of the veteran JD leader, Biju Patnaik), Lok Shakti Party (led by Ramakrishna Hegde, a former JD chief minister of Karnataka, who was expelled at the behest of his political rival in the state, H.D. Deve Gowda).

The second Vajpayee ministry survived 13 months in office. The cabinet that was sworn in was understandably dominated by the BJP: apart from Vajpayee, it included

L.K. Advani (Home), Yashwant Sinha (Finance), Jaswant Singh (MEA, from December 1998), Murli Manohar Joshi, Sushma Swaraj, Pramod Mahajan, Ram Jethmalani, Uma Bharati, Jagmohan, P.R. Kumarmangalam, and so on. But it also included a veritable galaxy of non-Congress politicians of that generation which had struggled against the Emergency from all across the country. They included George Fernandes and Nitish Kumar (Samata Party), Surjit Singh Barnala and Sukhbir Singh Badal (Shiromani Akali Dal), Suresh Prabhu (Shiv Sena), Ramakrishna Hegde (Lok Shakti), Navin Patnaik and Dilip Ray (BJD), M. Thambidurai (AIADMK), among others.

Vajpayee's second ministry was, in many ways, an exemplary exercise in how to run a coalition that was stitched together despite ideological incongruence. While Vajpayee steered clear of many of the truly divisive issues that would have rankled with his coalition partners (viz. revocation of Article 370, Uniform Civil Code, etc.), he seized the moment with the peaceful nuclear explosion (PNE) at Pokhran within weeks of coming to office - which the BJP used to convey a posture of hardline nationalism. The diplomatic isolation that India was threatened with was handled well by Jaswant Singh (who was yet to be a foreign minister), and Vajpayee went to the extent of extending an olive branch to Pakistan (which had followed India's PNE with its own tests), hosting prime minister Nawaz Shariff and even launching a bus service between the two countries. He also continued with economic liberalization in the face of opposition from the RSS.

However, given the dependence of the government on its regional allies, outfits like the AIADMK tried to utilize the opportunity, carpe diem. After repeated demands and tantrums, Jayalalithaa's ultimatum for the reinstatement of Admiral Vishnu Bhagwat or the dismissal of George Fernandes made the government draw the line. When Jayalalithaa pulled out from the governing coalition, the government lost the vote of confidence by only 1 vote in May 1999. However, before the elections could take place, a covert military incursion by Pakistan in Kargil, in the inhospitable climes of the J&K mountains, put a major challenge before the government. Vajpayee rose equal to it by having the military push back the Pakistani troops over a 3-month period, even as New Delhi successfully brought to bear tremendous international pressure for Islamabad to pull out without broadening the conflict. The nationalistic fervour generated by the Kargil war carried the BJP-led coalition to victory in the thirteenth general elections.

Chapter 9

FIRST MOVE TOWARDS CONGRESS DECLINE

The year 1977 marked the beginning of a period when the people seemed no longer ready to be in the thrall of the Congress. Once the Lok Sabha saw the first non-Congress government installed, the argument was made that the results showed that the Congress had lost the mandate of the people, hence state governments under the Congress had to be dissolved and go to the polls at the earliest. In state after state, the Congress did badly once the Emergency was revoked, losing power in many for the first time since elections began. Even though the Congress bounced back nationally in the Lok Sabha elections of 1980, Congress's hold over the assemblies never returned to the earlier degree of dominance.

1977

Bihar

In Bihar, the Congress government under CM Jagannath Mishra was toppled by the Janata government at the Centre, and assembly elections followed.

In the Bihar assembly, the Janata Party won a dramatic victory, winning 214 seats of the total 324, winning 42.7% of the vote share. The Congress came second with 57 seats (a vote share of 23.6%); the CPI won 21 seats and the CPI(M) won 4 seats; the Jharkhand Party won 2 seats, and the Akhil Bharatiya Shoshit Samaj Dal and the all-India Jharkhand Party won a seat each.

Once the election was over, the victorious Janata Party elected former Socialist Party (first SSP and then BLD) leader Karpoori Thakur, defeating Satyendra Narayan Sinha (formerly Congress(O)) by 114 votes to 84 as its legislative party leader. Thus, he became the chief minister. During his tenure as chief minister (June 1977–April 1979), Karpoori Thakur appointed, and tried to implement the recommendations of the Mungheri Lal Commission which recommended reservation of public jobs for the backward classes. However, resistance from within the Janata Party, especially its upper caste members, resulted in much watering down of the reservation scheme, that resulted in Karpoori Thakur stepping down in 1979, to be replaced by the Dalit MLA, Ram Sundar Das, who held office for the remaining period of the Janata Party government (April 1979–February 1980), and diluted the reservations policy. In the factional splits that followed in the Janata Party, Thakur remained with Charan Singh, and went on to mentor the next generation of Bihar politicians, such as Lalu Prasad Yadav, Nitish Kumar and Ram Bilas Paswan, as Bihar slid in to President's Rule.

A stamp commemorating Karpoori Thakur

Goa, Daman and Diu

In the 1977 elections to the assembly of Goa, Daman and Diu, in a curious deviation from the rest of India, the Congress actually did better, even though it did not manage to capture power.

The ruling Maharashtravadi Gomantak Party won 15 seats (down 3) out of the 30, with 38.49% of the vote share. The Congress won 10 seats (up 9), with a vote share of 28.94%. The Janata Party also, for the first time, gained a foothold in the assembly with 3 seats.

The incumbent chief minister Shashikala Kakodkar remained in office to start her second term, warding off major allegations of corruption and managing to survive resignations of major ministers like Pratap Singh Rane (all of whom lost their seats in the 1977 elections). However, the corruption allegations continued right through her second term, with other rebel MLAs emerging (Dilkush Desai, Dayanand Navrekar), who teamed up with the opposition Congress MLAs, bringing about a defeat of the government over a money bill in 1979. As Kakodkar resigned, Congress MLA Shankar Laad was about to stake claim to the formation of a new government. PM Morarji Desai recommended President's Rule for 6 months, averring his desire to not allow horse-trading in pursuit of political power in Goa.

Haryana

Haryana was another state where the incumbent Congress government of Banarsi Das Gupta was toppled, and President's Rule was imposed upon the claim that the Congress had lost its mandate with the Lok Sabha defeat and now had to go to the polls again.

In the elections that followed, the Janata Party swept the Congress out of power, winning 75 seats out of the 90 (with 46.7% of the vote share), reducing the ruling Congress to only 3 seats (a vote share of 17.15%); the Vishal Haryana party won 5 seats (with 5.96% vote share). The CPI, CPI(M), SUCI and RPI failed to win any seats at all.

Chaudhary Devi Lal was raised to the office of the chief minister. A one-time Congressman and a major force behind the creation of Haryana as a state before he left the Congress in 1971, Devi Lal had been among the earliest of Haryana politicians to be arrested under the Emergency, and among the more important leaders of the Janata Party from its inception. He held the office between June 1977 and June 1979, when his JP associate and cabinet minister, Bhajan Lal, defected with 40 MLAs, thus bringing the government down. Bhajan Lal formed a government with a wafer-thin majority, with the Congress behind him, but managed to hold on to the office for the rest of the assembly term (i.e. 1979–82).

Himachal Pradesh

Himachal Pradesh was one of those governments that were toppled in 1977 after the Lok Sabha elections, despite enjoying a majority on the floor of the assembly, and was brought under President's Rule for less than 2 months.

In the elections that followed, the Janata Party won 53 seats out of 68, with 49.01% of the vote share; the Congress won only 9 seats with 27.32% of vote share.

Shanta Kumar of the Janata Party (erstwhile BJS and later the BJP) was made chief minister, an office he held for a little over 2 years (1977–80), before his government collapsed over splits in the Janata Party, and he was replaced by Thakur Ram Lal at the head of a minority government which survived till the end of its term (February 1980–April 1983).

Jammu and Kashmir

In 1974, Mrs Gandhi came to an understanding with Sheikh Abdullah, who was then appointed to head the INC government in Jammu and Kashmir, because of the curious situation that the state Congress unit was basically the JKNC which had been forced to merge with the national outfit. Sheikh Abdullah remained in power through the Emergency years, and the assembly was dissolved only in the summer of 1977, after the Congress government in Delhi had fallen. In the assembly elections that were held in June 1977, perhaps the first free and fair election in the history of the state, Sheikh Abdullah revived the JKNC from the much-depleted Plebiscite Front he had set up after his fall from power in the 1950s.

Of the 76 seats in the assembly, the JKNC won 47 seats (46.22% of the vote share); the Janata Party came second with 13 seats (with a vote share of 23.72%, taking over from the Praja Parishad). The INC managed to win only 11 seats, while the Jamaat-e Islami Kashmir won only 1 seat.

While the JKNC won 40 of the 42 seats in the Valley itself, its tally for the Jammu area was only 7 seats out of 32; the INC won all its seats in Jammu and none in the Valley; the Janata Party won 2 seats in the Valley and the rest in the Jammu region – a signifier of the nature of polarization of the electorate.

Sheikh Abdullah was sworn in as the chief minister of the state, which he remained till his death in 1982. Thereafter, his anointed successor, his son Farooq Abdullah was sworn in as the new chief minister, as the JKNC government went on to complete its full term in power.

Kerala

The Kerala assembly completed its term in 1975, but elections had been deferred till the Emergency came to an end. By then the Delimitation of assembly Constituencies 1974 was implemented, increasing the total seats in the assembly to 140.

The INC went to the polls in alliance with the CPI, Kerala Congress, the IUML and RSP, collectively known as the United Democratic Front. The INC ended up winning 38 seats, the CPI 28, Kerala Congress 20, IUML 13, and RSP won 9. Obtaining the support of 8 independents, the UDF tally stood at 111 seats.

The opposition forces lined up behind the CPI(M) which won 17 seats, the BLD won 6 seats, all-India Muslim League (Opposition) won 3 and the Kerala Congress (Pillai group) 2 seats.

The UDF government was sworn in under Kannoth Karunakaran, who had led the initiative to put the alliance together. However, he had to resign within a month over the issue of police torture of a left-wing student during the Emergency when he held the portfolio of Home Ministry, and was replaced by A.K. Anthony. When the Congress split in January 1978, Karunakaran went with Indira to join the Congress(I), while Anthony remained with the Congress(Urs). However, as more and more leaders of the Congress(Urs) began to join the Congress(I) by the end of 1978, Anthony put in his resignation, and no other government could be formed – pushing Kerala to polls a couple of years before its term was to end.

Madhya Pradesh

The Madhya Pradesh government of Congress's Shyama Charan Shukla was among those toppled after the general elections of 1977, despite having a majority in the assembly, and President's Rule was imposed till assembly elections were held.

In the elections of 1977, the Janata Party ended with 230 seats out of the assembly's total 320, securing 47.28% of the total vote share. The INC finished with 84 seats (down 136), with 35.88% of the vote share. The ABRRP finished with only 1 seat.

Kailash Chandra Joshi (ex-Jan Sangh, and later to be of the BJP) was sworn in as the chief minister of Madhya Pradesh (June 1977–January 1978), but fell a victim to the Janata Party infighting before he was replaced by Virendra Kumar Sakhlecha (1978–80). In his turn he was to fall a victim to further infighting when he was replaced by Sundar Lal Patwa, whose government in turn lasted only 28 days. As the Janata experiment broke down, Joshi, Sakhlecha and Patwa – all ex-Jan Sangh – signed up with the newly-formed Bharatiya Janata Party.

Nagaland

The state of Nagaland had been gripped by a major insurgency that ran for decades since 1947, with varying strengths at different times. The Government of India was finally able to negotiate with the Naga underground to conclude the Shillong Accord in 1974, which meant to bring the insurgents back into the mainstream. But this went on to undermine the elected government in the state as the political landscape began changing somewhat in the wake of the accord. Hence the government collapsed because of defections and counter-defections, and after quite a few attempts at forming minority governments, the state was brought under President's Rule before new elections were held in 1977, two years ahead of time, with the assembly strength increased to 60 under the delimitation exercise of 1974.

In the 1977 elections, the United Democratic Front finished at the top of the tally with 35 seats, (up 10) with a vote share of 39.21%. The INC emerged as the principal opposition, for the first time, with 15 seats (a vote share of 20.19%), with 9 other seats being taken by independents and 1 seat by National Convention of Nagaland.

Vizol Koso returned to office as the chief minister (1977–80), but failed to complete his full term in power. In 1980, he was replaced by another major figure in Naga politics, Senayangba Chubatoshi Jamir (one of the signatories of the original Accord that brought Nagaland into the Indian Union), a fellow member of the UDF – he remained in office from April to June 1980. After Jamir's government collapsed, the UDF merged with the Naga National Party to form the Naga National Democratic Party in 1980. The NNDP then went forth to form a minority government under its leader, John Bosco Jasokie, whose government survived for of the rest of assembly term (June 1980–November 1982).

Orissa

The political landscape in Orissa changed significantly on the eve of the declaration of Emergency. In 1974, the Utkal Congress merged into the Bharatiya Lok Dal, which together with the SSP, Congress(O) and the BJS, constituted the Janata Party in the state.

In the elections that took place, the Janata Party won 119 out of 147 seats, with 49.2% of the vote share; the INC was reduced to 26 seats (a vote share of 31%); the CPI and CPI(M) won a seat each, while independents won 9 seats. The all-India Jharkhand Party and SUCI failed to win any seats at all.

Nilamani Routray was elected chief minister. An ex-Congressman, Routray went through the Utkal Congress and Bharatiya Lok Dal to end up with the Janata Party. He remained in office till February 1980, when the Janata Dal broke up. President's Rule was imposed in Orissa yet again.

Pondicherry

Pondicherry went to the polls to elect its assembly in 1977 after 3 years of President's Rule.

The AIADMK improved upon its previous performance to finish with 14 seats in the 30-seat assembly, with about 30.16% of the vote share. The debutant, Janata Party, got 7 seats (with 25.77% of the vote share); the DMK won 3, the INC won 2 and the CPI 1.

S. Ramaswamy was sworn in yet again, at the head of a minority government which collapsed after a year, and in 1978, Pondicherry returned to President's Rule for a little over a year.

Punjab

The government of Giani Zail Singh was among the ministries dissolved after the 1977 general election, despite having the numbers in the assembly.

In the elections that followed, the Shiromani Akali Dal fought with an electoral understanding with the Janata Party. The SAD won 58 out of the 70 seats it contested (31.41% vote share), while the Janata Party won 25 of the 41 seats it contested (14.99%), giving the combined figure of 83 seats. The INC was reduced to 17 seats (down 49) despite winning the highest vote share – 33.59%. The CPI(M) won 8 seats and the CPI won 7.

Former chief minister Parkash Singh Badal was sworn in as the head of the coalition government, which lasted only as long as 1980, when, subsequent to the break-up of the Janata Party, the Congress government at the Centre dissolved the Badal ministry without giving it an opportunity to prove its majority on the floor of the assembly, resulting in the imposition of President's Rule.

Tamil Nadu

M. Karunanidhi

The political landscape in Tamil Nadu changed dramatically between the elections of 1971 and 1977. The DMK witnessed a kind of consolidation of the power of M. Karunanidhi – thus successfully driving away people with some political heft. Satyavani Muthu, an influential Dalit leader, left the party in 1972 in order to set up the Thazhthapattor Munnetra Kazhagam (TMK) to raise Dalit issues. M.G. Ramachandran also fell out with Karunanidhi for publicly airing his grievances about corruption, and was expelled by the party in October 1972. MGR went on to set up the all-India Anna Dravida Munnetra Kazhagam in 1973, into which the TMK was eventually to merge. V.R. Nedunchezhiyan, finance minister to Annadurai and Karunanidhi, left the party with several senior leaders to set up the Makkal Dravida Munnetra Kazhagam (MDMK) in 1977. All these splits substantially weakened the DMK.

Yet another factor of change in Tamil politics was the passing of the old guard. As the INC split along the lines of Congress(O) and Congress(R), K. Kamaraj was successful in denying the Indira faction from gaining a foothold in Tamil Nadu in his lifetime - which made the Congress(R) befriend the newly emergent AIADMK and the rising star of M.G.R.. But the death of Kamaraj in 1975 turned the Congress(O) into a spent force, as a large number of its leaders, led by M.K. Moopanar, merged the party with the Congress led by Mrs Gandhi. The rest went on to join the Janata Party. In 1972, the death of another giant among the old guard, C. Rajagopalachari, reduced the Swatantra Party to a terminally weakened state. Many of its members joined the Janata Party, and the rump party did not contest the elections.

Jayaprakash Narayan's movement failed to generate much traction in Tamil Nadu in the lifetime of Kamaraj, and even after Kamaraj's death, JP's proximity with DMK - which had been in power quite long and had gained quite a reputation for corruption - did not change matters much. On the other hand, M.G.R. was happy to develop good ties with the INC, and eventually succeeded in toppling the Karunanidhi government in 1976 (one year after its term in office was completed) for not implementing the Emergency stringently.

When elections were held in 1977, the AIADMK entered into an electoral alliance with the CPI(M); the INC went with the CPI; the DMK and the JP went on their own strength.

Contesting for the first time, the AIADMK won 130 seats in the 234-seat assembly (polling 30.4% of the vote share); the CPI(M) won 12 seats, the AIFB won 1 seat and another independent candidate joined hands with the alliance partners to bring the alliance tally of 144 seats. DMK was reduced to 48 seats (with 24.9% vote share); the INC finished with 27 seats, while the CPI finished with a tally of 5 seats, finishing with an alliance tally of 32 seats; the Janata Party finished with a tally of only 10 seats.

Flush with victory, Maruthur Gopala Ramachandran was sworn in as the chief minister of Tamil Nadu. Shortly thereafter, when the Janata Party won the parliamentary elections, the AIADMK extended the new government full and unconditional support – thus saving itself from dissolution. When the Janata-led government collapsed in 1980, and Mrs Gandhi returned to office through fresh elections in 1980, her newfound ally in Tamil Nadu, the DMK, persuaded her to dismiss the AIADMK government, which was thus dismissed in February 1980, and President's Rule was imposed in Tamil Nadu.

Tripura

The Congress government of Sukhamoy Sen Gupta was toppled in 1977 towards the close of his term, and replaced by 2 short-lived minority governments – those of Prafulla K. Das (April–July 1977) and Radhika Ranjan Gupta (July–November 1977) of the Janata Party, before President's Rule was imposed.

When the assembly elections were held next, the CPI(M) swept the polls, winning 51 of the 60 seats, with a vote share of 47%. The Tripura Upajati Juba Samiti (TUJS) emerged as the second-largest party with 4 seats, the RSP came third with 2 and the AIFB fourth with 1 seat. The Congress, despite winning over 17% of the popular vote, was reduced to zero, as were the Janata and the CPI.

Nripen Chakraborty of the CPI(M) was sworn in as the chief minister, in which office he continued for the full term of the assembly (1977–82).

Uttar Pradesh

The Congress government of N.D. Tiwari was among those that were toppled by the Janata Party government in 1977, despite having a majority on the floor of the house, and President's Rule was imposed in the state.

In the assembly elections that were held in Uttar Pradesh in 1977, the Janata Party won 352 seats out of 427 seats in the assembly (cornering 47.76% of the vote share); the INC was reduced to 47 seats (down 168) with a vote share of 31.94%; the CPI won 9 seats to come third and the CPI(M) won just 1 seat.

Ram Naresh Yadav of the Janata Party was sworn in as chief minister in 1977, and remained in office till he lost a vote of no confidence in 1979, and was succeeded by Banarsi Das. Babu Banarsi Das remained in office till February 1980, when the Janata Party broke up, upon which Banarsi Das went with Charan Singh. Uttar Pradesh returned to President's Rule, without giving Babu Banarsi Das a chance to prove his government's majority on the floor of the assembly.

West Bengal

The West Bengal government of Siddhartha Shankar Roy was among those that were dissolved after the Janata Party won the parliamentary elections – a decision that was upheld by the Supreme Court, and the government was denied a chance to prove its majority on the floor of the assembly. During the parliamentary elections, the Janata Party and the CPI(M), led Left Front arrived at a seat adjustment, but similar attempts before the 1977 assembly elections proved fruitless despite the

Left Front offering 56% of the seat to the Janata Party and the CM's chair to the former chief minister (and now JP candidate), Prafulla Chandra Sen – the Janata Party insisted on being given at least 70% of the seats. This resulted in a triangular contest between the INC, the Janata Party and the CPI(M)-led Left Front.

In the elections that followed, to the great surprise of everyone, the Left Front swept the polls, winning 231 out of 294 seats. Of this tally, the CPI(M) won 178 seats out of 228 (with a vote share of 35.46%); the IFB won 25 seats out of 36 contested (vote share being 5.24%); the RSP won 20 of the 23 it contested (3.74% vote share), the RCPI won 3 out of the 4 it contested (a vote share of 0.52%), the Marxist Forward Block won all the 3 seats it contested; the Biplabi Bangla Congress won 1 of the 2 it stood for.

The Janata Party won 29 seats (20.02% vote share), while the Congress was reduced to only 20 seats in the assembly (albeit with 23.02%); the SUCI won 4 seats, while the CPI won 2 seats; the IUML and Workers' Party of India won 1 seat each. The Jharkhand Party, the all-India Gorkha League and the RPI drew a blank.

In 1977, the veteran opposition leader of the CPI(M), Jyoti Basu was sworn in as the chief minister – an office he was to hold till he retired in 2000 – one of the longest tenures as chief minister in the history of India (23 years).

1978

Andhra Pradesh

Andhra Pradesh went to the polls one year after the end of the Emergency. By then Mrs Gandhi was bouncing back, and had split the INC sufficiently to call it her own – Congress(I). The incumbent Andhra Pradesh chief minister, Jalagam Vengala

Rao, was slow in jumping ship at the end of a full 5-year term in office.

In the elections that were held for the 294 seats to the assembly, the Congress(I) won 175 seats, with a vote share of 39.25%. The Janata Party won 60 seats on the back of its vote share of 28.85% to come second; the rump Indian National Congress, under chief minister J.V. Rao, came third with 30 seats; the CPI(M) won 8 seats and the CPI 6.

Mari Chenna Reddy, who had once agitated for the demand of a separate Telangana and rewarded with the governorship of Uttar Pradesh for dropping that demand, was now appointed the chief minister of Andhra Pradesh (March 1978–October 1980). Faced with an internal party rebellion, Chenna Reddy had to step down, making way for Tanguturi Anjaiah, who ended up with the hitherto largest cabinet in the state, accommodating all geographical regions of Andhra Pradesh. He was in turn asked to step down by Mrs Gandhi in February 1982 to stem the tide of a rebellion, and succeeded by Bhavanam Venkata Reddy who remained the chief minister for the remaining term of the assembly (February–September 1982).

Arunachal Pradesh

Arunachal Pradesh constitutes that territory of north-eastern India which came under British suzerainty when an accord was signed in Simla between the British-Indian government and the then-independent authorities of Tibet. The 550-miles of the boundary of the two domains were drawn by Sir Henry McMahon, the eponym of the McMahon Line, which the Tibetan authorities signed in 1914 with the proviso that it would require China's consent to be valid. The KMT government of China refused to recognize the Simla Accord of 1914. The British Government of India waited for nearly 2 decades before plotting the McMahon Line on official maps, publishing the Simla Accord in 1937–38, and setting up administrations in the region. In 1954, these territories were reconstituted as the North-Eastern Frontier Agency (NEFA). The Sino–Indian War of 1962 was fought over the boundary between the two countries, with the People's Republic of China continuing to dispute the validity of the McMahon Line. At one stage, the Chinese even briefly occupied the Tawang region before pulling back behind the McMahon Line in 1963. Presumably with an intention of integrating NEFA with the rest of the Union, the region was made into a Union Territory in 1972, and renamed Arunachal Pradesh. Four years later, it was given a legislative assembly of its own, and the first elections to the state were held in 1978.

In the 30-seat assembly of the UT, the Janata Party fielded 29 candidates, the People's Party of Arunachal (founded in 1977 by Bakin Pertin, Oken Lego and L. Wanglat) fielded 21 and the Congress 1. The Janata Party won 17 seats (a vote share of 42.08%) and the PPA (30.24%) won 8.

A 5-member cabinet was sworn in under Prem Khandu Thungan, who had earlier been appointed the chief minister in 1977, elected unopposed on a Congress ticket to the parliament in 1977, had since crossed over to the Janata Party with Gegong Apang and others as cabinet members. In 1979, when the Janata Party government at the Centre collapsed, a minority government was set up under Tomo Riba of the People's Party of Arunachal, but short of numbers, the Riba government was dismissed after less than 2 months, in November 1979, and President's Rule was imposed in the state.

Assam

Years of Congress dominance in Assam began to show signs of withering first in the assembly elections of 1978, in the shadow of the Emergency, and also in that of the split in the Congress party.

In the elections of 1978, the Janata Party displaced the Congress to secure the highest tally in the 126-seat assembly by winning 53 seats (29.95% of the vote share), well short of the halfway mark. The rump INC, which was split by the creation of Congress(I), finished with 26 seats, while the newly created Congress(I) won only 8 seats. The CPI(M) finished third with 11 seats, while the CPI won 5. The Plains Tribal Council of Assam, confined primarily to the Bodo areas, finished with 4 seats.

Golap Borbora of the Janata Party, a loyal disciple of J.P. and then, Ram Manohar Lohia, imprisoned for more than a year-and-a-half, was sworn in as the first non-Congress CM of the state, albeit for a brief stint (March 1978–September 1979). He had to step down due to factionalism in the Janata Party and was succeeded by Jogendra Nath Hazarika, who remained in office for only 94 days before President's Rule was imposed by Mrs Gandhi after her return to power in New Delhi. In December 1980, Syeda Anwara Taimur of the Congress(I) was appointed the chief minister at the head of a minority government – the first Muslim woman to hold that office in India. It is believed that this was one of the triggers for the intensification of the Assam agitation targeting the Bengali and Muslim minorities of the state. The violent agitations ultimately led to Taimur stepping down and President's Rule being imposed for 6 months (June 1981–January 1982). At the end of 6 months, Kesab Gogoi – an ethnic Tai-Ahom politician of the Janata Party, who crossed over to Congress(I) in 1980 – was asked to form a minority government. The government thus formed lasted only about 65 days between January and March 1982. Gogoi resigned, being unable to pass the floor test, and President's Rule was imposed once again, which lasted till the dissolution of the assembly and the next elections.

Karnataka

The Karnataka Government of CM Devaraj Urs was dismissed and the assembly dissolved in December 1977, despite enjoying the confidence of the House. After a brief period of President's Rule, elections were held in the spring of 1978, by which time the Congress had also split.

In the elections, the performance of the Devaraj Urs government secured for Congress(I) (with which Urs had himself gone when the party was split by Mrs Gandhi) the highest number of seats in the 224-seat assembly – 149 seats (with a vote share of 44.25%). The Janata Party came second with 59 seats (37.95% of the vote share), the CPI came third with 3 seats and the rump INC with only 2 seats.

Devaraj Urs returned to the office of the chief minister in 1978, but in 1979 he was expelled from the Congress(I) as a result of differences with Mrs Gandhi over the return of Sanjay Gandhi to a position of influence in the party. He joined the Congress(S) with many of his men (which for a while even came to be known as Congress (Urs) when he became its president). His position as chief minister became unsustainable when the Congress(I) captured most of the Congress votes and most of Urs's associates left him for the Congress(I), making him step down in 1980. Gundu Rao became the new chief minister of Karnataka, and remained in office for the rest of the assembly term (1980–83).

Maharashtra

Maharashtra had to change its chief minister midstream just on the eve of the onset of the Emergency, when Vasantaro Naik was replaced by Shankarrao Chavan, who held the office (February 1975–May 1977) for almost the entire duration of the Emergency. When Congress lost a large number of Lok

Sabha seats in the general elctions of 1977, Chavan assumed responsibility of the Congress defeat and made way for a pro-tem chief minster in veteran Congressman and the original Maratha Strong-man Vasantrao Banduji (Vasantdada) Patil. The party split shortly after, with Y.R. Chavan, and his protégé, Sharad Rao Pawar, joining the Congress (Urs), while the others went over to the Congress(I).

In the assembly elections of 1978, the Janata Party emerged as the single largest party, finishing with 99 seats (with 27.99% of the vote share) out of the assembly total of 288; the INC (Urs) finished second with 69 seats (with 25.33% of the share, down 153 seats) and the Congress(I) finished with 62 seats (with 18.34% of the vote share) - indicating, even if the INC had not split, their seats would have come down dramatically. The Peasants and Workers Party India, in its best showing ever, won 13 seats, the CPI(M) won 9 seats, the AIFB won 3, the 2 factions of RPI won 2 seats each, the CPI 1, while the IUML and the Shiv Sena failed to win any seat at all.

The two Congress factions fought separately but came together to form a coalition government under Vasantdada Patil. However, by July 1978, Sharad Pawar broke away from the coalition and formed the Peoples' Democratic Front, in alliance with the Janata Party in order to be appointed chief minister of the state (July 1978–February 1980). Pawar's government was eventually toppled when Mrs Gandhi returned to power in 1980, and President's Rule was imposed.

Meghalaya

The assembly elections in Meghalaya in 1978 beat the pattern that was emerging in the rest of India around this time.

The INC, (which Williamson Sangma and some of his APHLC associates joined in 1976) emerged as the single largest party with 20 seats (28.96% of the vote share); the rump APHLC (led by B.B. Lyngdoh) was reduced to half its strength winning 16 seats (24.92% of the vote share); the Hill States Peoples' Democratic Party (HSPDP) of Hopingstone Lyngdoh won 12 seats (19.24% of the popular vote); the independents won 10 seats of whom 2 actually belonged to an outfit called Public Demands Implementation Commission (PDIC), which broke away from the APHLC in defence of the interests of potato farmers of Khasi Hills.

The APHLC and HSPDP teamed up with the 2 winners from PDIC to form a coalition, and staked claim for ministry formation. The 3 components of the coalition however failed to amicably choose a chief minister, and hence chose one by lots. The first to hold office in this manner was Darwin Diengdoh Pugh of the APHLC - who held the office between March 1978 and May 1979. He was succeeded by Brington Buhai Lyngdoh of the APHLC (May 1979–May 1981), the main architect of the coalition, who eventually got the Congress (led by Williamson Sangma) join it as well. During the last two years of the government, the office of the chief minister rotated back to Williamson Sangma (May 1981–February 1983), who held it till the end of the term of the assembly.

Mizoram

The Mizoram government under C. Chhunga had stepped down in May 1977, in order for the Government of India to have a free hand in concluding the Mizo Accord that was to bring to an end the insurgency that had afflicted the state till then. Mizoram thus had gone under President's Rule for a year, before elections to the second assembly could take place.

In the assembly elections held in 1978, the Mizoram People's Conference (MPC) swept the polls, winning 22 out of 30 seats, and independents winning the remaining seats. No national party managed to win a single seat.

Brigadier Thenpunga Sailo, an ex-service man and later a rights activist speaking out against the misuse of power by forces of the Indian military (who was the founder of the MPC), was sworn in as chief minister for a brief term (June–November 1978), before political unrest brought down his government, and President's Rule was imposed, and the assembly was dissolved.

1979

Mizoram

Mizoram went back to the polls in April 1979, and returned with a verdict similar to the year before, albeit with a reduced margin for the MPC.

The MPC emerged yet again as the single largest party in the assembly, winning 18 seats (down 4), with a vote share of 32.67%. The Congress(I) gained its toehold in Mizoram, winning 5 seats, with 23.88% of the vote share; the Janata Party also entered the assembly with 2 seats.

Brigadier T. Sailo was sworn in as the chief minister for the second time, which he held for the full term of the assembly (May 1979–May 1984).

Sikkim

The state of Sikkim went for its first assembly polls since its induction into the Indian Union in October 1979.

The princely state of Sikkim, ruled by a lineage of Tibetan Buddhist kings called the Chogyul, had befriended the British early in the nineteenth century, and had preserved such proximity right through to 1947 despite occasional periods when that relationship was disturbed – such as in 1861, when the British annexed the whole district of Darjeeling and the Terai, and reduced Sikkim to the status of a de facto protectorate that year by the treaty of Tumlong. In 1918, Sikkim was restored its independence, and the guarantees of independence were transferred to the Indian state when it came into being in 1947. Prime Minister Nehru was careful in his guarantee of Sikkim's independence once a popular vote to take Sikkim into the Indian Union failed. Sikkim was given the status of a protectorate where India was left in charge of its defence, external relations and communications.

With time, the political landscape in Sikkim veered in the direction of constitutional monarchy, and the political parties in Sikkim came to be associated with their Indian counterparts – such as the Congress, the Swatantra Party, the Janata Party. In the 1973 elections, as the pro-monarchy Sikkim National Party won 9 of the 18 elective seats to the 24-seat State Council, the Sikkim National Congress and the Sikkim Janata Congress, complaining about the manipulated electoral process, demanded free and fair polls, resulting in a tripartite agreement between the Chogyul, the political parties of Sikkim and the Indian government that a responsible government be formed under the supervision of the Election Commission of India.

The elections to thc fully elective 31-seat State Council was held in 1974, under the supervision of the Election Commission of India. The Sikkim National Congress swept these polls, wining 31 seats, with the Sikkim National Party winning just 1. Kazi Lendup Dorjee was sworn in as the head of the council of ministers that came into being.

However, in the wake of India's defeat in the China war, the usefulness of the existence of Sikkim as a buffer between India and China gradually lost its proponents, and given her growing responsibilities in the Kingdom, India resolved to take over

Sikkim in 1975. With Mrs Gandhi appearing invincible, and the decision finding a large swathe of support in both Sikkim and India, the incorporation of Sikkim into the Indian Union was announced in the Parliament in March 1975. The State Council was then made into the Sikkim legislative assembly, and Kazi Lendup Dorjee became the chief minister of Sikkim. Lendup Dorjee had merged the Sikkim National Congress into the INC, and would have led the party to the polls in 1979 had it not split into the Sikkim Prajatantra Congress and the Sikkim Congress (Revolutionary), and President's Rule being declared.

In the event, the Sikkim Janata Parishad won the 1979 elections with 16 seats (a vote share of 31.49) out of the assembly total of 31; Sikkim Congress(R) won 11 seats (with 20.58% of votes); the Sikkim Prajatantra Congress won 4 seats (15.76%). The Congress vote being split, the INC failed to win any seats at all, as did the Janata Party, the CPI(M) and the Sikkim Scheduled Caste League.

Nar Bahadur Bhandari, the leader of the Sikkim Janata Parishad, was sworn in as the chief minister (1979–84). Bhandari was dismissed a little while before the end of his term, and was succeeded by Bhim Bahadur Gurung of Sikkim National Congress at the head of a minority government. The Gurung government however turned out to be a very brief one in the absence of numbers in the assembly, thus returning Sikkim to President's Rule.

1980

Arunachal Pradesh

The first assembly elections in Arunachal Pradesh were held in 1978 when the Janata Party was in power in New Delhi. In those elections, the Janata Party gained power with 17 seats. But they could not hold on to power once the Janata government in New Delhi collapsed, and the state went under President's Rule.

In the second assembly elections, the state swayed the other way, wiping out the Janata Party and had the Congress finish on top with 13 seats (with a vote share of 42.58%), tied with the People's Party of Arunachal (with a vote share of 40.98%), with the remaining 4 seats being taken by independents.

Gegong Apang of the Congress(I), who had previously served as the Minister of Agriculture, was sworn in as the third chief minister of the state, he remained in office till the end of the assembly term.

Bihar

After months of turmoil, followed by President's Rule, Bihar went to elect its assembly in 1980.

In the polls that were held, Congress(I) emerged as the single largest party with 169 seats out of 324; the Janata Party (Secular) (which was later to become the Lok Dal) of Charan Singh won 42 seats, while the Janata Party (Secular, Raj Narain faction) won only 1. The CPI won 23 seats, the CPI(M) won 6 and the debutant, Bharatiya Janata Party, comprising the Hindu nationalist component of the Janata Party, finish with 21 seats. The INC (Urs) finished with a tally of 14 seats and the Janata Party with 13 seats. The Jharkhand Mukti Morcha (founded by Binod Behari Mahato and Shibu Soren) won 11 seats.

Jagannath Mishra was sworn in as the chief minister, in which capacity he served till 1983, when on the floor of the assembly he criticized the Government of India policy of paying Bihar a royalty that was considered disproportionately low. Mishra was immediately summoned to the Centre, was asked to resign and was replaced by Chandrashekhar Singh, one of the young turks of Bihar politics (apart from Satyendra Narayan Sinha, Sitaram Kesri, Kedar Pandey and Bindeshwari Dubey).

Goa, Daman and Diu

The assembly elections of 1980 finally brought to an end the rule of the Maharashtravadi Gomantak Party (MAG).

The Congress (Urs) emerged as the single largest party, winning 20 seats in the 30-seat assembly, with a vote share of 38.36%; the MAG finished with only 7 seats, its worst performance since the creation of the state of Goa, Daman and Diu (although MAG won 36.36% of the popular vote, only 2% behind the Congress(U)); the Janata Party, Congress(I), CPI(M) and the Janata Party (Secular) finished without any seats.

Upon winning, the Congress was immediately consumed by a power struggle between Wilfred de Souza and Ananta Narcina Naik. In the event Pratapsingh Raoji Rane, a former cabinet minister of the MAG government, was chosen as a consensus candidate to be sworn in as the chief minister – an office he held till the end of the assembly term.

Gujarat

Gujarat went for its assembly polls in 1980 after a short period of President's Rule.

The Congress(I) won 75 of the 182 seats, winning 40.7% of the vote share, while the INC(O) won 56 seats with 23.7% of the vote share; the BJS won 18 seats, while the debutant Kisan Mazdoor Praja Paksha won 12 seats and the Bharatiya Lok Dal (of Charan Singh) won 2 seats.

Madhav Singh Solanki was sworn in as chief minister for the second time, and this time he remained in office for nearly the whole term (June 1980–July 1985). During this ministry, the Gujarat government decided to implement the reports of the Bakshi Commission, introducing reservations for socially and economically backward classes. The decision led to a massive outbreak of protests against the seat reservations which culminated in the deaths of hundreds of protesters, forcing Solanki to resign. However, the decision to implement the reservation of seats helped the Congress forge a social coalition known as the KHAM – Kshatriya, Harijan, Adivasis and Muslims.

Kerala

Kerala came out of its brief bout of President's Rule in 1980, when it went for its assembly polls in January of that year.

The Congress went to the polls, split into Congress(I) and INC(Urs). The Kerala Congress also split into the Kerala Congress (Mani) and the Kerala Congress (Jacob) factions. The Muslim League (Opposition), now renamed itself All-India Muslim League (AIML). Most importantly, the long association between the Congress and the CPI finally came to an end as 2 alliances came into being before the assembly polls in Kerala. On the one hand stood the United Democratic Front(UDF) constituting of the Congress(I), KC(J), IUML, PSP, National Democratic Front and Socialist Revolutionary Party; on the other hand, stood the Left Democratic Front constituting of the CPI(M), CPI, Congress(U), KC(M), Kerala Congress (Pillai group), AIML and RSP.

The LDF prevailed in the elections, winning 93 seats in the 140-seat assembly, of which the CPI(M) raked in 35 seats, INC(U) got 21, CPI 17, KC(M) 8, AIML 5 and RSP 6. The UDF managed to win only 46 seats, of which Congress(I) won 17, IUML 14, KC(J) won 6, NDP 3 and PSP 1.

E.K. Nayanar was sworn in as the chief minister at the head of a CPI(M)-led government in January 1980. However, owing to the high-handed mode of functioning of the CPI(M) government, the INC(U), led by A.K. Anthony, and the KC(M) decided to pull out of the government in October 1981, causing the Nayanar government to collapse. The Congress(U) – which had become Congress (Socialist) by then, decided to support the UDF, and K. Karunakaran was sworn in yet again.

However, shortly after this, the Congress (S) split into the Anthony group (15 MLAs) and Chacko group (6 MLAS) which left the UDF. This resulted in a curious situation where both the incumbent UDF and the LDF had 70 seats each, making it necessary for the Speaker, A.C. Jose, to excercise his casting vote with the government at least 8 times to keep the ministry going for the next 3 months. The government collapsed in March 1982, when a KC member voted against the government. The assembly was dissolved and Kerala went to the polls yet again.

Madhya Pradesh

Madhya Pradesh had come under President's Rule in 1978, and went for its next assembly elections only in 1980, with the enhanced number of 320 seats as per the decision of the Delimitation Commission.

In the elections of 1980, the Congress(I) won 246 seats (with 47.52%), and thus had a clear majority. The newly-created BJP won 60 seats (with a vote share of 30.34%) to come second, the CPI and the Janata Party won 2 seats each; the Janata Party and RPI (Khobragade) won 1 seat each.

Arjun Singh of Congress(I) was sworn in as the chief minister, in which capacity he remained between June 1980 and March 1985. Singh managed to survive 2 major scandals – the Bhopal Gas tragedy of 1982 and the Churhat Lottery Scandal, where Arjun Singh's family ran the lottery, and Arjun Singh was widely believed to have won the lottery himself. He was eventually moved out of Madhya Pradesh when the next Congress government came.

Maharashtra

The Maharashtra assembly went to the polls in July 1980 for all its 288 seats.

The Congress(I) won 186 seats (up 124) in the election, with a vote share of 44.50%; the Congress(Urs) won 47 seats (a vote share of 20.49%); the Janata Party won 17 seats (down 82); the debutant, BJP, won 14 seats (with a vote share of 9.38%); the Peasants and Workers Party of India won 9 seats; the CPI and CPI(M) won 2 seats each.

Abdul Rahman Antulay of Congress(I) was sworn in as the chief Minister of Maharashtra, while Sharad Pawar became the leader of the Opposition. A.R. Antulay however had to step down on charges of corruption in 1982, for allegedly asking builders to make donations to trusts in the name of Indira Gandhi. Antulay was succeeded by Babasaheb Bhonsle, handpicked by Mrs Gandhi, overlooking many senior Congress leaders, which caused much dissension among the Congress state leadership. In February 1983, however, the legislature party removed Bhonsle and elected Vasantdada Patil as their leader, and hence Patil was sworn in as the chief minister (1983–85).

Manipur

Manipur came from 2 months of President's Rule in 1980 to hold assembly elections.

In the 60-seat assembly, the Congress(I) won 13 seats on the strength of 21.63% of vote share; the Janata Party won 10 seats while the Congress (U) won 6 seats and the CPI won 5. The Manipur People's Party got 4 seats; the Kuki National Party won 2 and CPI won 1, with the independents winning 19 seats.

Rajkumar Dorendra Singh was sworn in for his second term as the chief minister of Manipur, but only for a brief period (January–November 1980). He was succeeded by Rishang Keishing, who held the office for only 92 days (November 1980–February 1981), before President's Rule was imposed in the state.

Orissa

In Orissa, assembly elections were held under President's Rule in July 1980.

When the polls were held, the Congress(I) won 118 seats in the 147-seat assembly, with 47.78% of the vote share. The Congress(U) won 2 seats, the CPI 4 and the independents won 7 seats. The BJP failed to win any seats at all, as did all other components of the Janata Party.

Janaki Ballabh Patnaik, a died-in-the-wool Congressman, became the chief minister of Orissa for the first (1980–84) of his 3 terms in that office.

Pondicherry

Pondicherry went to the polls in 1980 to elect its assembly after a year under President's Rule.

The DMK emerged as the single largest party with 14 seats, with 27.73% of the vote share; the Congress(I) improved its tally considerably to finish with 10 seats (23.92% of the vote share), the Janata Party won 3 seats and the CPI(M) won 1.

M.D.R. Ramachandran was sworn in as the chief minister of a coalition government with the Congress. He served in that capacity till 1983, when the Congress(I) withdrew its support and Pondicherry returned to President's Rule without Ramachandran being given the opportunity of proving his majority on the floor of the house.

Punjab

President's Rule was imposed in Punjab in 1980 after Parkash Singh Badal's government had been toppled without a floor test. The state went to the polls to elect its 117-seat assembly in June 1980.

The Congress(I) managed to obtain a simple majority in the assembly, winning 63 seats with a vote share of 45.19%. The SAD won 37 seats wih 26.92% share of the votes; the CPI won 9 seats, CPI 5 and the BJP 1.

Darbara Singh was sworn in as the chief minister of Punjab in June 1980, presiding over the state when militancy increased rapidly, threatening law and order, with the demand for the creation of Khalistan. The situation degenerated so fast that, in 1983, Darbara Singh was asked to resign and Punjab returned to President's Rule.

Rajasthan

The Bhairon Singh Shekhawat government was dismissed in February 1980, and the state went under President's Rule for a little over 3 months before the state went for assembly polls – now with an increased total of 200 seats, as per the delimitation exercise.

In the elections that were held in June 1980, the Congress(I) won a comfortable majority with a tally of 133 seats, and a vote share with 42.96% of the popular vote. The BJP finished second with 32 seats (18.60% of the vote share); the Janata Party (Secular), led by Charan Singh, came third with 7 seats, while the rump Janata Party managed to win 8 seats; the Congress (U) won 6 seats, while the 2 communist parties won a seat each.

Jagannath Pahadia was sworn in as the chief minister, the first Dalit to hold the position in Rajasthan, albeit for only a year. He was replaced in 1981 by Shiv Charan Mathur, who remained in office almost for the rest of the assembly term (1981–85), before he had to resign over the killing of Man Singh, the Raja of Bharatpur.

Tamil Nadu

M.G. Ramachandran's AIADMK government went to the polls in 1980 two years before its full term in power because Governor Neelam Sanjeeva Reddy dismissed it for breakdown of the constitutional machinery of the state on account of farmers' protest over subsidized electricity.

In the elections that were held in 1980, the AIADMK (contesting 177 seats) went to the polls in alliance with the CPI(M) (16 seats), CPI (15 seats), the Gandhi Kamaraj National Congress (GKNC, 10 seats), AIFB (2 seats) and independents aligned with AIADMK (11 seats). The Congress(I), led in the state by G.K. Moopanar, went to the polls in alliance with the DMK – violently disagreeing over seat sharing first, before agreeing to roughly half-and-half (114 seats to DMK's 112, plus 6 for the IUML, running as independents) with the agreement that Karunanidhi was to be CM if the alliance won.

Of the total 234 seats in the assembly, the AIADMK alliance won a comfortable majority winning 162 seats. The AIADMK by itself won 129 seats (38.8% of the vote share), CPI(M) 11 seats, the CPI 9, the GKNC and the FB won 6 seats each. The DMK alliance won 69 seats, of which the DMK won 37 seats and the Congress(I) won 31 seats.

M.G. Ramachandran returned to the office of the chief minister, which he held on to for the full term of the assembly.

Uttar Pradesh

Uttar Pradesh went to the polls in 1980 while under President's Rule.

The Congress(I) swept the polls, winning 309 seats in the 425-seat assembly. The Janata Party (Secular) of Charan Singh came second with 59 seats, followed by the Congress(U) with 13 seats and the BJP with 11. The CPI won 6 seats, while the Janata Party and Janata Party (Secular) won 4 seats each and the Shoshit Dal only 1.

Vishwanath Pratap Singh was sworn in as the chief minister of the state in 1980. He earned a good reputation in cracking the whip on dacoity which had become a major problem in Uttar Pradesh. Having consolidated the upper caste vote of the Congress through his stand on dacoity, he tried to consolidate the lower caste vote by saving Phoolan Devi from police encounter. But he came under pressure over the outrage caused by the caste-based atrocity of the Behmai massacre (which was carried out by Phoolan Devi) and had to resign in 1982. Singh was succeeded by Sripati Mishra, who remained in office till the end of the assembly in 1984.

1982

Haryana

Haryana went to the polls in 1982.

In the elections that were held, no party came even close to a simple majority in the 90-seat assembly. The INC (which became the official name for the Congress(I) by then) emerged as the largest party, winning 36 seats (with 37.58% of the vote share); the Lok Dal came a close second with 31 seats (with 23.87% vote share); the BJP came third with 6 seats; the Janata Party was reduced to a mere 1 seat; the 2 communist parties failed to win a single seat.

Bhajan Lal was sworn in yet again and continued to hold the office of the chief minister till 1986, when he left the office and was replaced by Bansi Lal (1986–87), who served till the end of the assembly term.

Himachal Pradesh

Thakur Ram Lal managed to steer his minority government for nearly 2 years before elections were held to the 68-seat assembly in 1982.

In the elections that year, the INC won 31 seats (with 42.52% of the total vote), up 22 seats, although still short of a simple majority; the BJP was a close second with 29 seats with 35.16% of the popular vote. The Janata Party won only 2 seats.

Thakur Ram Lal continued as the chief minister, but only as long as 1983. His tenure was rocked by a series of corruption scandals, which culminated in 1983 when he had to step down in favour of Virbhadra Singh, a Union minister, who completed the remaining assembly term.

Kerala

The Kerala assembly elected in 1980 had a short life and had to return to the people again.

Battlelines were drawn between the UDF (constituting of Cong(I), Cong (Anthony), IUML, KC (Mani), KC (Joseph), Janata (Gopalan faction), NDP, SRP, PSP, RSP (Sreekantan Nair faction), DLP] and the LDF [constituting of CPI(M), CPI, Janata, Congress (Socialist), RSP, AIML, DSP and AIML).

The UDF emerged as the single largest bloc with 77 seats, of which 20 were taken by the Congress(I), 15 to the Congress (Anthony) and the IUML won 14. the KCJ won 8, the KCM won 6 seats, the NDP and the Janata(G) won 4 seats each, the SRP, PSP and DLP won a seat each.

The LDF won 63, of which the CPI(M) took 28 seats, the CPI 13, 7 seats went to the Congress(S); the RSP, AIML and Janata won 3 seats each.

K. Karunakaran of the Congress(I) was sworn in to the office of the chief minister, which he occupied for the full term (1982–87).

Nagaland

The Nagaland assembly went to the polls in 1982 to elect its house of 60 members. The UDF, which had emerged as the largest combination in the last assembly, had collapsed towards the middle of the term and many of its constituents merged with the Naga National Democratic Party (NNDP). The rump elements went with the INC to set up the UDF Progressive Alliance.

The INC-led combination won 24 seats, winning 32.08% of the popular votes; this held them to a tie with the NNDP, who also won 24 seats with 32.01% of the vote share. This probably qualifies as the closest outcome ever in any assembly election, since the difference between the INC plus the independents who decided to support it (1,40,420 votes) and the NNDP (1,40,112 votes) was of only 308 votes. Independents won the remaining 12 seats.

S.C. Jamir returned to the office of the chief minister at the head of the INC led coalition government of the Progressive United Democratic Front, which he held till 1986, when he was succeeded for a brief period by the former Naga Nationalist Organization (and, by then, the INC) leader, Hokishe Sema (1986–88).

West Bengal

The 1982 assembly elections in West Bengal was the point around which the political landscape of the state settled down for some time to come.

The Left Front inducted the CPI, West Bengal Socialist party (WBSP) and the Democratic Socialist Party (DSP) at the initiative of the CPI(M), even as some smaller parties were slightly uncomfortable with the mode of the expansion. On the other hand, the INC had split in Bengal after the 1977 elections, and by 1981, the Congress(I) and the Congress (S), led in West Bengal by Priya Ranjan Dasmunshi, were vying for the INC vote and decided to contest the elections together. Up north, in the hills, the Gorkha National Liberation Front of Subhash Ghisingh (which had gained prominence with the Gorkhaland agitation of 1980) gave a call for poll boycott and managed to mobilize much of the Hill people around it, which dented the popular participation in the polls by almost a third.

The Left Front won its second clear term in power, winning 238 of the 294 seats in the assembly. Of these, the CPI(M) won 174 seats by itself (38.49% of the popular vote); the AIFB won 28 seats, the RSP won 19, CPI 7, the RCPI and Marxist Forward Bloc 2 seats each; the WBSP and DSP won 6 seats between them and Biplobi Bangla Congress happened to be the only LF constituent that failed to win any seat. As a result of the GNLF vote boycott, the CPI(M) managed to win 3 of the 4 seats in the hill districts in that election.

The INC emerged as the largest Opposition party with 49 seats; the Congress (S) won 4 seats and the SUCI won 2 seats. The BJP, Lok Dal, JMM, IUML and Janata Party failed to win any seats at all. As a pointer to voter consolidation, of 432 independent contestants, only 1 managed to win an assembly seat.

Jyoti Basu was sworn in for a second time as the chief minister of the state, and came to hold it for the full second term. In an interesting turn, despite the good results of the Left Front, 4 of the incumbent cabinet ministers failed to win their seats in the 1982 elections – they were Ashok Mitra (Finance), Buddhadeb Bhattacharjee (Information), Partha De (Education) and Sudhindranath Kumar (Food).

1983

Andhra Pradesh

Andhra Pradesh had given the Congress a clear mandate in 1978, and yet, the government saw considerable instability in the 5 years that followed, having at least 3 chief ministers during those 5 years. Corruption and backstabbing became integral to the Congress politics of those years, bringing about a paralysis in governance – the kind that was seen in 1977 during the Diviseema floods, when between 14,000 and 50,000 people were feared to have died. Nandamuri Tarak Rama Rao, a celebrated actor of the Telugu film industry, was shocked to see the brazen indifference of the government of the day who were occupied with the ongoing faction fight within the Congress. Rama Rao took the initiative to raise funds and help with the rehabilitation of the flood-affected people. The persistence of the Congress political culture prompted a desire among a large number of people, hitherto outside politics, to replace the Congress brand of politics. Accordingly, in 1982, Rama Rao took the initiative to set up the Telugu Desam Party (TDP).

In the assembly elections of 1983, the TDP swept the polls, winning 201 of the 294 seats of the assembly, with a vote share of 46.4%. The INC was reduced to 60 seats (down 115), with a vote share of 33.64%. The CPI(M) won 5 seats, the CPI won 4 seats, the BJP 3 and the Janata Party only 1.

N.T. Rama Rao was sworn in as the first non-Congress chief minister of Andhra Pradesh in 1983. However, within a year, when he had to undergo an open-heart surgery in the USA, Rao was removed from office by Governor Thakur Ram Lal, and replaced by the Finance Minister of the cabinet, Nadendla Bhaskar Rao, who claimed to have the support of the majority of the MLAs. Recovering, Rama Rao returned to stake his claim to the office. With N.B. Rao holding out, Rama Rao started his Chaitanya Ratham campaign (a Chevrolet-van modified as a rath) to make people aware of Congress's attempts to undermine democracy by using the governor to topple an elected government. He courted the support of all non-Congress forces – the Janata Party, the BJP – in this 'struggle for democracy'. The adverse publicity that all this generated for the Congress prompted Mrs Gandhi to replace the governor, Ram Lal, with the veteran, Shankar Dayal Sharma, who restored Rao to the office. Soon after this upon the assassination of Indira Gandhi and the general elections, TDP swept the parliamentary seats from Andhra Pradesh. Rama Rao felt confident enough to bring forward the assembly elections and seek a fresh mandate in 1985, three years ahead of schedule.

HE MANAGED TO BEAT THE CONGRESS'S FAVOURED TACTICS OF HORSE-TRADING WITH THE SUPPORT OF RAMAKRISHNA HEGDE, THE CM OF KARNATAKA, BY REMOVING ALL HIS MLAS TO A HOTEL IN MYSORE – THE FIRST INSTANCE OF WHAT HAS COME TO BE KNOWN AS 'RESORT-POLITICS'.

Assam

After years of political instability and being in and out of President's Rule, Assam went to the polls in 1983 for election to its 109 seats in the assembly. But the All Assam Students' Union (AASU), which was at the forefront of the Assam Agitation that had begun in the 1980s, decided to boycott the polls.

In the absence of anyone representing the forces of the Assam Agitation, the INC was swept back to power with 91 seats in its kitty, and 52.53% of the vote share; the Congress(S) came second with 4 seats; the CPI(M) won 2 seats, while the CPI and the Plains Tribal Council of Assam won 1 seat each.

Hiteshwar Saikia, an Ahom leader who had served in the cabinets of Sarat C. Sinha, Taimur and Gogoi, was now sworn in as the chief minister of the state, which he held between June 1983 and December 1985. His greatest efforts were to bring the AASU leaders to the table and facilitate some kind of an understanding. He enjoyed the support of both Mrs Gandhi, and, after her assassination, that of the next prime minister Rajiv Gandhi. Accordingly, the discussions with the AASU facilitated the conclusion of the Assam Accord in 1985, whereupon the assembly was dissolved at the recommendation of Saikia, a full 3 years ahead of term, to bring the protagonists of the Assam Agitation into the political mainstream.

Jammu and Kashmir

The assembly elections of 1983 were the first to take place with Farooq Abdullah at the helm of the state, and turned out to be highly polarized across the main line of division in the state.

The J&K government had introduced a bill on resettlement which allowed the residents of the state who had left for Pakistan before 1954, to return, reclaim the properties they had left behind and resettle – in a bid to get people from Azad Kashmir back to the Indian side, with an eventual aim of uniting the two Kashmirs. This was skillfully twisted by Mrs Gandhi to raise the bogey of Muslim invasion of the Jammu plains, promising resistance to the same in the J&K assembly, and beyond, if need be.

Farooq Abdullah

The polarization produced just the results desired. The JKNC swept the Valley, winning 46 seats (with a vote share of 47.29%), all of which were in the Valley itself, losing its toehold in Jammu. The INC swept the Jammu region and Ladakh, winning 26 seats (of which only 1 was in the Valley). The Jammu and Kashmir People's Conference (of Abdul Ghani Lone and Maulvi Iftekhar Hussain Ansari) made its debut with 1 seat and 2 seats were won by independent candidates. From this election on, whenever the INC and JKNC went for seat adjustments, the INC fielded candidates in Jammu and the NC in the Kashmir Valley.

Farooq Abdullah was sworn in again as the chief minister of J&K. The Abdullah government collapsed in 1984, when his brother-in-law, Ghulam Mohammad Shah, broke away with a cluster of MLAs to create the Awami National Conference, and the INC decided to extend support to the latter, with Shah as the chief minister. During the Shah ministry, the situation in the Valley began to degenerate into a communal frenzy, assuming a particularly vulgar shape during the 1986 Kashmir riots – a series of killings targeting Kashmiri Hindus in the Anantnag district of the Valley. The Shah government was dismissed, and once an accord was arrived at between the prime minister Rajiv Gandhi and Farooq Abdullah, the latter was allowed to become the chief minister yet again in November 1986, and the road was paved for the next assembly elections where the INC and JKNC were meant to contest the assembly elections together, which were held in March 1987.

Karnataka

The Karnataka assembly, that was elected in 1977, had given the Congress a simple majority which was virtually squandered owing to factional fighting and backstabbing, which had become endemic in Congress culture. The party in Karnataka split along the lines of those who favoured the leadership of Mrs Gandhi, and those who favoured Devaraj Urs. This necessarily affected the party's performance in the next assembly elections which were held in 1983.

In the assembly elections of 1983, the 224-seat assembly returned with a hung verdict. The Janata Party emerged as the single largest party, winning 95 seats (up 36) with 33.07% of the popular vote; the INC (i.e. the Indira faction) won 82 seats (albeit with higher vote share of 40.42%); the BJP came third with 18 seats (7.42% of the popular vote); the CPI and CPI(M) won 3 seats each; the AIADMK took 1 seat and independent candidates won in 22 seats.

The leadership of the Janata Party, caught between its Lingayat and Vokkaliga lobbies, went to the Brahmin leader, Ramakrishna Hegde, as a compromise candidate. A master strategist, Hegde managed to put a coalition together, obtaining support from the 2 Left parties, the BJP and around 16 independents. As a consequence, Hegde, who had begun his political career as a Congressman, and had left the INC to join the Congress(O) following S. Nijalingappa, and then made it into the Janata Party in 1977, was sworn in as the first non-Congress chief minister of Karnataka in 1983. However, when the Janata Party did badly in the 1984 general elections (winning only 4 Lok Sabha seats out of 28), Hegde resigned in 1985 seeking a fresh mandate.

Meghalaya

The Meghalaya assembly, despite being a hung assembly, somehow managed to last its full term, sharing power with almost all parties that had won seats in the 1977 elections. The assembly elections of 1983, similarly, threw up a hung verdict.

The INC emerged as the single largest party, with 25 seats in the 60-seat assembly, with a vote share of 27.68%; the APHLC won 15 seats (with 24.92% of the vote share); the HSPDP won 15 seats (with 19.32%); the PDIC finished with 2 seats.

The APHLC, HSPDP and PDIC, along with 2 independent MLAs, came together to form the Meghalaya United Parliamentary Party, with B.B. Lyngdoh of the APHLC being sworn in as the chief minister – with the understanding that after two and a half years, Hopingstone Lyngdoh of the HSPDP would take over. However, this coalition lasted only 25 days. It had to be replaced by another coalition, the Meghalaya Democratic Forum – this time, led by the INC, with 4 dissidents of the HSPDP, 1 each of APHLC and PDIC who had voted against their own party's government. Williamson A. Sangma was sworn in as the chief minister yet again, this time, for the full term (1983–88).

Tripura

Tripura escaped the kind of political instability all other states were showing, especially the non-Congress states in the assembly elections of 1977. The 1983 election was similar in its outcome.

In the 1983 elections to the Tripura assembly, the CPI(M) lost some of its seats but remained in power with a clear majority. The CPI(M) won 37 seats in the 60-seat assembly (down 14), with a vote share of 46.78%. the INC came second with 12 seats, with a vote share of 30.51%; the Tripura Upajati Juba Samiti came third with 6 seats and the RSP with 2. None of the other parties that fielded candidates in this election – the BJP, the CPI, Congress (Secular), the Janata Party and the AIFB – managed to win any seats.

As after the last assembly election, Nripen Chakraborty was sworn in as the chief minister, and held the office till the end of the term in 1988.

1984

Arunachal Pradesh

The elections to the third assembly of the state of Arunachal Pradesh was held in 1984.

Chief Minister Gegong Apang led the INC to a clearer victory than in 1980. The INC won 21 of the 30 seats of the assembly, with 43.07% of the popular vote. The People's Party of Arunachal (PPA) won 4 seats as did independent candidates; the BJP won 1 seat and the Janata Party failed to win any.

Gegong Apang was sworn in yet again as the chief minister, which he continued to be for the full term of the assembly (1984–89).

Goa, Daman and Diu

The Union territory of Goa, Daman and Diu went to its next assembly polls in the year of 1984 for all 30 seats.

The incumbent chief minister of the INC, Pratap Singh Rane, led his party to another victory, winning 18 seats in the assembly, on the basis of 39.48% of the popular vote; the long-reigning MAG finished second with 8 seats (with a vote share of 21.12%); the Janata Party, the BJP and the 2 Communist parties failed to win any seats at all.

Pratap Singh Rane was sworn in as the chief minister of the UT of Goa, Daman and Diu, and remained in that capacity till 1987. In 1987, Goa was turned into a state, while Daman and Diu were separated from it and retained as a Union Territory. Rane continued as the chief minister of Goa till its first state legislative assembly elections in 1989, with an assembly strength of 40 seats.

Manipur

Elections to the 60-seat assembly of Manipur were held between December 1984 and May 1985.

The INC Chief Minister Rishang Keishing led his party to a victory with an incredibly slim margin, winning 30 seats. The Janata Party, with 4 seats, finished second, the Manipur Peoples Party finished third with 3 seats; and the CPI and the Kuki National assembly finished with 1 seat each. The independents finished with a handsome tally of 21.

Rishang Keishing was sworn in as the chief minister, which he remained till 1988, when he made way for Rajkumar Jaichandra Singh, a close associate of the prime minister, Rajiv Gandhi.

Mizoram

The Union Territory of Mizoram went to the polls for elections to its 30-seat assembly in April 1984.

The elections brought about a change of guard in the state, with the INC winning 20 seats, i.e. up 15 seats, (on a vote share of 39.81%); the long-ruling MPC won 8 seats (down 10) with a vote share of 35.54%, with 2 seats won by independents.

The INC leader, Pu Lal Thanhawla, was sworn in as the chief minister in 1984. Lal Thanhawla, began his life in government service before joining the insurgency led by the Mizo National Front (MNF). Captured and imprisoned, he joined the Congress after his release in 1967. His election, in a way, facilitated the dialogues that were begun by the Government of India to bring to an end the Mizo insurgency. The talks bore fruit after a year or so when Rajiv Gandhi signed the Mizoram Peace Accord with the MNF. One of the provisions of the Accord was that the MNF would be given a share of the power, Lal Thanhawla stepped down so that the MNF leader Laldenga, could be sworn in. Thus, Laldenga was sworn in as the chief minister in 1986, in which office he remained till 1988. Lal Thanhawla was made the first deputy chief minister of Mizoram.

In 1987, the UT of Mizoram was turned into a full-fledged state.

Tamil Nadu

In 1984, when the Congress brought forward the Lok Sabha election by a year, ostensibly seeking a fresh mandate but probably hoping to ride a sympathy wave, Tamil Nadu was the only state that brought the assembly elections forward for the same reason, since the ruling AIADMK had entered into a electoral coalition with the Congress. However, the chief minister, M.G. Ramachandran was diagnosed with kidney failure, for which he had to leave for treatment in the United States. With the top leaders of both his adversaries either dead or indisposed, M. Karunanidhi of the DMK decided to sit the 1984 election out – either in a rare gesture of chivalry (as the DMK claimed) or anticipating a sympathy wave to be blowing against the DMK (which was a pretty accurate prognosis). This was the only election since 1957 that Karunanidhi did not contest.

The Congress and the AIADMK entered into coalition arrangements based on what popularly came to be known as the MGR formula of 70:30 – in national elections, the national party would field candidates for 70% of the seats and the state parties would field candidates for 30%; in state elections, the provincial parties would field 70% of the seats, while the national parties would stick with 30%.

In the assembly election, as much as in the Lok Sabha elections, the sympathy wave gave the AIADMK-INC coalition a landslide of a victory. The AIADMK-INC-Gandhi Kamaraj National Congress won a whopping tally of 195 seats out of the assembly total of 234 (53.9% of the vote share). Of this, the AIADMK won 132 seats (gaining 3), the INC won 61 seats (gaining 30) and the GKC 2 seats. The DMK alliance finished with 34 seats (a vote share of 37%), of which the DMK itself won 24, CPI(M) won 5, Janata Party 3 and the CPI 2.

M.G.R. was sworn in as the chief minister for another term, which turned out to be his last. He died in office in 1987, and was succeeded by his widow, Vaikom Narayani Janaki Ramachandran, in 1988, albeit for only 23 days. The party was beginning to split in 3 groups – about 97 MLAs supported V.N.J. Ramachandran; about 33 decided to go with Ramachandran's protégé, Jayalalithaa Jayaram. The INC was wary of being caught in the middle, and decided to go with the winning side. When the government appeared for a floor test, the Speaker played a partisan role, making all 33 MLAs of the Jayalalithaa faction abstain from voting. The Speaker, who was supporting the V.N.J. Ramachandran faction, disqualified all of the supporters of Jayalalithaa and had previously disqualified 10 MLAs from the DMK. Thus, with the strength of the assembly reduced to 191, the Ramachandran faction secured 99 votes (and the DMK boycotted the floor test). This caused mayhem in the House, as the Speaker declared the government to have won the vote and urged the CM to call the police into the House.

In these circumstances, the Tamil Nadu government was dismissed under Article 356, and President's Rule was imposed on grounds of chaos in the assembly.

Chapter 10

FROM SYMPATHY WAVE TO RAPID DECLINE OF THE CONGRESS IN THE STATES

1985

Andhra Pradesh

The incumbent chief minister of Andhra Pradesh, N.T Rama Rao was heartened by the performance of his party, TDP, in the 1984 parliamentary elections, and sought a larger mandate than the one he received in 1983. Hence, the state went to the polls for its 294-seat assembly 3 years ahead of the time it was required to.

In the elections that were held, the TDP won by a landslide, winning 202 seats with a vote share of 46.21% – but ultimately a pointless victory because there was only 1 seat in addition to the earlier tally. Of course, some people of doubtful loyalties were dropped in course of the election. The INC lost 10 more seats to finish with 50 seats; the CPI and the CPI(M) finished with 11 seats

A stamp commemorating N.T. Rama Rao

each; the BJP won 8 seats and the Janata Party 3 – all of them gaining marginally, invariably at the expense of the INC. Even former chief ministers Kasu Brahmananda Reddy and Kotla Vijaya Bhasakara Reddy lost their seats.

Rama Rao continued as the chief minister till 1989, proving himself to be no better than his predecessors in terms of governance.

Assam

The Assam elections of 1985 were among the most significant political exercises ever undertaken in that state. The elections were held after 6 years of the Assam Movement (1979–85) which aimed at preventing the progressive feeling of marginalization that the ethnic and indigenous peoples of Assam Valley had been experiencing for some time, in the light of the huge numbers of Bengali-speaking people (mostly Muslims) that were there. Led by the All Assam Students Union (AASU), the Assam Movement worked with the agenda of driving out all illegal migrants into the valley from East Pakistan and (after 1971) from Bangladesh. Leaders of the Assam Movement believed that past and continuing immigration endangered the local people socially, economically, culturally, and generally speaking, existentially. It operated with the slogan of 'Bangal Kheda' (Drive Out the Bengalis) – targeting Bengali-speaking people that had acquired land and property, which the ethnic people considered often as fruits of exploitation. The movement spiralled out of control and degenerated into initially isolated, and then organized, acts of violence and pogroms targeting the Bengali-speaking people, illegal migrants or otherwise – such as the Nellie massacre of 1983 (claiming the lives of hundreds of people in 14 villages) or the Khairabari massacre of the same year (killing some 500 Bengali immigrants). Although the figures of the fatalities of the Assam Movement are disputed by both sides, the facts of these are not.

The Government of India had engaged in a dialogue process with the protagonists of the Assam Movement for months before they were able to conclude the Assam Accord. As per the Accord, the status of all those who had entered the valley before January 1966 were not to be disputed; the Government of India agreed to identify and deport all illegal immigrants who entered the country after 25 March 1971; the Government of India also undertook to erect physical barriers (such as walls, barbed wire fences, etc.) and deploy border patrols to prevent future illegal immigration. All police activities against leaders and participants of the Assam Movement were withdrawn and closed.

Immediately after the signing of the Accord, leaders of the movement – Prafulla Mahanta and Bhrigu Phukan of the AASU and Brij Kumar Sarma of the All Assam Gana Sangram Parishad (AAGSP) – decided to enter the political mainstream. Capitalizing on the success of their movement, they persuaded the various organizations associated with the movement to come together to form the Asom Gana Parishad, at the Golaghat Convention of October 1985.

In the election that took place for the state's 126-seat assembly in 1985, the INC was reduced to only 25 seats (down 66), and Congress (Socialist) won 4; the Plains Tribal Council of Assam won 3 seats and the CPI(M) won 2. Of the 92 seats taken by independents, 67 belonged to the Asom Gana Parishad, which was yet to be registered as a regional party by the ECI.

Prafulla Kumar Mahanta was sworn in as the chief minister of the Assam government at 33 years of age, the youngest person to do so in the country at that time. His government gained a bad name for corruption, and more importantly for allowing separatism associated with the United Liberation Front of Assam to gain ground unchallenged. Once the ULFA insurgency began to go out of hand, the Government of India dismissed the Mahanta government in 1990, and imposed President's Rule in Assam.

Bihar

The INC somehow stumbled through its factional squabbles to the 1985 assembly elections to win another mandate for the Bihar government.

The INC won 196 seats in the 324-seat Bihar assembly, with 39.30% of the vote share; Charan Singh's Lok Dal finished second with 46 seats (14.69% of the vote share); the BJP finished third with 16 seats, followed by the Janata Party with 13 seats and the CPI with 12; the JMM won 9; and the CPI(M), Congress (S) and SUCI won 1 seat each.

Veteran freedom fighter and trade unionist, and one of the young turks of the INC, Bindeshwari Prasad Dubey was sworn in as chief minister of Bihar, an office he held on to till 1988. His tenure was mired in corruption, but even worse, it was stained by caste-related atrocities, including the mass rape of women belonging to 26 backward caste families in Pararia village – an atrocity perpetrated by Bihar police, which the government consistently denied. Dubey also gained a bad name for harbouring political criminals. B.P. Dubey was eventually replaced in 1988 by his close associate (and yet another of the young turks of Bihar Congress), Bhagwat Jha Azad, who held office for just about a year (February 1988–March 1989). Bhagwat Azad, in his turn, was replaced by the last of the young turks of Bihar Congress to make it to the position of the chief minister of the state, Satyendra Narayan Sinha. S.N. Sinha was a Congressman with great promise, who despite having gone with the Syndicate (and supporting Indira Gandhi's expulsion) and then with Jai Prakash Narayan's Sampurna Kranti movement as a member of the Janata Party, eventually made it back to the INC, and resumed his good work for the party. His stint as the chief minister of Bihar, however, was much less illustrious than his political career generally, for he had to step down after a very short stint (March–December 1989) in favour of Jagannath Mishra, who remained in office the last 3 odd months of the assembly term which ended in 1990.

Gujarat

The 1985 elections to the 182-seat Gujarat assembly turned out to be a landmark election for the INC.

The incumbent Congress won the election by a landslide, winning 149 seats, with vote share of 55.55%. The Janata Party came second with a mere 14 seats (and vote share of 19.25%), while the rising force of the BJP won 11 seats (with a vote share of 11.96%). Both of the communist parties failed to win any seats.

The chief minister of Gujarat for the better part of the previous assembly term and the architect of the KHAM coalition that powered the Congress to electoral victories, Madhav Singh Solanki had demitted his office in the face of upper caste agitations in the summer of 1985. He was succeeded in the office of the chief minister by Amarsinh Chaudhary, who was the first person of Adivasi origins to hold that office. Amarsinh Chaudhary was sworn in as chief minister in the new assembly term as well, and he continued to hold that office till July 1989, when the office reverted to Solanki once more for the last few months.

The margin of the INC's 1985 victory was the biggest that any party was to have till the 2002 elections. It also turned out to be the last time the INC won the state assembly to date.

Himachal Pradesh

As in Gujarat, the INC had a landslide in the assembly elections for Himachal Pradesh as well, benefitting from the sympathy wave after Mrs Gandhi's assassination.

The INC won 58 of the 68 seats in the assembly, with a vote share of 55.86%. The BJP emerged as the main party of opposition, winning 7 seats, with a vote share of 35.87%; the Lok Dal managed to win only 1 seat.

The recently instituted chief minister, Virbhadra Singh was sworn in for his second term, which he served till the end of the assembly term in 1990.

Karnataka

The ruling Janata Party of Karnataka fared badly in the 1984 parliamentary elections, winning only 4 seats to the Lok Sabha from the state. Chief Minister Ramakrishna Hegde resigned saying his party appears to have lost its mandate and decided to seek a fresh one.

In the elections that followed, the Janata Party won 139 seats out of the assembly total of 224, with a vote share of 43.6%. The INC did poorly in terms of seats, winning only 65 seats, but did well in terms of its vote share, winning 40.82% of the popular vote, only marginally behind the Janata Party. The CPI won 3 seats, and the BJP and the CPI(M) won 2 seats each.

Ramakrishna Hegde returned to the office of the chief minister, which he continued to hold till 1988, when he had to step down over a scandal involving the government tapping into the phones of prominent businessmen and politicians in the state. His party associate, Somappa Rayyappa Bommai, became the new chief minister of the state for less than a year (August 1988–April 1989). Bommai fell victim to large-scale defections from the party, which made the governor of Karnataka, P. Venkatasubbaiah, dismiss his government without giving him the opportunity of a floor test, and impose President's Rule.

Bommai took this to the Supreme Court where, in a famous verdict (S.R. Bommai vs the Union of India), the Supreme Court made an elaborate observation about the circumstances in which Article 356 could and should be applied.

THE VERDICT DELIVERED IN 1994 IS THE PRINCIPAL POINT OF REFERENCE ON THE ISSUE OF ARTICLE 356, AND IS WIDELY ACCEPTED TO BE THE PRINCIPAL REASON WHY THE FREQUENCY OF IMPOSITION OF ARTICLE 356 HAS REDUCED CONSIDERABLY SINCE THEN.

Madhya Pradesh

Madhya Pradesh was yet another Congress-ruled state where the Congress benefitted from the sympathy wave following the assassination of Mrs Gandhi.

The INC won 250 of the 320 seats in the assembly, with a vote share of 48.87%; the BJP won 58 seats (down 2) with a vote share of 32.42%; the Janata Party finished with 5 seats and Congress (S) with 1.

The incumbent chief minister Arjun Singh was sworn in for another term, but he resigned the very next day after some differences cropped up with veteran MLA Shriyut Sriniwas Tiwari, upon which Motilal Vora was sworn in. Vora served as the chief minister till 1988, when Arjun Singh was brought back as chief minister, while Vohra was inducted into the Union cabinet. Arjun Singh, however, was forced to resign in 1989 over the Churhat Lottery Scam, organized by his family members where the first prize was believed to have been won by Arjun Singh himself. Upon Arjun Singh's resignation, Motilal Vora was reappointed the chief minister in which capacity he served between January and December 1989. However, the same factionalism that was responsible for the musical chair performances of Arjun Singh and Motilal Vora, in the five years of the assembly term, brought Shyama Charan Shukla back to the chief minister's chair for one last time in December 1989, which he continued to occupy till the end of that assembly term in March 1990.

Maharashtra

Maharashtra was one of those states where the sympathy wave of 1984 probably saved the incumbent Congress government.

The INC emerged as the single largest party winning 161 of 288 seats, with a clear majority and a vote share of 43.41%, but noticeably, the INC lost some 25 seats (as against what Congress(I) had won the last time). The Congress (Socialist), previously known as Congress (Urs), led by Sharad Pawar, won 54 seats (up 7 from 1980) with 17.28% of the popular vote; the Janata Party won 20 seats to come third and the BJP won 16 to come fourth. The PWPI won 13 seats, the CPI and the CPI(M) won 2 seats each.

Shivajirao Patil Nilangekar, a prominent educationist, was sworn in as the chief minister in June 1985. However, he had to step down after strictures were passed in the High Court against him for engaging in fraud and misuse of power in the conduct of MD examinations to favour his own daughter and a friend of hers. Former chief minister and Union Home Minister Shankarrao Chavan was appointed chief minister yet again, and he held the office between March 1986 and June 1988, when Rajiv Gandhi called Chavan back to the Union cabinet. By then Sharad Pawar had returned to the INC, merging his Congress (S) into the parent organization. As a kind of reward, Pawar was appointed the chief minister for the rest of the term (1988–90).

Orissa

In Orissa as elsewhere, the sympathy wave generated by the assassination of Mrs Gandhi helped in carrying an already strong Congress party over the winning post.

The incumbent chief minister J.B. Patnaik carried the INC towards an emphatic victory, winning 117 seats out of the assembly total of 147, with a vote share of 51.08%. The Janata Party came second with 21 seats, with a vote share of only 14.28%; the CPI and the BJP got 1 seat each.

J.B. Patnaik was sworn in for a second term in office, which he nearly completed before stepping down with the last few months of the assembly term to spare. Hemananda Biswal was sworn in to the office for the last few months (December 1989–March 1990).

Punjab

The 1985 assembly elections in Punjab mark an important point between virtually two eras in the state's politics.

From the time of independence, the Sikhs, who had, along with the Hindus, favoured partition of the British province of Punjab, had often expressed the feeling of being somewhat repressed in the Indian Union. While individual Sikhs who entered into public and private corporate life in the country never had any glass ceiling to overcome, the experience of the average Sikh in the political life in Punjab made many feel shortchanged by the partition. The tensions between the more urban Hindu-dominated areas and the more rural Sikh-dominated areas steadily grew to the point where the state of Punjab had to be trifurcated to create Haryana and Himachal Pradesh in such a way that the much reduced state of Punjab would constitute the largely agricultural regions of the state.

Tensions with the Hindu-dominated state of Haryana continued over sharing of river water, and large segments of people of the state of Punjab began to find the Central government often favouring Haryana over Punjab, to the detriment of Punjab's agricultural economy. Here lay the foundations of the mounting demand for autonomy that began to crystalize into the form that was first seen in the Anandpur Sahab Resolution of 1973 of the Shiromani Akali Dal – a declaration that the Government of India considered a seditious document. By that time the Green Revolution was getting into full swing, and the popular culture of Punjab was becoming materialistic in a way that caused a lot of people considerable discomfort – especially those who put a premium on the simplicity and humility that were considered essential to Sikhism. Hence the demands for autonomy converged with a sort of religious essentialism. These discomforts increased further with the growing inequalities ushered in by the Green Revolution.

The Akali Dal tried to ride these twin impulses to make a major impact in Punjab politics, under the leadership triad of Gurcharan Singh Tohra, Parkash Singh Badal and Surjit Singh Barnala – using the religious authority of the Shiromani Gurudwara Prabandhak Committee to obtain political power. As the Akali Dal grew in political strength incrementally over the years, the Congress(I) – especially Giani Zail Singh, with the support of Mrs Gandhi, decided to undermine the religious credentials of the Akali leadership and played up the critique of the Akali leadership mounted by the son of a preacher of Damdami Taksal, Jarnail Singh Bhindranwale. However, Bhindranwale, and many others who followed him, saw Punjab becoming nothing but a deeply flawed, materialistic, hedonistic society if it remained a part of India. Believing that only a social revolution could save the Sikh faith, Bhindranwale took the path of militancy reviving the dream of an independent Khalistan. This drew in more support than either the Akalis or any other political formation could ever mobilize. In these circumstances of law and order rapidly beginning to break down, the Congress government of Darbara Singh was dismissed and President's Rule was imposed in October 1983.

As authorities were beginning to get alarmed, Bhindranwale took shelter in the Golden Temple of Amritsar, the holiest place of the Sikhs, fully armed – to the consternation of both the SGPC and the police authorities of Punjab. Mrs Gandhi, working on intelligence that clearly indicated that the situation was getting out of hand, decided on military intervention. In June 1984, Operation Blue Star was carried out to physically eliminate the threat posed by Bhindranwale – causing considerable physical damage to the holy shrine of the Harmandir Sahib and the Akal Takht – two of the holiest places in Sikh faith. Apart from the physical damage, the collective trauma of the Sikh people at the desecration of their holiest shrine was beyond imagination. In a direct act of retaliation to this desecration, Mrs Gandhi was gunned down by her own Sikh bodyguards in October 1984. The assassination of Mrs Gandhi brought out an orchestrated blowback by Congress activists and functionaries, with some degree of state complicity, which resulted in the mindless killing of hundreds of Sikhs in many parts of India, with Delhi being the epicenter.

Needless to say, the pogroms of 1984 had a major impact on the politics of Punjab – both in the short and long runs. Once the situation appeared to have cooled down somewhat, elections were announced in preparation for the withdrawal of President's Rule for the state after more than a year and eleven months.

In the elections that year, the SAD won 73 of the 117 seats in the assembly, with a vote share of 38.01%; the INC, despite Operation Blue Star and the anti-Sikh pogroms, managed to win 32 seats, with a vote share of 37.86% – only a fraction behind the Akalis; the BJP finished with 6 seats, the CPI and the Janata Party won 1 seat each.

Surjit Singh Barnala, a former Union cabinet minister in the Morarji Desai government, was sworn in at the head of a Akali Dal government. He held the office during the 2 years (1985–87) when militancy spread rapidly across Punjab with financial support from Pakistan. As situation deteriorated rapidly, the Barnala government was dismissed and President's Rule was imposed yet again in Punjab – this time it was to last more than 4 years and 8 months.

Pondicherry

Pondicherry had been under President's Rule for more than a year and 8 months when it went to polls in 1985.

In the elections that year, the INC won 15 out of the 30 seats of the assembly, with a vote share of 32.28%; the DMK was reduced to only 5 seats, with a vote share of 29.08%; the AIADMK gained its toehold in the Union Territory winning 6 seats, while the Janata Party won 2 seats.

M.O. Hassan Farook Maricar was sworn in as the chief minister for the third time, which became his only tenure that lasted the full term of the assembly (1985–90).

Rajasthan

Rajasthan was a state where the Congress was clearly setting into a mode of decline. The sympathy wave after Mrs Gandhi's assassination appeared to have saved the government for the time being, but the writing appeared to be on the wall.

In the elections held in 1985 to the now increased size of 200 seats in the assembly, the INC finished with 113 seats, down 20, with a vote share of 46.57%. The second slot was taken by the rapidly ascendant BJP, winning 39 seats with a vote share of 21.24%. The Lok Dal won 27 seats, the Janata Party 10 and the CPI 1.

Hari Dev Joshi was sworn in as the chief minister, which he remained till 1988, when former chief minister Shiv Charan Mathur was brought back for a little less than 2 years (1988–89) before Hari Dev Joshi was brought back in yet again.

Sikkim

Sikkim went to the polls in 1985 after nearly 2 years under President's Rule. The chief minister whose government was toppled in 1983, Nar Bahadur Bhandari, dissolved the Sikkim Janata Parishad (thus dissociating himself from the Janata Party) and set up instead the Sikkim Sangram Parishad in 1984.

In the elections held to the 32-seat assembly, the Sikkim Sangram Parishad made a clean sweep winning 30 seats, with 62.20% of the vote share; contesting its first elections in the state, the INC won a seat, with another being taken by an independent candidate.

Nar Bahadur Bhandari was sworn back in as the chief minister, and this time he managed to serve till the end of the term in 1989.

Uttar Pradesh

The clearest indication of Congress's declining political heft could be seen in the elections to the Uttar Pradesh assembly, which in the 1985 elections had its strength increased to 425.

Riding the sympathy wave, the INC made it back to power with 269 seats, with 39.25% of the popular vote, but losing 40 seats in the process. Chaudhary Charan Singh's Lok Dal made its debut in the UP political circuit with 84 seats to finish in the second spot, with 21.43% of the vote share. The Janata Party finished with 20 seats, the BJP with 16 and the CPI with 6. The debutant Congress (Jagjivan), led by Bapu Jagjivan Ram who left the Congress(Urs) in 1981 to set the party up, finished with 5 seats, and the CPI(M) with 2; independents finished with 23 seats.

Narayan Dutt Tiwari, who had occupied the chief minister's office since August 1984, was sworn back in, only to have to step down in favour of Vir Bahadur Singh – who served as chief minister between September 1985 and June 1988, before being replaced by Narayan Dutt Tiwari yet again in a cabinet reshuffle powered by the proverbial Congress factional struggles. Thereafter, N.D. Tiwari continued in office till the end of the term in December 1989. He remains the last Congress chief minister to have held power in Uttar Pradesh.

1987

Haryana

Elections to the Haryana assembly in 1987 marked the rise of Chaudhary Devi Lal in the politics of the state.

In the elections held that year, the Lok Dal fought in a coalition with the BJP. Having successfully consolidated the votes, the Lok Dal had a landslide of a victory, winning 60 of the 90 seats in the assembly, with a vote share of 38.58%. The second slot was taken by its ally, the BJP, with 16 seats (vote share of 10.08%) – giving the coalition 76 seats. The Congress was reduced to only 5 seats (despite a vote share of 29.18%), while the CPI and CPI(M) won 1 seat each.

Chaudhary Devi Lal was sworn in as the chief minister of Haryana, and continued in office till 1989 when he joined the Union cabinet. He was succeeded by his son Om Prakash Chautala (December 1989–May 1980). When Chautala had to vacate the post of the chief minister for a brief while, it was held by former chief minister Banarsi Das Gupta (May–July 1990), before Chautala returned to assume the office once again for only 5 days, before it went over to Hukam Singh (July 1990–March 1991), before returning yet again to Chautala for the last 14 days of the assembly term in March–April 1991.

Jammu and Kashmir

Farooq Abdullah had been reappointed the chief minister of Jammu and Kashmir after his agreement with Prime Minister Rajiv Gandhi that the two parties would contest the assembly elections of 1987 together.

The elections that were held in March 1987 were widely understood to be one where Farooq Abdullah and his JKNC were doing the bidding of New Delhi – which, given the turn towards communal polarisation associated with the Congress in the 1983 election, was denounced as submission before the (Hindu) government of India, and bartering away the autonomy granted to Jammu and Kashmir in 1948. Most of the anti-establishment opinion and political outfits in the Valley therefore rallied around the Jamaat-e-Islami Jammu Kashmir (JIJK) and put together the Muslim United Front (MUF). Even at this date, the JIJK (led by Syed Ali Shah Geelani who wanted J&K to merge with Pakistan) favoured peaceful and constitutional process, and abjured the path of violence adopted by the Jammu and Kashmir Liberation Front, which wanted independence for the state through armed struggle. Despite mobilizing in the name of religion (saying Islam was in danger, and calling for implementation of Shari'ah in the Valley) the JIJK was still calling for resolution of the status of J&K in accordance with the Shimla Agreement, and freedom from interference of New Delhi.

In the elections of 1987, the JKNC won 40 seats, with a vote share of 32.98%, while its electoral ally the INC won 26 seats, with a vote share of 20.2%. The MUF candidates, contesting as unregistered and therefore as independent candidates won

4 seats (with more than 34% of the vote share) while the BJP debuted in the state winning 2 seats.

The 1987 election had logged the highest ever voter turnout in the state (74.88% of all eligible voters cast their votes, and 80% of all voters from the Valley having done so). It was widely believed that the votes were rigged, and had that not been the case the MUF could have won between 15 and 20 seats. In the final analysis, the JKNC-INC alliance, having won 66 of the 76 seats of the assembly, with only 63% of the votes, whereas the MUF won only 4 seats with 34% of the votes – the 1987 elections appeared to have been disproportionately rigged even by J&K standards.

Farooq Abdullah was sworn in as the head of the JKNC–INC coalition government, but in public perception he stood discredited with the manner of his electoral victory. Some unpopular decisions taken by his government (especially those raising power tariffs in 1988) brought the people out to protests, which elicited brutal police action – serving as a trigger for the JKLF's resorting to militancy yet again. Only by this time, outfits like Jaish-e-Muhammad and Lashkar-e-Taiba also entered the field among many other militant outfits, and targeted attacks and killings of Kashmiri Hindus began in earnest. As the acts of public protest and militancy snowballed, threatening the stability of the state, the hardline Jagmohan Malhotra (the extremely unpopular governor of J&K during 1984–89) was reappointed as the governor of Jammu and Kashmir. Farooq Abdullah resigned in protest of the decision, and Governor's Rule was introduced in the state. As Kashmir descended into an unprecedented level of violence, beginning with an open call for Kashmiri Hindus to leave the Valley that resulted in their exodus for fear of their lives, India grappled with the severest insurgency and challenge to its territorial integrity, the state remained under Governor's Rule (the Kashmiri equivalent of President's

Rule) for more than 6 years and 8 months (19 January 1990–9 October 1996).

Kerala

The fragmented political landscape of Kerala continued to worsen and polarise between the 2 assembly elections of 1982 and 1987.

Within 6 months of the assembly elections of 1982, Congress (Anthony) merged into the Congress(I); by August 1985 the AIML merged back into IUML, and within the 2 years that followed the Congress(S) and Janata(G) merged back into Congress(I). On the other hand, the Kerala Congress split again into 2 factions, followed by the NDP and SRP – 1 faction of each of the last 2 left the UDF. Even the BJP was able to float a Hindu–Munnani front for the first time in the fragmented landscape of Kerala.

In the elections that took place in 1987, the UDF consisted of the INC, IUML, Kerala Congress (Jacob), Kerala Congress (Mani), National Democratic Party (Panicker), SRP(S), RSP(S). The LDP constituted of CPI(M), CPI, RSP, Congress (Socialist, led by Sarat Chandra Sinha), Janata Party and Lok Dal.

The LDF won a clear majority, winning 73 seats of the 140-seat assembly. The CPI(M) won 38 seats, followed by the CPI winning 16 seats. The Congress (Socialist) won 6 seats, the Janata party 7, RSP 5 and Lok Dal won 1. The UDF won 53 seats with the INC winning 33 seats, the 2 Kerala Congress factions 5 seats between themselves, and the IUML won 15 seats. Of the 14 independent winners, 5 decided to support the LDF, while 8 went with the UDF.

Erambala Krishnan Nayanar was sworn in as the chief minister for the second time, and he held the office till 1991, when the CPI(M) brought the assembly polls forward by a year, only to lose it.

Mizoram

Mizoram had gone for what turned out to be its last assembly elections as a UT in 1984. In 1985, the Mizo insurgency came to an end with the Mizoram Peace Accord and a leader of the insurgency Laldenga was sworn in as the chief minister, and Mizoram was made into a state in accordance with the Mizoram Peace Accord in 1986. Thus, in 1987, Mizoram went for assembly elections as a state, with the strength of the assembly increasing to 40 seats.

The main force behind the Mizo insurgency and the chief protagonist in the accord, the Mizo National Front, was yet to receive their registration as regional party. Hence the MNF contested as independents and won 24 seats (43% of the popular vote); the INC led by Lal Thanhawla won 13 seats (32.99% of the popular vote), and the Mizoram Peoples' Conference led by Brig Sailo won 3 seats (with 23.7% of the vote share).

Laldenga was sworn in as the chief minister and served for just over a year when his government collapsed because of defections from his party. With no other party being able to form a government, President's Rule was imposed in Mizoram. Shortly after this Laldenga himself fell terminally ill with lung cancer and lost to it by 1990.

Nagaland

The Nagaland assembly went to the polls in November 1987 after a full term under the INC government led by S.C. Jamir, and then Hokishe Sema.

In the elections that followed, the INC improved its seat tally to win 34 seats out of 60 seats in the assembly, with 36.1% of the vote share. The Naga National Democratic Party finished with 18 seats, with 26.18% of the vote share. The Naga People's Front won 1 seat, and the BJP failed to win any.

Hokishe Sema was sworn in yet again as the chief minister, but defections from his party made his government collapse in 1988, and President's Rule was imposed in Nagaland yet again.

West Bengal

By the time West Bengal went to the polls to elect its assembly in 1987, the state had settled in for a kind of political stability under the Left Front, and Congress was out of power from the state for a decade. While Prime Minister Rajiv Gandhi did his best to galvanise the Bengal Congress, then led by Priya Ranjan Dasmunshi, two of its stalwarts from the 1970s, Somen Mitra and Subrata Mukherjee, fell out with the central leadership. Mrs Gandhi's trusted aide Pranab Mukherjee had also fallen out with Rajiv Gandhi, and broke away from the party setting up his own party, the Rashtriya Samajwadi Congress. Gandhi's attempts to reach an accord in the Darjeeling Hills also further emboldened Subhash Ghisingh, as the scale of violence mounted demanding Gorkhaland. It was in this backdrop of a fragmented political opposition and also a restive hill region that West Bengal voted for its assembly in 1987.

The outcome was somewhat of a foregone conclusion. The Left Front had yet another landslide, winning 251 seats out of the 294 seats in the assembly. Of this, the CPI(M) won 187 seats of its own, with a vote share of 39.12%; the AIFB won 26 seats; RSP 18, CPI 11, MFB 2 and RCPI 1; DSP and West Bengal Socialist Party (led by Kiranmaoy Nanda) won 6 seats between themselves. The Congress remained the dominant force of the opposition, and the second-largest party in the assembly, winning 40 seats (with a vote share of 41.12%, larger than the CPI(M)); the SUCI won 2 seats while the IUML won 1 seat. The BJP, the Janata Party and the Lok Dal failed to win any seats at all. Most interestingly, with the voters' consolidation done to near perfection, not a single independent managed to win a seat in the assembly.

The incumbent chief minister, Jyoti Basu, was sworn in again for his third full term in government. On the campaign trail, Rajiv Gandhi had passed comments at Basu being of an age where people tended to retire. Jyoti Basu was known to have retorted that he will have Rajiv retire before he hung up his boots. Within 2 years after 1987, Basu may be said to have kept his word when the Left Front became a part of the coalition led by V.P. Singh that brought Rajiv Gandhi down.

1988

Meghalaya

The political landscape of Meghalaya was becoming increasingly fragmented over the years, and the assembly elections of 1988 were no different.

The INC emerged as the single largest party with 22 seats (and a vote share of 32.65%); the Hill People's Union (set up in 1985 by breakaway politicians from the All Party Hill Leaders' Conference and from the Hill State People's Democratic Party) managed to win 19 seats; the rump HSPDP managed to win only 6 seats (down 9); APHLC (Armison Marak Group) and the PDIC managed to win 2 seats each; the CPI failed to win any, while independent candidates were able to win 9 seats.

Given yet another fractured verdict, Meghalaya reverted to yet another post-poll coalition – this time called the United Meghalaya Parliamentary Democratic Forum, comprising the INC, HPU and APHLC (AM group). Williamson Ampang Sangma, who had carried his associates from the APHLC to the INC in 1977, finally stepped aside, allowing Purna Agitok Sangma to be sworn in as the chief minister (February 1988–March

1990). In March 1990, he stepped down and was succeeded by B.B. Lyngdoh (March 1990–October 1991). The government collapsed in October 1991 with a spate of defections, and President's Rule was imposed in Meghalaya yet again.

Tripura

In 1978, the Tripura National Volunteer Force or the Tripura National Volunteers (TNV) began a militant campaign to separate Tripura from India. Led by Bijoy Kumar Hrangkhawl, the TNV was dominated by Christian tribals who were fighting against domination by the Bengali-speaking population that the CPI(M) had come to stand for in the politics of Tripura. In August 1988, the TNV finally signed an accord and joined the political mainstream, and the politics of reconciliation began after having displaced thousands and killing hundreds.

In the elections of 1988, the CPI(M) emerged as the single largest party, winning 26 seats out of the 60 seats of the assembly, with a vote share of 45.82%; the INC finished as the second-largest party with 25 seats (with 37.33% of the vote share); the Tripura Upajati Juba Samiti finished third with 7 seats, and the RSP won only 2 seats.

The INC formed a post-poll coalition with the TUJS, allowing Sudhir Ranjan Majumdar of the INC to be sworn in as the chief minister in February 1988, in which capacity he served till February 1992. In 1992 the government collapsed, whereupon President's Rule was imposed.

Chapter 11

THE DEFINITIVE DECLINE OF THE CONGRESS

1989 marks the definitive year of Congress's decline. Indeed the INC won 3 of the 6 general elections after that, and also continued to be a big player at the level of many states, but India seemed to have finally come out of the thrall of the party – both at the Centre and at the provinces – even though no other party appeared to be strong enough to replace it just yet.

1989

Andhra Pradesh

In Andhra Pradesh, the Congress bucked the national trend, riding on a very strong anti-incumbency wave against the reigning Telugu Desam, after 7 years in power in the state.

In the elections held in that year, the INC emerged as the single largest party with 181 seats (up 131) with 47.09% of the vote share. The TDP received a hammering, as in the Lok Sabha polls of that year, winning only 74 seats (down 128 seats). The CPI won 8 seats, the CPI(M) won 6 and the BJP won 5 seats. The All India Majlis-e-Ittehadul Muslimeen (which began as the Majlis-e-Ittehadul Muslimeen in 1927 as an anti-integrationist party but later took a pragmatic turn and accepted Hyderabad as integral to India, and had initially gained success only at the municipal level) won its first Lok Sabha seat in 1984 went on to win 4 assembly seats in the 1989 elections. The Janata Dal could gain only 1 seat.

Marri Chenna Reddy was sworn in yet again at the head of the Congress government in December 1989, but stepped down next year faced with factional fights. He was replaced by Nedurumalli Janardhana Reddy (December 1990–October 1992). Janardhana Reddy, during his short tenure, had to deal with both communal riots and naxalite insurgency by the People's War Group which he went on to ban. Janardhana Reddy stepped down in favour of Kotla Vijaybhaskara Reddy (October 1992–December 1994). K.V. Reddy's stint came to be known for introducing the mid-day meal scheme.

Goa

The Congress government in Goa managed to hold on to power, but only for a brief while before being replaced by a coalition government with the resurgent Gomantak Party.

In the elections, the INC won 20 seats in the 40-seat assembly (with a vote share of 40.52%); the MAG finished with 18 seats (polling 38.78% of the vote share). The Janata Dal, Shiv Sena, CPI, BJP, Janata Party, CPI(M) – none of them managed to poll enough votes to win a seat.

Pratap Singh Rane was sworn in as chief minister in January 1990, only to step down in favour of Churchill Alemao – a former leader of the United Goans Democratic Party who had helped form the Congress government despite its much reduced strength by putting together the Progressive Democratic Front. Allemao however held the office only for 18 days before the Front split, when 6 Congress MLAs broke off under the leadership of Louis Proto Barbosa to form a coalition with the MAG, with Barbosa as the chief minister, in April 1990. However, even the Barbosa-led coalition failed to survive beyond December 1990, when Barbosa's act of defection was struck down by the High Court. President's Rule was imposed for a little over a month. In January 1991, a section of the MAG broke away under Ravi Naik, who joined the INC and staked claim to form an INC government. Naik remained as the chief minister during January 1991–March 1993, with Wilfred de Souza as the deputy chief minister. In 1993, Wilfred de Souza took over as the chief minister (May 1993–April 1994), and after a 6-day stint by Ravi Naik in April 1994, continued as the chief minister for the rest of the assembly term (April 1994–December 1994).

Karnataka

The elections to the Karnataka state assembly, like Andhra Pradesh, went the way of the Congress.

Of the 224 seats of the assembly, the INC won 178, with a vote share of 43.76%. The Janata Dal came second with 74 seats, with a vote share of 27.08%; the BJP finished with 4 seats, the Janata Party along with the peasant's movement Karnataka Rajya Raitha Sangha finished with 2 seats each; and the AIADMK and the Muslim League with 1 seat each.

Veerendra Basappa Patil was sworn in for the second time as the chief minister in 1989, but in the wake of his failure to stem the tide of communal disturbances after the BJP's *ratha yatra* in 1990, Patil was asked to step down. He was replaced by Sarekoppa Bangarappa (1990–92) who in turn was succeeded by M. Veerappa Moily (November 1992–December 1994).

M. Veerappa Moily

Mizoram

Mizoram had seen some instability since its assembly elections in 1989 as more MLAs of the victorious MNF wanted cabinet posts than there were positions to fill.

After a period of President's Rule, when the assembly went back to the polls, the INC won a simple majority winning 23 out of the 40 seats, with 34.85% of the popular vote. The MNF won only 14 seats (down 10) with a higher proportion of the popular vote (35.29%). Mizoram People's Conference remained confined with a single seat with a disproportionately high vote share of 19.67%.

Pu Lalthanhawla was sworn in for the third time, this time for a period longer than the previous terms (1989–93).

Nagaland

Just like Mizoram, Nagaland also suffered from factional squabbles that brought in President's Rule after its last elections. When the state went to polls again in 1989, a clear verdict was provided by the people.

The Congress won a simple majority with 36 (up 2) out of the 60 seats of the assembly, and a vote share of 51.45%. The newly emergent party of the Nagaland People's Council (which eventually began to spread its roots among the Nagas of Manipur and Arunachal Pradesh) finished with 24 seats, with a vote share of 41.61%.

Senayangba Chubatoshi Jamir, who was with the United Democratic Front Progressive in the 1987 elections, merged his party with the INC before the 1989 elections. He was sworn in after the elections as the chief minister in 1989, but had to step down in the face of factional trouble in 1990. He was succeeded by K.L. Chishi, the leader of National Democratic Movement, who held the office for only 28 days at the head of a coalition government with the INC. Chishi's resignation was followed by the first Nagaland People's Council minority government under Vemuzo Phesao, who ruled between June 1990 and April 1992. Upon the collapse of the government in 1992, President's Rule was imposed in Nagaland yet again.

Sikkim

The Sikkimese government had been one of the few governments in north-east India to have shown any stability, thanks to the huge mandate that had been given to Nar Bahadur Bhandari of the Sikkim Sangram Parishad. In 1989, he was handsomely rewarded for the good work done by his government.

In perhaps the only election of its type, the SSP won all the 32 assembly seats, with over 70.41% of the popular votes being cast for the party. The INC failed to win any seat despite polling 18% of the popular vote. The debutant Rising Sun Party, led by Ram Chandra Poudyal, a former member of the Sikkim Congress (Revolutionary), created quite a stir in the run up to the elections, but failed to win any seat either.

In the event, Nar Bahadur Bhandari had another clear term, remaining chief minister till 1994 – which turned out to be his last term in office.

Tamil Nadu

After the mayhem in Tamil Nadu assembly, the state remained under President's Rule for a year, after which it went to the polls yet again. Both the Janaki Ramachandran faction and the Jayalalithaa faction of the AIADMK had applied for the AIADMK logo, but the ECI denied them both and put it on ice. The AIADMK (Jaya) faction was given the election symbol of a cock; the AIADMK (Janaki) faction was given the election symbol of 2 doves.

The INC initially considered aligning with the AIADMK (Jaya) faction, causing INC leader Sivaji Ganeshan to leave the Congress and float his own party, Thamizhaga Munnetra Munnani. Ganeshan went on to align with the AIADMK (Janaki). Eventually, the INC's alignment with the AIADMK (Jaya) also broke down, and the Congress contested on its own. By contrast, the DMK fought the elections as a part of the Janata Dal-led National Front, and had electoral understanding with the Janata Dal and the CPI(M). The CPI chose to align with the AIADMK (Jaya).

A stamp commemorating Sivaji Ganesan

When the elections were held, the DMK alliance won an emphatic victory with 169 seats (and vote share of 37.29%). The DMK won 150 seats by itself, the CPI(M) won 15 seats and the Janata Dal won 4. The AIADMK alliance won 30 seats, of which 27 were taken by the AIADMK (Jaya) (but, with 22.4% of the vote share) while the the CPI won 3 seats. The INC won 22 seats of its own strength, but the AIADMK (Janaki) could win only 2 seats (with just over 9% of the vote share). Janaki Ramachandran lost her own seat, which served as a sort of writing on the wall for her political ambition. The 2 factions of the AIADMK soon united under Jayalalithaa Jayaram and won 2 by-elections where polling had been deferred at the time of the assembly polls.

M. Karunandihi was sworn in as the chief minister for his third term, which was cut short in 1991 over his support for the LTTE, which had been fighting the Indian Peace-keeping Force on Sri Lankan soil. Despite the reluctance of Governor, Surjit Singh Barnala, the Union government led by Chandra Shekhar, had the DMK ministry dismissed, and imposed President's Rule even though the government still commanded majority on the floor of the house.

Uttar Pradesh

The year 1989 was a landmark election for the Uttar Pradesh assembly in the sense that it marked the beginning of the definitive decline of the Congress in the Hindi heartland.

In the elections that were held in November 1989, the Janata Dal, formed as a result of the merger of the various forces associated with the Janata movement of the 1970s (minus the BJS), ended up with a tally of 208 seats out of the 425-seat assembly (with a vote share of 29.71%). The Congress came second with 98 seats (with a vote share of 27.90%), down 175 seats; the BJP finished with 57 seats (up 41) albeit with a vote share of only 11.61%; the Bahujan Samaj Party (set up in 1984 by Kanshi Ram) had its first noticeable performance with 13 seats in this election. The CPI finished with 6 seats; the Lok Dal and the CPI(M) won 2 seats each, and the rump Janata Party, the Hindu Mahasabha and the Shoshit Dal won 1 seat each.

Mulayam Singh Yadav, who had begun his political career with the SSP, been put behind bars during the Emergency and previously held state cabinet berths during the Janata Party experiment, and later held party positions with the Lok Dal under Charan Singh, was now sworn in as the chief minister, with outside support from the BJP. The government, however, did not last as Mulayam handled the Ram Janambhoomi movement of the BJP with a heavy hand, launching police action against the karsevaks at Ayodhya in 1990, killing at least 16 rioters. When the BJP pulled out of the National Front at both the Union and the state levels in November 1990, Mulayam saved his seat for the time being by joining the Janata Dal (Socialist) under Chandra Shekhar, which was supported from outside by the Congress. However, once the Congress withdrew its support from the Chandra Shekhar government at the Centre, Mulayam's government also collapsed in April 1991, and the state went for mid-term elections in 1991.

1990

Arunachal Pradesh

Unlike in the Hindi-heartland states, the Congress continued to be of some significance in states far removed from the Centre. In Arunachal Pradesh, the elections were held for the 60 seats in the state assembly in 1990.

The INC won 37 seats with a vote share of 44.25%; the Janata Dal finished second with 11 seats with a vote share of 36.21%; the number of independent candidates who won seats in the assembly was also 11.

Gegong Apang, the incumbent chief minister, was sworn in for another full term.

Bihar

The inertia of the 1989 elections in the Hindi-heartland continued to decimate the Congress into the next year, with the Bihar assembly elections held in February of 1990.

In the elections held that year, the Janata Dal emerged as the single largest party, winning 122 seats in the 324-seat assembly, with 25.61% of the vote. The INC finished second with 71 seats (down 125) albeit with a marginally lower vote share of 24.78%; the BJP finished third with 39 seats (up 23), with a vote share of 11.31%; the CPI won 23 seats (up 11); the Jharkhand Mukti Morcha won 19 seats. The Indian People's Front (a front organization of the CPI(ML)) won 7 seats and the CPI(M) finished with 6 seats. The newly-formed Janata Party won 3 seats, the Marxist Coordination Committee won 2 seats; the Jharkhand Party and the Socialist Party won a seat each. Thirty seats were taken by independent candidates.

Given the fractured verdict, no party was in a position to form the government on its own strength. The Janata Dal was to stake its claim for the formation of government, but while Prime Minister V.P. Singh wanted former chief minister Ram Sundar Das to be sworn in again, Chandra Shekhar wanted Raghunath Jha. Lalu Prasad Yadav, the former leader of the Opposition in the assembly was suggested by Devi Lal, and when a legislature party poll was taken, Yadav won the majority votes. The BJP, which was supporting the Janata government from the outside in New Delhi agreed to do the same for Yadav – thereby giving the Janata Dal the required majority on the floor of the House.

Yadav was sworn in as chief minister in March 1990, but despite his dependence on the BJP in forming his government, Yadav did not hesitate to arrest L.K. Advani, when in December 1990 the latter was passing through Bihar on his Ratha-yatra to mobilize opinion in favour of the Ram Janambhoomi movement. The BJP promptly withdrew support to both V.P. Singh and Lalu Yadav's governments. However, while V.P. Singh's government collapsed, Yadav saved his government by obtaining support from the CPI (23 MLAs), CPI(M) (6), IPF (7) and JMM (19). Also, he managed to have 10 BJP MLAs, led by Inder Singh Namdhari, defect and support his government. Namdhari in fact joined the Lalu government subsequently. Hence, unlike the Janata government at the Centre, Lalu served as the CM of Bihar for the full term.

Gujarat

Even as late as 1990, Gujarat seemed ready to replace Congress, but unsure about whom to replace Congress with. Madhav Singh Solanki, who had earlier led INC to a clear victory, was saddled with an equally clear rejection, despite the fact that no one seemed particularly favoured.

In the 1990 elections to the 182 seats of the Gujarat assembly, the Janata Dal emerged as the single largest party with 70 seats (29.36% of the vote share); the BJP finished second with 67 seats (up 56 seats, and a vote share of 26.69%); the INC finished third with a mere 33 seats (down 116), despite having the largest vote share of 30.74%. While the Yuva Vikas Party won only 1 seat, BSP, CPI and the CPI(M) failed to win any seats.

The Janata Dal and the BJP entered into a post-poll understanding and formed a coalition government in March 1990, under the Janata Dal leader, Chimanbhai Patel. However, when the BJP pulled out of its coalition with the Janata Dal on 20 October 1990, at both the level of the Union and state governments, the 33 MLAs of the INC gave Chimanbhai Patel, who used to be in the Congress before he joined the Janata Party, outside support – one of the few governments where the INC extended support from outside without pulling it down after a while, because Patel and his Janata associates made it back to the Congress. Chimanbhai Patel remained in office till his death in February 1994, when he was succeeded by Chhabildas Mehta, the finance minister in Chimanbhai's cabinet, and who, like Chimanbhai, left the Congress to join the Janata Dal only to make it back to the Congress with Chimanbhai. Chabildas Mehta occupied the office from February 1994 to the end of the assembly term in March 1995 – leading, as it happened, technically the last Congress government since then to elections in Gujarat.

Himachal Pradesh

The 1990 elections to the assembly of Himachal Pradesh caught the Congress government under Virbhadra Singh in an anti-Congress wave.

In the elections to the Himachal assembly, the Bharatiya Janata Party prevailed in the state elections for the first time, winning 46 seats out of the assembly total of 68, with a vote share of 41.78%. The Janata Dal finished second with 11 seats (with less than 10% of the popular vote, and the INC was reduced to only 9 seats (albeit it had a vote share of 36.54%).

Shanta Kumar, who had earlier been chief minister of Himachal at the head of the Janata government, was now sworn in to the office of the chief minister at the head of a BJP government. An RSS Pracharak, Shanta Kumar's government enjoyed the confidence of the assembly when it was dissolved and Article 356 imposed after the destruction of the Babri Masjid by right-wing Hindu Nationalist karsevaks.

Madhya Pradesh

Madhya Pradesh was another of the states where the faction-ridden Congress was swept aside by a gale of anti-incumbency to give the BJP a clear mandate, only to have it taken away from them in a fell swoop.

In the elections of 1990, the BJP carried all before it winning 220 out of the 320 seats in the assembly (up 162) and with a vote share of 39.14%. The Congress under the incumbent Chief Minister Shyama Charan Shukla was reduced to 56 (down 194) with 33.38% of the popular vote; the Janata Dal won 28 seats, the CPI won 3 seats, the BSP 2, Krantikari Samajwadi Dal 1 seat, and independents won 10 seats.

Sunder Lal Patwa, who had once been sworn in as chief minister for less than a month in 1980, was now sworn in as the chief minister of the BJP government with a huge majority. But like Virbhadra Singh and the other BJP state governments in 1992, Patwa was also dismissed after the demolition of the Babri Masjid, and President's Rule was imposed in December 1992.

Maharashtra

Sharad Pawar, who had hopped all around the Congress political landscape only to finally return to the Congress in the late 1980s, led the Maharashtra Congress to the assembly elections in 1990.

In the 1990 elections, the INC remained the single largest party with 141 seats (down 20) in an assembly of 288, with 38.17% of the popular vote. The Shiv Sena exploded to the assembly level winning 52 seats (a gain of 52), with a vote share of only 15.94%. The BJP won 42 (gain of 26) seats with only 10.71% of the vote share. The Janata Dal won 24 seats; the PWPI won 8 seats; the CPI(M) won 3 seats and the CPI won 2; IUML, PRI (khobragade) and Congress (Socialist) won 1 seat each.

Sharad Pawar was sworn in as the chief minister of a minority government, which he knew was likely to prove unstable. Matters went into a tizzy when Congress President Rajiv Gandhi was assassinated in Tamil Nadu while campaigning for the general elections of 1991. P.V. Narasimha Rao, the former Andhra chief minister and member in Indira Gandhi and Rajiv Gandhi cabinets, was elected by the party as its new president. Pawar at that point maintained that the principle of 'one man, one post' should apply to the Congress, and that the president should not automatically be in the running for the office of the prime minister. Since Maharashtra had the largest number of Congress MPs at that time, Pawar fancied his chances as the prime minister. When Congress eventually won the general elections, Rao was elected by the Congress legislature party to be the prime minister. Rao chose to mollify Pawar's ambitions by making him the defence minister. Thus Pawar left for Delhi, as Sudhakar Rao Naik took over from him in Bombay in June 1991. However, Naik totally failed to control the communal frenzy that overwhelmed Maharashtra after the demolition of the Babri Masjid. Naik had to be replaced by Pawar yet again, who was sworn back in as the chief minister, in which capacity he served for the rest of the assembly term (March 1993–March 1995).

Manipur

The Manipur elections of 1990 fitted the pattern of neither incumbency nor anti-incumbency, so to speak.

In the elections that year, in the 54-seat assembly, INC won 24 seats only (down 6) with a vote share of 33.71%. The Janata Dal finished second with 11 seats, while Manipur Peoples' Party (MPP) – set up in 1968 by dissident Congressmen – won 9 seats. The Congress (Socialist) won 4 seats; the CPI won 3 seats, the Kuki National Party won 2 and even the National People's Party won 1 seat.

In a pretty interesting display of political imagination, a post-poll coalition was formed under the banner of the United Legislature Front (ULF, with 27 seats) that brought the Janata (11 seats), the MPP (9 seats), Congress(S) (4 seats), the KNP (2 seats) and the NPP (1). Rajkumar Ranbir Singh was elected as chief minister after great difficulty and complete chaos in the ULF meetings. At that stage results of 12 seats where polling was countermanded had not seen repolling yet. As the governor, Chintamani Panigrahi, did not invite the INC (the single largest party), Rajesh Pilot (Congress observer to the state) accused him of trampling upon democracy. Once repolling was done in the 12 seats, Janata and MPP were tied at 10 seats each. This led to further tussle over chief ministership which ended with Ranbir Singh agreeing to take Janata Dal leader Mayengbam Amutombi Singh as the deputy chief minister. Needless to say, this did not augur well for the government, which lasted only from February 1990 to January 1992 before multiple defections brought the government down and President's Rule was imposed.

Orissa

In 1990, the Congress government went to the polls riding a strong anti-incumbency in Orissa, as evident from the 1989 debacle in the general elections. In December 1989, the incumbent chief minister Janaki Ballav Patnaik was asked to resign after 9 years at the helm, and was replaced by Hemananda Biswal in December 1989.

In the elections held in March 1990, the Janata Dal won an emphatic victory, securing 123 seats (up 102) with a vote share of 53.69%. The INC was reduced to 10 seats (down 107) out of the assembly total of 147, with a vote share of 29.78%. The CPI came third with 5 seats, the BJP finished with 2, and CPI with 1 seat.

Biju Patnaik was sworn in as chief minister, which he served for the full term of the assembly (March 1990–March 1995).

Pondicherry

The Pondicherry assembly went to the polls in February 1990.

The Congress emerged as the single largest party with 11 seats (down 4), with a vote share of 25.04%; the DMK emerged as the second-largest with 9 seats (gaining 4), with 24.07% of the popular vote; the AIADMK won 3 seats, the Janata Dal 4 and the CPI 2. Since the DMK had an alliance with the Janata Dal and the CPI, they finished as the largest electoral bloc with 15 seats.

M.D.R. Ramachandran of the DMK was sworn in as the chief minister of Pondicherry for a second time. But the coalition did not last beyond a year (March 1990–March 1991), and Ramachandran had to step down as Pondicherry went for mid-term polls in 1991.

Rajasthan

A faction-ridden ridden Congress went to the assembly polls in Rajasthan in 1990, with the office of the chief minister being juggled between Hari Dev Joshi and Shiv Charan Mathur.

In the elections of 1990, this factionalism cost the Congress dearly. The BJP under Bhairon Singh Sekhawat romped home with 85 seats (up 46) with a vote share of 25.25%. The Congress, despite winning a larger share of the popular vote (33.64%) could manage only 50 seats (down 63); the Janata Dal finished with 55 seats (21.58% of the vote share).

Bhairon Singh Shekhawat was sworn in for his second term as chief minister, with support from the Janata Dal, led by Jagdeep Dhankhad (who later went on to become the vice president of India). Dhankhad eventually left the Janata Dal to join the INC towards the end of 1991. Shekhawat's government was dismissed and President's Rule was imposed after the 1992 demolition of the Babri Masjid.

1991

Assam

The rise of insurgency in Assam under the ULFA had resulted in the dissolution of the state assembly in 1989. The next elections to the assembly in the state were held in 1991.

In the 1991 elections, after a stint in the Opposition, the INC won a simple majority with 66 seats (up 41), and a vote share of 29.65%; the party that was ruling before President's Rule, the Asom Gana Parishad was reduced to 19 seats in what was its first election under its own banner. The BJP won 10 seats in what was its first proper venture in the state. The Notun Asom Gana Parishad (set up by Bhrigu Phukan and Dinesh Goswami, who had broken away from AGP to create the NAGP) won 5 seats. The CPI won 4 seats, the CPI(M) won 2 and the Janata Dal won 1 seat. The Autonomous State Demands Committee (ATDC, set up to demand a separate state for the Karbi Anglong district in Assam) finished with 4 seats.

One of the architects of the Assam Accord, Hiteshwar Saikia – a former chief minister and later Governor of Mizoram – was brought back and given charge of the Assam elections by Rajiv Gandhi. With the election won, Saikia was now sworn in for a second term as chief minister. During this second term (1991–1996), Saikia's tact and willingness to look away helped in the eventual reconciliation and rehabilitation of the ULFA insurgents into the political mainstream. Saikia died in office in April 1996, and was succeeded by Bumidhar Barman who led the party into the next general elections in May 1996.

Haryana

The government of Haryana was undergoing a period of baffling changes in the chief minister's office with multiple entries and exits of O.P. Chautala, who did not seem either willing or able to trust anyone in the CM's office, nor able to continue himself because of brushes with the law. The incumbent government finally went to the polls under Hukam Singh in 1991.

In the elections to the assembly that year, the INC returned to power with a simple majority, winning 51 of the 90 seats, and a vote share of 33.73%. The rump Janata Party remained in second place with 16 seats; the Haryana Vikas Party of Bansi Lal finished third with 12 seats and the Janata Dal fourth, reduced to just 3 seats. The BJP won 2 seats and the BSP won 1.

Bhajanlal Bishnoi was sworn in for his third term, which also turned out to be his only full term as the chief minister of the state.

Kerala

The state of Kerala, which had an LDF government installed from 1987, had seen the government do well in the 4 years it was in power, perform well in the Lok Sabha and municipal polls of 1990. Hence, confident by dint of its performance, the LDF government decided to go the assembly polls a year ahead of time.

The elections that were held in 1991 were won by the United Democratic Front, with 90 seats out of 140. The UDF constituted of the INC (55 seats), IUML (19 seats), Kerala Congress (Mani) (10 seats), Kerala Congress (Jacob) (1), RSP (2), Communist Marxist Party, Kerala (1).

The losing Left Democratic Front won 48 seats, of which the CPI(M) won 28 seats; the CPI 12; Congress (Socialist, SC Sinha faction) 2; Janata Dal 3; National Democratic Party 2.

The veteran Congress leader K. Karunakaran was sworn in for his fourth term in office. He ruled for four years (1991–95), but then had to step down owing to differences with the party central leadership. He was replaced by A.K. Anthony, who had by then returned after having once left the party and setting up his own party. Anthony led the party into the assembly elections of 1996, after a little more than a year (March 1995–May 1996) in office.

Pondicherry

Mid-term polls were held in Pondicherry in 1991 after the collapse of the Ramachandran government.

In the elections that were held in 1991, the INC contested in alliance with the AIADMK. While the INC won 15 of the 30 seats, with 30% of the vote share, the AIADMK won 6 seats (14.74% of the vote share) – hence commanding a two-thirds majority in the assembly. The DMK finished with 4 seats (despite having a vote share of 24.71%); its allies, the Janata Dal and the CPI, won a seat each.

V. Vaithilingam was sworn in as the chief minister of Pondicherry, in which capacity he served for the full term of the assembly (July 1991–May 1996).

Tamil Nadu

Dismissal of the DMK government in 1991 by New Delhi brought a new assembly election upon Tamil Nadu more than three years ahead of time. By then the three factions of the AIADMK – led by Jayalalithaa, Janaki Ramachandran and R.M. Veerappan – reunited, accepting Jayalalithaa's leadership. This this was followed by the restoration of the two leaves party symbol of AIADMK. The DMK on the other hand saw a split when Vijaya T. Rajendar broke away from the party to set up his own party Thyaga Marumalarchi Kazhagam (TMK), which began to eat into the DMK constituency. The year 1991 also saw the founding of the Pattali Makkal Katchi (PMK) – an outgrowth from the Vanniyar community, led by S. Ramadoss, which ate heavily into the DMK vote bank in northern Tamil Nadu. And finally, with election campaign going on in the month of May, Rajiv Gandhi was assassinated in Sriperumbudur by an LTTE assassination team.

The AIADMK formed an alliance with the INC and the Congress (Socialist, S.C. Sinha faction). The DMK contested in alliance with the CPI, CPI(M), Janata Dal and the debutant TMK.

With vote bank fragmentation, incumbency and finally sympathy for Rajiv Gandhi's assassination, the INC–AIADMK swept the assembly polls just the way they

Jayaram Jayalalithaa

had swept the Lok Sabha polls that were held simultaneously, winning 225 of the 234 seats in the assembly with 59.8% of the popular vote. The AIADMK won 164 seats (with a vote share of 44.4%); the INC won 60 seats (with 15.2% of the popular vote) and Congress (S) winning 1 seat. The DMK alliance managed to win only 7 seats (despite winning 30% of the popular vote), with the DMK and the TMK winning 2 seats each, while the CPI, CPI(M) and JD won 1 seat each. The PMK also managed to win 1 seat. This turned out to be DMK's worst performance since its emergence in 1957.

Jayaram Jayalalithaa was sworn in as the chief minister for her first term in office, which she held for the full term (June 1991–May 1996).

Uttar Pradesh

The Uttar Pradesh government of Mulayam Singh Yadav had been dismissed and President's Rule was imposed after Congress withdrew its support from the government. When the state went to the polls next, the decision to topple Mulayam proved counter-productive.

In the assembly elections of 1991, the BJP rode the wave of the Ram Janambhoomi movement to win a simple majority with 221 seats in an assembly of 425 seats, with a vote share of 31.45%; the Janata Dal, led by Mulayam Singh Yadav, finished second with 92 seats (18.84% vote share), while the INC came third with 42 seats (17.32% vote share); the rump Janata Party won 32 seats, while the BSP managed to win 11. The CPI won 4 seats, while the CPI(M), the Shoshit Dal and even the Shiv Sena (Pawan Pandey) won a seat each.

Riding the Ram Mandir-Babri Masjid wave, BJP nominated its OBC leader Kalyan Singh to the position of chief minister. Kalyan Singh's occupation of the chair helped the BJP to bring in karsevaks in their thousands in 1992, which led to the demolition of the mosque on 6 December 1992 by the karsevaks. Kalyan Singh was promptly dismissed along with the other BJP governments in the states where they were in power – another move that was to prove costly for the Congress as it would turn out.

1992

Punjab

The Punjab assembly was dissolved and President's Rule was imposed in 1987, less than 2 years since the last election. President's Rule remained in place for more than 4 years and 8 months, as India battled with one of its deadliest insurgency movements ever. By 1991, the insurgency appeared to have been contained, more through military subjugation than through gentle persuasion. In 1992, it was considered safe enough for the state to be returned to a representative form of government.

Although elections were indeed held, some taste of the rancour lingered, and became clear from the results as large numbers of voters seemed to stay away. The turn out was higher in the urban areas, averaging at 38.3%; in rural Punjab it averaged 15.1%; in the semi-urban areas the turn out stood at 26.5% and in the semi-rural constituencies the turn out stood at 25.3%.

The INC won 87 seats out of the 117 that were up for grabs, with a vote share of 43.83%; the BSP with 9 seats came second; the BJP with 6 seats came third. The CPI won 4 seats and the Akalis won only 3 seats; the CPI(M), the Janata Dal and the Indian Peoples' Front (a front organization of the CPI(ML) won 1 seat each.

Beant Singh was sworn in as the chief minister of Punjab in February 1992, and did his best to reduce the scale of insurgent activities in the state. Just as it seemed that his policies were working, he was assassinated in August 1995. Upon his death, the office was passed on to Harcharan Singh Brar (August 1995–November 1996). Brar resigned after factional struggle broke out in the wake of the party's poor performance in the 1996 general elections. The office was then passed on to Rajinder Kaur Bhattal (November 1996–February 1998) who led the state to the next elections.

1993

Delhi

In 1952, Delhi had a legislative assembly of its own, but was derecognized as a state in the States Reorganisation Act of 1956, and deprived of its legislative assembly. From the 1970s, demands were raised that Delhi should be given an assembly of its own, and should be recognized as a state yet again. In 1992, this demand was addressed as Delhi was reconstituted as the National Capital Territory, and furnished with its own legislative assembly by the sixty-ninth Amendment to the Constitution.

In the elections that were held in 1993 to elect Delhi's 70-seats strong assembly, the BJP emerged as the single largest party with 49 seats (47.82% of the popular vote share); the INC came second with 14 seats (with 34.48% of the popular vote), and 4 seats went to the Janata Dal. None of the other parties – BSP, CPI, CPI(M), Shiv Sena, AIFB – managed to win any seats.

An old RSS and Jan Sangh member who was instrumental in keeping the party relevant in Delhi's municipal politics for decades, Madan Lal Khurana, was sworn in as the chief minister of Delhi (December 1993–February 1996). Khurana had to step down in 1996, faced with allegations of corruption, and was succeeded by Sahib Singh Verma. S.S. Verma continued till

October 1998, when he left the office in favour of Sushma Swaraj faced with mounting onion prices. Swaraj led the BJP on to its next assembly polls after less than 2 months in office.

Himachal Pradesh

The Himachal assembly, which had been dissolved after the demolition of the Babri Masjid in 1992, went to the polls in 1993 after a short period of President's Rule.

In the elections that were held in the month of September, the INC won 52 of the 68 seats in the assembly, with a vote share of 48.82%; the BJP won only 8 seats despite receiving 36.14% of the popular vote; the CPI(M) won only 1 seat.

Virbhadra Singh was sworn in as the chief minister for the second term, which he served for the full term (March 1993–March 1998). J.P. Nadda became the leader of the Opposition.

Madhya Pradesh

The Madhya Pradesh assembly was among those that were dissolved in the wake of the demolition of the Babri Masjid in 1992. After a brief period under President's Rule, the state went to the polls to elect its new assembly in November 1993.

In the elections that were held to the 320-seat assembly, the INC finished with a clear majority, having won 174, winning (40.67% of the popular vote); the BJP finished second with 117 seats with 38.62% of the popular vote. The BSP won 11 seats with 7.05% of the popular vote; the Janata Dal won 4 seats, the CPI 2 seats, and the CPI(M), the Chattisgarh Mukti Morcha, the RPI won 1 seat each.

Digvijay Singh, a veteran Congressman from Indore, was sworn in for the first of his 2 consecutive terms as chief minister.

Meghalaya

The state of Meghalaya continued to have a fragmented assembly, always settling for multi-party post-poll coalitions. The elections of 1993 returned a similar verdict.

The INC emerged as the single largest party with 24 seats (up 2), with a vote share of 34.62%; the Hill People's Union came second with 11 seats (down 11); the Hill State People's Democratic Party won 8 seats; All Party Hill Leaders Conference (Armison Marak Group) managed to win 3 seats; the Meghalaya Progressive People's Party and Public Demands Implementation Convention managed to win 2 seats each. National parties like the BJP, Janata Dal, Janata Party, CPI and CPI(M) failed to win any seat.

At the stage of coalition building, for a change the INC took the initiative, and entered into a coalition with the APHLC (AM group) and a few independents to reach the figure of 30 seats. Salseng C Marak of the INC was thus sworn in as the chief minister, in which capacity he served for the full term of the assembly (1993–1998).

Mizoram

Mizoram had its last assembly elections in 1989 and hence did not have its election due before 1994. However, that year being the centenary year of the introduction of the Gospel into Mizoram a large number of celebrations were scheduled to mark the centenary. Hence elections were brought forward to 1993 instead.

In the elections held in November 1993, the INC emerged as the largest party in the 40-seat assembly, winning 16 seats, with a vote share of 33.10%; the Mizo National Front led by Pu Laldenga won only 14 seats albeit it won the larger share of the popular vote (40.41%); the BJP failed to win any seats.

Pu Lalthanhawla was sworn in as the chief minister for his third term (1993–98).

Nagaland

By the 1990s, Nagaland was beginning to witness a similar kind of stability as Mizoram.

In the assembly elections of 1993, the INC held on to 35 seats (down 1) out of the 60 seats of the assembly; the Naga People's Front won 17 seats (32.82% of the popular vote); while the Democratic Labour party won 1 seat; the BJP failed to win any seats.

Former Congress chief minister, S.C. Jamir, was sworn in as chief minister for the fourth time, in which office he managed to stay for the first full term (1993–98).

Rajasthan

Rajasthan was another of those states where the assembly was dissolved years ahead of schedule in the aftermath of the destruction of the Babri Masjid.

When the elections were held for the 199-seat strong assembly, the BJP came back to power albeit with a somewhat reduced strength, winning 95 seats with a vote share 38.6%. The INC came second with 76 seats on a vote share of 38.27% – beginning an era of a two-party political landscape in the state. The Janata Dal was reduced to 6 seats and the CPI(M) to only 1.

Bhairon Singh Shekhawat, whose government was toppled in 1992, returned to power for a full term (1993–98).

Tripura

Tripura came out of a brief period of President's Rule to head to the polls in February 1993.

In the elections that were held to the 60-seat Tripura assembly, the CPI(M) won 44 seats with a popular vote share of 44.78%; INC came second with 10 seats (32.73% of the popular vote); the RSP managed to win only 2 seats; the Janata Dal, AIFB and TUJS won 1 seat each; the CPI, BJP and Amra Bangali failed to win any seats at all.

Dasarath Deb was sworn in as the chief minister of the CPI(M) government, and remained in office for the full term of the assembly (1993–98).

Uttar Pradesh

The Uttar Pradesh assembly was one of those that were dissolved in the aftermath of the demolition of the Babri Masjid in December 1992. The state went to the polls for its 425-seat assembly in 1993 after a brief period of President's Rule.

In the elections held that year, the BJP remained the single largest party in the assembly, albeit with a reduced strength of 177 seats, with a vote share of 33.3%. The second slot was taken by the newly-founded Samajwadi Party with 109 seats, with 17.94% and the BSP came third with 67 seats (up 55), with a vote share of 11.12%. The INC won 28 seats and the rump Janata Dal won 27; the CPI won 3 seats, the CPI(M), the Janata Party and the Uttar Pradesh Kranti Dal won 1 seat each.

The Samajwadi Party was set up by Mulayam Singh Yadav and Beni Prasad Verma in 1992, just months before the Babri Masjid demolition, in course of the dismemberment of the Janata Dal. The SP (claiming to represent the OBC) entered into a post-poll alliance with the BSP (claiming to represent the Dalit constituency) to deny the (upper-caste dominated) BJP the opportunity to form a the government. After 2 rocky years, Mayawati pulled out from the coalition, bringing down Mulayam Singh Yadav in June 1995. She sought, and received, support from the BJP to form the government with herself as the chief minister. But in October 1995, the BJP withdrew support from the BSP-led government, and President's Rule was imposed in Uttar Pradesh yet again.

1994

Andhra Pradesh

Elections were held for the 294-seat Andhra Pradesh assembly after 5 years of Congress rule.

In the elections that were held in December 1994, the Telegu Desam party bounced back with 216 seats (up 142), a 44.14% of the popular vote. The INC, despite winning 33.85% of the popular vote, did miserably winning only 26 seats (down 155); the CPI won 19 seats, the CPI(M) 15; the BJP won 3 seats, the Majlis Bachao Tehrik 2 seats and the AIMIM won 1 – the Charminar seat returning Asaduddin Owaisi for the first time.

Since the TDP contested in alliance with the CPI and CPI(M), and roped in some other independents, the alliance had 269 seats under its belt (with figures of the TDP itself rising to 226). N.T. Rama Rao was thus sworn in for his third term in December 1994. This term however proved brief because of a revolt that developed within the party over the role beginning to be played by Rama Rao's second wife Lakshmi Parvathi, in the Rao household, the party and the government. This made a dominant section of the party to revolt in August 1995, under his son-in-law N. Chandrababu Naidu who forced Rama Rao to step down in

Asaduddin Owaisi

September 1995. Rama Rao vowed revenge, comparing himself with Mughal Emperor Shah Jahan, but did not last long after this – dying of a heart attack in January 1996. Chandrababu Naidu was sworn in at the helm of the TDP government in September 1995, and remained in office till the end of the term in 1999.

Goa

After considerable turmoil within the INC on account of a tussle between Pratapsingh Rane, Wilfred de Souza and Ravi Naik (all ex-MAG), the assembly elections of 1994, it was hoped would stabilize the political landscape in Goa. Unfortunately, the verdict of the 1994 elections was even less decisive than the last one had been.

The INC emerged the largest party, albeit weakened, winning 18 seats (down 2), with a vote share of 37.54%. The MAG came second with 12 seats (down 6) and a vote share of 22.24%; the BJP entered the assembly with 4 seats (up 4) and a vote share of 9.05%. Former chief minister Churchill Alemao's United Goans Democratic Party won 3 seats and 8.3% of the popular vote. None of the other parties – CPI, CPI(M), Shiv Sena, BSP, Janata Party, Samajwadi Party – managed to win any seat.

Pratapsingh Rane was sworn in yet again, at the head of a minority government, and successfully ran the government from December 1994 to July 1998. In 1998, Wilfred de Souza broke away from the INC with the entire Youth Congress and National Students Union of India (Goa chapter), and set up the Goa Rajiv Congress Party, entered into a coalition with the BJP and the MAG, and brought the Rane government down. De Souza was sworn in as the chief minister in July 1998, but the government collapsed in November 1998. The INC staked its claim to form yet another minority government, which was sworn in under Luizinho Faleiro, who held office for 77 days during November

1998–February 1999, before the assembly was dissolved and Goa went to the polls.

Karnataka

The INC government in Karnataka was severely hobbled by factionalism, as in many other states, and by the time the state went to the polls in 1994, Congress defeat in the elections was virtually guaranteed.

In the elections that were held to the 224-seat strong assembly, the Janata Dal won a clear victory with 115 seats (up 77) and a vote share of 33.54%. The BJP became the second-largest party with 40 seats (up 36) and a vote share of 16.99%; the INC came third with 34 seats (down 143), and vote share of 26.95%. The Karnataka Congress Party, set up in 1994 by former Congress chief minister, S. Bangarappa, who was expelled from the Congress in 1993 finished with 10 seats. The BSP, CPI(M), AIADMK, Karnataka Rajya Raitha Paksha and three other local parties won 1 seat each.

Haradhanahalli Doddegowda Deve Gowda, who began his political career in the Congress, then moved to the Congress(O), next to the Janata Party and moved on to the Janata Dal, was sworn in as the chief minister of Karnataka at the head of the Janata Dal government. He remained chief minister during December 1994–May 1996, after which he stepped down to become the prime minister of the United Front government. Upon Deve Gowda's resignation, Jayadevappa Halappa Patel was sworn in as the chief minister, who continued for the rest of the assembly term (May 1996–October 1999).

Sikkim

The Sikkim assembly, after having given a sweeping victory to Nar Bahadur Bhandari and his SSP – 32 seats in a 32-seat assembly – witnessed the inevitable anti-incumbency kick in.

In the assembly election of 1994, the newly-created Sikkim Democratic Front won 19 seats, with 42% of the popular vote, thus obtaining a simple majority in the assembly. The outgoing SSP was reduced to 10 seats (down 22) with a vote share of 35.08%. The INC managed to win 2 seats (up 2), whereas the debutant BJP, RSP and CPI(M) failed to win any seat at all.

Pavan Chamling, the architect of the SDF, was sworn in as the chief minister for the first of his 5 straight full terms in office.

1995

Arunachal Pradesh

The Arunachal Pradesh assembly had stabilized in course of the 1990s, overcoming the initial uncertainties of the exercise of franchise. That element of stability continued into the election of 1995.

In the 60-seat assembly of Arunachal, the INC finished with a simple majority with 43 seats (up 6), on a vote share of 50.50%; the Janata Dal managed to win 3 seats, the Janata Party won 2 seats, and independent candidates finished with a tally of 12 seats. The BJP fielded 15 candidates to draw a blank, with 11 candidates forfeiting their deposits.

Gegong Apang, the incumbent chief minister, was sworn back in for his fourth term (1995–1999). However, he could not complete the full term because of a split in the party in 1999, led by Mukut Mithi, who set up his own party. Arunachal Congress (Mithi). Losing the consequent vote of confidence, Apang stepped down and Arunachal Pradesh went for the polls in 1999.

Bihar

Coming to the office of the chief minister first at the head of a minority government with outside support, and then

Nitish Kumar

manipulating the political situation in order to stabilize the ministry, Lalu Prasad Yadav had by and large consolidated himself in the political landscape of Bihar. The assembly elections of 1995 simply reinforced this electorally as well, amidst considerable disquiet over electoral malpractice engaged in presumably by all sides, but most emphatically by Yadav.

In the 324-seat assembly of Bihar, the Janata Dal finished with a simple majority of 167 seats (up 45) with a vote share of 28%. The BJP emerged as the second-largest party with 41 seats (and a vote share of 13%); the INC finished third with 29 seats (and a vote share of 16.3%) and the CPI came fourth with 26 seats. Jharkhand Mukti Morcha, now led by Shibu Soren, won 10 seats; the Samata Party (which was set up in 1994 by George Fernandes and Nitish Kumar, breaking away from the Lalu-dominated Janata Dal, citing its casteist disposition) won 7 seats; the CPI(ML) won 6 seats while the CPI(M) managed only 2 seats. The JMM (Marandi) won 3 seats, and the SP, BSP and Jharkhand People's Party won 2 seats each.

Lalu was sworn in for the second term which came to an abrupt end in 1997, when he was mired in corruption allegations in connection with the fodder scam. Sentenced to a jail term, he vacated his office in favour of his wife, Rabri Devi who had no connection with politics till then. Rabri Devi remained in office from July 1997 to February 1999, before the assembly was dissolved and President's Rule was imposed.

Gujarat

Gujarat had already seen the beginning of INC's decline in 1990; in 1995, it witnessed the rise of BJP to political power in the state that it was to enjoy for the next 3 decades.

In the election that was held for the 182 seats of the Gujarat assembly in 1995, the BJP won 121 seats (up 54) with a vote share of 42.51%; the INC came second with 45 seats (up 12) and a vote share of 32.86%. Independents took 18 seats. The consolidation of votes was so fabulous that no other party – Janata Party, CPI, CPI(M), SP, BSP, Shiv Sena, RSP – was able to win a single seat, nor were they able, put together, to poll even a million votes among the 18 million that were cast.

Keshubhai Patel, a lifelong RSS operative and a founder-member of the Jan Sangh, and the deputy chief minister of the outgoing government, was sworn in as the chief minister. However, he stepped down after 7 months when his party colleague Shankarsinh Vaghela revolted against Patel. For the time being Suresh Mehta was sworn in as the pro tem chief minister. But, unrelenting, Vaghela split from the BJP in Gujarat and set up his own Rashtriya Janata Party (RJP) and staked claim to form a minority government with 46 MLAs, with Congress's support (44 MLAs) from the outside in October 1996. Vaghela remained in power from October 1996 to October 1997 before he stepped down in the face of threats by the Congress, and was replaced by Dilip Ramanbhai Parikh of the RJP as the compromise candidate. With the same political instability continuing, Parikh resigned in January 1998 but remained in a caretaker capacity till the elections were held in the month of March 1998.

Two years later, Congress withdrew its support for the RJP government, and Gujarat went to assembly polls yet again in 1998.

Maharashtra

Maharashtra is a patent case where Congress decline was more a product of its internal feuds than any opposition ascendancy.

In the 1995 assembly election, the INC emerged as the single largest party with 80 seats (down 61) in the 288-seat assembly, with 31% of the popular vote. In the second place emerged Shiv Sena with 73 seats (up 21) with a vote share of 16.39%; the BJP finished third with 65 seats (and a vote share of 12.8%). The Janata Dal won 11 seats; PWPI won 6 seats; the CPI(M) and the Samajwadi Party won 2 seats each. A number of national and regional parties drew a blank. Since the Shiv Sena and the BJP had contested the polls in alliance, the 138 seats won between the 2 of them brought them to power, at the head of the minority government.

Manohar Joshi of the Shiv Sena was sworn in as the chief minister of Maharashtra, in which capacity he served till February 1999, when a housing scam (where the beneficiaries were associated with his son-in-law) forced his resignation. He was succeeded by Narayan Rane, who held the office between February and October 1999, when Maharashtra went to the polls again.

Manipur

Even as Congress began to lose its hold on most states of northern India, in the North-East INC became associated with a kind of stability – Manipur being a good example.

In the elections of 1995, the INC under Reishang Keishing, emerged as the single largest party with 22 out of the 60 seats of the assembly, with 28.08% of the popular vote; the Manipur People's Party finished a close second with 18 seats, with 23.2% of the popular vote. The Janata Dal won 7 seats. The Samata Party, the CPI, the National People's Party and the Federal Party of Manipur won 2 seats each; the BJP and the Congress (Socialist) won 1 seat each.

Reishang Keishing was sworn back in at the head of a minority government with a strength of 27 seats. However, Reishang Keishing held the office till December 1997, and after he stepped down in the face of factional struggle, Wahengbam Nipamach

Singh – who quit as the head of Manipur State Congress party, (which split from the INC) led to the formation of a minority government, which remained in office between 1997 to 2000.

Orissa

Orissa was a state where the INC remained a strong force even as it weakened elsewhere in North India.

In the elections held in 1995, Congress won 80 of the 147 seats in the assembly (up 70) with a vote share of 39.08%; the Janata Dal won 46 seats (down 77), with a vote share of 35.41%; the BJP finished third with 9 seats (up 7) with 7.88% of the popular vote. The JMM, which was new to the political landscape of the state won 4 seats; the CPI and the Jharkhand People's Party won 1 seat each.

Janaki Ballabh Patnaik was sworn in as the chief minister yet again. After 4 years, in February 1999, when the Australian Missionary, Graham Stewart Steines, and his 2 young sons were burnt alive by a gang of right-wing thugs led by an RSS activist, Dara Singh, J.B. Patnaik was summoned to Delhi and summarily asked by Congress President Sonia Gandhi to assume moral responsibility and resign. After Patnaik stepped down, he was succeeded by Giridhar Gomang, an MP at that point, who served as the chief minister from February to December 1999. Curiously, 2 months later, when the 13-month-old Vajpayee government was faced with a no-confidence motion, Gomang was flown back to the Parliament, where he was yet to vacate his seat, to vote against the government. It is believed that had he not voted, the confidence motion would have come to a tie, in which the casting vote by T.M.C. Balayogi, the Speaker of the Lok Sabha, may have saved the Vajpayee government. It is quite interesting that parliamentary speakers are always assumed to be partisan, and not neutral, even after they enter the office of the speaker – and no one assumes otherwise.

1996

Assam

Hiteshwar Saikia, the incumbent chief minister of Assam who helped stem the tide of ULFA insurgency during the 1990s, suddenly died a few days before the 1996 assembly elections, and was succeeded by Bhumidhar Barman. This proved to be a body blow to the Congress. On the other hand, the faction of the AGP led by Bhrigu Phukan, that had broken away in 1993, merged back with the main party. Further, the AGP entered into an alliance with the CPI, CPI(M), Autonomous States Demand Committee (front organization of the CPI (ML) and United Minorities Front of Assam (UMFA, founded by Kalipada Sen). This strengthened the hand of the AGP significantly.

In the elections that were held in 1996, votes were cast for 122 of the 126 constituencies, with 4 more constituencies voting a few months later. The AGP finished as the single largest party with 59 seats, (29.7% of the popular vote). The INC, despite winning a larger share of the vote (30.56%), won only 34 seats (down 32). The ASDC won 5 seats, the CPI 3, the CPI(M) and the UMFA won 2 seats each – hence giving the AGP alliance 71 seats, and thus a clear majority in the assembly. The BJP won 4 seats and the Congress (Tiwari) faction managed to win 2 seats.

Prafulla Mahanta was sworn in as the chief minister, in which capacity he served for the full term of the assembly (1996–2001). Despite corruption allegations and a highly controversial counter-insurgency strategy of knocking out ULFA militants using those who had already surrendered (hence SULFA), Mahanta went on to finish his full term as the chief minister.

Haryana

The Congress succumbed to forces riding anti-incumbency quite predictably after 5 years at the helm in 1996. The Congress split

3 ways with Bansi Lal taking the largest chunk into his Haryana Vikas Party; a splinter faction went with the Indira Congress (Tiwari) group, while a rump remained with the INC.

In the elections held that year, the Haryana Vikas Party, led by Bansi Lal emerged as the single largest party with 33 seats (22.7% of the vote share) with his agenda of prohibition; the Samta Party (led by Devi Lal and Chautala) came up with a tally of 24 seats (20.6% of the vote share) and the BJP won 11 seats (8.9% of the vote share). The INC won 9 seats and the Indira Congress (Tiwari) won 3 seats, with 10 seats being taken by independent candidates.

Bansi Lal was sworn in as the chief minister yet again, this time at the head of a coalition with the BJP and 6 independents. He remained in office for 3 years (1996–99), before the BJP withdrew its support to the government. Thereupon, Om Prakash Chautala, who contested the elections on behalf of the Samta Party, but then reinvented the state unit of the party as the Indian National Lok Dal, staked its claim to form the government, with a breakaway group of MLAs from the Congress and outside support of the BJP. Chautala was sworn in as the chief minister in July 1999, and remained in office till the end of the assembly term in March 2000.

Jammu and Kashmir

Jammu and Kashmir had descended into a maelstrom of violence and militancy in the late 1980s, and after the resignation of Farooq Abdullah in 1989, President's Rule was imposed in the state which lasted for over 6 years. When the 1996 general elections were held, JKNC had boycotted the polls, demanding that President's Rule be lifted. Once the United Front government came to office, PM Deve Gowda promised Abdullah that J&K will be accorded 'maximum autonomy'. It was only on those terms that JKNC agreed to contest the assembly polls in 1996.

In the 87 seats of the J&K assembly that went to the polls, JKNC emerged as the largest party with 57 seats (up 17) with 34.78% of the vote share. The BJP shot up to the second slot with 8 seats (12.13% of the vote share) and the INC came third with 7 seats (down 19) with 20% of the vote share. The Janata Dal finished with 5 seats, the BSP won 4, while the Jammu and Kashmir Awami League (set up in 1995, comprising different anti-insurgent groups), J&K National Panther's Party; CPI(M) and Congress (Tiwari) won 1 seat each.

In a noticeable departure from most of the previous elections, seats in the Kashmir Valley were not won by the JKNC alone, INC and Janata Dal managed to win some. Seats in the Jammu region were won by parties from all shades. In other words, polarization along communitarian lines was not as complete as in some of the earlier elections. Farooq Abdullah was sworn in as the chief minister for what came to be his first (and only) full term in that office (1996–2002).

Kerala

By the 1990s, Kerala had developed a pattern of alternating governments in power. 1996 did not prove any different from this.

In the elections that were held in 1996, the outgoing UDF coalition won 59 seats (down 31), of which INC won 37 seats and the IUML won 13; Kerala Congress won 6 seats, with 3 others coming from the independents. By contrast the LDF coalition won 80 seats (up 32), of which the CPI(M) won 40 seats, the CPI won 18, Kerala Congress (Mani) won 5, Janata Dal won 4 seats; Indian Congress (Socialist) won 3 seats; RSP won 5; Kerala Congress (Joseph) won 2 and Kerala Congress (B) won 1 seat, along with some independent candidates.

The LDF candidate earmarked for the chief minister's post, V.S. Achuthanandan, lost his seat of Mararikulam, hence E.K. Nayanar was sworn in for yet another term, and was later elected through a bypoll. Nayanar held the position for the full assembly term (May 1996–May 2001).

Pondicherry

Pondicherry had come to enjoy some degree of stability under the Vaithlingam government in the early 1990s, but INC never really enjoyed the kind of dominance in Pondicherry the way it did in many other smaller states and Union Territories.

In the 1996 assembly elections, the INC remained the single largest party with 9 (down 6) out of the 30 seats, and a vote share of 25.34%. The DMK won 7 seats (up 3), with 22.90% of the popular vote, and the Tamil Maanila Congress won 5 seats (with 9.23% of the vote share), while the AIADMK won 3 seats. The CPI won 2 seats, while the PMK and the Janata Dal won 1 seat each.

R.V. Janakiraman was sworn in as the head of the coalition government of the DMK and the TMC. Janakiraman remained in office from May 1996 to March 2000. When the coalition government collapsed as a result of the TMC pulling out of the coalition, a Congress-led government was formed under the Congress leader P. Shanmugam (March 2000–October 2001) with the Tamil Maanila Congress now joining in a coalition with them.

Tamil Nadu

The political landscape in Tamil Nadu proved quite eventful since the ascent of Jayalalithaa-led AIADMK to political power.

The DMK, out of power, was beset with political problems, which eventually led to the expulsion of a leader of the second tier of the party, Vaiyapuri Gopalsamy aka Vaiko, in 1993. Vaiko went on to float his own party in 1994, the Marumalarchi Dravida Munnetra Kazhagam (MDMK).

In the meantime, the AIADMK government was beset with all sorts of corruption scandals and allegations of arrogance and high-handedness, and had become extremely unpopular by the end its assembly term. Thus, when the INC High Command decided to enter into electoral alignment with AIADMK, despite the advice of the state unit to the contrary, a large section of the state unit of INC broke away to set up the Tamil Maanila Congress under G.K. Moopanar and P. Chidambaram.

In 1996, when Tamil Nadu went to the polls, the INC contested it in coalition with the AIADMK, the two Muslim Leagues, and a few other parties; the TMC aligned with the DMK, AIFB and Indian National League. The MDMK aligned with the CPI(M), Janata Dal and Samajwadi Janata Party (led by Chandrasekhar). Congress (Tiwari) and PMK had initially thought of aligning with DMK, but finally settled for alignment among themselves. Subramaniam Swamy's Janata Party went with caste organization Devendra Kula Vellar Sangam. BJP went by itself.

In the 234-seat assembly, DMK had a landslide of a victory, winning 173 seats with a vote share of 42.07%; the TMC (M) won 39 seats with 9.3% of the popular vote; along with its other smaller allies, the alliance tally stood at 221 (up 219). The AIADMK on the other hand received a massive drubbing, and was reduced to 4 seats (albeit with 21.47% of vote share), while its ally the INC drew a blank. The CPI won 8 seats, the PMK won 4; the CPI(M), Janta Dal, Janata Party, BJP and Forward Bloc got 1 seat each. Jayalalithaa lost her own seat, as did virtually her entire cabinet.

M. Karunanidhi was sworn in yet again as the chief minister for the full term of the assembly (May 1996–May 2001).

Uttar Pradesh

Uttar Pradesh continued with its period of political instability in the 1996 assembly election with a badly fragmented political landscape.

The BJP remained the single largest party with 174 of the 425 seats, and a vote share of 32.52%. The SP held its ground with 110 seats (and a vote share of 21.8%); the BSP finished with 67 seats (19.64%); the INC won 33 (with a vote share of 8.35%). The Bharatiya Kisan Kamgar Party, (floated by Ajit Singh, the son of Charan Singh) won 8 seats; the Janata Dal won 7 seats, the CPI(M) and Congress (Tiwari) won 4 seats each; the Samta Party won 2, and the CPI and the Samajwadi Janata Party (led by Chandrasekhar) won 1 seat each.

In the totally hung assembly, President's Rule remained in force before Mayawati staked claim for government formation in March 1997 in a power-sharing arrangement of 6 months each with the BJP. Her term ended in September 1997, bringing Kalyan Singh to power. Kalyan Singh discontinued schemes, favouring Dalits, launched by Mayawati, prompting the latter to withdraw support from the government. Kalyan Singh, however, survived with the support from a breakaway faction of the INC, the Akhil Bharatiya Loktantrik Congress. Singh was briefly dismissed in February 1998 by Governor Ramesh Bhandari after ABLC withdrew its support, but was reinstated 2 days later. However, Singh was finally toppled in November 1999 in the face of a revolt by 36 BJP MLAs. He was succeeded by Ram Prakash Gupta (November 1999–October 2000) as the chief minister who then made way for Rajnath Singh (October 2000–March 2002).

West Bengal

Compared to the rest of India, West Bengal seemed to enjoy a unique kind of political stability. The Opposition Congress was in disarray, with the firebrand leader Mamata Banerjee at loggerheads with the state unit president Somen Mitra. As a result, the Left Front, with its consolidated vote bank, romped home with another term albeit with a reduced margin.

In the elections that were held in 1996, the Left Front won 203 out of the 294 seats. Of this, the CPI(M) alone won 153 seats (vote share of 37.16); the AIFB won 21 seats; the RSP won 18; the CPI won 6 and the Marxist Forward Bloc and the DSP won 2 seats each, while Biplobi Bangla Congress won 1 seat. The INC won 82 seats (albeit with a vote share of 39.48); while the Gorkha National Liberation Front won 3 seats, and the BJP drew a blank.

Jyoti Basu was sworn back in for a fifth straight term as the chief minister. Despite the overwhelming majority won by the Left Front, there was growing disaffection with the government. Loss of all seats in metropolitan Calcutta and most of the industrial towns aside, 9 sitting cabinet ministers failed to get re-elected. Disaffection within the CPI(M) and a revolt by the home minister, Buddhadeb Bhattacharjee saw to his being appointed as deputy chief minister in 1999, and then his elevation to the position of the chief minister after Jyoti Basu was persuaded to step down in November 2000 following 23 years in power – a record at that time (bested only by Pavan Chamling and Navin Patnaik since then.)

1997

Punjab

By the mid-1990s, the militancy that had come to characterize Punjab had been almost snuffed out, and normalcy returned to the political landscape of the state. In the first elections held under such normal circumstances, the Congress received a thorough drubbing.

In the elections of 1997, the SAD and its ally, the BJP, won 93 seats out of the total 117 in the assembly. Of this, the SAD won 75 seats (a vote share of 37.64%) and the BJP 18 (vote share of 8.33%); INC was reduced to 14 seats (albeit with a vote share of 26.38); the CPI won 2 seats and the BSP and the Akali Dal (Mann) won 1 seat each.

Parkash Singh Badal was sworn in as the chief minister of the SAD-BJP coalition government, which went on to last the full term (February 1997–February 2002). This alliance at the state level proved to be one of the two most durable alliances of the BJP, both provincially, and nationally, ending its status of a political pariah since 1992.

1998

Delhi

Sheila Dikshit

Delhi assembly had seen some turmoil, shuffling the office of the chief minister between three BJP functionaries – Madan Lal Khurana, Sahib Singh Verma and Sushma Swaraj. The party paid the price for this in 1998.

In the elections held that year, the INC registered an emphatic victory, winning 52 of the 70 seats in the Delhi assembly, with a vote share of 47.75%. The BJP was reduced to the second spot with 15 seats (34.02% of the popular vote). The Janata Dal won only 1 seat.

Sheila Dikshit, former Union minister under Rajiv Gandhi, was sworn in as the chief minister, in which capacity she served till the end of the term.

Gujarat

The political instability seen in Gujarat was partly because of rifts within the BJP and partly because of Congress meddling in an attempt to somehow hold on to political power in the state. The assembly became unworkable by January 1998, and thus, Gujarat went to the polls nearly 2 years ahead of schedule.

In the elections held that year, the BJP managed to win 117 seats (down 4) out of the 182 seats of the assembly, on the strength of 44.71% of the popular vote. The INC remained a distant second with 53 seats with a vote share of 34.85%. The All India Rashtriya Janata Party, the breakaway faction of the BJP, led by Shankar Singh Baghela, managed to win 4 seats (with a vote share of 11.68%) and the Janata Party also finished with 4 seats.

Keshubhai Patel was sworn back in as the chief minister in March 1998, and remained in office till October 2001, when he stepped down because of failing health, but also because of growing allegations of corruption, abuse of power and bad government. The BJP central leadership decided to appoint a fresh face, untainted by allegations of any kind of association with the previous government – thus Narendra Modi was sworn in as the chief minister of Gujarat. Shortly after the appointment, in February 2002, Gujarat was consumed by anti-Muslim mass violence in the wake of an act of arson in a railway compartment full of karsevaks in the station at Godhra. With thousands dead, calls were raised for the immediate removal of Modi from power in Gujarat by BJP's allies in the Union government – especially the Telugu Desam and the DMK. Publicly reprimanded by no less than the prime minister A.B. Vajpayee himself, Modi himself put in his resignation in April 2002, but the BJP central leadership (at the behest of Advani) had him withdraw it. Thereupon, Modi sought a fresh mandate and brought elections forward to December 2002, going against the advice of the Election Commission, who believed conditions were not right as many displaced by the anti-Muslim carnage still remained displaced.

Himachal Pradesh

After 5 years under Virbhadra Singh's Congress rule, Himachal Pradesh went back to the polls in 1998. The political landscape saw the brief spurt of a new political party, the Himachal Vikas Congress, a party floated by former Union minister from the Congress, Sukh Ram. Charged with receiving kickbacks from the telecom scam, Sukh Ram was expelled by the Congress because he was becoming an easy target of the BJP. He ended up costing the INC its power in the state.

In the elections that were held that year, the INC and the BJP came to a tie. While the INC won 31 seats (down 21) out of 68, with a vote share of 43.50%, the BJP won 31 seats (up 23) with a vote share of 39.01%. The Himachal Vikas Congress won 5 seats with 9.62% of the vote share and emerged as the deciding factor in the assembly.

The BJP swiftly entered into negotiations with the HVC, and formed the government under Prem Kumar Dhumal who served as the chief minister from March 1998–March 2003.

Madhya Pradesh

The 1998 elections were the last elections before the creation of Chhattisgarh, hence the last in which the MP assembly had 320 seats.

In the elections of 1998, the INC by and large held on to its position, winning 172 seats (down 2), with a vote share of 40.59%. The BJP won only 119 seats (up 2) but managed to secure 39.28% - only about 1% votes behind the INC. The BSP held on to its 11 seats as before; the Samajvadi party won 4 seats; the Janata Dal, the RPI and Gondvana Ganatantra Party won 1 seat each.

Digvijay Singh was sworn in for his second term, which he served as chief minister for the full term of the assembly (1998–2003).

The 1998 election clearly showed that while the BJP was gaining ground by consolidating all the anti-Congress votes, the Congress was losing its voters among the Dalits, OBCs and tribal communities quite consistently. It was partly to offset the loss of support among the tribal communities of the region that Congress eventually decided to not oppose the creation of the state of Chhattisgarh, made up mostly of the tribal regions to the east of Madhya Pradesh, and to work out so that Congress leadership in the new state ended up with Ajit Jogi, a major critic of Digvijay Singh.

Chhattisgarh was detached from Madhya Pradesh under the Madhya Pradesh Reorganisation Act of 2001, and the new state was assigned 90 seats, while the state of Madhya Pradesh was left with 230 seats, for which it went to polls in 2003.

Meghalaya

The landscape of Meghalayan politics had been changing almost continually, facilitating the rise of the Congress by bringing about mergers with regional political players. In 1997, a major consolidation of the non-Congress components of Meghalayan politics came about when the Hill People's Union, some members of the Hill State People's Democratic Party and Public Demands Implementation Convention merged to create the United Democratic Party.

In the elections that followed, the INC emerged as the single largest party with 25 (up 1) out of the 60 seats of the assembly, with a vote share of 35.03%. The debutant UDP won 20 seats, with 26.99% of the vote share. A new party, People's Democratic Movement managed to win 3 seats, as did the rump HSPDP and the BJP. The Garo National Council, demanding a separate state of Garoland won 1 seat. 16 of the 26 ministers lost their seats, and the incumbent chief minister himself barely scraped through by a margin of 285 seats.

The elections having thrown up a hung assembly, S.C. Marak staked his claim for government formation, believing INC had the support of 3 independents and 3 members of HSPDP. Within 11 days of the swearing in, however, Marak realized that his government would not win the floor test in the assembly, because only 5 independents and 3 MLAs of the PDM were actually found committing themselves. This was believed to be partly the result of a threat issued from a Khasi insurgent group, Hynniewtrep National Liberation Council (HNLC), that threatened anyone cooperating with the continuation of Garo domination of Meghalayan politics. Thus, Marak (who, like Sangma, was a Garo), unable to reach out to MLAs with offers of cabinet berths, stepped down in favour of his long-time (Khasi) rival B.B. Lyngdoh who was sworn in as chief minister in March 1998. As in the past, B.B. Lyngdoh, this time at the head of the UDP, proved quite deft in negotiating a post-poll coalition, seeking (and receiving) support of the 3 BJP and 3 rump HSPDP MLAs, the lone GNC MLA, plus 4 of the independents – with the same offer as Marak (cabinet berths, but without any threat from the HNLC).

However, by July 1998, the UDP-led coalition broke down as the chief minister came under relentless pressure for cabinet berths for virtually all the MLAs. On the morning of 27 July 1998, Lyngdoh resigned as chief minister only to come back in the evening at the head of a UDP-Congress coalition under a power-sharing arrangement in which the UDP led the government in the first half of the coalition term, and Congress was to take the reins in the second where the order of succession was decided by the toss of a coin. However, by October 1998, Lyngdoh changed horses midstream and returned UDP to the original coalition with the BJP and PDM. This was partly because of difficulties within the Congress. In June 1999, these difficulties led Purna Ajitok Sangma to break away from the Congress with 9 MLAs, creating the Nationalist Congress Party, and then the

NCP joined the ruling coalition. Lyngdoh remained the chief minister of this government till March 2000, when faced with major corruption allegations, he stepped aside in favour of Evansius Kek Mawlong of the UDF. The Mawlong government worked from March 2000 to December 2001, when it collapsed because some MLAs supporting it pulled out after Mawlong was accused to have made a packet in the construction of the Meghalaya House in Kolkata. At this point, the INC and NCP came together to form a coalition government under the independent MLA, Flinder Anderson Khonglam, who was sworn in as the chief minister and remained in office for the rest of the assembly term (December 2001–March 2003).

Mizoram

Mizoram had seen Congress rule for a steady 3 terms since the conclusion of the Mizoram Peace Accord under Pu Lalthanhawla. This changed finally in 1998.

In the elections held that year, even though the INC won the popular vote by securing a vote share of 29.77%, it was reduced to only 6 seats (down 10) in the 40-seat assembly. The Mizo National Front emerged as the single largest party with 21 seats (with a vote share of 24.99%), followed by Mizoram People's Conference (of Brig. T. Sailo) which won 12 seats with a vote share of 20.44%). The BJP, Samta Party, Lokshakti Party, Janta Dal and RJD – all failed to win any seats.

One-time secessionists, MNF, under Laldenga had been one of the signatories of the Mizo Accord, but could hold power only briefly, after which he served as the Opposition. By 1998, Laldenga was dead and had been succeeded by Zoramthanga (former finance minister of Mizoram). Thus, it was Zormathanga that was sworn in as chief minister of Mizoram, and remained so for the full term of the assembly (1998–2003).

Nagaland

The 1990s constituted a kind of a milestone for the Naga conflict. A large section of the Naga people had initially sought to remain outside the Indian union, and under the leadership of the Naga National Council, they waged a struggle for independent Nagalim, till the NNC came forward to sign the Shillong Accord, renouncing violence. Some Naga leaders – such as Thuingaleng Muivah of the Tangkhul tribe, Isak Chishi Swu of the Somi tribe and S.S. Khaplang – were opposed to this, broke away from the NNC to set up the National Socialist Council of Nagaland (NSCN). Subsequently the group broke up even further, with the S.S. Khaplang-led NSCN (Khaplan) faction favouring resumption of dialogue, while the NSCN (Isak-Muivah) faction favoured resistance. A lot of inter-factional conflict followed alongside conflict with the Indian government. In 1997, finally, the NSCN-IM and NSCN-K signed a ceasefire agreement among themselves and with the Government of India, agreeing to refrain from attacks on each other. However, when the NSCNs and the tribal body, Naga Hoho, issued a call that elections be postponed, the Government of India refused to accede to the call. This made the NSCN-K to abrogate the ceasefire agreement and both the NSCN factions called for a boycott of the assembly elections, supported by the BJP.

In the elections that were held in the shadow of the boycott, INC remained the only major party standing in the field, thus obtaining a crushing majority by winning 53 seats in the 60-seat assembly, while the independents won the remaining 7 seats. Of its 53 seats, 43 were won uncontested.

S.C. Jamir, the incumbent chief minister was sworn in for his second straight full term (1998–2003).

Rajasthan

The elections in Rajasthan during the 1990s put in place virtually a pattern of built-in anti-incumbency for all reigning chief ministers. 1998 brings out this pattern quite well.

After 5 years of BJP rule under Bhairon Singh Shekhawat, the party received a drubbing being reduced to 33 seats (down 62) with a vote share of 33.23%. The INC returned to power with a handsome tally of 153 seats (up 77), with 49.95% of the popular vote. The Janata Dal won 3 seats, BSP 2, RJD and CPI 1 each, plus 7 independents.

Ashok Gehlot, an OBC leader of the Mali caste, was sworn in as the chief minister for the first of his 3 full terms in that capacity.

Tripura

Tripura was starting to become an arena of political stability by the 1990s. The 1998 elections were no different.

After a full term under Dasarath Deb, the CPI(M) went to the polls only to retain power with 38 seats (down 6) out of 60 seats, with a vote share of 45.49%. The INC improved its tally to 13 seats (up 3) to remain the second-largest party, drawing 33.96% of the votes. The Tripura Upajati Juba Samiti won 4 seats, RSP 2, CPI 1, while 2 independents also sat in the assembly.

After the elections, Manik Sarkar was sworn in as the chief minister for the first of his 4 straight, full terms (1998–2003).

Chapter 12

BEYOND THE BALLOT 1977–99

The Loss of a Reviled Strategist and the Onset of Congress Decline 1980–83

Sanjay Gandhi has remained, in public memory, synonymous with the excesses of the Emergency and hence as the principal instrument of the first serious attempt at subverting Indian democracy. However, for the Congress(I), he was the master strategist who was attributed with making Mrs Gandhi's dramatic return to power possible. Sanjay chose a large number of the candidates, and his Youth Congress provided organizational support to Mrs Gandhi. Sanjay had built the Youth Congress into a powerful fighting force loyal to the Nehru–Gandhi family. Thus, in the first 6 months after the massive victory in 1980 general elections, Sanjay Gandhi was calling the shots both in the party and the government, further weakening the institutional character of the party and facilitating the rise of a parallel organization – Sanjay Gandhi's Youth Congress. The party's victory in the assembly elections of June 1980 in 8 out of the 9 states in which elections were held was immediately attributed to Sanjay's power and his political acumen in winning elections. Sanjay Gandhi was effectively being groomed to succeed his mother when, on 23 June 1980, he unexpectedly died in an air crash.

Mrs Gandhi took months to recover from Sanjay's death. After that, she turned to her elder son, Rajiv, an airline pilot, as her possible successor. After a period of considerable reluctance and despite strong reservations of his wife Sonia, Rajiv Gandhi became the general secretary of the Congress(I) as the party definitively steered itself towards a dynastic character.

Sanjay's sudden death led to an imbalance in the inner party equilibrium. In many states where the Congress was in power, chief ministers lacking local support bases of their own were retained in power provided they were able to contribute resources to party coffers - which diverted resources that might have been more useful for developing the various constituencies. Some political analysts have identified this period as significant in the party's loss of the ability to govern and to distribute patronage effectively. In 1983, the Congress(I) suffered assembly election defeats in Karnataka and Andhra Pradesh. By-elections told the same story. It seemed that Mrs Gandhi was losing her grip over the country when she was assassinated in 1984.

Allahabad Bypoll: Victory before Victory - 1988

In 1988, the outcome of a by-election in a single parliamentary constituency which took place one and half years before the general elections of India turned out to be the indicator of the change that was to come in India's political landscape in 1989. Held on 16 June 1988, it was a prestige fight between the ruling Congress party, led by Prime Minister Rajiv Gandhi, and the Opposition, which more-or-less found a face in Vishwanath Pratap Singh. At the same time, the opposition camp was struggling to close its ranks.

Amitabh Bachchan, the megastar of the Bollywood film industry and a close friend of Rajiv Gandhi, had joined the Congress and had been given a ticket in the 1984 election.

Contesting from Allahabad parliamentary constituency, Bachchan defeated the Janata Party stalwart Hemwati Nandan Bahuguna (a former UP chief minister and union finance minister, and a heavyweight leader of the Opposition) by a margin of 1,87,000 votes to the great surprise of all concerned.

In April 1987, when the scandal over the acquisition of howitzer guns from the Swedish company, Bofors, surfaced, reports published in an Indian newspaper and a Swedish newspaper alleged that Bachchan and his brother Ajitabh had been recipients of kickbacks in the deal that took place between India and the Swedish company. Under pressure, Bachchan resigned from the Lok Sabha in July 1987, vacating the Allahabad seat.

The pressure was largely the result of the probe announced by the then defence minister Vishwanath Pratap Singh, who was appointed to that office in January 1987, after the Bofors deal had been concluded. Singh, who was then a member of the Rajya Sabha, himself had to resign from the cabinet on 11 April 1987, under tremendous pressure from within the Congress party and the cabinet, largely on account of the probe he announced without consulting anyone. It was widely believed that Singh was pushed out of the Finance Ministry earlier because he was looking into the accounts of the Bachchan brothers. After Singh resigned from the post of defence minister as well, the Congress expelled V.P. Singh. He thus had to resign from the Rajya Sabha as well, where he was the party leader since 1984.

When V.P. Singh took his case to the people through a series of public meetings, he began from Allahabad, which he had represented in the Lok Sabha before Bachchan. Singh was quite categorical in highlighting Bachchan's complicity, and when Bachchan vacated the seat, Singh promptly filed his nomination from that constituency to wage his 'crusade' against corruption that he accused Rajiv Gandhi and his government of. Singh projected the bypoll as a referendum on corruption and, more importantly, on the Rajiv Gandhi government. By that time, Singh had already floated the Jan Morcha along with Arun Nehru and Arif Mohammed Khan, 2 other defectors from the Congress. However, Singh filed his nomination as an independent candidate since the Jan Morcha did not get the official recognition from the Election Commission at that date.

A huge section from the Opposition, including the Left parties, the Janata Party, Lok Dal, and almost the entire national opposition came to stand behind V.P. Singh in the bypoll. Jaipal Reddy, then deputy leader of the Janata Party in Parliament, said, 'Singh's resignation confirms that there is no place for an honest man in Rajiv Gandhi's government. It is evident that Rajiv Gandhi has given up even the pretensions of cleanliness.' L.K. Advani (then BJP president) said, 'I think it is very difficult for any Congressmen to be anywhere near the top and remain clean. I think Mr Singh has made a sensible choice.' In V.P. Singh, the Opposition leaders found a credible, clean, strong and vibrant face.

At one point Singh had said that if the Congress did not give ticket to Bachchan, he would withdraw. He stayed on nonetheless even when Bachchan did not contest the election, saying this was a collective decision by the Opposition and his personal choice shouldn't be more important. In reality, V.P. Singh represented the entire opposition block in the Allahabad by-election.

On the other hand, the Congress took a defensive stance all along. Media reports suggested that after waiting for a year till no charges could be proved against him, Bachchan himself wanted to contest the bypoll as a way of salvaging his personal reputation – sources indicate that Rajiv Gandhi himself was in favour of his candidature. However, forces from within the Congress persuaded PM that this by-election should not become a referendum on the Gandhi government – which the Opposition was certain to portray it as, had Bachchan lost. The party decided to field a low-profile candidate whose victory could bring V.P. Singh's career to an end; but if that candidate were to lose, the party would not be much affected. This low-profile candidate was Sunil Shastri, the son of former Prime Minister Lal Bahadur Shastri (who had won the Allahabad seat twice in 1957 and 1962, consecutively).

Even Sunil Shastri (MLA from Gorakhpur Urban) was surprised by the decision to field him against V.P. Singh, in solidarity with whom he resigned his position in the UP cabinet. Shastri had been campaigning for Singh and was meant to join the Jan Morcha when he was offered the ticket. Supposedly, Shastri had been told that he was to be a dummy candidate, who would file his nomination and then withdraw in favour of Bachchan.

During the poll campaign, V.P. Singh emphasized that the battle was being fought between the prime minister and himself, and Sunil Shastri was none other than a pawn in the hands of the prime minister. The Jan Morcha leader travelled to those villages, where few campaigners had reached in 4 decades and V.P. raised many inconvenient questions for the prime minister. Singh's entire campaign was based on the issue of morality and principles in politics.

The Congress countered this saying first that V.P. was a traitor and a hypocrite. Shastri was projected as a clean, young Congressman with claims to his late father's legacy and on whose victory the further development of the constituency depended.

On 18 June, V.P. won the battle defeating his closest contender Sunil Shastri by a handsome margin of 1,10,751 votes. Senior journalist Khushwant Singh observed that 'The wind is blowing in the direction of Gandhi's ouster.'

Defeating the Weakened Giant – 1989

In 1989, the National Front led by V.P. Singh gained a head-start over the ruling Congress(I) by being able to field more than 400 candidates under a common banner. The seat-sharing arrangement was arrived at after long-drawn-out negotiations, whereby the parties, comprising the Front, decided not to put up candidates against each other. Consequently, the Janata Dal's dominance was accepted in Uttar Pradesh, Bihar, Haryana, Karnataka and Orissa. The BJP put most of its candidates in Madhya Pradesh, Rajasthan and Gujarat, while Telugu Desam Party and DMK were acknowledged as the only parties in Andhra Pradesh and Tamil Nadu respectively. The communists, or the Left, were left to contest from West Bengal and Kerala. This one-to-one contest gave the Congress the toughest fight ever from the Opposition since 1977.

The Congress(I) was pitted against a whole bunch of experienced and highly influential campaigners from the Oppositions. They all had a formidable grip over their constituencies. Ramakrishna Hegde, N.T. Rama Rao and Karunanidhi were canvassing in the south. The north was managed by Bhairon Singh Shekhawat, Devi Lal, Atal Bihari Vajpayee, Lal Krishna Advani and Chandra Shekhar. V.P SIngh focussed on Uttar Pradesh and Bihar (these two states together send 139 members to the Lok Sabha – about 25% of its strength).

Hercules and the Augean Stables: T.N. Seshan

An IAS officer 1955 batch under the Tamil Nadu cadre, Seshan served in many bureaucratic positions including the secretary to the Atomic Energy Commission and joint secretary at the Department of Space. As the CEC (December 1990–December 1996), he changed the process of conducting elections in the nation and introduced a list of 150 malpractices during elections. Stringent directives were issued by the CEC forbidding bribing or intimidation of voters, distribution of liquor during the elections, use of official machinery for poll campaigning, appealing to voters' caste or communal feelings, use of religious places for campaigns and use of loudspeakers without prior written permission. He also enforced a strict limit to poll expenses by candidates in every constituency.

> Constitutional posts are meant to ensure governance without fear or favour of the political masters of a country. But very few persons appear to make the posts meaningful. One such person was Tirunellai Narayana Iyer Seshan, aka T.N. Seshan, the tenth Chief Election Commissioner of India. He was among the few members associated with the office that posterity is likely to remember, principally because he took on whichever political stalwart tried to interfere with his assigned responsibility of smooth conduct of elections. He has been widely credited for ushering in electoral reforms that changed the face of Indian elections, by dramatically reducing the extent of electoral malpractices.

Still more importantly, Seshan had initiated the process of cleaning up the electoral system by purging the system of false voters. The introduction of voters' photo identity cards was a measure towards this goal. He also saw to it that the model code of conduct, till then considered a document of academic interest, was taken seriously by the parties and candidates. Despite facing a volley of criticism, that he had exceeded his jurisdiction, from the various ruling forces at the Centre as much as the states, during his tenure, Seshan made the EC vibrant by asserting its rights under the Constitution, and without expecting rewards from the political class by remunerative or prestigious offices after retirement. He put the Election Commission on a high pedestal and was instrumental for its visibility, arguably for the first time in independent India.

Needless to say, on account of his reforms in the process of overhauling the election system, T.N. Seshan had to face the wrath of a section of political leaders, who spoke of him as a megalomaniac, a mad dog, or even a mad ox. In 1995, he had rescheduled assembly elections in Bihar as many as 4 times, because he was not satisfied with the arrangements in place for the voting process. Which is why Lalu Prasad Yadav was less concerned about his political adversaries, though Seshan is known to have worried him.

While finalising the dates for any election, Seshan was not known to be mindful of the preferences of his political master. Presumably, that is the reason why, after his retirement, he was neither given an extension in service, nor any sinecure, nor a seat in any legislature (union or state). However, in 1996, T.N. Seshan received the Ramon Magsaysay Award for his role in cleaning up the electoral process in the country – which is perhaps a better recognition for public service than anything from one's own political master.

'Historic, Political Blunder' – 1996

In 1996, after the eleventh Lok Sabha elections returned a hung parliament, the first Vajpayee government gave up after 13 days unable to cobble up the requisite numbers on the floor of the house, and P.V. Narshimha Rao was given the cold shoulder by almost all non-Congress, non-BJP forces. The search began for a combination of all non-BJP political forces, with someone from some party other than the Congress, but acceptable to it.

On the evening of 10 May 1996, V.P. Singh, keen to have a third-front government sworn in, rang up the veteran communist leader Jyoti Basu, chief minister of West Bengal, to communicate that the Janata Dal and other allies were unanimous in seeking Basu as the leader of the third front and the prime minister. Before the day was out, Congressmen also indicated their acceptance of their old adversary. Communist lore claims that Basu had been offered the post of prime minister of India twice before that. First, when the BJP withdrew support from the V.P. Singh government in 1990 and second, when the Chandrasekhar government fell in 1991, as a fallout of his tussle with the Congress. In both cases, Rajiv Gandhi was claimed to have proposed the elevation of his old adversary, but Basu as much as the collective leadership of the party declined the offer right out of hand. However, the situation in May 1996 was totally different from the situation of November 1990 and March 1991 – the need to stem the rise of the BJP appeared paramount to all concerned.

Basu himself was sceptical of the viability of a government constituting such a diverse range of political forces; besides, there was no telling how long such a government may be supported by the Congress. But he was also alive to the fact that if a diverse non-BJP coalition came to power, it would need a leader experienced in the art of coalition government – a virtue that Basu had aplenty, being at the helm of a coalition government for nearly 19 years by then. Hence, at the CPI(M) Politburo, Basu expressed his doubts, but also said that he was ready to join the government. According to him, 'It would be politically correct under the "circumstances". Most of the Politburo members felt otherwise. Basu argued that in politics there are moments when one has to rise to the occasion and one has got to cater to the need of the hour and the pleas of the people, our infallible judge.' After a prolonged debate that stretched out for more than a day, the Central Committee decided by 35 votes to 20 (with 4 undecided) against joining the government.

The leaders of what was now coming together as the third front persisted in asking the Politburo to reconsider its decision, which resulted in a special session of the Central Committee – but the majority still remained averse to joining the government.

Later, in an interview to the *Asian Age* in January 1997, Basu termed it as a 'historic, political blunder' of the CPI(M) party. Even a member of the BJP later admitted that if Jyoti Basu had emerged as the Third Front leader, it may not have been that rickety.

The year 1996 was the closest that the Indian Left made it to the highest political office of the country.

Jagadambika Pal: the Chief Minister with the Briefest Stint – 1997

In 1996, the Uttar Pradesh assembly polls had led to a hung assembly followed by the imposition of President's Rule. In March 1997, the BJP and BSP formed an alliance, and the BSP top leader Mayawati, became chief minister. In September 1997, Kalyan Singh of the BJP became chief minister, in accordance with the power-sharing adjustment and agreement between the two parties. However, in October 1997, the BSP withdrew its support from the Kalyan Singh government, purportedly because of the disagreement on the implementation of the Scheduled Castes and Scheduled Tribes (Prevention of Atrocities) Act. The Kalyan Singh government, though, managed to survive with the support of a breakaway faction of the BSP and that of the Congress, called the Akhil Bharatiya Loktantrik Congress, led by Naresh Agarwal. However, after only 4 months, the Loktantrik Congress withdrew its support to the government and, under the leadership of Jagdambika Pal, the party put a claim for government formation before Governor Romesh Bhandari that they had adequate numbers. On 21 February 1998, Bhandari dismissed Singh's government and asked Pal to swear in on the same night.

Jagadambika Pal was, thus, sworn in at 10.16 p.m. on 21 February 1998, along with 17 ministers. Naresh Agarwal, the chief of the Loktantrik Congress became deputy chief minister. Pal was asked to prove his majority on the floor of the assembly by 24 February; that is within 72 hours. However, a division bench of the Allahabad High Court stayed Governor Bhandari's order, and on 23 February it reinstated Kalyan Singh as the chief minister, and by the afternoon of 23 February, Pal's stint as chief minister was over. The dismissal of Singh's government had been termed 'unconstitutional' by the Allahabad High Court because Governor Bhandari did not let Singh prove his majority on the floor of the assembly, which Kalyan Singh managed to prove easily in the floor test at the assembly.

Pal's stint of 40 hours as the chief minister of Uttar Pradesh remains the briefest stint as chief minister in the history of the Indian Republic.

One Vote is Enough – 1999

On April 17 1999, a confidence vote was called in the Lok Sabha. When the count came in, the Vajpayee government had lost the confidence of Parliament by a single vote, the final count being 269–270.

The BJP left no stone unturned to win the confidence vote. Pramod Mahajan, then minister for Information and Broadcasting, and Food Processing, was given the task of floor management to gather the required numbers once the AIADMK pulled its 18 MPs out of the NDA. Mahajan tried hard but failed because of 4 different factors that went against Vajpayee on that occasion. Any one of them was damaging enough; together their effect was lethal.

First, the Bahujan Samaj Party (BSP), which had 5 MPs, had its leader Kanshi Ram assure Vajpayee that his party would not vote against the government. Even on the morning of the confidence vote, Mayawati, the second-in-command of the BSP, went to see Vajpayee, touched his feet, and assured him of the BSP's support. Then her MPs went into Lok Sabha and voted against the government.

Second, the National Conference had 2 MPs. J&K Chief Minister and National Conference Chief Farooq Abdullah had instructed the party's vote should go with the NDA government. While one of the 2 MPs, Omar Abdullah abided by the instruction, the other MP Saifuddin Soz voted to bring down the government – arguably because Farooq Abdullah had sidelined Soz in order to promote his own son, Omar.

Probably the most knotty issue was the vote cast by Giridhar Gamang. A Congress MP elected from Koraput parliamentary constituency, Gamang had been sent to Bhubaneshwar as chief minister of Orissa in February 1999. Thus, in April 1999 Gamang was, at the same time, an MP in the parliament as also, leader of the treasury benches in Orissa, with nearly 4 months in hand within which he had to be elected in the state assembly, and vacate his seat in the Parliament.

The BJP and its NDA partners, as well as a section of political analysts, believe that the morally correct position would have required Gamang to abstain. Had he done so, the vote would have ended with a tie, and then the Lok Sabha Speaker, Ganti Mohana Chandra Balayogi, could have used his casting vote to save the government. (Nobody bothered to ask whether the speaker occupying a position that was meant to be non-partisan should vote at all.) But Gamang voted against the government, and pushed the country towards an untimely election. Later, upon joining the BJP in 2015, Gamang maintained that in April 1999 he was still subject to the party whip, and could not have done otherwise.

Another act of oversight by the BJP was no less decisive. Arunachal Congress MP Wangcha Rajkumar had assured Vajpayee, months before the floor test in the Lok Sabha, having broken away from the provincial Congress party, he would be happy to vote with the NDA in the event of a floor test. At the time he made that promise, there was no immediate threat to the Vajpayee government. Unfortunately, when the moment came, no one remembered to approach Rajkumar, and he voted against the government since no one approached him for his vote.

Every vote counts.

The Vajpayee Lift-off – 1999

In November 1998, at the onset of the last quarter of the 13-month Vajpayee government, 4 assembly elections held for Delhi, Madhya Pradesh, Mizoram and Rajasthan took place. The Congress emerged as the big winner taking Delhi, Madhya Pradesh and Rajasthan with a clear majority. Even in Mizoram, where it won only 6 seats in the state assembly, out of 40, it got the highest vote share. This was a big victory for the new president Sonia Gandhi who had personally involved herself with these elections.

The results were a setback for the BJP, who even after rejecting the idea that this was nothing short of a referendum on the central government, could not but carry out a post-mortem. The general consensus seemed to be that price-rise was the principal factor behind the BJP's poor performance. There was the additional consideration that while the BJP had managed to retain its traditional base among the nation's middle class, it fared particularly badly in the areas dominated by Muslims, Scheduled Castes and Schedule Tribes – opening up the question whether the Congress was consolidating *its* traditional vote bank. When the Vajpayee government fell on April 1999, and the twelfth Lok Sabha was dissolved, the government's popularity figures were pretty disconcerting.

In a fateful decision, the ECI, after meeting representatives of all recognized national and state-level parties decided that, given the impending monsoon season as also the strain of holding 2 general elections within 13 to 15 months, the earliest feasible date for the elections to the thirteenth Lok Sabha would be the month of September. The polls were scheduled to be held between 5 September and 3 October 1999 – 127 days, or a little over 4 months since the twelfth Lok Sabha was dissolved.

The gap of 4 months emerged as a crucial factor in Indian electoral history because it was during that period that the Kargil conflict broke out in which India won a decisive victory driving out Pakistani intruders by the end of July, and the interim government of A.B. Vajpayee gained its lift-off, claiming to 'dedicate ourselves anew to preserving the honour and territorial integrity of our motherland.'

Overlooked was the fact that the BJP-led NDA government had fallen on 17 April 1999. The party, which only a few years back had been considered a political pariah, seemed to have redeemed itself by leading the country into victory over its principal antagonist. Thus, even though the BJP seemed to barely hold its ground with 182 seats (marginally better than the 179 it won in 1998), its allies secured 117 seats for the NDA. The Telugu Desam Party of Andhra Pradesh came back with 29 seats, the Shiv Sena won 15 seats, the DMK triumphed in 12 seats in Tamil Nadu. The NDA had got 299 seats, which meant a comfortable majority in the Lok Sabha total of 544, allowing Vajpayee the numbers that helped him give India a stable government after nearly half a decade of political instability.

The Foreign Origin Issue and Split within the INC – 1999

Even as troops were moving into position in Kargil in May 1999, the Congress was left facing yet another crisis over the foreign origin of its newly-elected president, Sonia Gandhi, which severely weakened the party in its last bastion in western India, Maharashtra.

Sonia Gandhi was first offered the post of president of the Indian National Congress in May 1991, immediately after the assassination of her husband, former prime minister Rajiv Gandhi – which she refused out of hand. During P.V. Narsimha Rao's regime, Sonia Gandhi kept herself and her children far away from politics in a deliberate manner although loyalists like Arjun Singh and others repeatedly tried to use Mrs Gandhi as a counter-weight to the prime minister.

This changed somewhat after the fall of the Rao government once out-of-power Congress began to appear somewhat ramshackle under the leadership of Sitaram Kesri. Those in the party opposed to Kesri repeatedly implored Mrs Gandhi to assume leadership of the party, and persuaded her to accept primary membership of the party at its eightieth Plenary Session, which took place in Kolkata in August 1997. After the Congress faced its second consecutive defeat in the general election of March 1998, Kesri was toppled and Mrs Gandhi was anointed/appointed the president of the Indian National Congress. Sonia Gandhi, who hails from a small village in Italy, was the grand old party's sixth president with non-Indian origin, but the first one since 1947.

Mrs Gandhi's appointment was a desperate attempt to hold the party together, and save it from a hapless leadership. By that time, the Congress had been ripped apart – leaders such as G.K. Moopanar and P. Chidambaram left the Congress and formed the Tamil Maanila Congress (TMC) in Tamil Nadu; Mamata Banerjee, the firebrand leader of West Bengal, also did the same and the All India Trinamool Congress (AITC) was born; Arjun Singh, Rajesh Pilot, Narayan Dutt Tiwari and some other senior and prominent leaders were in open revolt against the president Sitaram Kesri. At this point in time, from senior leaders to rank and file workers of the Congress party were badly searching for a personality capable of holding the party together, and most agreed that Mrs Gandhi was the best choice available at that time despite her Italian origin. In the 2 decades that followed, Mrs Gandhi remained at the helm of the Congress.

However, 14 months after Sonia took charge, the most serious revolt against her authority surfaced.

The revolt took place on the evening of 15 May 1999 at a Congress Working Committee meeting to finalise the list of party candidates for the upcoming Goa assembly election, as well as to work out the alliances for the parliamentary poll. Purportedly, on a cue from Sharad Pawar, the proverbially mild-mannered Purna A. Sangma slowly built a case on how Mrs Gandhi's foreign origins were being taken by the BJP into the remotest corners of the country as an election issue – to an extent that the Congress risked losing the forthcoming election that autumn. Sharad Pawar then chimed in, praising Sonia Gandhi's contribution in unifying the party and revamping the organisation, and then cautioned that the Congress has not succeeded in answering the BJP's campaign about Mrs Gandhi's foreign origins – much in the same vein as Jagjivan Ram's challenge to the authority of Indira Gandhi in 1977.

Sonia Gandhi's acolytes in the CWC, led by Arjun Singh, accused Pawar, Sangma and the third CWC member to support them, Tariq Anwar, of betrayal, and eventually had them expelled from the party. The trio went on to form the Nationalist Congress Party (NCP).

Contrary to what the trio said in the CWC meeting, they were not much disturbed by the impact of the BJP's nationwide campaign on Sonia Gandhi's foreign origins. In fact, in May 1999, the Congress was quite hopeful that come the elections, the party would regain power at the Centre. So much so that Sharad Pawar was himself given the responsibility by Mrs Gandhi to secure letters of support from other non-BJP parties after the elections for her candidacy as prime minister.

Pawar had been among the signatories on both occasions when Sonia Gandhi was approached to assume leadership of the party, and was also pivotal in the ousting of Kesri and his replacement by Mrs Gandhi. A general consensus exists that

Pawar aspired to the position of the prime minister for himself, and that in 1991 he lost the race for both prime ministership and Congress presidentship to P.V. Narsimha Rao because of the silent support Rao received from Sonia Gandhi. In May 1999, Pawar (then 58 years of age) seemed to have thought that if Sonia Gandhi took charge, his prospects of securing the prime job in the country would never materialize again.

Some political observers are of the view that in Pawar's scheme of things, in the event of no political party or group securing the majority in the thirteenth Lok Sabha, the Congress would have had a good chance to gain support of other political parties – but not if Mrs Gandhi was at the helm. Former prime minister Chandra Shekhar, Samajwadi Party leader, Mulayam Singh Yadav, and Samata Party leader, George Fernandes, convinced him to this effect. Also, as long as Sonia Gandhi was Congress chief, Chandrababu Naidu, Mayawati, and Jayalalithaa would not extend their support.

Pawar played his hand aiming at the prime minister's seat. By creating his separate party, he put paid to that possibility altogether. The low-hanging fruit could have been his old job as the chief minister of Mahararashtra, but even there he did not manage to fare much better. In the following Maharashtra assembly elections, which took place along with the parliamentary polls in 1999, Pawar's NCP finished behind the Congress and got only the third place by getting 58 seats. The Congress emerged as the single largest party having 76 seats. The NCP damaged the fortunes of the Congress candidates in many seats, and then went for a post-poll alliance with the Congress to form the government and to keep the BJP–Shiv Sena alliance away from power. Therefore, the political party, which came into being by challenging Sonia Gandhi's leadership, joined hands with her party immediately afterward, only for power.

In the 1999 Lok Sabha elections, Pawar's new party ate into a sizeable amount of the Congress's committed vote share. The

INC stood in the third place (10 seats) finishing behind the Shiv Sena (15 seats) and the BJP (13 seats) in terms of number of seats in Maharashtra. The NCP secured only 6 seats. Therefore, the BJP–Sena alliance fared better by winning 28 out of the 48 seats. It became evident that the birth of the NCP had dented the Congress badly, making it lose what till then was a veritable stronghold for the Congress in western India.

The INC has had a large number of splits since 1947, but none proved more debilitating, electorally and politically, than that of 1999 and the rise of the NCP in Maharashtra as an alternate point of rallying voters who had historically voted for the Congress.

BOOK III

THE AGE OF BJP ASCENDANCY (1999 ONWARDS)

Chapter 13

THE AGE OF STABLE GOVERNMENT 1999 ONWARDS

1999: The NDA and the First Stable Coalition

The thirteenth general elections were staggered over a month and were scheduled in 5 phases between September and October 1999 – the first time ever.

The Vajpayee government's exemplary treatment of its allies, both while in government and in making seat adjustments for even the smallest political outfit to garner electoral mileage, helped remove the tag of unacceptability that had been pinned onto it in 1996. The other factor that worked in its favour was the elevation of Sonia Gandhi to the position of the president of the Congress, which increased the prospects of her becoming the Congress candidate for the prime minister's post if the party was able to gather the requisite number of seats. Senior party leaders like former Chief Minister of Maharashtra and Defence Minister Sharad Pawar, former Speaker of the Lok Sabha Purna Sangma and Tariq Anwar demanded that her name should not be in the running, on account of her foreign origin – an issue that the BJP was already making much of. When the Congress top brass skirted the issue, Pawar, Sangma and Anwar broke away from the Congress and set up the Nationalist Congress Party (NCP), thereby weakening the party in Maharashtra – one of the bastions of Congress politics.

The incumbent Bharatiya Janata Party led a 20-party National Democratic Alliance (NDA) into the polls and emerged with a stable non-Congress political coalition with a simple majority on the floor of the House for the first time, helping it form the first non-Congress and coalition government that lasted a full term of 5 years. The NDA picked up 269 seats in the Lok Sabha, and received a boost when a further 29 seats, taken by the Telugu Desam, were made available by way of outside support – in return for which T.M.C. Balayogi of the TDP was made the Speaker of the Lok Sabha.

In terms of the tally of seats and vote share, the BJP chalked up 182 seats, with a vote share of 23.75%; the Congress continued to have a higher popular vote share (28.3%), but was reduced to only 114 seats. The CPI(M), with 33 seats, came in the third position (with just over 5% share of the votes), while the TDP had its greatest performance ever with 29 seats (albeit with only 3.65% of the vote). A new party, made up of old players, the Janata Dal (United) was created just before the elections when the rump Janata Dal split once again upon a section of it choosing to go with the NDA. This rump group, led by Sharad Yadav, merged with the Lok Shakti of Ramakrishna Hegde – which had already served in a BJP-led government – came to constitute the Janata Dal (United), or JD(U). In 2003, the Samata Party (led by Nitish Kumar and George Fernandes) merged with the JD(U) – thereby contributing a total tally of 21 seats. The faction of the erstwhile Janata Dal, that chose to stay equidistant from both, the Congress and the BJP, came to be called Janata Dal (Secular) or JD(S), led by H.D. Deve Gowda, and was reduced to only 1 seat – that of the leader himself. Of the other regional parties that were in the NDA, Shiv Sena chalked up a tally of 15 seats yet again; its new ally from Tamil Nadu, the DMK, brought in another 12, while its old allies the PMK got 5 and the MDMK got 2; the BJD got in 10; the Trinamool Congress (TMC) led by Mamata Banerjee, which had split earlier from the Congress, now entered the NDA with 8 Lok Sabha seats under its belt; the Shiromani Akali Dal was reduced to only 2 seats, but the Jammu Kashmir National Conference (led by Farooq Abdullah) brought in 4 more seats, and the Rashtriya Lok Dal (which broke away from the Janata Dal in 1996), led by Ajit Singh, contributed 2 more seats to the ruling alliance.

The SP came fifth with 26 seats, almost double the strength of its provincial rival, the BSP with 14 seats. The Indian National Lok Dal of O.P. Chautala got 5 seats; the RSP continued to retain its 4 seats; the AIFB, Rashtriya Lok Dal (led by Ajit Singh), Muslim League Kerala State Committee and Akhil Bharatiya Loktantrik Congress won 2 seats each. The JD(S), CPI(ML), Bharipa Bahujan Mahasangh, AIMIM, MGR Anna DMK, Kerala Congress, Kerala Congress(M), SAD(M), Samajwadi Janata Party (Rashtriya) (led by Chandra Shekhar), PWPI, HVC, MSCP, SDF – all of these won 1 seat each. Independents won in 6 seats. A total of 131 parties, out of the 175 who fielded candidates, failed to win any seats.

Despite the fragmentation of the political landscape, the BJP-led NDA enjoyed sufficient leverage in most states in order to provide a stable coalition that could survive the full term in office. In Bihar, the NDA won 41 seats, of which the BJP won 23 and JD(U) won 18 seats; the RJD won 7 seats, the INC 4 and others 2. In Uttar Pradesh, the BJP went by itself and won 29 of the 85 seats; the SP won 26 seats; the BSP won 14, the INC 10 seats; the Akhil Bharatiya Loktantrik Congress and Rashtriya Lok Dal won 2 seats each, the SJP(R) and an independent candidate won a seat each. In Rajasthan, the BJP won 16 seats, while the INC took 9. In Himachal Pradesh, the BJP won 3 seats and the Himachal Vikas Congress won 1 seat – the first time ever that the INC failed to win any Lok Sabha seat from the state. In Madhya

Pradesh, the BJP won 29 seats, while the INC won 11. In Jammu and Kashmir, the JKNC won 4 seats, while the BJP won only 2. In Delhi, the BJP won all 7 seats. In Punjab, the INC salvaged its situation a bit, winning 8 seats, the SAD won 2 and the BJP 1 – bringing the NDA tally to 3. In Haryana, the BJP and the INLD of Chautala contested the elections in alliance and won all 10 seats in the state. In Gujarat, the BJP won 20 seats, while the INC won 6 seats. In Maharashtra, the NDA carried 28 seats, of which the Shiv Sena won 15 and the BJP 13; fighting on their own, the INC won 10, the NCP won 6, the Bharipa Bahujan Mahasangh, JD(S), PWPI and an independent took 1 seat each. In Orissa, the NDA took 19 seats, of which the BJP took 10 seats and the BJD won 9; the INC won the remaining 2 seats. In West Bengal, the Left Front won 29 of the 42 seats – with the CPI(M) winning 21 seats, the CPI winning 3, the RSP winning 3 and the AIFB winning 2 seats; the NDA won 10 seats of which the Trinamool Congress (TMC) won 8 seats and the BJP won 2; the INC won 3 seats by itself. The solitary seats of Chandigarh and Daman and Diu were taken by the INC, while the Dadra and Nagar Haveli seat was taken by the BJP.

In south India, of the 42 seats in Andhra Pradesh, the NDA won 36, of which the TDP won 29 seats, the BJP 7; the INC won 5 seats, while the AIMIM won 1 seat. In Karnataka, the INC stood its ground winning 18 seats, while the NDA won 10 seats, of which the BJP won 7 seats and the JD(U) won 3. In Kerala, the INC and the CPI(M) won 8 seats each, while the IUML won 2 and the Kerala Congress and Kerala Congress (M) won 1. In Tamil Nadu, the NDA won 26 seats, of which the DMK won 12 seats, the PMK won 5, the MDMK and BJP won 4 seats each, and the MGRADMK won 1 seat; the AIADMK won 10, the INC won 2 seats, while the CPI(M) won 1. Both the seats in Goa were won by the BJP. The solitary Lok Sabha seat in Pondicherry was taken by the INC, as was the one of Lakshwadeep. The seat in Andaman and Nicobar Islands was taken by the BJP.

In the North-East, of the 14 seats from Assam, the INC won 10, the BJP won 2, the CPI(ML) and an independent contestant won 1 seat each. The INC won both the seats in Arunachal Pradesh; the 2 seats in Manipur were taken by the MSCP and NCP. In Meghalaya, the INC and the NCP won 1 seat each. In Mizoram, the solitary seat was taken by an independent candidate and, in Nagaland, by the INC. In Tripura, both the seats were won by the CPI(M), while the solitary seat in Sikkim was taken by the Sikkim Democratic Front (SDF).

The NDA government of Vajpayee had the occasion to appoint 73 ministers during its 5-year term, of whom 55 were from the BJP. It was an interesting amalgamation of 2 generations of Hindu nationalist right-wing politicians and left-wing politicians of the Janata camp (all of whom had come of age during the era of Congress domination and decline), and a cluster of regional leaders who were coming of age at the turn of the millennium. Most of the BJP ministers were veterans of the right wing – Advani (Deputy PM, Home), Jaswant Singh (MEA, Finance) or of the Janata clan – like Yashwant Sinha (Finance, MEA), George Fernandes (Defence). The second generation of BJP leaders – viz. Arun Jaitley, Sushma Swaraj, Rajnath Singh, Ravi Shankar Prasad, Uma Bharti, Pramod Mahajan, and so on – which was used to project the image that the BJP was a party of the future, failed to live up to the promise they had started with. By contrast, the regional leaders who had served in the Vajpayee government went on to rise higher in the regional political space and served as chief ministers of their respective states – Navin Patnaik (Orissa), Nitish Kumar (Bihar), Mamata Banerjee (West Bengal), Manohar Joshi (Maharashtra) and Omar Abdullah (J&K).

The 5 years of the Vajpayee government went with mixed ratings. While Vajpayee was feted for continuing with liberalisation of the Indian economy and improving the country's ties with the US, he came under pressure owing to the government's stand on the 2002 Godhra incident and the carnage that followed in BJP-ruled Gujarat. From then onwards, there were often occasions when an image began to do the rounds that Advani was the more forceful of the two, and discussions indicated that in the next general election, Advani should be the prime ministerial candidate. Such discussions began to circulate from as high as the office of party president Venkaiah Naidu, before Vajpayee threatened to resign. Immediately the party fell in line, and Vajpayee was projected yet again as the face of the party in the elections. Having won the state elections in Rajasthan, Madhya Pradesh and Chhattisgarh, the BJP was considered to be riding on a 'feel good factor'. Hence, the government requested President A.P.J. Abdul Kalam to dissolve the thirteenth Lok Sabha 6 months before its term ended, confident of victory. By then, the Congress finally learnt from the error of its ways and tried to cobble together an alliance of anti-BJP forces in the country, which eventually took the form of the United Progressive Alliance (UPA), and helped pull a surprise by defeating the NDA at the fourteenth general elections, held in 2004.

2004: The Stable Tenure of the UPA

The general elections of 2004 were held in 4 phases: 20 April, 26 April, 5 May and 10 May 2004.

THE GENERAL ELECTIONS OF 2004 WERE THE FIRST TO BE CARRIED OUT ENTIRELY WITH ELECTRONIC VOTING MACHINES.

This was the first election in a very long time to have 2 broad coalitions of forces (social and political) lined up on either side – with the BJP and its allies on the one hand (NDA), and the Congress and its allies on the other (the United Progressive

Alliance, or the UPA) – without a viable third alternative being on offer. While the NDA was a properly constituted alliance of more than 20 parties at the time of the election, Congress's efforts did not quite lead to a proper and formal alliance when the polls started. The Congress, however, was able to arrive at alliances or seat adjustments at the regional level, sufficiently enough to have the contours of the alliance in place when it went to the polls – thus the Congress contested with the CPI(M)-led Left Front in West Bengal, Tripura and Kerala, but managed to accomplish seat adjustments with them in Punjab and Andhra Pradesh.

While technically the Congress won the elections, it was actually more like the BJP lost it. The Congress barely improved its seats tally over 1999, winning 144 seats on the basis of a 26.53% vote share; the BJP came second, being reduced to 138 seats (22.16% of the votes). The CPI(M) improved its performance to win 43 seats (with 5.66% of the votes) – the highest ever. The 2 parties that kept equal distance from both alliances – the SP, led by Mulayam Singh Yadav, and the BSP, led by Mayawati, won 36 and 19 seats respectively. The other major party of north India to put up a handsome performance was Lalu Yadav's RJD, winning 24 seats on less than 3% of the votes. The AIADMK was wiped out, while the DMK swept Tamil Nadu with 16 seats of its own bat. The Shiv Sena won 12 seats, the BJD won 11 seats, the CPI won 10 and the NCP won 9. The SAD won 8 seats, the PMK won 6, the Telangana Rashtra Samithi, TDP and JMM won 5 seats each. The Lok Janshakti Party and MDMK won 4 seats each; the Rashtriya Lok Dal, AIFB and the RSP won 3 seats each; the TMC, AGP and JKNC won 2 seats each; the IUML, Naga People's Front, AIMIM, RPI, NLC, Kerala Congress, SJP(R), JKPDP, IFDP, MNF, Bharatiya Navashakti Party and SDF won 1 seat each. A total of 179 parties failed to win any seats.

The regional breakup of the NDA and the UPA show roughly co-equal strength of the 2 main alliances. In Bihar, the UPA won

29 seats, of which the RJD won 22, the LJP won 4 and the INC won 3; the NDA won 11 seats, of which the JD(U) won 6 seats and the BJP won 5. In Uttar Pradesh, the SP won 35 seats, the BSP won 19; the NDA won 11, of which the BJP won 10, the INC won 7, the RLD won 3 and independents won 2. In the newly-created state of Uttarakhand, the BJP won 3 of the 5 seats, while the INC and SP won 1 each. In Himachal Pradesh, the INC won 3 and the BJP 1 seat. In Jammu and Kashmir, the JKNC won 2 seats, the UPA 3 (of which the INC won 2 seats and PDP 1), and 1 went to an independent candidate. In Punjab, the NDA took 11 seats, of which the SAD won 8 seats and the BJP won 3, the INC won 2. In Haryana, the INC won 9 seats and the BJP won 1. In Rajasthan, the BJP managed to win 21 seats, while the INC won 4. In Gujarat, the BJP won 14 and the INC won 12. In Madhya Pradesh, the BJP won 25 and the INC 4. In the new state of Jharkhand, of the 14 Lok Sabha seats, the UPA won 12, of which the INC won 6 seats, the JMM won 4, the RJD won 2; the BJP and the CPI(M) won 1 seat each. In the other new state of Chhattisgarh, the BJP won 10 seats and the INC 1. In Maharashtra, the INC and the BJP won 13 seats each; the Shiv Sena won 12 seats, and the NCP 9 seats – thus, the NDA to UPA score was 25 to 22. In Orissa, the NDA took 18 seats of which the BJD won 11 and BJP 7. The INC won 2 seats. In West Bengal, the Left Front won 35 seats, of which the CPI(M) won 26, the CPI, RSP and AIFB won 3 seats each. The INC won 6 seats and the TMC won only 1 seat, while the BJP drew a blank. The INC took the solitary seat in Chandigarh, and that of Daman and Diu. Dadra and Nagar Haveli was won by the BJP. In Delhi, the INC took 6 seats, while the BJP took 1.

In Andhra Pradesh, the INC won 29 seats, and its ally TRS another 5; the TDP won 5 seats. The CPI, CPI(M) and AIMIM won a seat each. In Karnataka, the BJP won 18 seats, the INC 8 and JD(S) 2. In Kerala, the CPI(M) won 12 seats, the CPI won 3 seats; KEC, IUML and IFDP won 1 seat each along with an independent candidate. In Tamil Nadu, the DMK won 16 seats, the INC won 10 seats, taking the UPA tally to 26. The NDA won 9 seats of which the MDMK won 5 and the PMK 4. The CPI and CPI(M) won 2 seats each. The solitary seat of Pondicherry was taken by the PMK for the first time; that of Lakshwadeep was taken by the JD(U), also for the first time. The Andaman and Nicobar Islands seat was taken by the INC. The 2 seats of Goa were split 1 each between the INC and BJP.

In Assam, the INC took 9 seats, while the BJP and its ally, the AGP, won 2 seats each. In Arunachal Pradesh, the BJP took both the seats. In Meghalaya, the INC and TMC won 1 seat each. The solitary seats in Mizoram and Nagaland were taken by the MNF and NPF respectively. In Manipur the INC took 1 seat, while an independent won the other. The 2 seats of Tripura were won by the CPI(M). The seat in Sikkim was retained by the SDF.

Once it became clear that the NDA would not be able to come close to 200 seats, the Congress was finally able to forge its coalition, and chalked up a tally of 214 seats. The UPA constituted of the RJD, the NCP, DMK, NDMK, the Jharkhand Mukti Morcha, apart from altogether new allies like the Lok Janshakti Party (led by Ram Vilas Paswan), Telangana Rashtriya Samiti (TRS) and Jammu and Kashmir People's Democratic Party (PDP). The Left Front with its tally of 59 seats, the SP with its 36 (plus 3 Rajya Sabha MPs) and the BSP with its 19, decided to support the UPA, from the outside, along with many other smaller parties and independents from time to time.

Owing to discordant voices inside the party and outside, the president of the Congress, Mrs Sonia Gandhi, stepped aside and installed Dr Manmohan Singh as the thirteenth prime minister of India. The cabinet of Manmohan Singh, during its full term of 5 years, appointed a huge council of ministers (77), of which 29 were of the cabinet rank (the Congress fielding 21, the RJD 3, the DMK 2, and 1 each from the LJP, PMK and the NCP). The more important members of the cabinet were veterans like Pranab Mukherjee (Defence, Finance, Foreign), P.

Sonia Gandhi

Chidambaram (Finance, Home) and be the Natwar Singh (Foreign), Lalu Prasad Yadav (Railways), Sharad Pawar (Agriculture), Arjun Singh (HRD), Shivraj Patil (Home), Kamal Nath. It also turned out to be first government to have a plurality of women (3) in the cabinet – Ambika Soni, Renuka Chowdhury and Meira Kumar (daughter of Jagjivan Ram).

The UPA government took to a centre-left line in accordance with the Common Minimum Programme drafted by a team of UPA and Left leaders (especially Jyoti Basu and Harkishen Singh Surjit). The government served its tenure almost without any serious crisis till Manmohan Singh went on to sign the 1-2-3 Nuclear Deal, and then moved to deepen relations with the US. The Left Front, especially its Kerala lobby, represented by Prakash Karat, was firmly opposed to the close alignment with the US, and decided to withdraw support from the government on this issue. The government survived the confidence vote on this issue in 2008, largely thanks to the support provided by Mulayam's SP on the floor of the House, and allegedly to money that was freely spent to ensure some amount of cross voting – 7 members of the UPA cross-voted against the government; at least 4 members of the Opposition who cross-voted in favour of the government. Eleven members remained undecided, including Mamata Banerjee – the sole member of the TMC in Parliament.

Prakash Karat tried to persuade Mulayam so that the latter's party would support the Left on the issue of the nuclear deal. Despite 2 meetings held between Yadav and Karat, the Samajwadi Party chief was not convinced with the view of the general secretary of the CPI(M). Amar Singh, a top leader of the

Samajwadi Party and a close aide of Mulayam, announced that the SP wanted all secular forces to remain united. 'A division in secular forces will be harmful for the country.' Again, A.P.J. Abdul Kalam, the former president of India and a towering nuclear scientist, issued a statement in support of the nuclear deal and urged Mulayam to support the government.

Meanwhile, a furious CPI(M) leadership (mainly the Karat lobby) asked Speaker Somnath Chatterjee to step down and vote against the government. Chatterjee chose not to oblige them. As a result, he was expelled from the party a day after the trust vote. Though the BJP had always supported the Indo–US pact, they voted against the government. They claimed that they would negotiate a better deal if they came to power. Eventually, the UPA government won the no-trust motion, with 275 votes against 256, while 10 members abstained.

Somnath Chatterjee

The trust vote had immense political significance. This was one of the factors that bolstered the Congress-led UPA to win the general elections in 2009 with more seats compared to the result of 2004. The Left parties snapped all ties with the Congress and UPA, but Congress found a new ally in West Bengal, which went on to benefit the UPA for the next few years.

2009: the UPA Lingers

Elections to the fifteenth Lok Sabha were held in April–May 2009. The UPA went to the polls with the incumbent prime minister Manmohan Singh as its designated prime ministerial candidate. The NDA had declared, as early as 2007, that L.K. Advani would be its prime ministerial candidate at the next general elections. The CPI(M)-led Left Front tried to go to the polls with its own combination of parties that wanted to keep equal distance from both the BJP and the Congress.

When the poll results came in, the Congress came with a much larger tally than it managed since 1984, winning 206 seats (with a vote share of 28.55%) on its own strength; the BJP was reduced to 114 seats (with a reduced vote share of 18.8%). The SP and the BSP, both of which went on their own after coalition talks with the Congress failed, came up with the third and fourth highest tallies - with 23 and 21 seats respectively. The CPI(M) was pushed down to the seventh slot with only 16 seats, while its regional rival and now a UPA constituent, the Trinamool Congress chalked up 19 seats to be the sixth largest party in the Lok Sabha, just behind the JD(U) which won 20 seats. The DMK, yet another UPA constituent, chalked up 18 seats.

The UPA victory did not change the political landscape that had come into being by then. In Bihar, the NDA won 32 seats of which JD(U) won 20 and the BJP won 12 seats; the UPA managed only 6 seats, of which RJD won 4 and INC won 2; independents won 2. In Uttar Pradesh, the SP won 23 seats, the INC won 21, the BSP 20, the NDA won 15 of which the BJP won 10 and the RLD 5; with an independent winning 1 seat. In Himachal Pradesh, the BJP won 3 seats and the INC won 1. In Uttarakhand, the INC won all 5 seats from the state. In Jammu and Kashmir, the UPA won 5 of the 6 seats, of which the INC won 2 and the JKNC won 3. In Haryana, the INC won 9 of the 10 seats, with the remaining seat being taken by the Janhit Congress, which was a splinter-group led by Bhajan Lal. In Punjab, the INC won 8 seats, while the NDA won 5, of which the SAD won 4 and the BJP won 1. In Rajasthan, the INC won 20 seats, while the BJP won 4 and an independent candidate took 1. In Gujarat, the BJP won 15 seats while the INC won 11. In Madhya Pradesh, the BJP was able to preserve its dominance, winning 16 seats while the INC won only 12, and the BSP won 1 seat. In Chhattisgarh, the BJP won 10 seats while the INC managed to win only 1. In Jharkhand, the NDA won 9 of the 14 seats from the states, with the BJP taking 8 and 1 being taken by the Jharkhand Vikas Morcha (prajatantrik); the UPA won 3 seats of which 2 were taken by the JMM and 1 by the INC. In West Bengal, the UPA finally defeated the Left Front to take 25 seats out of 42, of which the TMC won 19 seats and the INC won 5; the CPI(M) won 9 seats, the CPI won 2 seats, the AIFB won 2 seats, RSP, SUCI and the BJP winning a seat each. In Orissa, the BJD, fighting by itself, won 14 seats, the INC won 6, the CPI(M) won 1 seat. In Maharashtra, the UPA won 25 of 48 seats, of which the INC won 17 seats and the NCP won 8; the NDA won 21, of which the Shiv Sena won 11, the BJP 9 seats, the Swabhimani Paksha won 1 seat. The Bahujan Vikas Agadi and an independent candidate won 1 seat each. The INC won all 7 seats in the NCR of Delhi and the solitary seat in Chandigarh. The BJP won the seats of both Dadra and Nagar Haveli and of Daman and Diu.

In Andhra Pradesh, the INC retained its stronghold, winning 33 of the 42 seats; the TDP won 6 seats and the TRS won 2. In Karnataka, the BJP held on to its gain winning 19 seats of the 28 Lok Sabha seats, while the INC won 6 seats, an JDS won the remaining 3 seats. In Kerala, the INC won 13 seats, the IUML won 3 seats, KC(M) and CPI(M) won 1 seat each. In Tamil Nadu, the UPA won 20 of the 39 states, where the DMK won 18 seats, the INC and VCK winning a seat each; the AIADMK won 4 seats and MDMK, CPI and CPI(M) all winning a seat each. The solitary seats in both Lakshwadeep and Puducherry were taken by the INC; that of Andaman and Nicobar Islands was taken by the BJP. In Goa, the INC and BJP won a seat each.

In the North-East, Assam saw the INC taking 7 of the 14 seats, the BJP won 4 seats, the AGP, AIUDF and Bodoland People's Front won a seat each. In Meghalaya, the INC and NCP won a seat each. In Arunachal Pradesh, the INC won both the seats. The solitary seat of Mizoram was taken by the INC; the solitary seat of Nagaland went to the NPF. In Tripura, both the seats were retained by the CPI(M), while that in Sikkim it was retained by the SDF.

In all, the UPA chalked up 262 seats (with about 48.25% of the votes), backed up by support from the SP, BSP, RJD (4 seats) and JD(S) (3 seats) – giving the government a comfortable 322 seats in a House of 543. Manmohan Singh became the first prime minister of India since Nehru to return to office after a full term, and complete the second term as well. The top rung of the cabinet remained unchanged: Pranab Mukherjee (Finance), P. Chidambaram (Home, Finance), A.K. Anthony (Defence), Sharad Pawar (Agriculture and Food Processing). Among the new faces were old hands like Sushil Shinde, S.M. Krishna and Vilasrao Deshmukh who were moved to the Union cabinet after they lost public confidence in the states. The ex-Congress and former NDA ally Mamata Banerjee held the Railways portfolio for 2 years before finally succeeding in her life's mission of defeating the Left Front government in state elections in 2011, whereupon she became the chief minister of West Bengal. The second Singh government had 6 women in the cabinet – Ambika Soni, Jayanti Natarajan, Kumari Selja, Meira Kumar, Girija Vyas and Mamata Banerjee – the highest number till then.

By 2012–13, the UPA II government seemed to have run out of ideas, and became stranded in a mire of corruption allegations. One scam after another – the 2G scam, Commonwealth Games scam, coal scam – made the government a spent force long before its term came to an end in 2014. It seemed that the Congress was tired, the prime minister was tired, and when elections were finally held in 2014, it was clear the people had become tired – the Congress was reduced to its lowest tally since elections began in India.

2014: The BJP on a Roll

The sixteenth general elections proved to be a resounding verdict against the INC, and indicated a kind of electoral consolidation that had gone missing from Indian politics for decades. Held in 9 phases spanning over a month during April–May 2014, it involved 834 million registered voters, which was surpassed by the number in 2019.

The country gave a clear mandate to the NDA which won a clear majority for the first time since 1984, with the BJP winning 282 seats, and more importantly 31% of the votes – exceeding that of the INC for the first time ever by any political party. The INC was reduced to mere 44 seats courtesy 19.31% of the vote share – both figures being the lowest ever polled by the party. An AIADMK clean sweep of 37 Lok Sabha seats helped it become the third-largest party (with only 3.27% of the votes) while the TMC came fourth with 34 seats (with only 3.84% of the vote share). The BJD, the only party that broke with the BJP and yet prospered, finished with 20 seats; the Shiv Sena climbed slowly up to 18 seats, and the TDP was reduced to 16 seats – all regional allies of the BJP at one point of time or another, whose relations were beginning to sour.

A major realignment of the votes could be seen in at least two parts of India that saw the INC's decline matched by the rise of new forces. Andhra Pradesh, which had been a bastion of sorts for the INC, was divided into 2 states of Telangana and Andhra Pradesh towards the close of the UPA II ministry – largely in a bid to undermine the NDA constituent Telangana Rashtriya Samiti (TRS, set up in 2001 by K. Chandrasekhar Rao with the one-point agenda of a separate state for Telangana region). Eventually, the mileage from the creation of the state of Telangana was gained entirely by the TRS, which won 11 seats with a meagre 1.22% of the vote share. In the rump Andhra Pradesh, on the other hand, the son of the Congress chief minister Y.S. Rajsekhar Reddy broke from his father's party and set up his own outfit - the YSR Congress - and seemingly carried whatever votes of the Congress remained with himself, winning 9 seats on the basis of only 2.53% of the votes. The other place from which the INC was virtually wiped out was the National Capital Region of Delhi, where a powerful anti-corruption movement against the Congress projected an anarchist figure, Arvind Kejriwal, who by November 2012 set up a political outfit - the Aam Aadmi Party (AAP). In the 2014 elections, the AAP ended up winning 4 seats from Delhi, gaining seemingly its entire vote at the expense of the INC.

As new regional power-centres were beginning to emerge, others were beginning to fade out. The CPI(M) and CPI - 2 parties that had constituted an important voice for the Opposition - finished with 9 and 1 seats respectively. Lok Janshakti Party finished with 6 seats. The SAD, for a long time the mouthpiece of the Sikh voter, was reduced to 4 seats; same for the RJD, once a dominant force in Bihar politics. The JDU, JDS, INLD - all of whom have aligned with either the INC or the BJP at various times, found themselves reduced to barely 2 seats or so. The AGP, reduced to 0 seats, came to appear as a spent force.

The figures for the 2014 elections reveal a major mismatch between votes polled and seats won, even more so than previous Indian elections. The vote share of the BJP (31%) was the lowest ever to land a party with a simple majority without having to rely on its allies. The BSP polled the third-largest vote share in the elections (4.14%) but failed to win a single seat, and the SP could only 5 seats on the strength of 3.34% share of the votes. On the other hand, the Shiv Sena won 18 seats on the strength of only 1.84% vote share and the BJD won 20 seats on the strength of only 1.71% of the votes, but the DMK failed to win a single seat despite winning 1.74% of the votes.

The fact that more seats were being won with much less share of the votes brings out the continued fragmentation of the electorate. And the fact that governments were becoming more stable was indicative of the fact that parties were beginning to negotiate the fragmentation of the vote better. This was especially clear from the landscape of the Lok Sabha elections, and in particular from the complexion of the NDA that won the elections. The NDA constituted of 23 parties of which 11 did not win any seats at all, and 5 parties won only 1 seat each - but seat adjustments with these 16 parties made it possible for the remaining 7 parties, and especially the BJP to consolidate the votes and thus win as much as they eventually did. Thanks to such consolidation in the NDA, while the BJP won more than 2 of every 3 seats it contested (282 of 427), the Shiv Sena won 18 of the 20 seats it contested.

The effects of the consolidation become particularly apparent in looking at the regional break-up of seats. In Bihar, the BJP won 22 of 40 Lok Sabha seats; the LJP finished second with 6 seats, and Rashtriya Lok Samta Party (led by Upendra Kushwaha, ex-JDU) won 4 seats, chalking an NDA tally of 32 seats; the RJD won 4 seats, the JDU and the INC won 2 seats each and the NCP won 1 seat. In Uttar Pradesh, the BJP won the largest number of seats, 71, followed by SP at 5 seats and the INC and Apna Dal won 2 seats each. The BSP was wiped out from the Lok Sabha. In Uttarakhand, the BJP won all 5 seats. In Jharkhand, the BJP won 12 of the 14 seats, with 2 remaining seats being taken by the JMM of the UPA. In Himachal Pradesh, the BJP won all 4 seats. In the Delhi-NCR region, the BJP won all 7 seats. In Jammu and Kashmir, the 6 seats were split between the BJP and the PDP at 3 each. In Haryana, the BJP won 7 seats, INLD won 2 and INC won only 1. In Punjab, the INC won 3 seats, SAD won 4 seats, BJP won 2 seats and AAP won 4 seats as well. In Rajasthan, the BJP had a clean sweep of all 25 seats; in Gujarat, it was much the same with the BJP winning all 26 seats. In Madhya Pradesh, the BJP had an emphatic victory with 27 seats and the INC won only 2 seats. In Maharashtra, the NDA won 42 of the 48 seats from the state, of which the BJP won 23 seats and Shiv Sena won 18 seats and the Swabhimani Paksha won 1 seat; the INC won 2 seats and NCP won 4 seats. In Chhattisgarh, the BJP won 10 seats, while the INC won only 1 seat. In West Bengal, the AITMC won 34 out of the 42 seats, the CPI(M) and the BJP won 2 seats, the INC being left behind with 4 seats. In Orissa, the BJD finished with 20 seats, with 1 seat being won by the BJP. The solitary seats of Chandigarh, Dadra and Nagar Haveli, and Daman and Diu all went to the BJP.

While the BJP by and large dominated the north of India; in the south, the INC found its strength severely corroded. In the rump Andhra Pradesh with 25 Lok Sabha seats after the creation of Telangana, the NDA won 17 seats of which TDP accounted for 15 seats, and 2 for the BJP; the YSR Congress finished with 8 seats. In Telangana, the TRS won 11 of the 17 seats; the INC won 2 seats, and the BJP, TDP, YSRC and AIMIM won 1 seat each. Karnataka, which once used to be an INC stronghold, the BJP held its ground winning 17 of 28 seats, with the INC winning 9 seats and the JDS 2 seats. In Kerala, the INC won 8 seats, CPI(M) won 5 seats, while IUML and independents won 2 seats each. The CPI, the Kerala Congress and RSP were all reduced to 1 seat each. In Tamil Nadu, the AIADMK wiped the floor with the Opposition, winning 37 of 39 seats, with both the BJP and PMK winning a seat each. The solitary seat of Puducherry was won by the N.R. Congress; and Lakshwadeep was won by the NCP. The BJP won the Lok Sabha seat for Andaman and Nicobar Islands.

In the North-East, 2014 began the process of BJP's attempts at dominating the region. In Assam, the BJP won 7 seats and the INC and AIUDF won 3 seats each, plus 1 independent. In Arunachal Pradesh, the BJP and INC managed to win a seat each. In Meghalaya, the INC and National People's Alliance won a seat with each other. In Manipur both the seats for the Lok Sabha were taken by the INC. In Mizoram, the INC won the solitary Lok Sabha seat from the state, but that in Nagaland went to the Naga People's Front (NPF). In Tripura, the CPI(M) retained both seats. In Sikkim, the SDF was also able to retain its seat in the Lok Sabha.

A week after the results were declared, Narendra Modi, the highly successful and immensely popular chief minister of Gujarat was elected the leader of the Parliamentary party, who was thereupon invited to form the government by President Pranab Mukherjee. The government that was formed lasted its full term of 5 years and constituted of 71 ministers of whom 66 came from the BJP, of which 26 were of the cabinet rank. Only 3 cabinet ministers of the NDA were from allied parties (1 each from the Shiv Sena, Lok Janshakti Party and Shiromani Akali Dal). This lopsided distribution of the cabinet was indicative of the much-reduced dependence of the BJP on its allies in the formation of the government at the Centre. Despite the imbalance in the distribution of ministerial berths, the NDA survived because of the efficacy of its electoral adjustments at the state level for most of its regional allies, where the BJP gave them precedence in the legislative assembly elections and municipalities and local boards, and helped them gain power (such as, for the Shiv Sena in Maharashtra and the Shiromani Akali Dal in Pujnab). This is largely the reason why the NDA survived Narendra Modi's first government despite allies being progressively marginalized right up to the seventeenth general elections.

2019: The NAMO Elections

The seventeenth general elections were held during April–May 2019 after a full term of the Lok Sabha – the second one since 1984 where an incumbent government returned to office. The polls saw the highest turnout ever – over 67% of the total eligible voters came out to vote – which the government claimed to be a testament to the popularity of the prime minister. There is indeed little doubt that PM Modi enjoyed phenomenal popularity, as much due to some of his populist policies as to incidents like the Pulwama attacks – something that was handsomely translated into votes and seats for the ruling combine.

THE 2019 ELECTIONS ARE ONLY THE SECOND OCCASION WHEN A RULING FORMATION HAS BEEN RETURNED TO POWER WITH A LARGER MAJORITY, AND WITH AN ENHANCED VOTE SHARE OVER THE PREVIOUS ELECTION.

The BJP won the Lok Sabha election by a decisive margin, winning 303 of the 543 Lok Sabha Seats, with a vote share of 37.3% – the highest ever polled by any party other than the INC. The INC held on to 19.46% of the vote share, improving its tally marginally to 52. The DMK swept back to the third position in the seats tally with 24 seats, and the YSR Congress came up to the fourth slot with 22 seats (with a vote share of 2.53%), which it shared with the much-reduced TMC that claimed its 22 seats with about 4.06% share of the votes. The Shiv Sena finished with 18 seats, followed by the JDU, which had been in alliance with the BJP since 2005, and then broke out of it in 2014 only to return to the NDA in 2017, managed to win 16 seats (with only 1.45% share of seats). The BJD came down to 12 seats, although still very much in charge of its own regional base in Odisha. The TRS with 9 seats enjoyed a similar dominance in its own regional base of Telangana. The LJP stood with a modest 6 seats, the NCP and SP with a much reduced strength of 5. The CPI(M) was reduced to its worst performance ever since coming into existence, with a mere 3 seats – at par with the JKNC, TDP and IUML. The CPI also shrunk to a paltry 2 seats, at par with the SAD and the AIMIM. At the base of the Lok Sabha, remain parties like the AIADMK, JDS, AAP, JMM, AIUDF, RSP, AJSU, VCK, NDPP, NPP, KCM, NPF and MNF - each with a seat. More than 500 parties failed to win any seat in the seventeenth Lok Sabha elections which had the highest number of registered and unregistered parties ever contesting.

The regional map of political domination also changed somewhat in 2019. In Bihar, the NDA made a nearly-clean sweep of the Lok Sabha seats, winning 39 of the 40 seats of the state, with the BJP winning 17, the JDU 16 and the LJP 6; INC managed to win the only seat for the UPA. In Jharkhand, the NDA won 12 seats out of 14, with the BJP winning 11 and the All Jharkhand Students Union taking 1; the INC and JMM won a seat each. In Uttar Pradesh, the NDA won 64 seats out of 80, of which the BJP won 62 and Apna Dal (Sonelal) won 2. The SP and BSP, which contested in alliance, won 15 seats of which the BSP won 10 and SP 5. The INC was reduced to only 1 seat. The BJP won all the 5 seats for Uttarakhand, and all 4 seats for Himachal Pradesh. In Jammu and Kashmir, the BJP won all the 3 seats for Jammu and Ladakh; the JKNC won all the 3 seats for the Valley. In Punjab, the INC won 8 seats, the BJP and the SAD won 2 seats each, and the AAP won 1. In Haryana, the BJP won all the 10 seats for the state. In Rajasthan, the BJP won 24 of the 25 seats, with the INC winning the remaining seat. In Gujarat, the BJP won all 26 seats from the state. In Madhya Pradesh, the BJP won 28 out of the 29 seats from the state, with the INC taking the remaining 1 seat. In Chhatttisgarh, the BJP won 9 of the 11 seats, with the INC picking up the remaining 2. In Delhi NCR, the BJP made a clean sweep of all the 7 seats. In Maharashtra, the NDA won 41 of the 48 seats, with the BJP winning 23 seats and the Shiv Sena winning 18; 4 of the 5 seats of the UPA were won by the NCP, and the once hegemonic INC finished with only 1 seat. In West Bengal, the TMC won 22 seats, the BJP won 18, and the INC won 2 seats - the once hegemonic CPI(M) was wiped out altogether.

In Odisha, the ruling BJD held on to 12 seats, the BJP won 8 and the INC 1. The solitary seats of Chandigarh, and Daman and Diu were taken by the BJP; Dadra and Nagar Haveli was won by an independent candidate.

In the south, the INC lost most of its foothold, but the BJP failed to go beyond Karnataka. In Andhra Pradesh, the YSRC won 22 seats, while the TDP finished with 3 – the INC was wiped out. In Telangana, the TRS won 9 seats, the BJP 4 and the INC 3. In Karnataka, the BJP won 25 of the 28 seats of the state, with the INC, JDS and an independent candidate winning the remaining 3 seats. In Kerala, the INC had its only respectable showing, winning 15 of the 20 seats. The IUML won 2 seats and the KCM, RSP won a seat each. This gave the UPA 19 seats from the state. The ruling CPI(M) was left with only 1 seat. In Tamil Nadu, the NDA had a respectable showing, winning 38 of the 39 seats, of which the DMK won 24, the INC won 8, the CPI and CPI(M) 2 seats each, the IUML and the VCK a seat each. The AIADMK, a constituent of the NDA, won the solitary seat for the alliance. In Goa, the BJP and the INC took a seat each. The solitary seat in Lakshwadeep was taken by the NCP; the Puducherry and Andaman and Nicobar Islands seats were taken by the INC.

In the North-East, the INC weakened considerably without the BJP gaining, except in Assam and Tripura, but the winners were mostly members of the NDA. Of the 14 seats in Assam, the BJP won 9 seats, INC 3, AIUDF 1 and an independent won 1 seat. The BJP won both seats in Arunachal Pradesh. In Meghalaya, the INC and the National People's Party (an NDA constituent) won a seat each. In Manipur, the BJP and Naga People's Front (NPF) won a seat each. Both the solitary seats of Nagaland and Mizoram were won by NDA constituents, viz. the National Democratic Progressive Party and the Mizo National Front. Both the seats in Tripura were taken by the BJP. The solitary seat in Sikkim went to Sikkim Krantikari Morcha.

The BJP victory was understood and projected to be on account of the charisma of the prime minister, thus overlooking the role played by the consolidation of votes by means of electoral alliances. As a consequence, 73 of the 76 ministers in the second government of PM Modi happened to be from the BJP. Because of the still-reduced dependence of the BJP on its allies, fewer ministerial portfolios were on offer after the 2019 elections and even fewer of their choice – resulting in JD(U)'s decision to not join the cabinet at all. Subsequently Shiv Sena, JD(U) and the Shiromani Akali Dal also pulled out of the NDA because of differences on policy issues and the treatment they were subjected to. The virtual disintegration of the original NDA, with the departure of all its allies from the 1990s, has so far not dented the BJP at the union level. However, the impact is beginning to show in the provinces (such as Punjab, where the BJP has been swept out of reckoning, and Bihar, where the BJP has now been in power 3 times and in Opposition twice in the last five years) – but whether it has any bearing on the Lok Sabha elections of 2024 remains to be seen.

Chapter 14

THE AGE OF NON-CONGRESS STATE GOVERNMENTS 1999–2004

1999

Andhra Pradesh

With the passing away of N.T. Rama Rao, an age of politics had come to an end in Andhra Pradesh. The question of whether Telugu Desam would survive NTR was swiftly resolved by the party's performance in 1998, for the first time in alliance with the BJP. The factions led by NTR's son and that by his second wife were blown away by Chandrababu Naidu's faction of the party.

Chandrababu Naidu

In the elections held in that year, the Telugu Desam lost quite a few seats, and yet managed to win a comfortable majority with 180 seats (down 36) out of 294, with vote share of 43.87%. The INC won 91 seats (up 65) with 40.61% of the vote share. The BJP won 12 seats (up 9), with 3.67% of the popular vote. The AIMIM bagged 4 seats (up 3) and the CPI(M) 2 seats (down 12). The CPI failed to bag any seats at all.

Albeit with a reduced number of seats, the victory of the TDP was quite emphatic. Thus, Chandrababu Naidu was sworn in for the second time, and for the first full term as chief minister.

Arunachal Pradesh

As late as 1999, Arunachal Pradesh remained firmly a Congress territory, even though dissent among the legislature party saw the long-incumbent Gegong Apang ejected in 1999 from the leadership of the legislature party.

In the elections held in 1999 in the 60-seat assembly, the INC swept the polls winning 53 seats (up 10), with a vote share of 51.78%. The NCP won 4 seats, and the Arunachal Congress managed to win 1 seat. The BJP failed to win any seats.

In a strange twist of the kaleidoscope, the Congress selected Mukut Mithi, leader of the Arunachal Congress (Mithi) faction, to become the chief minister – he remained in office from 1999 to 2003. The former chief minister Gegong Apang, who left the Congress with a large body of the MLAs to set up a faction of the Arunachal Congress, entered into coalition with other allies to constitute the United Democratic Front. Soon after in August 2003, the UDF merged into the BJP to create a minority government in the state with the blessings of the governor. In 2004, when the NDA lost the general elections, Gegong Apang stepped down from the chief minister's office and left the BJP.

Goa

The assembly elections in 1999 marked a major transition in the political landscape of Goa, witnessing the rise of the BJP as a major player in the state's politics. The BJP had entered the Goa assembly in alliance with the MAG in 1994, but working hard among the newly domiciled in Goa in the 5 years that followed, along with its emphasis on Hindutva, the BJP flourished, gradually swallowing the vote base of its ally the MAG.

In the elections held that year, the INC emerged as the single largest party in the 40-seat assembly with the thinnest possible majority, winning 21 seats. Coming out of almost thin air, the BJP won 10 seats, while traditional players in Goan politics such as the MAG won 4 seats, and the United Goans Democratic Party only 2 seats. The Goa Rajiv Congress Party, a splinter group of the INC also won 2 seats.

Luizinho Faleiro, leader of the Congress in Goa, was sworn in as chief minister in the month in June 1999, but the government soon collapsed in November 1999 when the Congressman Francisco Sardinha broke away with some MLAs, and staked claim to form government with the support of the the BJP. In the new Sardinha government, the BJP was given 3 ministerial portfolios. Shortly thereafter, 4 more Congress MLAs (including the leader of the legislature party Ravi Naik) crossed the floor to join the BJP, followed by 5 more that had split earlier from the INC. Buoyed by the additional support of the 2 MAG allies, the BJP now staked claim to government formation. Accordingly, the Sardinha government resigned and the first BJP government was sworn in under Manohar Parrikar in October 2000. The Parrikar government remained in office for a little over 1 year and 7 months, before the government lost its majority on the floor of the assembly and collapsed, leading to fresh elections in 2002.

Karnataka

In an age when the INC was veritably wiped out in the north, and weakened even in the traditional bastion of Andhra Pradesh, the party won a resounding victory at Karnataka assembly elections of 1999. This was partly as a result of the split in the Janata Dal, brought about by the decision of the incumbent faction of the Janata Dal led by Chief Minister J.H. Patel that merged along with the Samata Party and the Lok Shakti Party of Ramakrishna Hegde into what came to be known as the Janata Dal United in 1998, which then entered the National Democratic Alliance led by the BJP, and won majority of the Lok Sabha seats from Karnataka. The segment of the Janata Dal that did not want to align with the BJP broke away to form the Janata Dal (Secular), splitting the Janata Dal votes.

As a consequence, in the 1999 elections to the 224-seat Karnataka assembly, the INC won a convincing majority of 132 seats (up 98) with a vote share of 40.84%. The BJP emerged as the second-largest party in Karnataka for the first time with 44 seats (up 4) and a vote share of 20.69%. The JDU came third with 18 seats (and vote share of 13.53%), while the JDS performed miserably with 10 seats – polling nearly 24% of the votes between the two of them. The independents carried 19 seats, indicating fragmentation of the electorate.

The veteran leader Somanahalli Mallaiah Krishna was sworn in as the chief minister of Karnataka. The former PSP legislator had joined the INC in 1971, and served in the Union cabinets of both Mrs Gandhi and Rajiv Gandhi, before becoming president of the Pradesh Congress Committee. He stayed in office for the full term (1999–2004), even as the Opposition ranks were being led by 2 prospective chief ministers – B.S. Yeddyurappa (BJP) and Siddaramaiah (then leader of the JDS).

B.S. Yeddyurappa

Maharashtra

The 1999 assembly elections in Maharashtra were the first where the political landscape became totally fractured, pulling in 4 different directions, making political alignments essential for stable governments to be formed. On the one hand, the incumbent Shiv Sena remained at the helm for a full term with support from its coalition partner the BJP. On the other now stood arraigned the INC, and its breakaway component, the Nationalist Congress Party, led by Sharad Pawar, who quit the INC refusing to accept Sonia Gandhi as party's prime ministerial candidate.

In the elections that were held, the Shiv Sena–BJP coalition lost a fair number of seats they had previously won. The INC emerged as the single largest party, winning 75 seats (down only 5, despite the loss of the Sharad Pawar faction), with a vote share of 27.2%; the Shiv Sena occupied the second slot with 69 seats (down 4) with vote share of 17.33%; the NCP came third with an impressive tally of 58 seats (and a vote share of 22.6%), while the BJP took 56 seats (down 9%) with a vote share 14.54%. The PWPI won 5 seats; the Bharipa Bahujan Mahasangh (founded in 1994 by Prakash Ambedkar); the JDS, CPI(M) and SP won 2 seats each.

Because of the 4-way fragmentation of the electorate, no party came close to forming a government. Pre-poll coalition of the Shiv Sena–BJP came up to only 125 seats, a good 19 short of the halfway figure of 288 seats. In the light of the circumstances, the INC and the NCP formed a post poll coalition (with 133 seats) and staked claim to the government, with Vilasrao Deshmukh of the INC being sworn in as the chief minister (1999–2003) and Chhagan Bhujbal of the NCP as the deputy chief minister. Eventually, Deshmukh had to step down as a result of inner-party power-struggle, and was replaced in

January 2003 by Sushil Kumar Shinde, who held the office till the end of the assembly term in December 2004).

2000

Bihar

The political situation in Bihar was appearing pretty dismal for quite some time, since Lalu Prasad Yadav stood at the helm in Bihar. Upon his being awarded a prison term and installation of his Rabri Devi in power, the BJP–JDU alliance carried 199 of the 326 assembly segments. The Congress, fearful that Lalu's corrupt image cost it votes broke their alliance with the RJD, decided to go it alone in the 2000 assembly elections; the RJD was left with only the 2 communist parties. On the other hand, Nitish Kumar pulled out of the JDU (led in Bihar by Sharad Yadav and Ram Bilas Paswan) floating the Samata Party with the veteran socialist George Fernandes. But despite his closer alignment with the BJP, he could not get them to project him as the CM-designate of the NDA.

In the elections that followed to the 324-seat Bihar assembly, the RJD pulled off a surprise show winning 124 seats of its own bat, to emerge as the single largest party. The BJP came second with 67 seats, followed by its election ally the Samata Party with 34 seats. The Congress came fourth with 23 seats, ahead of JDU's 21. The JMM won 12 seats; BSP finished with 5 seats; the CPI won 5 seats; the CPI(M) finished with 2 seats.

The NDA and its allies could pull up only 151 seats, and they decided to stake claim to form a government led by Nitish Kumar (since BJP's own strength did not measure up to much). Yet, controversially, the governor disregarded Rabri Devi's claim for government formation and invited Nitish Kumar instead, who was sworn in as chief minister in the month of March 2000. However, Nitish resigned after 7 days, unable to prove his majority on the floor of the house. Thereafter, Rabri Devi was sworn in at the helm of a government backed by both the communist parties and the Congress (with the latter accounting for 20 ministers in Rabri Devi's cabinet). Rabri Devi held the office of the chief minister for the full term of the assembly (March 2000–March 2005).

Haryana

The 2000 elections to the Haryana assembly brought about a change of government in a predictable fashion.

In the elections that were held that year to the 90 seats of the state assembly, the Indian National Lok Dal, led by O.P. Chautala, won 47 seats, with a vote share of 29.61%. The INC won only 21 seats, albeit it won the popular vote securing 31.22%. The BJP won 6 seats, and the BSP and NCP won 1 seat each.

Om Prakash Chautala was sworn back in as the chief minister, this time for the full term of the assembly (March 2000–March 2005).

Manipur

The elections to the Manipur assembly in 2000 saw the beginning of a trend of political forces being weaned away from the Congress.

In the elections that year, the breakaway formation of the INC, the Manipur State Congress Party, won 23 of the 60 seats in the assembly, with a vote share of 26.28%. The rump INC managed to retain only 11 seats (down 11), with a vote share of 18.31%. The BJP won 6 seats (up 5), with a vote share of 11.28%, as did the Federal Party of Manipur (founded by Gangmumei Kamei) with vote share of 9.44%. The NCP managed to win 5 seats and the Manipur People's Party won 4 seats. The Samata Party, the RJD, the JDS and JDU won 1 seat each.

The incumbent chief minister from MSCP, Wahengbam Nipamacha Singh was sworn back in as the chief minister at the head of United Front (constituting of 23 MSCP, 6 of the FPM, with 3 defecting MLAs from NCP and 1 from MPP. The Nipamacha Singh government remained in office till February 2001, when one by one its allies defected. Singh's government was replaced by Radhabinod Koijam, who took 11 of the 12 MLAs into the Samata Party, and persuaded Singh to step down in his favour. Radhabinod Koijam was sworn in as the chief minister in February 2002, at the head of the 33-minister-strong United Front government, with only 1 Congress MLA remaining in the Opposition. In May 2001, 18 MLAs of the Nipamacha faction of the MSCP broke from the party to constitute the Progressive MSCP, and then merged into the BJP. Shortly thereafter, with some more joining in, the BJP suddenly came to have 26 MLAs in the assembly – its leader in the state, Dorendra Singh, a former Congressman who now wanted to be the chief minister. A no-confidence motion was brought against Koijam, and he was easily voted out in June 2001. But this resulted in a full blown spat between the BJP and the Samata Party, and the BJP considered it prudent to impose President's Rule in Manipur (instead of appointing a BJP-led government), citing break-down of law and order after the Koijam government's failure to pay salaries of policemen had resulted in a strike by Manipur police. President's Rule remained in place for 277 days before elections were held in 2002.

Orissa

The assembly elections of the year 2000 marked a kind of milestone in ushering in an era of political stability in the state that was unprecedented. This was marked by the collapse of the Congress as a ruling party and the rise of the Biju Janata Dal as the main political force in the state.

The Biju Janata Dal was set up in 1997 by Naveen Patnaik, the son of the stalwart of Orissa politics, Biju Patnaik, after the death of his father. It was basically a breakaway faction of the Janata Dal under the leadership of Naveen, who took his party into an alliance with the NDA. Patnaik gained a seat in the Union cabinet of the 1999 Vajpayee administration, after the BJD won 10 Lok Sabha seats from Orissa – which essentially primed the BJD for the assembly elections of 2000.

In the elections of 2000 to the 147-seat Orissa assembly, the ruling INC got a drubbing, being reduced to 26 seats (down 54), with a vote share of 33.77%. The BJD won 68 seats by itself with only 29.39% of the vote share, and its electoral ally, the BJP, won 38 seats (with vote share of 18.19%). The JMM won 3 seats in the tribal areas, while the CPI, CPI(M), JDS and Trinamool Congress (TMC) won 1 seat each.

Naveen Patnaik was sworn in on March 2000, for his first full term (2000–2005) as the chief minister of Orissa.

2001

Assam

The state of Assam became one of the few states where the Congress bucked the national trend to return to power in 2001, thanks to the force of anti-incumbency operating against the AGP government of Prafulla Mahanta.

In the elections that were held in 2001, out of the 126 seats of the assembly the INC won 71 seats (up 37) with a vote share of 39.75%. The AGP managed to win only 20 seats (down 39) with a vote share of 20.02%. The BJP emerged as the third-largest party with 8 seats (up 4), and a vote share of 9.35%. The

NCP managed to win 3 seats, the Autonomous State Demand Committee managed to win 2 seats; the SP, the Samata Party and TMC won a seat each. The CPI, CPI(M) and other parties contesting the elections failed to win any seats.

Tarun Gogoi, who till then was active more in New Delhi than in the state circuit, was sent back to the state and was sworn in as the chief minister of Assam for the first of his 3 full terms (May 2001–May 2006) at a stretch in that office.

Kerala

The political landscape in Kerala has had an interesting feature develop over the years, apart from the near complete consolidation of the electorate along bipolar lines of alignment – the virtually routine change of government. 2001 was no different.

In the 2001 elections to the 140-seat assembly, the Congress-led UDF trounced the CPI(M)-led LDF and returned to power in the state. The UDF won 99 seats (up 40), while the LDF managed only 40 seats (down 80). Among the UDF constituents, the INC emerged as the largest party in the assembly winning 63 seats (with vote share of 31.4%); the IUML won 16 seats, the Janadhipatya Samrakshana Samiti won 4 seats; the JDS won 3; the Kerala Congress (Joseph) won 2; RSP 2; and the CMP won 1. Among the LDF constituents, the CPI(M) won 24 seats to be the second-biggest party in the assembly; the Kerala Congress (Mani) won 9 seats; the CPI won 7. While the BJP failed to win a single seat, the JDS won 3 seats and the NCP 2.

Arackaparambil Kurien Anthony was sworn in as the chief minister (May 2001–August 2004). He stepped down in 2004 after the party's poor performance in the Lok Sabha polls of 2004, and was succeeded by Oomen Chandy for the rest of the assembly term (August 2004–May 2006).

Pondicherry

Politics in the UT of Pondicherry remained comfortably ensconced in favour of the INC, and this continued to be so in the elections of 2001.

In the elections held that year to the 30-seat assembly, the INC led by chief minister Sanmugam won 11 seats with a vote share of 22.78%. The DMK remained the second-largest party, with 7 seats (vote share of 17.54%), and the AIADMK came third with 3 seats (12.54% of the popular vote). The debutant, Puducherry Munnetra Congress, won 4 seats. The Tamil Maanila Congress won 2 seats and the BJP opened its account in the territory with 1 seat.

The INC with its pre-poll ally Tamil Maanila Congress had a tally of 14 seats; with external support from the AIADMK, they were able to form the government, with T. Shanmugam being sworn in once again. But this time his stint in this office was brief (May 2000–October 2001), and was succeeded by Natesan Krishnasamy Rangaswamy who held the office for the rest of the term (2001–06).

Tamil Nadu

The DMK managed to finish its full term in office in 2001, deftly switching from the Congress to the NDA when it came to power in 1999. In so doing, it lost its old ally the Tamil Maanila Congress, which went over to join forces with the AIADMK, INC and PMK, as well as CPI, CPI(M), AIFB, IUML, INL, Tamilaga Makkal Munntera Kazhagam, and so on. On the other hand the DMK-led NDA alliance included the BJP and 14 other smaller parties.

In the elections that followed, the AIADMK-led alliance won 196 (up 138) of the 234 seats, winning 50.1% of the vote share. Of this the AIADMK won 132 seats (up 127, with 31.27 of the vote share); the TMC(M) won 23 seats (down 15); PMK won 20 seats (up 16); the INC won 7; the CPI(M) won 6 seats, and the CPI 5; the AIFB won only 1 seat. The DMK alliance won a total of 37 seats, of which 31 was won by the DMK; the BJP won 4 seats, and the MADMK won only 2 seats.

J. Jayalalithaa was sworn in as the chief minister, even though she was debarred from contesting elections because she had been found guilty of corruption. Jayalaithaa's swearing in was invalidated on the same ground, which resulted in the swearing in of O. Paneerselvam as interim chief minister till Jayalalithaa was acquitted in December 2001. Thereupon, after winning the Andapatti bypoll, Jayalaithaa was sworn in as the chief minister in March 2002, in which office she remained till May 2006.

West Bengal

On the face of it, the assembly elections of 2001 simply marked another victory of the Left Front in West Bengal, beating all possible records of anti-incumbency. However, the elections showed that the Left domination was beginning to fray. The Left Front realized this early on, and tried to salvage its position by replacing the veteran chief minister Jyoti Basu with his deputy Buddhadeb Bhattacharjee to lead the party into the polls.

In the elections held that year, the Left Front won 197 of the 294 seats in the assembly, of which the CPI(M) alone won 143 seats; AIFB won 25 seats, RSP won 17; CPI won 7; the WBSP won 4, and Biplobi Bangla Congress won 1 seat. The Trinamool Congress (TMC) emerged as the main force of the Opposition with 60 seats, breaking away from the INC, which won 26 seats. The GNLF won the 3 hill seats of Darjeeling, Kalimpong and Kurseong as before.

While the incumbent chief minister Buddhadeb Bhattacharjee was sworn back in 2001 and went on to serve his first full term in office, not all was hunky-dory. This was the first time since 1977 that the CPI(M) failed to win a majority in the assembly by itself, and also the only time since 1971, when no single party won the majority on the floor of the West Bengal assembly.

2002

Goa

After 19 month-plus BJP government in Goa during 2000–02, the political landscape of Goa shifted decisively in favour of the national parties and against the regional parties.

In the elections that were held to the 40-seat assembly, the BJP won 17 seats (up 7 since 1999), while the INC finished close with 16 seats. The UGDP finished with 3 seats and the MAG won only 2 seats, while the NCP won only 1 seat.

Manohar Parrikar was sworn back in office in 2002, and managed to run his government for only 3 years, even as one of his allies the UGDP and its Catholic base became increasingly uncomfortable with the free rein that was being given to the Hindu nationalist forces, such as the RSS. Parrikar also systematically tried to get Opposition legislators to cross the floor and join the BJP under the benevolent gaze of Governor Kedar Nath Sahni. However, when the NDA government lost the 2004 elections, the governor was changed, and the coming of the former Congress chief minister of Nagaland, S.C. Jamir (with a gaze no more benevolent) as the governor of Goa turned the tables on Parrikar. The Congress resumed the same game that Parrikar had been playing, and its support for Anatasio Monserrato (ex-UGDP) and other disgruntled ministers served to bring the Parrikar government down in 2005.

Pratapsingh Rane was sworn in as the chief minister of a minority government in February 2005 for just a month, but stepped down in the absence of the required numbers on the floor of the house. President's Rule was imposed for a few months, and then Rane staked claim for government yet again having successfully convinced enough number of MLAs to back him. Rane was thus sworn back in office in June 2005, and he remained in office till June 2007 when the next elections were held.

Gujarat

Assembly elections were held in Gujarat nearly 8 months ahead of schedule, partly because of the criticism of the role played by the chief minister during the carnage of 2002, and partly to capitalize on public opinion in favour of the ruling party. The incumbent chief minister resigned in July 2002 to seek a fresh mandate, which he secured handsomely.

In the elections that were held, the BJP blew away all fears of anti-incumbency to win 127 seats (up 10) out of 182, with a vote share of 49.85%. The INC emerged a distant second with only 51 seats, albeit with a vote share of 39.28%. Two seats were taken by the Janata Dal.

Narendra Modi was sworn back in as the chief minister of Gujarat, in which office he served for the full term of the assembly (2002–07).

Jammu and Kashmir

A measure of political stability returned to Jammu and Kashmir under chief minister Farooq Abdullah who had his first full term as chief minister, which came to an end with the 2002 assembly elections, held in the face of a boycott call from the Hurriyat Conference.

In the assembly elections that were held that year, the JKNC remained the single-largest party, but saw its strength drastically diminish, winning only 28 seats (down 29), with a vote share of 28.24%. The INC occupied the second slot, winning 20 seats (up 13), with a vote share of 24.24%. The debutant People's Democratic Party (PDP, founded in 1999 by the former Union Home minister, Mufti Muhammad Sayeed) finished with a tally of 16 seats; the BJP finished with 8 seats and the BSP with 4. The Panthers Party and JK Awami League won 1 seat each.

The year 2002 was the first election in which the stranglehold of the JKNC on the politics of the Valley was challenged through electoral means by a force (PDP) from within the Valley. The INC went on to forge a post-poll arrangement with the PDP, under which the PDP was to have its nominee the chief minister for the first 3 years, followed by the Congress nominee for the last 2. In accordance with this arrangement, Mufti Muhammad Sayeed was sworn in as the chief minister of the state in November 2002. After 3 years, he stepped down in favour of Congress's Ghulam Nabi Azad who held office for the rest of the term (2005–08).

Manipur

Manipur was under President's Rule during June 2001–March 2002 before it went for the assembly elections of 2002.

In the elections that were held in 2002 for the 60-seat assembly, the INC won 20 seats (up 9), with vote share of 26.18%; the Federal Party of Manipur came second with 13 seats (up 7) with vote share of 18.14%; the Manipur State Congress Party finished with 7 seats (down 16). National parties also began to grow their roots in the state, with the CPI winning 5 seats, the BJP winning 4, the NCP and Samata Party 3 each. The Democratic Revolutionary People's Party (represented by Biren Singh and Thokchom Meniya) and Manipur People's Party won 2 seats each.

In absence of the requisite numbers to form a government of its own, the INC joined the Secular Democratic Front with the Manipur State Congress Party, the NCP and the CPI. Okrom

Ibobi Singh of the Congress was sworn in as the chief minister of Manipur, in which capacity he served for the full term of the assembly (2002–07).

Punjab

Punjab witnessed a strong anti-incumbency after 5 years of the Akali government under Chief Minister Parkash Singh Badal. The SAD went to the polls in alliance with the BJP, while the INC had a pre-poll alliance with the CPI.

Captain Amarinder Singh (left)

In the elections that were held in 2002 for the 117-seat Punjab assembly, the INC won 62 seats by itself (with vote share of 35.81%), and its ally the CPI fetched 2 more (with 2.15% of the vote share). On the other hand, the SAD won 41 seats (with 31.08% of the vote share), while its ally the BJP won 3 seats (with vote share of 5.67%).

Captain Amarinder Singh, from the royal house of Patiala, was sworn in as the chief minister for the Congress, who held the office for the full term of the assembly.

Uttar Pradesh

After 5 years of political instability since the 1997 elections. Uttar Pradesh went to the polls for its 403-seat assembly in 2002. But there was little change in the political landscape of the state.

In the elections that were held in 2002, the Samajwadi party emerged as the single largest party with 143 seats (up 36), with vote share of 25.37%. The BSP finished second with 98 seats (up 32 seats) with vote share of 23.06%; the BJP finished third with 88 seats (down 68), and vote share of 20.08%. The INC, heavily depleted in strength, finished with 25 seats (and vote share of 8.96%), and the Rashtriya Lok Dal (led by Charan Singh) won 14 seats. The CPI(M) and Janata Dal won 2 seats each, and many other smaller parties (such as the Apna Dal, Akhil Bharatiya Loktantrik Congress, etc.) won a plurality of seats.

Given the fractured verdict, President's Rule had to be imposed for 56 days, before Mayawati became chief minister for the third time in May 2002, with the BJP extending support. The BJP proved to be a divided house, with Kalraj Mishra resigning his party presidency at the state level, who was then replaced by Vinay Katihar. Turmoil in the BJP had its impact on the state politics as well, with Mayawati finally having to step down in August 2003. Thereupon, Mulayam Singh Yadav staked claim to form another minority government with the support of disgruntled BSP MLAs. The SP government survived the rest of the term of the assembly (August 2003–May 2007), largely because the BJP let him be, hoping to gain political advantage from lowering of levels of hostility.

A noticeable feature of the 2002 elections to the UP assembly was that this particular election was the worst manifestation of criminalization of politics. A trend began to be noticeable from the 1990s, where candidates relying on muscle power (*Bahubalis*) and often those with criminal records were being given party tickets in elections, and such criminals were often also beginning to win such contests – the worst offenders being in Uttar Pradesh and Bihar. The Uttar Pradesh assembly polls saw the eventual election of 206 people with criminal records in an assembly of 403 seats. It could be said, the criminals had won a simple majority in the 2002 elections in the state.

Uttarakhand

In September 1998, the Uttar Pradesh Reorganisation Bill proposed the creation of the state of Uttarkhand in what used to be Garhwal kingdom. The Indian Parliament passed the Uttar Pradesh Reorganisation Act of 2000, bringing the state of Uttarakhand into being. In the Interim Uttarakhand assembly that came into being with elected members of the 2 houses of Uttar Pradesh, the BJP had 23 seats, the SP had 3, with the BSP and INC 2 seats each. The leader of the house was initially Nityanand Swamy, but was subsequently replaced by Bhagat Singh Koshiyary.

At the first assembly elections to the state of Uttarakhand in 2002, the INC finished with 36 seats out of 70, with vote share of 26.91%. The BJP finished second winning 19 seats (with 25.45% vote share); the BSP won 7 seats, the Uttarakhand Kranti Dal won 4, and the NCP won 1 seat.

Narayan Datt Tiwari, former chief minister of Uttar Pradesh and leader of the once-breakaway Congress (Tiwari) faction, had returned to the Congress in 1997. He was sworn in as the first elected chief minister of Uttarakhand, in which capacity he served for the full term of the assembly (2002–07).

2003

Chhattisgarh

Chhattisgarh came into being in 2000, as a result of legislation passed by the Madhya Pradesh government, which was then endorsed by the Government of India. On account of the distribution of the assembly constituencies and their incumbent positions, Ajit Jogi served as the first chief minister of the state, and took it into the first assembly elections in 2003.

In the elections held to the 90-seat assembly, the BJP won a simple majority with 50 seats (and vote share of 39.26%). The INC finished with 37 seats (with a vote share of 36.71%). The BSP won 2 seats, and the NCP won 1 seat.

Raman Singh, a dyed-in-the-wool BJP man from its earliest days, was sworn in as the chief minister of Chhattisgarh in December 2003, in which capacity he served the full term of the assembly, and the first of his 3 consecutive full terms.

Delhi

The assembly elections of Delhi in 1998 had brought a degree of stability to the political landscape of the state under the steady hand of Sheila Dikshit. The INC reaped the benefits of that stability in a terrain that had been dominated by politicians historically more aligned to the BJP.

In the elections that were held in 2003, the Congress won 47 seats (down 5) in the 70-seat assembly, with a vote share of 48.13%. The BJP came second with 20 seats (up 5), with a vote share of 35.22%. The NCP and JDS won 1 seat each.

Given the unambiguous nature of the victory, the incumbent chief minister Sheila Dikshit was sworn back in for the second (2003–2008) of her 3 full terms in that office.

Himachal Pradesh

By the early 2000s, a measure of political stability had emerged in the politics of Himachal Pradesh that ran along the lines of a kind of bi-party political consolidation.

In the elections to the 68-seat assembly of Himachal Pradesh, the INC managed to win 43 seats (up 12), with 41% of the popular vote. By contrast, the incumbent BJP was reduced to 16 seats (down 15), with 35.38% of the vote share. One seat each were taken by the Himachal Vikas Congress, Loktantrik Morcha Himachal Pradesh and Lok Jan Shakti party, with 6 seats being claimed by independent candidates.

The veteran Congress leader Virbhadra Singh was sworn in for his third full term as chief minister (2003–2007).

Madhya Pradesh

The Congress government in Madhya Pradesh fell victim to a very strong anti-incumbency after 10 years of Digvijay Singh as the chief minister.

In the first elections since separation of the state of Chhattisgarh, the Madhya Pradesh assembly came down to 230 seats. The BJP won a handsome majority with 173 seats (up 90), with a vote share of 42.50%. The INC got a major drubbing, being reduced to 38 seats (down 86), with vote share of 31.61%. The SP won 7 seats, the Gondwana Ganatantra Party won 3, and BSP and the Rashtrita Samanta Dal won 2 seats each. The NCP, JDU and CPI(M) won 1 seat each.

The firebrand Hindutva politician Uma Bharati was appointed the chief minister of the state in the December 2003, but had to step down in August 2004 under pressure from the party top brass after being accused of Hubli riots of 1994. Even as Uma Bharati fell out publicly with Deputy Prime Minister L.K. Advani, and floated her own outfit the Bharatiya Janashakti Party after being expelled for indiscipline, the Babulal Gaur was appointed chief minister (August 2004–November 2005) largely as a stop-gap chief minister. Once it was decided that Bharati was too much of loose cannon in a party like the BJP, the chief minister's baton was passed on to the state unit president, Shivraj Singh Chauhan, who held the office for the rest of the assembly term (2005–08). Chauhan had lost his own assembly election in 2003 at Raghogarh against Digvijay Singh, but made it back to the assembly through a by-election at Budhni. He has been winning the Budhni assembly seat ever since.

Uma Bharati

Meghalaya

The assembly elections in 2003 was in a way a continuation of the pattern of fragmented verdicts as in the past, but a novel feature of this election was the virtually complete marginalization of regional parties and relative dominance of national parties.

In the elections to the 60-seat assembly, the INC emerged yet again as the single-largest party, with 22 seats (down 3) with vote share of 29.96%. The debuting NCP emerged as the second-largest outfit with 14 seats, and a vote share of 19.40%. The UDP was reduced to 9 seats (down 11), its breakaway outfit Meghalaya Democratic Party (MDP) won 4 seats. The HSPDP, Khun Hynneutrip National Awakening Movement (KHNAM) and the BJP won 2 seats each; the Garo National Council and People's Democratic Movement and the Khasi Farmer's Democratic Party failed to win any seats. The same was true for the SP, CPI and the Samata Party.

The NCP tried to form a government under its leadership, but that failing the INC staked its claim after forming a coalition – Meghalaya Democratic Alliance – constituting of the UDP, MDP and KHNAM. D.D. Lapang of the INC was sworn in as the chief minister and Donkupar Roy of the UDP was made the deputy chief minister. Lapang remained in office from March 2003 to June 2006. When faced with internal party squabble, he stepped down in favour of his loyalist J. Dringwell Rymbai (June 2006–March 2007), only to resume the office from March 2007 to March 2008.

Mizoram

By 2000s, Mizoram began to enjoy a kind of political stability, largely thanks to the steady hand of Chief Minister Zoramthanga.

In the 2003 election to the 40-seat assembly of Mizoram, the MNF led by the incumbent Chief Minister Zoramthanga was able to retain a simple majority with 21 seats, winning a vote share of 31.69%. The INC finished second with a tally of 12 seats (up 6), albeit with a vote share of 30.06%, only marginally less than Zoramthanga; the Mizoram People's Conference (of Brigadier T. Sailo) was reduced to 3 seats (down 9). The debutant Zoram Nationalist Party (a breakaway faction of Mizo National Front (Nationalist), which in turn was a splinter group of MNF) won 2 seats; the Maraland Democratic Front and the Hmar People's Convention, 2 outfits devoted to the interests of small tribal groups in the state won a seat each. The BJP, JDU and the CPI failed to secure any seats, and the latter won only 1 vote more than the Ephraim Union (who got 123 votes) – a party that believes the Mizos are one of the 10 lost tribes of Israel.

Having secured a clear majority, the chief minister Zoramthanga was sworn in for the second full term in office (2003–08).

Nagaland

Nagaland assembly experienced a major tremor during the S.C. Jamir (1998–2003) government. Home Minister Neiphiu Rio resigned from the Congress in 2002, accusing the chief minister S.C. Jamir of being an obstacle to a negotiated settlement of the Naga issue. Rio joined the Naga People's Front (NPF, earlier known as the Naga People's Council), and put together a coalition – the Democratic Alliance of Nagaland – with the BJP, the JDU and the Samata Party.

In the elections to the 60-seat assembly that followed in 2003, the incumbent Congress remained the single largest party despite losing heavily, finishing with a tally of 21 seats (down 32), with a vote share of 35.86%. The debutant NPF won 19 seats, with a vote share 29.76%; the debutant BJP won 7 seats; the Nationalist Democratic Front (led by K.L. Chishi, which later merged with the BJP) won 5 seats; the JDU won 3 seats, and the Samata Party won 1 seat.

Neiphiu Rio was sworn in as the chief minister of Nagaland in March 2003, and remained in office for nearly 5 years, being dismissed by the governor only 2 months before the end of his full term, when President's Rule was imposed for reasons considerably less than satisfactory.

Rajasthan

By the 2000s, Rajasthan was one those states which appeared to have settled in for a bi-partisan consolidation of the electoral landscape where the two dominant parties were taking turns in every alternate election.

In 2003, the incumbent Congress government of Chief Minister Ashok Gehlot was voted out, with the party winning only 56 seats (down 97) of the 200-seat assembly. The BJP won 120 seats (up 87). The Indian National Lok Dal finished third with 4 seats, the JFU and BSP won 2 seats each, while the Lok Janshakti Party and the CPI(M) won 1 seat each, and 14 seats being taken by independents.

Vasundhara Raje Scindia

Vasundhara Raje Scindia, the Rani-ma of the royal Dholpur family, was sworn in as the chief minister for the full term of the assembly (December 2003–December 2008).

Tripura

Tripura continued to see near complete consolidation of the political landscape between the CPI(M) and the INC.

Manik Sarkar

The incumbent CPI(M) government of the chief minister Manik Sarkar won yet another clear majority with 38 of 60 seats, with vote share of 46.82%. The INC retained its previous tally of 13 seats, with vote share of 32.84%. The Indigenous Nationalist Party of Twipra (led by Bijoy Kumar Hrangkhawl) came third with a tally of 6 seats, the RSP won 2 seats, and the CPI won 1 seat. The BJP, the CPI(M) and the TMC failed to win any seats at all.

Manik Sarkar was sworn back in for the second (2003–08) of his 4 consecutive terms in the office of the chief minister.

2004

Andhra Pradesh

By 2004, Andhra Pradesh was firmly embedded in the NDA, and Chandrababu Naidu had successfully projected Hyderabad as one of the most important beacons of the India Shining campaign that NDA went to the general elections with. The outcome for the incumbent chief minister Chandrababu Naidu in Andhra Pradesh was much the same as for the NDA in the general elections of 2004 – a decisive defeat at the hands of the Congress and its pre-poll allies, the CPI, CPI(M) and the Telangana Rashtra Samiti.

In the elections to the 294-seat assembly, the INC won 185 seats (up 94), with vote share of 38.56%. The TDP finished second with 47 seats (down 133) despite having a high vote share of 37.59%, the TRS finished third with 26 seats (with vote share of 6.68%), the CPI(M) won 9 seats, and the CPI 6. The AIMIM stood steady at 4 seats and the BJP only 2.

The INC and its allies having chalked up 226 seats among themselves, Yeduguri Sandinti Rajasekhara Reddy, the leader of the Opposition in the outgoing assembly, was now sworn in as the chief minister, in which office he remained for the full term (2004–09).

Karnataka

The assembly elections of 2004 marked a watershed in the state of Karnataka, as a turning point of the steady rise of the BJP in the state.

Hit by anti-incumbency, the S.M. Krishna government was thrown out of power. The BJP emerged as the single largest party winning 79 seats in the 224-seat assembly, with 28.33% of the vote share. The INC won the popular vote with 35.27% vote share, but could not make it to more than 65 seats. The JDS finished with 58 seats (20.77% of the vote share), while the JDU finished with only 5 seats.

Confronted with the first hung assembly in the history of Karnataka, the Congress and the JDS came to form a post-poll coalition. Dharam Singh – a former state cabinet minister with excellent rapport with the JDS leader H.D. Deve Gowda – was sworn in as the consensus candidate for the position of the chief minister in May 2004. However, his government collapsed in February 2006 when JDS leader (and son of Deve Gowda) Haradanahalli Deve Gowda Kumaraswamy brought down the coalition government with 46 MLAs from his party, in order to form a coalition government of his own with the BJP. He remained in office from February 2006 to October 2007. His stint as the chief minister was on the basis of a power sharing arrangement under which he was meant to transfer power to the coalition partner BJP, but this he refused to do when his period came to an end, and resigned instead from the office. This caused the state to be put under President's Rule for the time being. Later, Kumaraswamy changed his mind and agreed to support B.S. Yediyurappa. Thus, Yediyurappa was sworn in as chief minister on 12 November 2007, but once again as disputes surfaced over distribution of portfolios, Kumaraswamy refused to extend his support, forcing Yediyurappa to resign, and President's Rule to be imposed once again, which remained in place till Karnataka went to the polls again in 2008.

Orissa

While the NDA failed to perform any electoral miracle nationwide, Orissa continued to be held by the NDA under Naveen Patnaik, who was becoming perhaps the most proficient chief minister of the country.

In the elections to the Orissa assembly, brought forward to coincide with the Lok Sabha elections, the BJD–BJP alliance clinched a comfortable victory, winning 93 seats between the two of them. Of this the BJD won 61 seats (down 7), with 27.36% vote share; the BJP won 32 seats (down 6), with vote share 17.11%. The INC emerged as the third-largest party winning 38 seats, even though it secured the largest vote share in these elections (34.82%). The JMM won 4 seats, 2 seats were won by a splinter group of the BJD, the Orissa Gana Parishad; the CPI and the CPI(M) won 1 seat each.

Naveen Patnaik was sworn in for his second full term as chief minister (2004–09) at the head of the coalition government. But by 2008, relationship began to strain between the 2 allies, with Hindu hardliners causing communal tensions in the tribal regions, in particular the Kandhamal region where Bajrang Dal instigated communal riots against Christians in 2007. Patnaik waited for his full term and then launched a severe critique of the BJP, and broke away from the NDA just on the eve of the next assembly elections in 2009.

Sikkim

Assembly elections in Sikkim were dominated by the incumbent Sikkim Democratic Front (SDF), who carried with the state's winner-takes-all pattern of elections.

In the 2004 elections to the 32-seat assembly, the SDF won 31 seats with 71.09% of the votes polled. The INC was the only other party with a single seat in the assembly, having received 26.13% of the votes. Both national parties like the BJP and the CPI(M) and state parties like Sikkim Himali Rajya Parishad and Sikkim Sangram Parishad failed to win any seats at all.

Given the unequivocal nature of the victory, Pavan Kumar Chamling was sworn back in again for the second of his 5 consecutive full terms as the chief minister.

Arunachal Pradesh

The 2004 assembly elections were held in Arunachal Pradesh in the backdrop of the defeat of the NDA in the general elections, and Gegong Apang's political somersault.

In the 2004 elections to the 60-seat Arunachal assembly, the INC swept the polls as earlier, winning 34 seats, with share of 44.41% of the vote share. The BJP under Kiren Rijiju emerged as the second-largest party with 9 seats (albeit with only 2.63% vote share). The NCP and the Arunachal Congress won 2 seats each, while the independents won 13 seats.

With the INC back in the driving seat, Gegong Apang stepped down as the chief minister of the minority BJP government, and was sworn back in as chief minister of the Congress government (August 2003–April 2007). Gegong Apang was finally toppled from office in 2007, when he was replaced by Dorjee Khandu, who continued in that office till the 2009 assembly elections. At the time of Apang's removal, the dissidents' claim for support of Arunachal Congress, 2 NCP and 11 independent MLAs provided the clinching argument for Khandu's elevation. In June 2009, 8 of the 9 BJP MLAs (i.e. all excluding Kiren Rijiju) joined the INC, raising its tally to 41.

Maharashtra

The defeat of the NDA in the general elections of 2004 was reinforced in Maharashtra by the defeat of the NDA allies, the BJP and Shiv Sena in the hands of the INC–NCP alliance.

In the elections to the 288-seat Maharashtra assembly, the NCP emerged the single largest party, winning 71 seats, with 18.75% of the vote share. Its electoral ally the INC won 69 seats with vote share of 21.06%. The Shiv Sena won 62 seats, with vote share of 19.97%; its electoral ally the BJP won 54 seats, with 13.67% of the vote share. The CPI won 3 seats and the Peasants and Workers Party of India won 2 seats; 4 other parties including Bharipa Bahujan Mahasangh (led by Prakash Ambedkar) won 1 seat each.

Vilasrao Deshmukh of the INC was sworn in as the chief minister of Maharashtra, in which office he remained from 2004 to 2008. He had to resign in 2008, in the aftermath of the 26/11 Bombay attacks, whereupon he was succeeded by Ashok Chavan, the son of former Congress stalwart, S.R. Chavan, for the rest of the assembly term (December 2008–November 2009).

Vilasrao Deshmukh

Chapter 15

THE INDETERMINATE YEARS IN THE STATES 2005–15

2005

Bihar

In 2005, Bihar witnessed something that has never happened in the realm of Indian politics – neither till then nor since. Elections to the legislative assembly of Bihar were held twice in the same calendar year.

In the elections to the 243-seat Bihar assembly, the RJD remained the single largest party with 75 seats, but much depleted (down 28), with a vote share of 25.07%; the principal challenger, the JDU chalked up a tally of 55 seats (up 17) with a vote share of 14.55%, and its ally the BJP won 37 (down 2) with a vote share of 10.97% – bringing the NDA tally to 92 seats. The Lok Janshakti Party (LJP, founded in 2000 by Ram Vilas Paswan after he left the Janata Dal), which contested the polls in alliance with the RJD and the INC, won 29 seats with a vote share of 12.62%; the INC finished with a tally of 10 seats with only 5% of the popular vote – virtually stamped out of the Bihar political landscape. The CPI(ML) won 7 seats, the Samajwadi

Party 4, the CPI and the NCP finished with 3 seats each and CPI(M) won 1. More than 40 other parties failed to win a seat.

With the RJD and its allies standing at 112, and the NDA at 92, neither bloc was in a position to come any close to forming a government. Accordingly, President's Rule was imposed in Bihar on 7 March 2005, which was to last till November 2005. However, in a lawsuit brought against the imposition, the Supreme Court ruled the imposition of President's Rule without giving elected legislators the time to try to form a government was unconstitutional, and a mala fide act. Thus, Bihar went back to the polls once again in the month of November.

In the October–November elections to the Bihar assembly, the NDA powered ahead of the RJD and its allies. The JDU emerged as the largest party in the assembly winning 88 seats (up 33) with a vote share of 20.46%; its ally the BJP emerged as the second-largest party with 55 seats (up 18) with 15.65% of the vote share. The RJD was pushed back to the third place, winning 54 seats (down 21) despite having the largest vote share (23.45% of the popular vote), the LJP was reduced to 10 seats (down 19 since February) and the INC was limited to only 9 seats. The CPI(ML) finished with a tally of 5 seats, the BSP with 4, the CPI 3, the SP 2 and the CPI(M) and the NCP with 1 seat each.

Nitish Kumar was sworn in as chief minister of Bihar, in which capacity he served for the full term of the assembly (2005–10); Sushil Modi of the BJP was brought back from the Lok Sabha and charged with the leadership of the BJP in the assembly, and was inducted into the government as deputy chief minister of the state.

Haryana

Elections to the Haryana legislative assembly in 2005 delivered a landslide against the incumbent long-time chief minister

Om Prakash Chautala, beginning a brief period of Congress resurgence in the political landscape of the state.

In the elections held in 2005, the INC won a landslide victory with 67 seats (42.46% of the vote share). The incumbent INLD was reduced to 9 seats, with 26.77% of the vote share; the BJP was reduced to 2 seats (10.36% of the popular vote), and the BSP and the NCP had 1 seat each.

Bhupinder Singh Hooda, the leader of the opposition in the previous assembly, was sworn in as chief minister, and remained in office for the full term of the assembly (2005–10).

Jharkhand

The Jharkhand state came into being in November 2000, and its first interim assembly was drawn from the Bihar legislative assembly, by taking into consideration the victorious candidates in the assembly constituencies that came to constitute the new state – which produced a hung assembly, led by Babulal Marandi of the BJP as its chief minister.

In the first elections held for the 81-seat Jharkhand assembly in 2005, a hung assembly was returned. The BJP won 30 seats with a vote share of 23.57%; its NDA ally, the JDU chalked up a tally of 6 seats (with only 4% of the popular vote). The JMM emerged as the second-largest party with 17 seats and a vote share of 14.29%, while its UPA ally, the Congress could win only 9 seats with 12.05%. The RJD, fighting by itself, won 7 seats, the AIGB, the All Jharkhand Student's Union and (curiously) the United Goans Democratic Party) won 2 seats each, and the NCP, CPI (ML) and the Jharkhand party failed to win any seats.

After the elections, one of the pioneers of the Jharkhand movement, Shibu Soren of the JMM, with INC support, staked the claim to form a government despite not having the numbers, and was even given the opportunity by a UPA-appointed governor, Syed Sibte Razi. However, predictably Shibu Soren failed to cobble together his government, and resigned after 9 days in March 2005. With 36 seats, the NDA formed a minority government under Arjun Munda, an ex-JMM politician and then a member of the Babulal Marandi cabinet. He remained in office for a little over a year (March 2005–September 2006), with support from Madhu Koda - former member of the Marandi cabinet, who, upon being denied his assembly ticket, contested as an independent candidate in the 2005 election, won the seat and decided to support the BJP-led government in return for a portfolio. In 2006, he along with two other MLAs withdrew support and brought down the Munda government. As a compensation for this, when the UPA (INC, RJD, JMM, NCP) staked claim for government formation, they made Madhu Koda the chief minister (September 2006–August 2008).

The Koda government collapsed in August 2008 when Shibu Soren wanted to become CM once again and withdrew support from the government. Koda stepped down and Soren assumed the position of the chief minister, only to fail to enter the assembly by losing the Tamar assembly seat. Thus Soren resigned and President's Rule was imposed in Jharkhand (January–November 2009).

2006

Assam

The 2006 elections to the legislative assembly of Assam returned the incumbent Tarun Gogoi back to the chief minister's office, but with a much reduced strength.

Tarun Gogoi

In the elections held that year to the 125-seat assembly, the INC emerged as the single-largest party with 53 seats (down 18) and 31.08% of the popular vote. The AGP won 24 seats with a vote share of 20.39%; its electoral ally in the NDA, the BJP won 10 seats, with 11.39% of the vote share. The Assam United Democratic Front, (set up in 2005 by Badruddin Ajmal, and speaking for the Bengali Muslim population of Lower Assam and Barak Valley) won 10 seats. The CPI(M) won 2 seats, the NCP, the CPI, Asom Gana Parishad Pragatisheel and Autonomous State Demand Committee won 1 seat each. There were, in addition 22 independents who won their seats in the assembly.

Falling short of the requisite numbers for a simple majority, the INC courted support from independent MLAs in addition to the sole NCP MLA. When such support was obtained, Tarun Gogoi was sworn back in for his second consecutive full term (2006–2011) as chief minister.

Kerala

The assembly elections in Kerala in 2006 conformed to the pattern that obtained for quite some time, of not returning any incumbent to power. The INC-led UDF government – led first by A.K. Anthony and later by Oommen Chandy – was beaten convincingly by the LDF.

In the elections that were held in 2006 to the 140-seat Kerala assembly, the LDF won 98 seats (up 51). Of this the CPI(M) alone won 61 seats (with a vote share of 31.45%); the CPI won 17 (a vote share of 8.09%); the Kerala Congress (Mani) won 7, the

JDS 5. The Indian National League, the NCP, the Kerala Congress (Balakrishna Pillai), the Congress (Secular), and the Kerala Congress secular had 1 seat each. By contrast the UDF won only 42 seats (down 57). Of this the INC won 24 seats (with a vote share of 24.09%), IUML won 7 seats, the Kerala Congress won 4, RSP 3, and the JSS 1.

Vellikakathu Sankaran Achuthanandan was sworn in as the LDF chief minister in 2006, and he remained in that office for the full assembly term (May 2006–May 2011).

Tamil Nadu

The 2006 elections to the Tamil Nadu assembly ran along lines similar to previous patterns that had developed over several years – the two Dravid parties take turns in power in alliance with smaller regional and national parties; national parties which contest alone do not manage to get their feet on the ground. Predictably the incumbent AIADMK was voted out, and DMK voted back in.

The incumbent AIADMK aligned with the MDMK (led by Vaiko), Viduthalai Chiruthaigal Katchi (VCK, aka Dalit Panthers), INL, INTUC, Moovender Munnetra Kazhagam (of the Thevar caste), Tamil Maanila Muslim League, Forward Bloc and JDS. On the other hand, the DMK aligned with the INC (into which TMC had merged in 2002), PMK, CPI, CPI(M), IUML, Puratchi Bharatam, Forward Bloc (Vallarasu). Desiya Murpokku Dravida Kazhagam (DMDK) was set up by Tamil actor K. Vijaykanth as a third option for the Dravid political landscape. The DMDK – just like the Lok Paritran (a party of IIT graduates with the agenda of saving the people) – decided to contest by themselves.

In the 234-seat Tamil Nadu assembly, the DMK and its allies won 163 seats (up 71), of which the DMK by itself won 96 seats (up 65) with 26.5% of the vote share; the INC won 34 (up 4) seats with 8.4% vote share; the PMK won 18 seats, the CPI(M) won 9 and the CPI won 6 seats. By contrast the AIADMK alliance won 69 seats (down 64), of which the AIADMK won 61 seats (down 72) with a vote share of 32.6%, the MDMK won 6 seats and the VCK won 2 seats.

This was the first time in the Tamil Nadu assembly that no party had the majority seats in the assembly since 1952. The DMK's Karunanidhi was sworn in as chief minister for the fifth (and as it happened to be the final) term (2006–2011).

West Bengal

The elections to the West Bengal assembly were pretty unremarkable in their outcome, returning incumbent chief minister Buddhadeb Bhattacharjee to power for his second and his party's seventh consecutive term.

In the elections that were held in 2006, the Left Front won 235 seats, of which the CPI(M) alone accounted for 176 seats (up 33) with a vote share of 37.13%; the AIFB won 23 seats, the RSP won 20; the CPI won 8 seats, the WBSP won 4, the RJD and DSP (PC) won 1 seat each. The TMC, which contested as a part of the NDA won 30 seats, while the BJP and the JDU failed to win any seats but tried to leave their mark. The INC won 21 seats and the GNLF won 3. Eventually in a number of bypolls, the Left Front lost 4 of their seats to the TMC.

Buddhadeb Bhattacharjee was sworn in for the last of his terms as the chief minister (2006–11).

Pondicherry/Puducherry

The elections to the 30-seat legislative assembly of Pondicherry in 2006 were a pretty mundane affair.

The incumbent UPA alliance, which constituted of the INC, the DMK, PMK and the CPI won a clear majority. Of this, the INC won 10 seats, the DMK 7, the PMK 2 and the CPI 1 seat.

Among the Opposition were the AIADMK (3 seats), Puducherry Munnetra Congress (3) and MDMK won 1 seat.

N. Rangaswamy was sworn back into power, where he remained between October 2006 to September 2008, when he stepped down in favour of his colleague in the Congress, V. Vaithlingam who held office for the rest of the assembly term. In the midst of all this, in October 2006 the name of the UT was changed from Pondicherry to Puducherry.

2007

Goa

Elections to the assembly of Goa took place in June 2007, appearing as fractured in its verdict as the last time.

In the elections held that year, the INC won 16 seats in the 30-seat assembly, its ally the NCP won 3 seats and the Save Goa Front won 2 seats. The incumbent BJP saw its strength reduced to 14 seats, the MAG to only 2 seats and United Goans Democratic Party to 1.

The INC staked the claim for government formation, but factional struggles pushed Pratapsingh Rane aside. Digambar Kamat, another Congress politician (who at one point of time even joined the BJP), was sworn in as the chief minister, and remained in the office between June 2007–March 2012. Forming the government with support from the NCP and SGF, eventually the INC had the SGF merged into it.

Gujarat

Elections to the legislative assembly of Gujarat, held in December 2007, helped set a pattern in the state's political landscape, and ushered in a period of considerable political stability.

In the elections held that year, the BJP won 117 seats (down 10) in the 182-seat assembly, with vote share of 49.12%. The INC finished second with 59 seats (up 8), with a vote share of 38%. The NCP finished third with 3 seats, the JDU with 1, while only 2 independents were successful – indicating how complete the consolidation of BJP's stranglehold on Gujarati politics had become by then.

The definitive architect of that consolidation, the incumbent chief minister Narendra Modi was sworn back in for his second full term at the helm of the state (2007–2012). The continuation of the twice-defeated former BJP leader, Shankarsinh Vaghela, as leader of the Opposition, went some distance in explaining the cause of CM Modi's success.

Himachal Pradesh

Elections to the legislative assembly of Himachal Pradesh in 2007 confirmed that Himachal Pradesh had more or less settled with a bi-partisan political consolidation with the two main parties taking turns at the helm of affairs. Anti-incumbency appeared to have become institutionalized.

In the elections held in December that year, the BJP won a comfortable majority, with 41 seats in the 68-seat assembly, (a vote share of 43.78%). The INC finished second with 23 seats, with 38.9% of the vote share. The BSP won 1 seat and independents 3.

Former Chief Minister Prem Kumar Dhumal was sworn in as the chief minister for his second full term in that office (2007–12). The outgoing Chief Minister Virbhadra Singh, resumed his earlier role as leader of the Opposition.

Manipur

The political landscape of Manipur appeared to stabilize somewhat in 2007, as the incumbent government managed to improve its hold on power, improving its tally of seats in the assembly.

The INC was able to win a simple majority of its own bat, winning 30 seats in the 60-seat assembly, with 34.3% of the vote share. Its allies in the governing Secular Progressive Front, the NCP, who won 5 seats, and the CPI (4), gave the Front 39 seats in the assembly. The Front's other constituent, Manipur State Congress Party failed to win any seats. The Opposition was led by Manipur People's Party with 5 seats. National outfits like the BJP, SP, RSP, CPI(M), JDU and JDS and regional parties like the Naga National Party and PDA – all failed to win any seats at all.

The architect of the victory, the incumbent Okram Ibobi Singh, was sworn back in as chief minister for his second consecutive full term (2007–12) in that office.

Punjab

The Punjab legislative assembly went to the polls in 2007, witnessing a fierce contest that continued with a kind of bilateral consolidation of the electorate.

The incumbent Congress chief minister Amrinder Singh decided to go it alone in 2007, and in a way paid the price by losing the election despite the really hard fight he put up. The INC finished second with 44 seats (down 18) with a vote share of 40.90%. The SAD, however, did not benefit much from the seats lost by the Congress, winning only 48 seats (up 8), with a vote share of 37.09%. The principal beneficiary of votes lost by the INC was its national rival and the SAD's NDA ally, the BJP, which won 19 seats (up 16) with 8.28% of the vote share. Apart from these 3 parties, only 5 independent candidates were successful in reaching the assembly. The CPI and CPI(M) – which had historically been steady in gaining a few seats in the Punjab assembly – were wiped out.

With 68 seats in the 118-seat assembly, the NDA duo of SAD-BJP formed the government, and Parkash Singh Badal was sworn in for the fourth time, and for his second full-term in office (2007–12), as Captain Amrinder Singh sat as the leader of the Opposition.

Uttarakhand

The second Uttarakhand assembly saw a turning of the tables as the incumbent INC were voted out in a clear mandate for the BJP.

The BJP emerged as the single largest party with 34 seats in the 70-seat assembly, with 31.90% of the vote share. The INC won 21 seats with a vote share only marginally lower than the BJP, standing at 29.59% of the popular vote. Since the BJP did not gain a simple majority of their own, they entered into a post-poll arrangement with the Uttarakhand Kranti Dal (led by Diwakar Bhatt), which won 3 seats, plus 3 more independents. The BSP managed to win 8 seats in the assembly.

Gaining power, the BJP in Uttarakhand began to look somewhat like the Congress, in the sense during the assembly term (2007–12), they gave the people of the state 2 chief ministers for the price of 1. Initially, retired major general Bhuvan Chandra Khanduri was sworn in as the CM in 2007, but he had to step down in 2009, when Ramesh Pokriyal Nishank became the chief minister. However, Khanduri once again made it back to the CM's office in 2011, and remained there till the next general elections in 2012.

Uttar Pradesh

The Uttar Pradesh assembly elections of 2007 were unusual in a way that after a long time it resulted in a government with a simple majority, which was relatively more stable than before.

In the elections held in 2007, the BSP won an outright majority with 206 seats (up 139) with a vote share of 30.73%. The outgoing party-in-power, the SP was reduced to 97 seats (down 46) with 25.43% of the vote share. The BJP came third with 51 seats (down 37) and a vote share of 16.97%, while the INC was confined to only 22 seats (down 3). The RLD of Ajit Singh barely hung on with 10 seats (down 5) and the Akhil Bharatiya Loktantrik Congress (of Jagadambika Pal), the JDU, the Jan Kranti Party, the Jan Morcha all finished with 1 seat each. A total of 116 parties that fielded a candidate failed to win any seats including the RJD and Lok Janshakti Party.

Mayawati, the leader of the BSP, was sworn in as chief minister for her only full term in office till date (2007–12). Her success in the 2007 elections was attributed to her attempt to step outside a Dalit box that gave her the core voters of the BSP, and her forming of a rainbow coalition (embracing both the Dalits and the upper castes). She also gained a reputation for reigning in the 'Mafia Raj' that Mulayam was reputed to have allowed during the SP stint in power. Mayawati improved law and order, and reined in corruption by members of the ruling party (if only by concentrating all acts of corruption in her own hands, as her critics would often say).

The 2007 elections in a way bore further testimony to the criminalization of politics in the state. It is estimated that 1 in every 3 BSP candidate had a criminal record, nearly 1 in every 4 SP and BJP candidates had the same. The INC turned out to be the cleanest of the lot, fielding only 1 criminal in every 5 for the assembly. However, unlike in the 2002 elections, only 100 candidates with criminal records against them became successful – presumably a tribute to the efforts of the ECI by the deployment of security personnel at an unprecedented level in conducting the elections.

2008

Chhattisgarh

Elections to the legislative assembly of Chhattisgarh were held in 2008, which the incumbent BJP government was able to win quite comfortably in what was well on the way to become a bi-partisan landscape.

In the elections held for the 90-seat assembly, the BJP won 50 seats, with 40.35% of the vote share. The INC won 38 seats with 38.62% of the popular votes. The BSP came third with 3 seats, the NCP drew a blank, as did the independents.

Raman Singh was sworn back in for a second term, which lasted for the full term of the assembly.

Delhi

The elections to the legislative assembly of Delhi in 2008 ran along the lines of the previous 2 elections. Sheila Dikshit reaped the benefits of a sound approach to administration and thus the Congress managed to hold on to Delhi with a degree of ease.

The INC won 43 seats (down 4) with a vote share of 40.31%. The BJP remained in second place, winning 23 seats (up 3) with a vote share of 36.34%. The BSP won 2 seats, the Lok Janshakti party and the tally for independents stood at 1 each.

Sheila Dikshit was sworn back in as the chief minister for her third and last time for the full term of the assembly (2008–13).

Jammu and Kashmir

The INC-PDP government under Ghulam Nabi Azad was brought down over the Congress decision of transferring 99 acres of land in the Kashmir Valley to the Amarnath Shrine Board for the well-being of pilgrims. The demonstrations against this by the All Parties Hurriyat Conference brought out huge crowds. Realizing the unpopularity of the decision, the PDP backed out from the decision, and withdrew their support from the government in July 2008 – months before the assembly term ended.

In the elections of 2008, the assembly remained nearly as hung as before. The JKNC remained the single largest party in the state, winning 28 seats (same as 2002) with a vote share of 23.07%; the JKPDP won 21 seats (up 5) with a vote share of 15.39%. The INC won 17 seats (down 3), with a vote share of 17.71%; the BJP won 11 seats (up 10, its best results ever, presumably boosted by their protests after the withdrawal of the land transfer), and the J&K Panthers Party won 3 seats (down 1).

This time round, the JKNC entered into a post-poll coalition with the INC, and Omar Abdullah became the youngest chief minister at the age of 38, who remained in that office for the full term of the assembly (January 2009–January 2015).

Karnataka

Karnataka had gone through turmoil since 2003 elections, with Kumaraswamy and Yeddyurappa contesting over the chief minister's office, dragging Karnataka into President's Rule.

In the elections that followed in 2008, the BJP emerged as the single largest party winning 110 seats (up 31), with a vote share of 33.86%. The INC finished second with 80 seats (up 15), even though it won the popular vote with 34.76%. The JDS finished with 28 seats (down 30), with a vote share of 18.96%. All other parties in the fray finished with a blank, and only 6 independents ended winning their seats.

Falling short of simple majority by only 3 seats, the BJP negotiated with the 6 independent MLAs, and went past the majority figure. Thus B.S. Yeddyurappa was sworn in as the chief minister (May 2008). After 3 years in office, Yeddyurappa had to step down in August 2011 charged in a corruption case on illegal mining. He was replaced by his protégé, Devaragunda Venkappa Sadanand Gowda. However, upon becoming chief minister, Sadanand Gowda fell out with his mentor, and lost the confidence of the legislature party (with the full support of Yeddyurappa), and was asked by his party to step down in July 2012. He was replaced by Jagdish Shettar, who held the office between July 2012 and May 2013.

Madhya Pradesh

By 2008, Madhya Pradesh was starting to become a BJP stronghold under the able rule of Shivraj Singh Chouhan, who led his party to the polls that year.

In the elections to the assembly, the BJP retained its majority winning 143 of the 228 seats (down 30), with a vote share of 37.64%. The INC finished second with only 71 seats (up 33) with 32.89% of the popular vote. The BSP won only 7 seats, while the Bharatiya Jana Shakti Party, founded by Uma Bharati finished with 5 seats. The SP won only 1 seat, while independents won 3.

Despite losing almost 1 in every 5 seats between 2003 and 2008, Chouhan was sworn back in as the chief minister for his second full term in office (2008–13).

Meghalaya

The Meghalaya Democratic Alliance that had formed the government after the 2003 elections had broken up long before the 2008 elections. Thus the INC contested against the UDP and the MDP.

In the election to the assembly held that year, the INC finished as the single largest party with 25 seats, and vote share of 32.88%. The NCP win 14 seats, with 20.4% of the popular vote.

The UDP finished in the third place with 11 seats (18.6% of the popular vote). The HSPDP won 2 seats, with 3.89% of the vote share. The BJP and the Khun Hynniewtrep National Awakening Movement managed to win 1 seat each, while independents won 5 seats.

Being the leader of the largest party in the assembly, D.D. Lapang was invited by the governor to form the government, but Lapang gave up after trying for 9 days to secure the required numbers for the floor test shortly after. Donkupar Roy of the UDP who had claimed the support of 31 MLAs in the 60-seat assembly (NCP, UDP, HSPDP, BJP, KHNAM and 2 independents) was next invited to form the government. Donkupar Roy was sworn in to the office of the chief minister in March 2008. The Roy government survived just for a year, after which it was dismissed and President's Rule was imposed in Meghalaya. After about 52 days, D.D. Lapang was sworn back in as chief minister for some time (May 2009–April 2010) at the head of the Meghalaya United Alliance (INC, UDP plus independents). Upon Lapang's stepping down, Deputy CM Mukul Sangma was sworn in, and he went on to hold the office for the remaining term of the assembly (2010–13).

Mizoram

In the elections to the 2008 legislative assembly of Mizoram, anti-incumbency finally kicked in to remove Zoramthanga from power after 2 straight terms.

In the elections held in December 2008, the INC swept back to power with 32 seats (up 20), and a vote share of 38.9%. The MNF was reduced to only 3 seats (down 17) with 31.54%; the MPC won 2 seats and Zoram Nationalist Party, while the Maraland Democratic Front won only 1 seat.

Pu Lalthanhawla was sworn in as the chief minister for the fourth time, and his second full term in office (2008–13).

Nagaland

Nagaland had come to see a kind of political stability without the INC under Neiphiu Riu of the NPF who led a coalition government for nearly a whole term before the arrangement broke down. When Nagaland went to the polls in 2008, that particular sort of political stability seemed to triumph over political fragmentation which had come to characterize the state's political landscape.

The NPF finished at the top of the seats tally winning 26 seats (up 7) in the 30-seat assembly, with a vote share of 33.6%. The INC came close enough with 23 seats (up 2), albeit with a higher vote share of 36.3%. The BJP and the NCP, aligned respectively with the NPF and the INC won 2 seats each, while independents claimed 7 seats.

In the circumstances, Neiphieu Riu was sworn back in as chief minister of the Democratic Alliance of Nagaland for his first full term (2008–13), with the support of some independent candidates.

Rajasthan

The template of bi-partisan political domination of the politics of Rajasthan, with the INC and the BJP taking turns, seemed to continue in the 2008 elections, as in the years before.

In the elections held in 2008, the incumbent BJP government of Vasundhara Raje Scindia was thrown out of power by the INC. The Congress won 96 seats (up 40) in the 200-seat house, with a 36.82% vote share. The BJP was reduced to 78 seats (down 42), with 34.27% of vote share. The BSP won 6 seats, the CPI(M) 3, the JDU, SP and the Loktantrik Samajwadi Party won 1 seat each, with 14 seats taken by the independents.

Famed as a troubleshooter for the party, Ashok Gehlot was brought back in as the chief minister of the officially minority government – which, thanks to Gehlot's political stratagem, survived for the full term of the assembly (2008–13).

Tripura

The political landscape in Tripura continued to be dominated by the CPI(M), in continuation of the template effective for the previous four decades (barring a short period).

In the elections to the assembly, the CPI(M) won 46 (up 8) of the 60 seats, with a vote share of 48.01%. The INC remained in the second slot, winning 10 seats (down 3), with a vote share of 36.38%. The RSP won 2 seats, while the CPI and Indigenous Nationalist Party of Tripura won 1 seat each.

The emphatic victory of the CPI(M) secured Manik Sarkar a third full term in power (2008–13), underlining the CPI(M)'s complete stranglehold on the state's politics.

2009

Andhra Pradesh

Andhra Pradesh went for the polls for its legislative assembly in 2009, simultaneously with the Lok Sabha elections. By then, the UPA in the state had come apart as the Left parties (CPI and CPI(M)) had pulled out after the Indo–US nuclear treaty of 2008. Thus, in the assembly elections, the INC took on the BJP on the one hand, and the new third front – which included the Telugu Desam, the TRS and the Left parties.

In the assembly elections that year, the INC managed to retain its simple majority despite losing quite a few seats. The Congress won 156 seats (down 29) with a vote share of 36.55%. The TDP won 92 seats (up 45) with a vote share of 28.12%; the new party Praja Rajyam (started by Telugu actor Chiranjeevi) won 18 seats, with a vote share of 16.3%; the TRS won 10 seats (down 16); the AIMIM increased its tally to 7. The CPI won 4 seats, the BJP 2, and the CPI(M) and the Lok Satta Party won 1 seat each.

Despite the diminution of seats, the electoral victory brought Y.S. Rajasekhar Reddy back to the office of the chief minister for his second term – the first Andhra chief minister from the Congress since 1969 to actually return to office. However, his death in a tragic helicopter accident in September 2009 cut his life short. The office of the chief minister was then assigned to the finance minister Konijeti Rosaiah, who remained in office from September 2009 to November 2010 – even as YSR's son, Jagan Mohan Reddy, decided to capitalize on his father's popularity to claim his succession from the party. When that was rejected he floated his own party – the YSR Congress. After that he and his mother contested 2 assembly seats and won them in defiance of the Congress. Rosaiah was succeeded by Nallari Kiran Kumar Reddy, the Speaker in the assembly, who held office in the 4 years that simultaneously saw the rise of Jagan Reddy in Andhra politics, and the intensification of the Telangana agitation by TRS leader K. Chandrasekhar Rao. As the politics of Jagan and Rao gained momentum, the Andhra Congress veritably hurtled out of control, split between the 2. In one of the last decisions of the UPA II government pertaining to Andhra, the state was split into two halves – Telangana and Andhra Pradesh – in 2014. Soon after, N.K.K. Reddy resigned both as chief minister and as a party member in protest against the decision, and floated his own party, the Jai Samaikyandhra Party. Upon his resignation, the assembly was dissolved, as the 2 new states went to the polls for their respective assemblies in 2014.

Arunachal Pradesh

After replacing Gegong Apang, Chief Minister Dorjee Khandu had merrily increased the INC's strength in the assembly by keeping his doors open for the NCP, BJP and independent legislators alike, thus pushing the Congress's tally up to 41 out of 60 MLAs by the time elections were announced in 2009. Despite being aligned with the INC as affiliates to the UPA, the NCP and TMC decided to fight on their own in the state.

In the elections held that year to the 60-seat assembly, the INC virtually held on to the tally they had finished with in the last assembly, winning 42 seats, with a vote share of 50.38%. The NCP and the TMC won 5 seats each, while the People's Party of Arunachal won 4 seats and the BJP won 3 seats.

Former chief minister Gegong Apang and his son both lost their seats, putting them away from the fray in the leadership of the party. This smoothened the swearing in of Dorjee Khandu as the chief minister for his second term (2009–11). His tenure, however, was cut short by a tragic helicopter crash in April 2011, as he flew back from Tawang to Itanagar. Upon his death, the baton of leadership was passed on to Jarbom Gamlin, but his government was toppled in October 2011 by fellow Congressman Nabam Tuki, who then became the chief minister and remained in office till the end of the assembly term in 2014. Tuki continued on the path taken earlier by Dorjee Khandu – 4 PPA legislators joined the Congress in February 2014, followed by 4 TMC MLAs and all 5 NCP MLAs in October – pushing the party's tally up to 55 in the 60-seat assembly.

Haryana

In the assembly elections held in 2009 for the state of Haryana, the incumbent Congress government returned to power with some difficulty.

In the 90-seat assembly, the INC won 40 seats (down 27), with a vote share of 35.08%. The INLD became the second-largest party with 31 seats (up 22) with a vote share of 25.79%. Former CM Bhajan Lal's outfit, the Haryana Janhit Congress, that had broken away from the INC, won 6 seats, while the BJP won 4, the BSP and SAD won 1 seat each, and the independents had a tally of 7. Of the 7 legislators of the HJC, 6 soon crossed the floor to join the INC (leaving Kuldeep Bishnoi as the sole MLA of HJC in the assembly), giving the INC government the majority they needed, receiving, in addition, support from the independent legislators.

Jharkhand

The 2009 elections for the Jharkhand legislative assembly was a 3-cornered contest. On the one hand was the BJP, which ruled for a part of the first assembly; on the other hand was the Congress, the chief opposition in the state; in the third corner stood the JMM, which had consistently campaigned for a separate state of Jharkhand.

In the elections that were held in the month of December 2009 to the 81-seat assembly, the BJP won 18 seats (down 12), with a vote share of 20.18%. The JMM increased its tally from the previous election by 1 seat to finish tied at 18 with the BJP, with 15.20% of the vote share. The INC finished third with 14 seats, with 16.16% of the vote share. Former chief minister Babulal Marandi's Jharkhand Vikas Morcha (Prajatantrik) finished with 11 seats. The All Jharkhand Students' Union and RJD finished with a tally of 5 seats each; the JDU won 2 seats and 6 other smaller and regional parties won 1 seat each.

In December 2009, the JMM–BJP entered into a post-poll alliance, allowing Shibu Soren to be sworn in as the chief minister. However, the government barely survived 6 months, when the BJP withdrew its support to Soren, and the government collapsed in May 2010, followed by imposition of President's Rule in the state. After a period of over 100 days, Arjun Munda was sworn in as chief minister in November 2010 with support from the JMM. Munda remained in office till January 2013, when the JMM withdrew its support, thus toppling the government. After yet another brief period of President's Rule, Hemant Soren, the son of Shibu Soren, was sworn in as the chief minister - this time with JMM being supported by the INC and the RJD. Soren remained in that office till the end of the assembly term in 2014.

Maharashtra

The elections to the Maharashtra assembly in 2009 saw the INC–NCP-led UPA returning to power in the state, defeating the Shiv Sena–BJP *mahajuti* of the NDA. According to analysts, this was possible only because of the split in the Shiv Sena, as Raj Thackeray left the party to set up his own outfit, the Maharashtra Navanirman Sena (MNS), which split the Marathi vote that Shiv Sena had successfully consolidated.

In the elections held in 2009, the INC won 82 seats, with 21.01% of the vote share, while its ally the NCP won 62, with 16.37% of the vote share. The Shiv Sena won 45 seats with 16.26% of the vote share while its ally, the BJP, won 46, with 14.02% of the popular vote. The MNS won 13 seats, the PWPI and the SP won 4 seats each, and other regional and local parties won another 29 seats among themselves.

Ashok Chavan of the INC was sworn back into power, but he lasted only 1 year (November 2009–November 2010), and had to step down in view of his involvement with the Adarsh Housing Society scam. He was replaced by Prithviraj Chavan who remained in office for the rest of the term of the assembly (2010–14).

Orissa

The Orissa legislative assembly elections of 2009 turned out to be a major milestone in the politics of Orissa. After 11 years of political alignment, the BJD fell out with the BJP, presumably over seat distribution, and snapped ties with the NDA shortly after the elections were announced. The BJP immediately pulled out of the outgoing government, but with both the BJP and INC walking out of the assembly on the day of the floor test, Patnaik's government was saved by a technicality. Patnaik then blamed the BJP for the Kandhamal anti-Christian riots to make the break unambiguous, and also declared the BJD to be equally distant from both the INC and the BJP, negotiating an alignment with the CPI and the NCP.

In the elections that were held in the month of June, Patnaik's decision was vindicated spectacularly, with the BJD winning a two-third's majority with 103 seats (up 42) in the 147-seat assembly, with a vote share of 38.86%. The INC finished in the second place with 27 seats (down 11) with 29.10% of the vote share. The BJP won 6 seats (down 26), with 15.05% of the popular vote. The BJD's ally in the elections, the NCP won 4 seats and the CPI won 1.

Given the emphatic victory, Naveen Patnaik was sworn back in as the chief minister for his third consecutive term (2009–2014).

Sikkim

The 2009 elections to the Sikkim legislative assembly went along pretty predictable lines as before, thanks to the incumbent chief minister from the SDF, Pavan Chamling.

In the elections held that year, the SDF had a clean sweep, winning all 32 seats in the assembly, with a vote share of 65.91%. The INC, led by former Sikkim chief minister and mentor of Pavan Chamling, Nar Bahadur Bhandari drew a blank in seats, despite having 27.64% of the vote share.

Owing to the repeated emphatic victory, Pavan Chamling was sworn in for his fourth consecutive term as the chief minister (2009–14).

2010

Bihar

The incumbent JDU–BJP coalition in Bihar had performed poorly in the 2009 general elections, as RJD handed out a major defeat. Thus, when it came to the 2010 assembly elections, the JDU tried to be a bit circumspect, and create a distance with its coalition partner, the BJP, because the UPA campaign revolved around Gujarat CM Narendra Modi's responsibility for the carnage of 2002. Nitish refused to show up for joint political campaigns if Modi was the lead speaker.

In the 2010 elections for the Bihar assembly, the NDA turned the tables on the Lok Sabha results. The JDU emerged as the single largest party with 115 seats (up 27), with a vote share of 22.58%. Its NDA ally, the BJP won 91 seats (up 36) with a vote share of 16.49%. The RJD finished third with only 22 seats, with a vote share of 18.84%. The Lok Janshakti Party of Ram Vilas Paswan won 3 seats (down 7); the INC finished with 4 seats, and the CPI and the JMM secured 1 seat each.

Nitish Kumar was sworn in for another term as the chief minister for the NDA government in 2010. He continued to hold the office till May 2014, when he resigned accepting the moral responsibility for his party's poor performance in the 2014 Lok Sabha elections. Upon his resignation, Jitan Ram Manjhi (who had started in the INC, then went to the RJD and finally the JDU) became the chief minister for less than a year (May 2014–February 2015). In February 2015, the JDU instructed him to step down so that Nitish Kumar could resume his stint. Upon Manjhi's refusal, he was expelled from the party, and was in addition asked to prove his government's majority on the floor of the house. Nitish suspected that Manjhi was encouraged by the BJP to queer Nitish's pitch, and almost vindicating that suspicion, the BJP declared its support for Manjhi. However,

Manjhi, predictably could not muster the requisite numbers, so he stepped down. Nitish Kumar was sworn back in, and he led his party and government to election for a new assembly in 2015.

2011

Assam

Around the time of the 2011 elections for the assembly in Assam, the tide began to turn in the direction of politics that characterized the state. In the first 3 decades or so after 1947, the politics of Assam revolved around language, as Assamese was sought to be imposed on other linguistic minorities – this resulted in the evolution of the entire region of the Indian North-East. In opposition to Assamese domination, with the emergence of new states like Meghalaya and Nagaland took place. Then from the 1980s, in a way the agenda that fueled the ascent of the AGP revolved around the question of ethnicity, which took the form of a fight for space between the Assamese and other 'sons of the soil' and the immigrant Bengali population. The year 2011 begins the period when this ethnicity-oriented politics gradually declined to make way for one pushing the state in the direction of communal mobilization.

In the elections held in 2011, the INC finished with 78 seats (up 25) out of 128, with a vote share of 39.39%. The surprise element in the election was the party that took the second spot – AIUDF (led by Badruddin Ajmal, a party speaking for the Bengali-Muslim population of southern Assam and Barak valley) which won 18 seats (up 8) with 12.57%. The Bodoland People's Front won 12 seats (6.13% of the popular vote) and the AGP 10 (despite winning 16.29% of the popular vote). The BJP got 5 seats and the TMC won 1.

Tarun Gogoi became the second Congress chief minister of Assam (after B.P. Chaliha) to be returned to power for 3 consecutive terms (2001–16). But far more than his electoral victory, what alarmed many people was how a party of immigrant Bengali-Muslims could outperform 2 parties representing the ethnic people of Assam (i.e. AGP and BPF), stoking feelings of how the Assam Accord had been reduced simply to a piece of paper. The BJP consciously began to steer the narrative away from Assamese-outsider binary into the Hindu/ Buddhist Assamese–Bengali (Muslim) binary. Sarbananda Sonowal leaving the AGP to head for the BJP in February 2011 bears witness to this trend.

Kerala

For a very long time, Kerala had been seeing power alternating between the 2 main coalitions that dominated the political landscape – usually by very clear margins. Elections to the 2011 assembly did not disturb this general schema of alternating power, but it turned out to be uncharacteristically tight – with the UDF taking power back from the LDF after 5 years, by a margin of only 4 seats.

The composition of the 2 fronts remained static at its core, but a few members were always falling in or out. In 2011, the UDF constituted of the INC, IUML, Kerala Congress (Mani), RSP, Kerala Congress (Jacob), Communist Marxist Party (John) and AIFB. On the other hand the LDF constituted of CPI(M), CPI, JDS, NCP, Kerala Congress (Scaria Thomas), Congress (S), Communist Marxist Party, Kerala Congress (Balakrishna Pillai), Indian National League. Besides the two, the NDA (represented by the BJP and the JDU) constituted the third front, and several other national parties – such as the BSP, AIADMK, Shiv Sena, and so on also contested on their own.

In the elections of 2011, the UDF won in 73 seats, (with a vote share of 45.83%) of which the INC alone won in 38, and the IUML in 20; the KC(M) won 9 seats, the RSP won 2 seats, the Kerala Congress (Jacob) and Kerala RSP won 1 seat each. The LDF won in 67 seats (with a vote share of 43.63%), of which the CPI(M) won in 45, the CPI in 13, the JDS in 4, the NCP in 2, and the LDF-aligned independents in 2. The NDA, which had fielded candidates in all 140 constituencies failed to win any seats, but secured over 6% of the popular vote.

Oomen Chandy became the chief minister of Kerala for the second time, and for his first full term in that office (2011–16).

Puducherry

The 2011 elections for Puducherry assembly marked a kind of intrusion of Tamil Nadu's politics in the enclave of Puducherry, with what could have been far-reaching consequences.

The 2 main combinations in the election revolved around 2 chief ministers, 1 incumbent, 1 ex-. On the one hand, incumbent chief minister V. Vaithlingam was leading a bloc comprising the INC, DMK, PMK Viduthalai Chiruthaigal Katchi. On the other hand was the former chief minister N. Rangaswamy, at the head of a bloc comprising the All India N.R. Congress, the AIADMK, the CPI(M), the CPI and the DMDK.

In the elections that were held, the AINRC won 15 seats in the 30-seat assembly to become the single largest party. The INC with 7 seats finished second; the AIADMK finished in the third place with 5 seats, the DMK won 2 seats and 1 went to an independent.

To the great chagrin of J. Jayalalithaa, N. Rangaswamy completely ignored the AIADMK, won over the sole independent MLA to secure a simple majority for his party, and had himself sworn in as the chief minister of the Union Territory for the second full term (2011–16). The decision to ignore the AIADMK at the time of government formation was to prove costly after the elections of 2016.

Tamil Nadu

The politics of Tamil Nadu, as much as a few other states, had begun to revolve around a two-party template with power alternating between the two. The DMK had come to power with a huge majority in 2006. It had engaged in a lot of development of infrastructure, but by the time its term ended it was mired in a lot of corruption allegations as well – pertaining to the 2G scam, excessive sand-mining, among others. Further, the problem of rolling power cuts, high food prices and so on, prompted the DMK to go full-out towards populism – distributing things such as laptops for free. To this the AIADMK promised sewing machines, mixers and grinders in addition to laptops – cementing the dawn of the age of competitive populism.

There was, as usual a lot of wrangling before the contours of the 2 main political blocs attained their final shape. On the one hand was the incumbent DMK-led front – including (apart from the DMK) the INC, PMK, Viruthalai Chiruthaigal Katchi, Kongunadu Munnetra Kazhagam, IUML, Moovender Munnetra Kazhagam (MMK) and the Perunthalaivar Makkal Katchi (PMK); as against the 8-party DMK front stood the AIADMK front, constituting (apart from the AIADMK), the DMDK, CPI(M), CPI, Mannithaneiya Makkal Katchi (MNMK), Puthiya Tamilakam (PT), AIFB, All India Samathuva Makkal Katchi, RPI, All India Moovender Munnani Kazhagam and Tamil Nadu Kongu Ilaiganar Peraival.

In the elections that were held in 2011 for the Tamil Nadu assembly, the AIADMK-led alliance won 203 seats (up 30), with a little over 50% of all votes cast. Of this, the AIADMK by itself won 150 seats (up 93) with 38.4% of the popular vote; the

DMDK won 29 seats (up 28), the CPI(M) 10 (up 9), the CPI 9 (up 3), the MNMK and the PT won 2 seats each, the AIFB won 1 seat. The DMK alliance, by contrast, was reduced to 31 seats (down 126), of which the DMK alone accounted for 23 seats, and the Congress 5 and the PMK 3.

The principal force behind the landslide victory, J. Jayalalithaa was sworn in as the chief minister for the fourth time. During this term, she engaged in her variety of competitive populism, launching 'Amma' brand of services (canteen, bottled water, salt). Midway into her term, in 2014, Jayalalithaa was convicted with having accumulated assets disproportionate to her income, ruled disqualified from holding office, and sentenced to prison. Jayalalithaa stepped down and was replaced by O. Paneerselvam who filled in her shoes from then to May 2015, when Jayalalithaa had herself acquitted, and resumed her office for the rest of the term (May 2015–December 2016), which also happened to be her last.

West Bengal

THE WORLD'S LONGEST SERVING ELECTED COMMUNIST GOVERNMENT WAS FINALLY DEFEATED AFTER 34 YEARS IN POWER, BEATEN AS MUCH BY AN OBDURATE OPPOSITION LEADER WHO DID NOT KNOW HOW TO ACCEPT DEFEAT AS BY A RANGE OF VESTED INTERESTS WITHIN THE RULING PARTY THAT STOOD BLOCKING THE WAY OF A CHIEF MINISTER DESIRING TO CHANGE HIS PARTY IN TANDEM WITH CHANGING TIMES.

The 2011 elections to the West Bengal assembly turned out to be a landmark election of the sort that happens about once a generation. The three-and-a-half decade long rule of the Left

Front, characterized by an increasingly militant trade unionism in the background of a incrementally moribund industrial economy, had made West Bengal virtually out-of-sync with the rest of post-liberalisation India. Unlike his predecessor Jyoti Basu, Buddhadeb Bhattacharjee during his 2 terms tried to fight his own government's old reputation of militant anti-industrial activities by bringing back industrial entrepreneurship to the state. The greatest obstacle in the path of that re-industrialisation was the issue of land acquisition for industry. The one truly progressive achievement of the Left Front government was to carry out land reforms in its first 2 terms in power in such a way that it helped provide sustenance and promote agricultural self-sufficiency among the rural population. But while sustenance was guaranteed, industry languished, and no alternative horizon of economic opportunities ever opened up in West Bengal. When Bhattacharjee pushed for industry, a large segment of the rural people were too fearful of losing their one means of livelihood. Hence, despite a reasonable compensation package offered by Tata Motors for the land they wanted to acquire around Singur to set up a manufacturing plant for the Nano brand of cars, the resistance to land acquisition snowballed, and finally got the indomitable leader of the TMC, Mamata Banerjee, to assume the leadership of that resistance. Similar fears of land acquisition for industry near Nandigram had the local party honchos along with the police resort to the kind of heavy-handedness that comes only from the hubris and illusion of invincibility generated by long years in power. It was from these 2 incidents that the countdown of the Left Front could be said to have begun, as became clear from back-to-back electoral reverses in municipal, panchayat and Lok Sabha elections.

Mamata Banerjee had been a Congresswoman at one stage, who left her party when she found the state unit not serious enough in confronting the Left. She floated her own party, breaking up the Congress and accommodating many

Congressmen even as she aligned with the NDA under Vajpayee (even serving in his cabinet as a minister). When her alliance with the NDA failed to dislodge the Left in 2006, she abandoned it to align with the UPA in 2009 (after the Left Front quit the UPA over the Indo–US Nuclear Deal) – realizing that it was essential to prevent fragmentation of the Opposition vote, of which the Congress had a considerable share till then.

In the assembly elections of 2011, the ruling Left Front was reduced to 62 seats, of which the CPI(M) accounted for 40 (plus 2 added by by-elections that followed); the AIFB won 11, the RSP 7, CPI 2 seats and the SP and DSP won 1 seat each. The UPA won 228 seats, of which the TMC accounted for 184 (plus 6 which were won during the by-elections), the INC won 42 seats, the SUCI and an independent won 1 seat each.

In a politically canny decision, having won a majority of the seats by itself, the TMC was quick to deny the INC the spoils of victory, veritably distancing the TMC from the UPA. Mamata Banerjee was sworn in as the chief minister in 2011, which was the first of her stints for the full term of the assembly (2011–16).

2012

Goa

Elections to the legislative assembly in Goa in 2012 showed clear signs of anti-incumbency weighing in heavily on the considerations of the electorate, influenced by allegations of corruption, inefficiency and nepotism in the INC government of Goa.

In the elections to the 40-seat assembly that were held in the month of March, the BJP won a simple majority on its own strength, with 21 seats (up 7) against a vote share of 34.68%; its NDA ally the MAG won 3 seats (up 1), with 6.72%. The INC was reduced to 9 seats (down 7) with 30.78% of the vote share. The Goa Vikas Party finished with 2 seats, while the NCP and the United Goans Democratic Party failed to win any seats at all.

The architect of the victory, Manohar Gopalkrishna Prabhu Parrikar was sworn in as the chief minister for his second term in March 2012. He subsequently stepped down from the office in November 2014 to join the Union government as the minister for Defence. At that time he was replaced by Laxmikant Parsekar, who held the office for the rest of the term of the Goa assembly (2014–17), and resigned after the 2017 assembly election where he lost his seat.

Manipur

Manipur for nearly a decade was already under Congress rule, helmed by Chief Minister Okram Ibobi Singh. Forces of anti-incumbency were not strong enough to challenge Singh effectively.

In the 2012 assembly elections, the INC had a veritable landslide even after 2 terms, winning 42 seats (up 12) out of 60, with a vote share of 42.4%. The Trinamool Congress (TMC) emerged as the second-largest party, with 7 seats and with a vote share of 17%. The Manipur State Congress Party, a splinter group of the Congress, finished third with 5 seats; the Naga People's Party claimed 4 seats, the NCP and LJP won 1 seat each. Two years later, in 2012, the MSCP merged with the INC, pushing the latter's tally to 47.

Okram Ibobi Singh was sworn back in as the chief minister for a third consecutive term (2012–17).

Punjab

Punjab politics had tended to become by-and-large bipolar, with the SAD and the INC constituting its 2 poles, with a heavy force of anti-incumbency being operational most of the time. The year 2012 happened to be one of the few elections that the forces of anti-incumbency did not prevail.

The SAD–BJP alliance led by incumbent Chief Minister Parkash Singh Badal won 68 seats (up 1) of which the SAD secured 56 seats (up 8, with 34.73% of the vote share) and the BJP won 12 (down 7, with 7.18% of the vote share). The INC secured 46 seats (up 2, with 40.09% of the vote share). Three seats were taken by independent candidates.

Given the emphatic nature of the victory, the incumbent chief minister, Parkash Singh Badal, was sworn back in for his fifth term in that office (2012–17).

Uttarakhand

The political trajectory of Uttarakhand had from the very beginning been bipolar, with the INC and the BJP alternating in the formation of government. The 2012 elections to the 70-seat Uttarakhand assembly remained true to this trajectory.

In the elections held in 2012, the incumbent party in power, the BJP won 31 seats (down 4) with a vote share of 33.13%. The INC emerged as the single largest party with 32 seats (up 11) with a marginally higher vote share of 33.79%. The BSP and independents won 3 seats each, while the Uttarakhand Kranti Dal won 1 seat. The INC immediately entered into negotiations and managed to rope in all the BSP, UKD and independent MLAs to support the government.

Thus, secure with a majority on the floor of the house, Vijay Bahuguna was sworn in as the chief minister in March 2012. His tenure in the office was, however, cut short because of severe criticism of his handling of the floods in June 2013. He was eventually forced to step down in January 2014 in favour of Harish Rawat. Rawat's tenure as chief minister (February 2014–March 2016) was also cut short by the defection of 9 INC MLAs, and the governor decided to impose President's Rule without a floor test. This was ruled unconstitutional by the Uttarakhand High Court, and the Rawat government was reinstated on 25 March. That verdict was then overturned by the Supreme Court the very next day, and President's Rule was reimposed subject to a floor test for the Rawat government. When a trust vote was formally moved, Rawat won the vote and was thus reinstated in office in March 2016, where he carried on till his defeat in the 2017 elections.

Uttar Pradesh

Elections to the legislative assembly of Uttar Pradesh in 2012 came after 5 years of the BSP government under CM Mayawati. The government had come under criticism from all sides on account of its reputation for corruption being concentrated in the office of the CM. It was also heavily criticized for erecting statues all around the state to the BSP leader Mayawati, her mentor Kanshi Ram and the party's symbol (elephants), at considerable cost to the public exchequer. Her government's policy of making land acquisition easy for entrepreneurs also occasioned considerable disquiet among the rural people.

In the elections that followed in 2012, the SP returned with a simple majority, winning 224 seats (up 127) with a vote share of 29.15%. The BSP was reduced to 80 seats (down 126) with a vote share of 25.91%; the BJP finished third with 47 seats (down 4) and a vote share of 15%, while the INC finished fourth with 28 seats (up 6) and 11.63% of the popular vote. The Rashtriya Lok Dal managed to win 9 seats, and some other parties managed to win 1 or 2 seats respectively.

As the SP president Mulayam Singh Yadav stood aside, his son Akhilesh Yadav was sworn in as the chief minister, in which capacity he served for the full term of the assembly.

Gujarat

The Gujarat assembly elections of 2012 were the last contested by Narendra Modi as the incumbent chief minister, contesting for his fourth term in power before leaving for New Delhi.

In the elections that year, the incumbent BJP came back with a convincing majority, winning 115 of the 182 seats in the assembly (down 2) with a vote share of 47.85%. The INC finished with 61 seats (up 2), with a vote share of 38.93%. Gujarat Parivartan Party, founded by the former BJP CM Keshubhai Patel, finished ignominiously with 2 seats; the NCP won 2 seats while the JDU won 1. Eventually, the GPP merged into the BJP.

The incumbent Narendra Modi was sworn in for his fourth term as chief minister, which he eventually did not serve for the full period, leaving for New Delhi to assume the role of the prime minister instead in 2014. He was succeeded by Anandiben Patel, the first female chief minister of the state. In a rare display of principle, she stepped down from the office in August 2016 when she turned 75 years of age. Vijay Rupani then took over from her in August 2016, and led the party into the next assembly election in 2017.

Himachal Pradesh

Himachal Pradesh in 2012 continued to stick to the template of bipolar contest between the INC and BJP, each forming governments in alternate sessions.

In the elections held in 2012, the INC came back to power with 36 seats (up 13) in the 68-seat assembly, with a vote share of 42.81%. The BJP won 26 seats (down 16) with a vote share of 38.47%. Independent candidates managed to win 5 seats.

Virabhadra Singh was sworn in for the fourth term in the government (2012–17), while the outgoing Prem Kumar

Dhumal went to resume his position as leader of the Opposition, also for the fourth time.

2013

Tripura

The political landscape of Tripura was characterized by the domination of the CPI(M) for more than 2 decades. That continued even in the elections of 2013.

In the elections of 2013, the CPI(M) won a crushing majority, securing 49 seats (up 3) with 48.11% of the vote share. The INC remained the second-largest party with 10 seats, and a vote share of 36.53%. The CPI won 1 seat. The INPT, BJP, RSP and even independents failed to win a seat.

Having won probably the cleanest victory in his political life, Manik Sarkar was sworn in for the fourth consecutive full term (2013–18).

Meghalaya

The political landscape of Meghalaya has historically been fragmented, and although the INC has steadily grown in size and often come to power, governments in Meghalaya have historically tended to be very fragile coalitions. In some ways, 2013 marked a change in that respect.

In the elections held in 2013, the incumbent party, the INC, won 29 seats (up 4) with a vote share of 34.8%; the UDP won 8 seats (down 3) with a vote share of 17.1%; the debutant National People's Party (set up by Purna A. Sangma after his expulsion from the NCP in 2012) won 2 seats; the HSPDP won 4 seats (up 2). The NCP secured 2 seats (down 13), while another debutant, the North East Social Democratic Party and the olden Garo National Council won 1 seat each. Independents won 13 seats.

Mukul Sangma was sworn in at the head of a Congress government, supported unconditionally by the NCP and 11 independents. An important point about this election is that traditionally strong among the Khasis, under Mukul Sangma, the Congress gained ground even among the Garos, winning 13 of the 24 seats in the Garo Hills, which earlier used to be NCP strongholds associated with Purna A. Sangma.

Nagaland

By 2013, Nagaland had begun to appear like being a pocket borough of Neiphieu Rio and of the Naga People's Front. The assembly elections of 2013 gave reasons to be convinced by this argument.

In the elections for the 60-seat Nagaland assembly, the incumbent NPF secured 38 seats (plus 12) with a vote share of 47%. The INC was the second-largest party with 8 seats (down 15) with a vote share of 24.9%. The NCP won 4 seats, the BJP and the JDU won 1 seat each, with 8 independent MLAs being successful.

Neiphieu Rio was sworn in for the third time as the chief minister of Nagaland. However, not all may have been alright with Rio in his own party. Accordingly, in 2014 he appeared for the Lok Sabha, and after winning the sole seat from Nagaland by a landslide (a margin of 4,00,225 votes, second only to the margin by which Narendra Modi won his 2014 elections), he resigned from his office and the Nagaland assembly. His designated successor was Taditui Rangkau Zaliang, who held the office during May 2014–February 2017. Zaliang had to step down from the position of the chief minister in February 2017, after protests broke out against his proposal that a third of the seats in local body elections should be reserved for women. He was succeeded by Shurhozelie Liezietsu, an octogenarian leader of the NPF who was not even an MLA at that time. He remained in office only for 4 months (February to July 2017) after which T.R. Zeiliang resumed his office which he held on to till the end of the term (July 2017–March 2018).

Karnataka

The politics of Karnataka had entered into a period of turmoil during 2008–13, with Yeddyurappa being instrumental to forming the first BJP government in Karnataka, then being forced to step down and witness being marginalized by his own protégé Sadanand Gowda and his adversary Jagdish Shettiar. Yeddyurappa, when he was the chief minister, faced revolts from the Reddy brothers (Karunakara, Somasekhara and Janardhana). By 2012 Yeddy himself raised the banner of rebellion when he quit the party and set up the Karnataka Janata Paksha (KJP). In the meantime, the INC and the JDU outperformed the BJP in local body elections. Thus, once the polls were announced, the BJP appeared very shaky.

In the elections to the 224-seat Karnataka assembly in 2013, the INC won 122 seats (up 43), with a vote share of 36.6%. The JDS won 40 seats (up 12) with a vote share of 20.2%, while the BJP too won 40 seats (down 72) with a marginally lower vote share of 19.9%. Yeddy's debutant KJP won 6 seats, and the Badavara Shramikara Raitara Congress won 4 seats.

In the new assembly, Siddaramaiah (who joined the Congress after being expelled by the JDS in 2005, and had originally been with the Janata Dal) was sworn in as the chief minister, and was only the second person to complete a full 5-year term (2013–18) in that office.

Delhi

The 2013 assembly elections for Delhi marked a watershed in 2 ways. After a little over a decade of dominating Delhi politics, and reshaping the urban sprawl in many ways, Sheila Dikshit ran out of steam. Nearly as importantly, the INC brand of state-driven development was replaced by populism on steroids in the form of the Aam Aadmi Party (AAP).

In the elections that were held that year, the INC was reduced to a rubble, with 8 seats (down 35), comprising 24.55% share of the popular vote. The BJP emerged as the single largest party with 31 seats (up 8) with 33.07% of the vote share. The debutant AAP emerged as the second-largest party, with 28 seats and a vote share of 29.49%. The JDU, SAD and an independent each won 1 seat only. The outgoing chief minister lost her own seat to Kejriwal in the New Delhi constituency.

The results were poised so tentatively that neither could any of the 3 parties form a government on their own respective strengths, nor could they rope in independents or rogue MLAs to cross the floor. Hence, with the sword of President's Rule hanging over their heads, BJP leader Harsh Vardhan declined the offer by Lt. Governor Najeeb Jung to form the government. The AAP leader Arvind Kejriwal did not seek support from any parties, but voiced its positions on 18 issues. The Congress communicated their positions on 16 of these and accordingly offered AAP outside support so that President's Rule could be avoided in the NCR. Hence Kejriwal was sworn in as the chief minister in December 2013.

The Kejriwal government lasted only 49 days because it resigned in February 2014 upon failing to have its signature promise of the Jan Lokpal Bill clear the Delhi assembly. The Lt. Governor then went on to impose President's Rule in Delhi, and Delhi went for its next assembly polls in 2015.

THE 2013 DELHI ELECTIONS SAW THE INTRODUCTION OF NOTA (NONE OF THE ABOVE) BEING INSERTED AS AN OPTION FOR THE VOTERS IN AN ASSEMBLY ELECTION. IT ALSO SAW THE INTRODUCTION OF THE VVPAT (VOTER-VERIFIED PAPER AUDIT TRAIL) MACHINES IN AT LEAST 1 CONSTITUENCY.

Rajasthan

The politics of Rajasthan being determinedly bipolar at the assembly level followed the template of 2 parties taking turns. The 2013 elections turned out to be no different, although the margins were noticeably different.

In the elections to the 200-seat Rajasthan assembly held in 2013, the BJP won 163 seats (up 85) with 45.2% of the vote share – its best performance ever in the state. The INC was reduced to 21 seats (down 75) with 33.1% of the vote share – its worst performance ever in the state. The National People's Party (set up in 2012 by P.A. Sangma, and represented in Rajasthan by Kirori Lal Meena) managed to win only 4 seats. The BSP won 3 seats, the National Unionist Zamindara Party (party of Guar farmers led by Kamini Jindal) won 2 seats and independent candidates were successful in 7 seats.

Vasundhara Raje returned to the office of the chief minister for her second full term in power (2013–2018), and Ashok Gehlot went back to wait in the wings as the leader of Opposition in the assembly.

Madhya Pradesh

By 2013, Madhya Pradesh was already appearing to be a BJP stronghold as the Congress continued on its path of almost terminal decline. The incumbent Shivraj Singh Chouhan was even beginning to be spoken of as a PM candidate within the BJP, by people who did not particularly like Narendra Modi.

In the elections held in 2013, with VVPAT on trial, the BJP won 165 seats (up 22) of the 230 seats in the assembly with 45.7% of the vote share. The INC finished second with 58 seats (down 13) with 37.1% of the popular vote. The BSP won 4 seats, and the independents 3.

Shivraj Singh Chouhan was breezily sworn in for his third consecutive full term in power (2013–18).

Chhattisgarh

Not unlike Madhya Pradesh, of which it was a part for a long time, Chhattisgarh was becoming a beacon of BJP's developmental model, and was beginning to show signs of becoming a BJP stronghold under the incumbent chief minister Raman Singh.

In the 2013 elections to the 90-seat assembly, the BJP won 49 seats (down 1) with 42.3% of the vote share. The INC won 39 seats (up 1) with 41.6% of the vote share. The BSP was the only other party to win a seat, and only 1 independent candidate ran successfully – indicating how completely consolidated the bipolar political landscape had become.

Raman Singh was sworn in for his third consecutive full term (2013–18) in the chief minister's office, while Ajit Jogi remained firmly ensconced as the leader of the Opposition.

Mizoram

Mizoram's politics had come to be dominated by the INC and the Mizo National Front taking turns. With the INC in power, the MNF forged an alliance – the Mizoram Democratic Alliance – involving itself, the Mizoram People's Conference (of Brigadier T. Sailo) and Maraland Democratic Front to take on the veteran incumbent chief minister Pu Lalthanhawla. The 2013 assembly elections saw the use of VVPAT EVMs in 10 of the 40 constituencies in which elections were held.

In the elections held in 2013, the INC swept the polls yet again, winning 34 seats (up 2), with a vote share of 44.9%. The MDA won the remaining 6 seats, with MNF winning 5 of these and the MPC 1. The BJP, which ran in the polls, drew a blank.

Pu Lalthanhawla was sworn in for his fifth term as the chief minister of Mizoram (2013–18), while Zoramthanga returned to being the leader of the Opposition.

Chapter 16

THE AGE OF BJP DOMINANCE 2014–23

2014

In 2014, assembly elections were held for 8 states, of which Andhra Pradesh, Odisha and Sikkim went to the polls simultaneously with the Lok Sabha. Arunachal Pradesh, Haryana, Jammu and Kashmir, Jharkhand and Maharashtra went to the polls later.

Andhra Pradesh

In October 2013, the Houses of Parliament approved bifurcation of the state of Andhra Pradesh to carve out the state of Telangana, and the gazette notification from the President's office listed the creation of the 2 states in June 2014. Hence, elections to the Andhra Pradesh legislature took place with the knowledge that they would constitute the assembly for 2 states – Telangana and (Coastal) Andhra Pradesh – but could not but be held as though for a united assembly, since the state went to the polls at a time it still was one.

In the elections to the last assembly of Andhra Pradesh which had both Telangana and the coastal Andhra Pradesh, the TDP won 117 seats (up 24) out of the assembly total of 294, with a vote share of 32.53%. The second place was taken by debutant YSR Congress (YSRC, founded and led by Jagan M. Reddy), which won 70 seats, with a vote share of 27.88%. The Telangana Rashtra Samithi (TRS led by K. Chandrasekhar Rao) won 63 seats (up 53). The rump INC was reduced to 21 seats (down 135), with 11.71% - easily among the party's worst performances in the state. The BJP managed to win 9 seats (with only 1.29% of the popular vote), while the AIMIM managed to retain their 7 seats, the BSP gained 2 seats, while the 2 communist parties managed to win 1 seat each.

Given the contours of the 2 incoming states in terms of constituencies, (coastal) Andhra Pradesh was to constitute of 175 of the above 294 constituencies. Thus, in the coastal Andhra state, the TDP with 102 seats emerged as the single largest party, followed by YSR Congress's 67, 4 of the BJP and Navodayam Party and independents winning 1 seat each.

Of the 119 seats of the incoming Telangana assembly, the TRS won 63, the INC 21, TDP 15, AIMIM 7, BJP 5, YSRC 3, BSP 2, and CPI, CPI(M) and an independent candidate took 1 each.

Thus, in the month of June 2014, Nara Chandrababu Naidu was sworn in as the chief minister of the rump state of Andhra Pradesh for a full 5-year term (2014–19), with Jagan M. Reddy as the leader of the Opposition.

Similarly, K. Chandrasekhar Rao was also sworn in as the chief minister of Telangana in June 2014.

Odisha

The 2014 elections to the Odisha assembly were held simultaneously. The Lok Sabha outcome, however, had no bearing on the assembly, because the people of Odisha seemed to be happy enough with the incumbent chief minister to hand him yet another term.

In the elections to the 147-seat Odisha assembly, the incumbent BJD won 117 seats (up 14) with 43.4% of the vote share. The INC won 16 seats (down 11), with 25.7% of the vote share; the BJP won 10 (up 4) with 18% of the popular vote. The CPI(M) and Braja Kishore Tripathy's Samata Kranti Dal took 1 seat each.

Naveen Patnaik was sworn in for his fourth consecutive full term in office (2014–19).

Sikkim

Politics in the state of Sikkim had a pretty unusual trajectory. It had been under the rule of 1 party (SDF) and ruled by the same chief minister (Pavan Chamling) for 4 consecutive terms. More importantly, the SDF's seat tally in the assembly had, by 2009, increased to a point where it could increase no more – having taken all the 32 seats of the assembly. Thus in 2014, the tally had to come down. Prem Singh Tamang, aka Prem Singh Golay, a prominent associate of Chamling, broke with him after 2009, and became a vocal critic of the chief minister. In February 2013, he set up a new political party, the Sikkim Krantikari Morcha, and projected it as the true voice of opposition.

In the elections that were held, the incumbent SDF lost 10 seats to finish at 22 seats, with a vote share of 55%. The debutant SKM won the remaining 10 seats, with a vote share of 40.8%. Neither of the 2 national parties won even a single seat.

Pavan Chamling was returned to power for the fifth term, which he went on to complete in 2019.

Arunachal Pradesh

The assembly of Arunachal Pradesh seemed to have been marching in the same direction as the rest of India. Suddenly in 2014, as India appeared to have changed its direction, Arunachal Pradesh was found to be continuing in its own way, returning its incumbent Congress government to power. But it saw a rare U-turn in its politics within 2 years of the assembly elections.

In the elections held that year to the 60-seat Arunachal assembly, the incumbent INC won 42 seats, with a vote share of 49.5%. The BJP won 11 seats (up 8); the People's Party of Arunachal won 5; the NCP, the Naga People's Front and the debutant AAP failed to win any seats at all.

The incumbent chief minister Nabam Tuki was sworn back in to the office. In December 2014, Tuki dropped Kalikho Pul, the minister of Health and Family Welfare. In April, Pul was sacked by the INC for anti-party activities upon accusing Tuki of financial impropriety. By November that year, full-fledged trouble erupted as the deputy Speaker of the assembly too began to criticize the government and the party openly, which led to INC MLAs demanding that he be removed. The BJP now stepped in to demand removal of the Speaker Nabam Rebia, a brother of the chief minister, instead. In this turmoil, the new governor J.P. Rajkhowa, a retired IAS officer, instructed the government to bring the assembly session forward by a month to December 2015. When the session started, the Speaker disqualified 14 of the 21 MLAs who were singing out of tune, but this was contested by the deputy Speaker. In the circumstances, the Speaker decided to not convene the assembly back into the session, and the government locked the assembly out. Thirty-three rebellious MLAs met in a convention centre and passed a resolution in the name of the assembly to depose the incumbent Speaker and elect a new one. In reply, Tuki razed the convention centre to the ground. The rebel MLAs then went to a hotel and elected Kalikho Pul as their leader, and therefore the chief minister – since they constituted the majority among the 60 MLAs.

In this crisis, as both sides resorted to the courts and a standstill came about, the governor recommended, and the Union government obliged by imposing President's Rule. After a brief period, the governor had Kalikho Pul reappointed as the new chief minister of the state. In July 2016, the Supreme Court ruled the deposition of the INC government unconstitutional, and ordered its immediate reinstatement. By that time the governor had been deposed, and the new acting governor, Tathagata Roy (a hardline BJP leader from West Bengal) obliged by reappointing Tuki, but asked him to prove his majority on the floor of the house the very next day. Tuki swore himself in, but on the morning of the floor test, realizing he had indeed lost his MLAs, resigned. Pema Khandu, the son of the former chief minister Dorjee Khandu, was sworn in, and passed the floor test, thanks to the rebel MLAs.

In September 2016, Pema Khandu left with all 42 other INC MLAs to join the People's Party of Arunachal, but they fell out with the PPA, and 7 (including Khandu) were expelled from the party. Khandu took 33 other ex-INC MLAs out of the PPA, and took his flock of 36 MLAs to join the BJP in January 2017. Thus, the BJP, which had 11 MLAs when the assembly had convened, finished with 47 MLAs, a speaker and a chief minister in Pema Khandu, who remained in office as the CM of the BJP government for the rest of the term (July 2016–2019).

Maharashtra

The Maharashtra assembly elections of 2014 followed upon the spectacular victory of the NDA in the Lok Sabha elections, with the BJP attaining majority by itself. This impacted on the assembly polls as the BJP demanded more seats (130) to contest in the assembly than what its regional ally, the Shiv Sena was willing to offer. So the BJP broke its oldest political alignment with the Shiv Sena going back over two-and-a-half decades, and went on to contest alone. The ruling alliance of the INC and NCP had a similar problem, because based on their performance at the Lok Sabha, the NCP wanted 144 seats from the INC and a rotation of the office of the chief minister, and since there was no progress on either issue, the NCP severed its relations with the INC for the assembly elections. Hence, the elections of 2014 were 4-cornered after a long time.

In the polls that followed to the 288-seat assembly, the BJP became the single largest party with 122 seats (up 76), with 27.81% of the vote share. The Shiv Sena won 63 seats (up 19) with 19.35% of the vote share. The INC came third with 42 seats (down 40) with 17.95% of the vote share. The NCP finished fourth with 41 seats (down 21) with a vote share of 17.24%. The PWPI won 3 seats, AIMIM and Bahujan Vikas Agadi won 2; MNS, SP, CPI(M), Bharipa Bahujan Mahasangh and Rashtriya Samaj Paksha won 1 seat each.

The BJP did not have enough seats to claim a majority. The NCP offered it outside support, but the BJP waited for a bit to have the Shiv Sena come around, since it was considered a natural fit for the party and its agenda. Shiv Sena's leader Uddhav Thackeray eventually came around, and the two formed a coalition government, with Devendra Fadnavis being sworn in as chief minister (October 2014–November 2019).

Haryana

Haryana exemplifies the ascendancy of the BJP in the provinces as much as anywhere else after the coming of the government of Narendra Modi. Having never been in power in a state that had proven to be proverbially corrupt, the BJP seemed to sweep into power from nowhere – in a manner they had never done before, nor were they suspected as being able to do.

In the elections held in October 2014 for the 90-seat assembly, the BJP won 47 seats (up 43), with a vote share of 33.2%. The INLD was reduced to 19 (down 12) with a vote share of 24.1%. The outgoing ruling party INC was reduced dramatically to the third place, winning only 15 seats (down 25), with a vote share of 20.6%. The Haryana Janhit Congress (led by Bhajan Lal) fought the elections in alliance with the BJP to win only 2 seats; the SAD and BSP won 1 seat each, and independents won 5.

Manohar Lal Khattar, an RSS veteran, BJP functionary and first-time MLA was sworn in as the chief minister of the state.

Jammu and Kashmir

The assembly polls of Jammu and Kashmir in 2014 were the last before the special status under Article 370 was revoked, and its statehood was rescinded.

Before the election, the INC broke its alliance with the JKNC, turning the contest into a 4-cornered one, as it turned out. Despite calls of boycott by All Parties Hurriyat Conference, the turnout for the elections actually improved.

The PDP, led by Mehbooba Mufti (daughter of former CM Mufti Muhammad Syed), became the largest party in the state with 28 seats (up 7) with a vote share of 22.7%. The BJP emerged as the second-largest party, winning 25 seats (up 14) with a vote share of 23%. The JKNC finished third with 15 seats (down 28) and a vote share of 20.8%, while the INC finished fourth with 12 seats (down 5) and 18% of the vote share. J&K People's Conference, led by Sajjad Lone, had 2 seats and the CPI(M) won 1 seat.

The JKNC initially offered to join a BJP-led government, but this faced some resistance within the party. JKNC then offered to support the PDP government from the outside. But even this was rejected out of hand. The BJP and PDP then opened negotiations over power-sharing as outgoing Chief Minister Omar Abdullah resigned and the state was brought under President's Rule in January 2015. On 1 march 2015, Mufti Muhammad Sayeed was sworn in for the full term of 6 years, with Nirmal Kumar Singh as his deputy; 12 cabinet ministers were to be drawn from both the parties, there was to be no rotation of the CM's office, but PDP would be required to support the NDA in Parliament, and Mehbooba Mufti herself at a later date was to join the Modi government at the Centre.

Mufti Muhammad Sayeed died in office in January 2016. His daughter Mehbooba Mufti reopened coalition negotiations and after 2 months was appointed the first female chief minister of J&K, and shortly thereafter she won a by-election from Anantnag to enter the assembly. Two years later, in June 2018, as the rape of a 8-year old Muslim girl by a few Hindu men at Kathua became politicized (with Hindu leaders from Jammu trying to prevent the accused from being arrested), Mufti resigned. By then, the security situation in the state had begun to degenerate, especially around the Amarnath Yatra, and the Union government wanted to take a hard stand. Thus, the BJP formally announced the end of the alliance, as Governor's Rule was imposed. Within a year, the BJP in an unusually bold move abrogated Article 370, ending J&K's special status, and subsequently J&K was stripped of its statehood, and reduced to a Union Territory.

Jharkhand

Jharkhand, like most other states that went to the polls after the BJP victory in the Lok Sabha election of 2014, swung merrily into the direction of the BJP after witnessing the turmoil that JMM governments could produce.

In the elections held for the 81-seat Jharkhand assembly, the BJP won 37 seats (up 19) with 31.26% of the popular vote. The JMM finished in the second place with 19 seats (up 1), with 20.43% of the vote share. The JVM(P) of Babulal Marandi finished with 8 seats, and the INC won 6 seats. The All Jharkhand Students Union won 5 seats, while the BSP, the CPI(ML), the Marxist Coordination Committee and two other parties won 1 seat each. Two months later, 6 of the 8 JVM(P) MLAs joined the BJP and pushed the BJP tally to 43.

In December 2014, Raghubar Das was sworn in as the first non-tribal chief minister of Jharkhand. He remained in office for the full term of the assembly, only to be defeated in the 2019 assembly elections.

2015

Delhi

Election to the assembly of Delhi was made necessary by the failure in government formation by members of the previous assembly.

In the elections that were held in 2015 to the 70-seat assembly, the AAP delivered a spectacular victory winning 67 seats (up 39) and a vote share of 54.3%. The BJP finished with only 3 seats (down 28) and a vote share of 32.2%. The INC was wiped out, as much as the BSP, SAD, INLD – all of whom drew blanks.

Arvind Kejriwal

Arvind Kejriwal, a former bureaucrat and a one-time recipient of the Magsaysay Award, was sworn in as the chief minister of Delhi in February 2015. His government appears to have been motivated by the force of populism, but during his second term in government (2015–2020), he has virtually overhauled Delhi's healthcare through his *muhalla* clinics experiment.

Bihar

Elections to the Bihar legislative assembly in 2015 took place in the backdrop of breakup of the BJP's decade-and-a-half-long tie with Nitish Kumar and the JDU. Nitish had been opposed to the elevation of Narendra Modi to the office of the prime minister, and unlike other PM aspirants in the NDA, he decided to break with the BJP rather than accepting Modi. He became a part of the process whereby in April 2015, 6 parties - the SP, RJD, JDU, JDS, INLD and Samajwadi Janata Party (Rashtriya) - decided to reconstitute the Janata Parivar and fight the Bihar elections together. Soon it was joined by the INC and the NCP (which left after some months). The NDA, on the other hand, went for the smaller parties - like Lok Janshakti Party (led by Ram Vilas Paswan), Rashtriya Lok Samta Party (led by Upendra Kushwaha) and the Hindustani Awam Morcha (Secular). The Left fought independently of both these blocs. The SP then left the Janata Parivar and aligned with the NCP and others to constitute the Socialist Secular Morcha. In August 2015, it was declared that the JDU and the RJD will contest 100 seats each, and 40 would go to the Congress, and that Nitish Kumar was to be the CM candidate for the *mahagathbandhan*.

In the elections that were held in 2015, the *mahagathbandhan* won 178 seats of which the RJD became the single largest party winning 80 seats (up 58), with a vote share of 32.92%; the JDU won 71 seats (down 44) with a vote share of 29.21%; the INC won only 27 seats (up 23), with 11.11% of the popular vote. The NDA won 58 seats, of which 53 were won by the BJP with a vote share 21.81%, the Lok Janshakti Party 2, RLSP 2 and HAMS 1. Of the 6 parties of the Left Front, only CPI(ML) won 3 seats, the rest drew blanks. The entire Socialist bloc led by SP failed to win a single seat among them.

Nitish Kumar was sworn in as the chief minister of Bihar for the fourth time in November 2015, with 2 sons of Lalu Yadav (Tejaswi and Tej Pratap) of the RJD joining the cabinet, Tejasvi being the deputy chief minister. The RJD and JDU had 12 ministers each in the cabinet, while the INC had 4. However, Nitish Kumar's discomfort with the RJD, especially with the deputy CM (when corruption charges were levelled against him) increased sufficiently for him to swallow his pride, dump the *mahagathbandhan*, and to form a coalition with the BJP and be sworn in as the chief minister at the head of a JDU-BJP coalition government, with Sushil Modi as his deputy CM. The NDA thus got back into power for the rest of the assembly term (2017–20).

2016

Assam

The political landscape of Assam began to undergo a change at the time of the 2016 assembly elections. Tarun Gogoi, the INC chief minister who had been in power for 3 terms was facing all the disadvantages of a very strong anti-incumbency. Additionally, the Supreme Court-mandated National Register of Citizens, promised under the Assam Accord to seek out aliens from among the citizens, was meant to be completed by 2016. Originally an agenda that brought the AGP into being as a political force, it appeared to have petered out somewhat, and AGP had weakened. AGP functionaries like Sarbananda Sonowal migrated to the BJP where the AGP agenda of flushing out aliens (i.e. Bangladeshi immigrants) was given a communal twist of Hindu-Muslim without diluting the citizen-alien tensions. The arrival of the dynamic Congressman Himanta Biswa Sarma into the BJP gave the BJP a kind of edge that harmed the incumbent Congress very hard.

In the elections that followed to the 126-seat Assam assembly, the BJP emerged out of the shadows to become the single largest party winning 60 seats (up 55), with a vote share of 29.5%. Its NDA ally, the AGP which contested only 24 seats won 14 (up 4), while the Bodoland People's Front –

another ally – won 12 seats. The INC, after 3 full terms in power, virtually seemed to collapse into a rump of only 26 seats (down 52), with a vote share marginally higher than of the BJP, at 30.9%. The AIUDF won 13 seats (down 5).

Sarbananda Sonowal resigned from his position in the Union council of ministers to swear in as chief minister of Assam, with Himanata Biswa Sarma as his deputy. He held the office for the entire duration of the assembly, May 2016–May 2021.

West Bengal

West Bengal had witnessed Mamata Banerjee evicting the Left Front after 3 decades in power, with the support of the INC. However, while the consolidation of voters helped TMC, the INC did not benefit from the little role they thought they had played. In the 5 years of Banerjee's first term, while her populism broadened the mass base of her party, she did not win much accolades for her administrative skill. But the viciousness with which TMC party-workers attacked former Left operatives of lower levels (and occasionally Congress functionaries as well) over local elections, many sensed it was unsafe to be supporting the Opposition.

In the election of 2016, accordingly, while the TMC stood in splendid isolation, with the support of only the Jana Andolan Party of Harka Bahadur Chetri of the Hills, a broad coalition of forces was gathered, comprising the INC, CPI(M), CPI, AIFB, RSP, DSP, RJD, JDU and NCP. Apart from this, the NDA comprising the BJP and Gorkha Janmukti Morcha (GJM) was also in the field.

Of the 294 seats in the assembly, the TMC won 211 seats, (up 27), with 44.91% of the vote share. The INC finished second with 44 seats (up 2) and a vote share of 12.75%; the CPI(M) came third with 26 seats (down 14), with 19.75% of the vote share. The BJP won 3 seats (with 10.16% vote share) and the same for the RSP and GJM; the AIFB won 2 seats; the CPI and an independent candidate won as well. No other party won any seats.

With nearly 3 seats in every 4, CM Banerjee was sworn back in for her second full term in office (2016–21).

Kerala

Kerala provincial politics continued to be played out along the lines of bipolarity, with the 2 principal political formations – the LDF and the UDF – alternating. Oomen Chandy of the INC had ruled for a full term and was now faced with the systemic anti-incumbency at the time of the assembly polls.

At the time of the elections, the incumbent UDF constituted of 7 parties – the INC, IUML, KCM, JDU, RSP, KCJ and CMP. The LDF, by contrast constituted of the CPI(M), CPI, JDS, NCP, KC (Skarla Thomas), Congress (secular), Janadhipatya Kerala Congress, Indian National League, Kerala Congress (Balakrishna Pillai), CMP and RSP (Leninist). The BJP found some fellow travellers in the Bharath Dharma Jana Sena, KC (Thomas), Janadhipatya Sanrakshana Samiti and Janadhipatya Rashtriya Sabha.

When thc clcctions were held, predictably the LDF won with 98 seats (up 23). The CPI(M) finished as the largest party in the assembly, winning 58 seats, the CPI won 19, the JDS 3, and the C(S), JDS, KC (B) and CMP won 1 each, plus 5 independents came their way. The UDF won only 47 seats, of which the INC won 22, the IUML 18, KC (M) 6 and KC(J) 1. The BJP won its first seat ever in Kerala in this election.

Pinarayi Vijayan, the long-time CPI(M) party secretary of Kerala was sworn in as chief minister, which he served for the full term of the assembly (2016–21).

Puducherry

The INC had been one of the planks of politics in Puducherry, and even when out of power, the INC was never very far from it – as became clear in the assembly elections of 2016. The incumbent CM N. Rangaswamy had hung on to power tenuously on the strength of smaller allies. When the anti-incumbency set in, he could not withstand it.

In the elections that were held to the 30-seat assembly, the INC won 15 seats (up 8) of its own, with 30.6% of the vote share; its electoral ally the DMK winning 2 seats, the UPA coalition had a simple majority. The outgoing party-in-power AINRC, won 8 seats (down 7), with 28.1% of the popular vote. Contesting by itself, the AIADMK won only 4 seats; the BJP failed to win any.

Velu Narayanasamy of the INC was sworn in as the chief minister, in which capacity he served for a full 5-year term (2016–21).

Tamil Nadu

Elections to the Tamil Nadu assembly in 2016 constituted a kind of landmark because of 2 reasons. The AIADMK became the first party in Tamil Nadu to be returned to power after a full assembly term since 1984, and also because this was the last election contested by both M. Karunanidhi and J. Jayalalithaa – 2 remaining stalwarts of Tamil politics of the previous half century.

The AIADMK forged a 7 party alliance involving small outfits with local significance – viz. Manithaneya Jananayaka Katchi, Republican Party of India, All India Samuthava Makkal Katchi, Tamil Nadu Kongu Ilaingar Peravai and Mukkulathor Pulipadai. The DMK forged an 8 party alliance, involving small and medium-sized parties like INC, IUML, Manithaneya

Makkal Katchi (MMK), Puthiya Tamilakam, Perunthalaivar Makkal Katchi (PMK), Tamil Nadu Peasants and Workers Party and Samuga Samathuva Padai. Vijaykanth's DMDK forged an alliance with Vaiko's MDMK, CPI, CPI(M), Tamil Maanila Congress, and VCK. The NDA in Tamil Nadu was represented by the BJP in alliance with Indhiya Jananayaga Katchi. Besides, a number of parties, such as the PMK and AIMIM went without any alliance.

In the elections that were held, the AIADMK lost a few seats but returned with a convincing majority, winning 134 seats (down 14) out of 234, with a vote share of 40.88%. The DMK finished a distant second with 89 seats (up 66), with a vote share of 31.39%. The only 2 other parties to win any seats at all were the INC (8 seats) and the IUML (1 seat).

J. Jayalalithaa was sworn back to the office of the chief minister in May 2016, the first incumbent CM of Tamil Nadu to be so since M.G. Ramachandran in 1984. In December 2016, she passed away after a period of hospitalization. She was succeeded in December 2016 by her trusted follower Ottakarathevar Paneerselvam, who had stood in for Jayalalithaa twice before when (2001–02, 2014–15) she had to vacate her office temporarily on corruption charges. However, OPS had to face an ugly power struggle with Jayalalithaa's close friend and associate, Sasikala Natarjan, which had him resign from the office of the chief minister in early February 2017. OPS was expelled from the party shortly after, and the assembly leader of the Sasikala faction of the AIADMK, Edapaddi K. Palaniswamy, was sworn in as the chief minister on 16 February 2017. In August 2017, the two factions of the AIADMK mended fences, and OPS returned as the deputy chief minister and the coordinator of the party. In the years that followed, OPS was steadily marginalized by E.K. Palaniswamy, and finally, ostensibly in a bid to end the dual leadership model followed since 2017, OPS was expelled from the party in 2022.

2017

Punjab

Punjab, like some other states, had been dominated by 2 parties – the SAD and the INC. The 2017 elections followed this model, but saw the rise of a third force that was to change the template in the next election.

Parkash Singh Badal, the veteran chief minister of Punjab had maintained a long association with the BJP, which continued into the assembly elections of 2017. The INC led by former chief minister, Capt. Amarinder Singh, contested on its own, while the AAP joined the fray in the assembly elections in Punjab for the first time.

In the elections held in 2017, the INC won 77 seats (up 31) with a vote share of 38.5%. The AAP displaced the SAD to break into second spot with 20 seats, polling 23.7% of the vote share. The SAD was reduced to 15 seats (down 41) with a vote share of 25.2%. The BJP shrunk to the fourth place with 3 seats (down 9) and a vote share of 5.4%. The only other party to win any seats was the Lok Insaaf Party (led by Simranjit Singh Bains), which won 2 seats. The Akali Dal (Mann) faction, BSP, CPI and Revolutionary Marxist Party of India polled reasonably poorly.

The triumphant Maharaja of Patiala, Capt. Amarinder Singh was sworn back in as the chief minister for his second term in March 2017. During his tenure, though, trouble began to brew in the Punjab Congress, with Navjot Singh Sidhu mounting repeated attacks on the CM as being inaccessible, and neglecting duties of office. By 2021, the spat was serious enough for Amarinder to be summoned to Delhi and be told that MLAs do not have confidence in him anymore. Singh resigned in September 2021, after ensuring that Sidhu did not succeed him in the office. The Congress, alarmed by the AAP cultivating the Dalit constituency of the state, decided to appoint Charanjit Singh Channi in

September 2021, who continued to hold the office till the end of the assembly term in March 2022.

Uttar Pradesh

The political landscape of Uttar Pradesh had changed dramatically since the 1990s, which was notorious for its instability in the wake of the decline of the INC. From 2007, however, the UP electorate had been voting stable, single-party governments to power – almost as if understanding that no two parties can be trusted to function as responsible coalition partners. Thus, the BSP ruled on its own during 2007–12 and was voted out; the SP ruled from 2012–17 by itself, with Akhilesh Yadav at the helm. In 2017, it came to be the turn of the BJP to have a go at power in UP on its own strength.

In the elections that were held in 2017 for the 403-seat UP assembly, the BJP surprised all pollsters (except for those of *Dainik Bhaskar*) and presumably even the BJP itself, winning 312 seats (up 265) with a vote share of 39.67% – the largest tally for nearly half a century. The outgoing ruling party SP was reduced to the second spot with 47 seats (down 177) with a vote share of 21.82%; the BSP came third with 19 seats and a vote share of 22.23%. The INC managed only 7 seats (down 21) with 6.25% of the vote share. Apna Dal (Sonelal), representing mostly the Kurmi community, finished with 9 seats, and Suheldev Bharatiya Samaj Party (led by O.P. Rajbhar) won 4 seats. The Rashtriya Lok Dal and the Nirbal Indian Shoshit Hamara Aam Dal or NISHAD (representing Nishad, Kewat, Bind, Beldar, Gond, Mallah and other Dalit groups) won 1 seat each.

While the Opposition as usual complained of tampering of EVMs for this spectacular result for the BJP, it would seem that the BJP successfully crafted a social coalition of upper, middle and lower caste groups, without appearing to be dominated by the upper caste groups alone. Its promise of being tough on law and order also helped, after the reckless reputation of the SP government under Akhilesh Singh in this regard.

Not having projected a CM face to start with, the BJP in Uttar Pradesh was now divided over its CM face. While the Brahmin lobby rooted for one of their own (such as Kalraj Mishra and Lalji Tandon), the Kshatriyas wanted Rajnath Singh to return from the Union cabinet for a second term. With the two factions determined not to let the other faction prevail, a rank outsider, Yogi Adityanath's name was mooted for the post instead. Associated with the Gorakhnath temple in UP, Adityanath's advantage turned out to be that he was a Rajput leader who did not even belong to the main party structure of the BJP. Coming from a long tradition of Hindu monks associating initially with HMS and later the BJP who did not consider themselves bound to the party, Adityanath's past activities for the Hindutva brigade had taken him to the parliament and he had often been used as a star campaigner for the party. Thus, it was essentially as a wild card entry that his name was mooted and, despite some reservations at the highest level of the BJP, approved.

Yogi Adityanath (born Ajay Mohan Bisht) was thus sworn in as the chief minister of UP in March 2017, in which capacity he served for the full term of the assembly (2017–22).

Uttarakhand

Uttarakhand had been operating the revolving door template of alternating governments at every election since it came into being. This persisted even during the 2017 assembly elections, as the Congress government of Harish Rawat was shown out.

In the 2017 elections to the 70-seat Uttarakhand assembly, the BJP came back to power with 57 seats (up 26) with a vote share of 46.5%. The INC was reduced to only 11 seats (down 21) with a vote share of 33.5%. Of the other parties, neither the

SP, nor the BSP or the Uttarakhand Kranti Dal managed to win any seats.

An old RSS hand Trivendra Singh Rawat was sworn in as the chief minister in March 2017, in which position he remained till September 2021, when opposition against him grew among both party people and the people at large. He was replaced in September 2021 by Tirath Singh Rawat, who held the office till July 2021, when he was replaced by Pushkar Singh Dhami, who led the party into the assembly elections of 2022.

Manipur

The 2017 elections to the Manipur assembly turned out to be quite fateful in the long run. After a kind of stability had been provided by the INC CM Okram Ibobi Singh for 15 years, the state finally managed to move away in a new direction, leading to the formation of the first BJP government ever in the state. The rise of the BJP in this north-eastern state was largely the doing of the then Deputy CM of Assam, Himanta Biswa Sarma, who pioneered the formation of the North-Eastern Democratic Alliance (NEDA), involving small but important regional parties and political figures into a political alliance/alignment/understanding with the BJP.

In the 2017 elections to the 60-seat assembly, the INC lost 19 seats to finish at 28 seats, with a vote share of 35.1%. The BJP finished second with 21 seats (up 21) with a vote share of 36.2%. The Naga People's Front, which rules Nagaland in alliance with the BJP as part of the NDA, won 4 seats with a vote share of 5.1%; the National People's Party (led by Conrad Sangma), which as a member of the NEDA, ran in alliance with the BJP, also won 4 seats. The LJP, another NDA constituent, won 1 seat. Thus, the BJP plus its allies chalked up 30 seats in the Manipur assembly, and NEDA was in a position to form a government on its own.

Nongthombam Biren Singh was sworn in as the BJP-led NDA/NEDA government in 2017. A Meitei leader who began his political career in the Democratic Revolutionary People's Party, before joining the INC in 2003, and serving as a minister in the Ibobi Singh government, Singh finally joined the BJP in 2016. Biren Singh held office for the full term of the assembly (2017–22), overcoming an internal party revolt by 3 MLAs who resigned and 6 others who joined the Congress by turning 5 INC MLAs into joining the BJP in 2020.

Goa

The BJP had wriggled its way into the Goa government, won elections, and emerged as the political alternative to the INC under the leadership of Manohar Parrikar, who then joined union cabinet in 2014. Goa was held by Laxmikant Parsekar till the end of the assembly term in 2017. The assembly elections of 2017 showed that they loved it enough to not let it go.

In the elections of 2017 to the 40-seat assembly, the INC emerged as the single largest party with 17 seats (up 8) with a vote share of 28.4%. The BJP was reduced to the second spot with 13 seats (down 8) with a vote share of 32.5%. The MAG, an NDA constituent, won 3 seats; the debutant Goa Forward Party (GPF, led by Vijay Sardesai) won 3 seats, the NCP won 1 seat and 3 seats were won by independent candidates.

Despite winning the larger number of seats, the INC proved remarkably slow in moving for government formation. They probably assumed that the Goa Forward Party, being founded on ant-BJP plank would automatically support INC. Hence INC leaders like Luizinho Faleiro were responding somewhat slowly to the GFP, both before and after the elections. This made the GFP respond more favourably to the BJP in talks on government formation. Its leader Vijay Sardesai made the GFP support conditional upon Parrikar returning to Goa as the chief minister.

The BJP obliged. Parrikar returned in March 2017 to be sworn in as the CM of Goa for a third term, with MAG, GFP and support from independents. The GFP had all 3 of its MLAs made ministers in the cabinet, with Vijay Sardesai being made the minister of Town and Country Planning and of Agriculture. Leading GFP functionaries, including then party president, Renuka da Silva, were appointed to prestigious (and occasionally remunerative) public institutions and organizations.

Manohar Parrikar held the office of the CM for just two-and-a-half years, before he passed away from pancreatic cancer in October 2018. He was succeeded by Pramod Sawant who remained CM for the rest of the term (2018–22).

Gujarat

By 2017, Gujarat had become a BJP stronghold, hence there was little by way of challenge to the thrall the party held the state in. For a brief period after the elevation of Narendra Modi to the office of the prime minister, the patidar agitation of 2015 (seeking OBC status for the community) caused a few flutters, but the replacement of Anandiben Patel by Vijay Rupani put the dampener on these issues.

In the assembly elections of 2017, the BJP came back to power with a slightly reduced margin, winning 99 seats (down 16) in the 182-seat assembly, with a vote share of 49.1%. The INC recovered somewhat, winning 77 seats (up 16) with a vote share of 41.4%. Among the other contenders, the debutant Bharatiya Tribal Party (led by Chhotubhai Basava) won 2 seats and the NCP 1, with 3 successful independent candidates.

The incumbent chief minister Vijay Rupani was sworn back in, and remained in office till September 2021. An ex-RSS man, Bhupendrabhai Patel, was sworn in as the chief minister in September 2021, who then led the party into the 2022 assembly elections.

Himachal Pradesh

Himachal Pradesh is a state which has in the last several decades, stuck to the template of the revolving door approach to political power in a 2-party setting. The BJP and the INC had been alternating in power for over 2 decades, and 2017 continued with that template as well, with the incumbent Virabhadra Singh being shown out by the incoming BJP government.

In the elections that were held in 2017, the BJP won 44 seats (up 18) with a vote share of 48.8%. The outgoing INC was reduced to 21 seats (down 15) with 41.7% of the vote share. Independents took 2 seats and the CPI(M) won 1.

In an interesting development, though, Prem Kumar Dhumal, 2-time chief minister of HP and BJP's CM-face in 2017 elections, lost his own seat. He was thus passed over in favour of Jai Ram Thakur – an ABVP functionary, 6-time MLA and former cabinet minister of HP – who was sworn in as the chief minister, and served for the full term of the assembly (2017–22).

2018

Tripura

The elections to the Tripura legislative assembly in 2018 constituted a major milestone. The CPI(M), a party predominantly catering to the Bengali community domiciled in the state, had established a stranglehold on the people of Tripura. After five assembly terms, the people presumably looked for a change, and presumably found in the BJP, an alternative strong enough to take on the five-term-old chief minister Manik Sarkar. The BJP put together a social coalition of the Bengali community with the hill tribes of Tripura, mobilized with the help of the NDA ally, the Indigenous People's Front of Tripura (IPFT), which possibly accounts for their success.

In the elections held in February 2018, to the great surprise of everyone concerned, the BJP won 36 seats out of the 60 seats in the assembly, with a vote share of 43.59%; its ally, the IPFT won 8 seats, making the NDA tally 44 in all. The CPI(M) was reduced to 16 seats (down 33). No other party won any seats. The INC, losing all 10 seats it won the last time, received only 1.79% of the vote share (as against over 36% in 2013) – indicating the entire vote that used to be cast for the INC probably went to the BJP, which never received much votes before this election.

Biplab Deb, son of Bengali refugees from East Pakistan who rose to become the state president of the BJP in 2017, was sworn in as the chief minister of Tripura in March 2018. Deb held the post till 2022, when he was replaced by Manik Saha, (a former Congressman who joined the BJP in 2016), who led the party to the elections in 2023.

Meghalaya

Elections to the legislative assembly in Meghalaya in 2018 came after a full term of 5 years under a coalition led by INC chief minister Mukul Sangma.

The elections returned a hung assembly in Meghalaya, as has almost always been the case. The INC remained the single largest party with 21 seats (down 8) out of 60 with a vote share of 28.5%. The NPP, led by Conrad Sangma, finished second with 20 seats (up 18), with a vote share of 20.6%. The United Democratic Party, led by Metbah Lyngdoh, won 6 seats (down 2) with a vote share of 11.6%. The debutant People's Democratic Front (PDF) won 4 seats, the HSPDP and the BJP won 2 seats each, the NCP won 1, and the independents took 3 seats.

As it always happened in the past, finishing as the largest party never helped any parties gain power. In 2018, Conrad Sangma, the son of Purna A. Sangma, was more successful with his attempts at forming a coalition, which constituted the NPP,

UDP, PDF, HSPDP and the BJP – commanding a total of 34 MLAs in the assembly.

Conrad Kongkal Sangma was sworn in as the chief minister in March 2018. He took the constituents of his coalition into both the NDA and the NEDA.

SANGMA HELD OFFICE FOR THE FULL TERM OF THE ASSEMBLY (2018–23) – THE FIRST MEGHALAYA CM TO HAVE EVER COMPLETED A FULL TERM IN OFFICE WITHOUT FACING ANY CHALLENGE TO HIS AUTHORITY.

Nagaland

Nagaland had seen a kind of stability develop with the NPF-led governments of Neiphiu Rio before he was toppled from within his party, the Naga People's Front (NPF), under the leadership of T.R. Zeliang, who as chief minister took Nagaland into the assembly elections of 2018. Rio set up his own party, the Nationalist Democratic Progressive Party (NDPP). Two months before the elections were due, the BJP suddenly came into being in the state of Nagaland as a party to reckon with when former chief minister K.L. Chishi, along with a dozen lawmakers, joined the party. The BJP also broke its alliance with the ruling NPF, and forged a coalition instead with NDPP.

In the elections to the 60-seat assembly held in 2018, the NPF won 26 seats (down 18) with a vote share of 38.8%. The debutant NDPP won 18 seats, with a vote share of 25.2%. The BJP, curiously emerged as the third-largest party with 12 seats (up 11) with a vote share of 15.3%. National People's Party (NPP) won 2 seats, the JDU won 1 seat, as did an independent candidate. As in Meghalaya and Tripura, the INC was wiped out in Nagaland as well.

With the NDA coalition (NDPP–BJP–JDU) winning a simple majority of 31 seats, Neiphiu Rio was sworn into office for the fifth time in March 2018, leading a cabinet of 12, of whom 6 belonged to the BJP, 5 (including Rio himself) to the NDPP, and 1 minister was an independent MLA who gave his support to the Rio government. Two NPP MLAs also later merged into the NDPP, being greased by the wheels of power. Rio's government survived the full term of the assembly (2018–23).

Karnataka

Elections for the assembly in Karnataka were held in May 2018 after 5 years of Congress government under the CM Siddaramaiah. Despite the best efforts of the BJP, which pumped in large amounts of resources and had the prime minister and the home minister of the country pull out all stops, all indications had begun to emerge of a hung verdict.

In the elections to the 224-seat assembly, the BJP under former chief minister B.S. Yeddyurappa emerged as the single largest party with 104 seats (up 64), with 36.5% of vote share. The INC finished second with 80 seats (down 42) and 38.14% of the vote share; the JDS finished as the third-largest party with 37 seats (down 3). The Pragnyavantha Janatha Party, the BSP and independents each won 1 seat.

B.S. Yeddyurappa staked claim for government formation, and the BJP being the single largest party, the governor obliged; hence Yeddyurappa was sworn in as chief minister in May 2018. However, Yedyurappa was being given a window of 15 days to prove his majority on the floor of the house, at a time when the INC and the JDS had already agreed upon forming a post-poll coalition. The INC–JDS moved court saying this was aiding horse-trading, and the Supreme Court, concurring, reduced the window to 3 days. Yeddyurappa resigned on the morning of the third day, unable to gather enough support from the other side of the floor. The INC–JDS coalition was then sworn into power with H.D. Kumaraswamy as the chief minister. Kumaraswamy held the office for 14 months before his government collapsed. In a span of 2 days, 16 MLAs from the JDS and INC resigned their seats, and 2 independent MLAs extended support to the BJP. This reduced the numbers of the INC-JDS coalition to 101, 4 short of the majority mark in the reduced assembly, with the BJP tally standing at 107. Kumaraswamy lost the trust vote on the floor of the house, and resigned in July 2019. On July 2019, Yedyurappa was sworn in once again as the chief minister, but dissidence within the party forced him to step down in July 2021. He was replaced by Basavraj Bommai (the son of S.R. Bommai of the Janata Dal), who remained in that office till assembly elections of 2023.

Chhattisgarh

From the first elections after its creation, Chhattisgarh had been ruled by the BJP. The incumbent chief minister Raman Singh had an impressive record as an administrator for 15 years. In 2018, as anti-incumbency finally caught up with him, the Congress won a landslide victory with a new leader, Bhupesh Baghel, who came to virtually revamp the party after the expulsion of former leader Ajit Jogi and the death of 31 top leaders of the state unit of the party in a Naxalite attack in 2013.

In the elections to the 90-seat assembly, the INC won 68 seats (up 29) with a vote share of 43%. The BJP was reduced to 15 seats (down 34) with a vote share of 33%. The debutant Janata Congress Chhattisgarh, set up by Ajit Jogi, after his expulsion from the INC, won 5 seats, and the BSP won only 2 seats.

Bhupesh Baghel was sworn in as the chief minister in December 2018. In the 5 years of his first term (2018–23) in office, Baghel made his mark with efficient administration and welfare policies.

Madhya Pradesh

The Madhya Pradesh assembly elections of 2018 began as a battle of the titans and ended with the high drama tapering into a damp squib. The BJP had been in power since 2003, with 2 straight terms under Shivraj Singh Chauhan, while the Congress had last been in power under Digvijay Singh during 1993–2003. While Chauhan was battling anti-incumbency, the Congress was weighed down with its trademark factionalism – Kamal Nath, Digvijay Singh and Jyotiradiya Scindia, each crucial to the party and CM aspirant.

In the elections held in 2018, the INC had the narrowest of victories, winning 114 seats (up 56), with a vote share of 40.89%. The BJP was close behind in seats, having won 109 seats (down 56), but marginally ahead in vote share: 41.02%. The remaining 7 seats in the assembly were taken by the BSP (2), SP (1), independents (4).

Despite being instrumental in the INC victory, Jyotiraditya Scindia was bypassed and Kamal Nath was sworn in as the chief minister of Madhya Pradesh (December 2018–March 2020), largely owing to Digvijay Singh putting his weight behind his one-time rival in order to weaken the rising star, Scindia. Despite being offered positions in New Delhi and organizationally, Scindia's justified ambitions kept being thwarted by these two old guards of the Congress. By March 2020, Scindia's patience ran out, and he crossed the floor to join the BJP with 22 MLAs. Reduced to a minority in the assembly, Kamal Nath had to step down, and Shivraj Singh Chouhan became the chief minister yet again, despite having lost the election. Jyotiraditya Scindia was rewarded by the BJP with a seat in the Rajya Sabha and eventually a berth in the Union cabinet, with the portfolio of civil aviation. Shivraj Singh Chouhan, wiping out the memory of his defeat, carried on with the business of the government, and took the BJP into the assembly elections of 2023.

Mizoram

The assembly election of 2018 in Mizoram was a pretty routine affair of an incumbent government being shown out of power – except that this was somewhat different.

After its coming to power in the Centre, the BJP had gone about bringing INC politicians over to their side, thus undermining the Congress in the region. Right before the 2013–18 assembly term ended, a number of such politicians resigned from the Congress and joined the BJP.

In the 2018 elections to the 40-seat Mizoram assembly, the Mizo National Front (MNF) won 26 seats (up 21) with a vote share of 37.7%. The 6-party alliance of Zoram People's Movement finished with 8 seats, and a vote share of 22.9%. The INC won 5 seats (with a vote share of 29.98%), and the BJP 1.

The MNF, which has been a constituent of the NDA since 2014, having successfully ended Pu Lalthanhawla's victory run, its leader Zoramthanga was sworn back in as the CM in December 2018.

Once the INC government was defeated in Mizoram in 2018, there was no Congress government left anywhere in the North-East for the first time since 1952.

Rajasthan

Well into the first term of the Modi government in New Delhi, Rajasthan remained one of the few places where the revolving door of politics continued, with the incumbent government of Vasundhara Raje being shown out of power at the end of her term.

In the elections to the 200-seat Rajasthan assembly, the INC won 100 seats (up 79) with a vote share of 39.3%, to emerge as the single largest party. The BJP came second with 73 seats (down 90), and a vote share of 38.77%. Among the other parties contesting in these elections, the BSP won 6 seats, the debutant Rashtriya Loktantrik Party (led by Hanuman Beniwal) won 3 seats, the CPI(M) and the Bharatiya Tribal Party won 2 seats each, the RLD won 1, and 13 seats were claimed by independents.

Sachin Pilot, the son of the veteran Congressman Rajesh Pilot, had been pivotal in the revival of the INC after the drubbing it got in 2013. Thus, after the victory of 2018, many thought that Pilot should have been made the chief minister. But mindful of the wiliness of the old guard, a fearful Congress top brass appointed Ashok Gehlot for his third term as chief minister, making Pilot the deputy chief minister. Soon after the Scindia defection in Madhya Pradesh, it almost seemed like the Congress would lose Pilot as well, but the crisis was tackled successfully, and Gehlot went on to hold the office of the CM till the end of the term.

Telangana

The first Telangana legislative assembly was dissolved in 2018, 9 months ahead of its term-end, as K. Chandrasekhar wanted to renew his mandate. The INC, TDP, Telangana Jana Samithi (TJS) and the CPI came together to form the Praja Maha Kutumi bloc; the BJP contested the election by itself.

In the elections that were held in 2018 for the 118-seat Telangana assembly, the TRS won 88 seats (up 25), a vote share 46.87%. The INC won 19 seats (down 2) with 28.43% of the vote share; the TDP won 2 seats, and the CPI failed to score – thus the alliance had a tally of only 21 seats. The AIMIM held on to its 7 seats with only 2.71% of the vote share. The BJP, AIFB and an independent won a seat each.

Kalvakuntla Chandrasekhar Rao was sworn in for his second term as chief minister in December 2018, in which capacity he played out for the full term.

2019

Andhra Pradesh

The rump state of Andhra Pradesh, after the creation of Telangana, was ruled during the first 5 years by the TDP, with N. Chandrababu Naidu as the chief minister. In the 5 years that followed, while Naidu tried to build the state a new capital city at Amaravati, he appeared to have run out of steam. Jagan Mohan Reddy, the leader of the Opposition, patiently went about mobilizing opinion against the developmental model of governance of Naidu, and showed signs of populism in his own approach.

While the 4 main parties – TDP, INC, YSRC and BJP – decided to fight by themselves, the Jana Sena Party (led by Telugu film star Pawan Kalyan) stitched an alliance with the BSP, CPI and CPI(M).

In the 2019 elections to the 175-seat Assembly of Telangana, YSRC had a landslide victory, winning 151 seats (up 84) with a vote share of 49.95% – a fantastic achievement by any measure. The outgoing TDP was reduced to 23 seats (down 79), with a vote share of 39.17%. The only other party to win a seat was the Jana Sena. The INC and the BJP were not merely wiped out, their deposits were confiscated in each of the 174 constituency they contested from.

Yeduguri Sandinti Jagan Mohan Reddy was sworn in as the chief minister of Andhra Pradesh. In course of his years in office, he established his trademark populist policies. However, his decision to discontinue with the new capital at Amaravati was overturned by the court. He remains in office as this book goes to press.

Arunachal Pradesh

Arunachal Pradesh had been among the earliest states to join the NDA bandwagon under Pema Khandu between assembly elections. In 2019, the Khandu-led BJP government came up for its first test at the ballot box.

In the 2019 election to the 60-seat assembly, the BJP won 41 (up 30) seats with 50.86% of the popular vote.; its ally, the JDU, won 7 seats, the National People's Party won 5 seats – pushing the NDA tally to 53 seats. The INC won 4 seats and the People's Party of Arunachal won 1. Independents won 2 seats.

Pema Khandu was sworn back in as the chief minister in May 2019, in which position he remains as of date.

Odisha

The politics of Odisha has sort of plateaued out in a way that it might actually appear that the 2 decades under BJD rule has virtually insulated Odisha from the main currents of politics of the national mainstream, even though the assembly polls were held along with the Lok Sabha polls. This was reinforced when the assembly elections were held in the state only to bring the incumbent chief minister back to power for a record fifth term, while BJD also won 12 of the 21 Lok Sabha seats from the seat.

In the elections to the 147-seat assembly, the BJD lost 5 seats to finish at 112 seats, with a vote share of 44.71%. The BJP finished second with 23 seats (up 13) with a vote share of 32.49%. The INC wilted at 9 seats (down 7) with only 16.12% of the popular vote. The CPI(M) and an independent candidate won a seat each.

Naveen Patnaik was sworn back in for the fifth term in May 2019. Once he completes the current term, he will be only the second Indian politician to be in the chief minister's office for 5 consecutive full terms.

Sikkim

The elections to the Sikkim assembly in 2019 were a milestone, in the sense that it brought an end to the 25-year long rule of the SDF Chief Minister Pavan Kumar Chamling, the longest continuous stint any Indian chief minister has had so far.

In the elections to the 32-seat assembly, the Sikkim Krantikari Morcha (founded in 2013 by Prem Singh Tamang, aka Prem Singh Golay, ex-SDF minister) won 17 seats (up 7) with 47.03% of the vote share. The outgoing SDF won 15 seats (down 7) with a marginally higher vote share of 47.63%. The INC was wiped out in the state, with less than1% votes polled, and the BJP failed to grow any roots for itself.

Prem Singh Tamang was sworn in as the chief Minister in 2019, and remains in office as of date. The SKM had considered joining the NDA before the elections, but decided against it. However, after forming the government on their own strength, they joined the NDA and NEDA after all.

Haryana

Elections to the Haryana assembly were held in 2019, along with the Lok Sabha polls. The M.L. Khattar government, which had brought to an end 10 years of Congress rule under B.S. Hooda, failed to obtain a majority by itself, and had to form a coalition government. The myth of the Modi effect clearly needs better evidentiary base.

On the eve of the elections, a new party, the Jannayak Janata Party, was launched in 2018, by Dushyant Chautala grandson of Om Prakash Chautala, who remains imprisoned on corruption charges. Dushyant Chautala and his brother Digvijay Chautala were expelled from the INLD by their uncle, claiming to be the sole inheritor of the Chautala legacy (not one to be particularly proud of). The JJP claims the legacy of Chaudhry Devi Lal. In 2019, they ended up playing the king-maker - much along the lines plotted by Devi Lal himself.

In the elections to the 90-seat assembly, the BJP remained the single largest party with 40 seats (down 7) with a vote share of

36.49%. The INC remained the second-largest party with 31 seats (up 16) and a vote share of 28.08%. The JJP finished with a surprise tally of 10 seats polling 14.08%, reducing the parent outfit of INLD to only 1 seat. Haryana Lokhit Dal also finished with 1 seat.

Falling short by 6 seats, Khattar opened negotiations with Dushyant Chautala. The JJP agreed to join the NDA and support the BJP in return for entry into the Haryana cabinet with the post of deputy chief minister for Dushyant Chautala. By consenting to this arrangement, Khattar was sworn back in as the chief minister of Haryana for a second term that began in 2019. The BJP-JJP alliance broke down in March 2024 over seat-sharing for the nineteenth Lok Sabha elections, leading to the resignation of Khattar, and departure of Dushyant Chautala and the JJP from the cabinet. Khattar was replaced by his associate Nayab Singh Saini, who was sworn in as the chief minister of the state.

Jharkhand

The elections to the Jharkhand assembly held in 2019 brought about a change in the government, showing the BJP out of power and bringing back the UPA. The idea of the Modi wave did not seem to have reached the state. With the BJP and JVM of Babulal Marandi fighting among themselves, consolidation of the vote bank did not work out in favour of the NDA.

In the elections that were held for the 81-seat Jharkhand assembly, the JMM won 30 seats (up 11) with a vote share of 18.72%. The BJP won 25 seats (down 12) with a much higher vote share (33.37%). The INC finished with 16 seats (up 10) with a vote share of 13.88%. The JVM won 3 seats, AJSU won 2, and the RJD, NCP and CPI(ML) won 1 seat each.

With the UPA allies having won 47 seats, Hemant Soren of the JMM was sworn in for the second term to the office of the chief minister in December 2019.

Maharashtra

The BJP–Shiv Sena government, that came into being in 2014, remained in power for the full 5-year term. When Maharashtra went to the polls, they once again went as a team. Similarly, the INC and the NCP also went for a pre-poll alliance before the 2019 elections were held.

In the elections to the 288-seat assembly, the BJP won 105 seats (down 17) with 25.75% of the vote share, while the Shiv Sena won 56 seats (down 7), with a vote share of 16.41%. The NCP won 54 seats (up 13) with a vote share of 16.71%. The INC won 44 seats (up 2), with 15.87% of the popular vote. Among other parties, the Bahujan Vikas Aghadi won 3 seats, the AIMIM, SP and Prahar Janshakti Party won 2 seats each. A whole range of parties including the MNS, PWPI and CPI(M) won only 1 seat each.

The Shiv Sena demanded rotational chief ministers for two-and-a-half years each, which Uddhav Thackeray claimed to have been agreed during negotiations over alliance formation. With the incumbent CM Devendra Fadnavis not agreeing to this, Uddhav Thackeray pulled out of the NDA. In these circumstances, President's Rule was imposed in Maharashtra. Back channel discussions began between Uddhav, Sharad Pawar and Balasaheb Thorat to work out a formula for power-sharing. By the time this was going to be officially communicated, the ambitious state unit president of the NCP, Ajit Pawar, approached Fadnavis, offering him NCP support if he should form the government. Fadnavis merrily went about having himself sworn in as chief minister in November 2019 with Ajit Pawar as the deputy, only to be tripped up when the NCP as a party refused to support the BJP. Fadnavis resigned on 26 November 2019. On 28 November, Uddhav Thackeray was sworn in as the chief minister of Maharashtra Vikas Aghadi, a post-poll coalition between the Shiv Sena, INC and NCP.

In June 2022, the MVA disintegrated when a majority of the Shiv Sena under Eknath Shinde quit the MVA and rejoined the

NDA. On 29 June 2022, Thackeray resigned without facing the floor test which he felt he was sure to lose. On 30 June 2022, Eknath Shinde was sworn in as the chief minister of Maharashtra, with Fadnavis as his deputy. Subsequently, Ajit Pawar took a bulk of the NCP with himself and joined the Shiv Sena-BJP combine, assuming office as the deputy CM. Thackeray moved court saying he represented the real Shiv Sena, but the Supreme Court expressed its helplessness in restoring Thackeray to the office *because he had already resigned*. Maharashtra awaits the next assembly election for the people's verdict on the matter.

2020

Delhi

The assembly elections for the state of Delhi in 2020 ran along pretty much the same lines as they had done on 2015. The AAP government of Delhi had delivered quite impressively on Delhi's health infrastructure. But as much as capitalizing on the Delhi government's own achievements, the AAP made the BJP's stonewalling of the Delhi government – ranging from its interactions with Delhi's Lieutenant Governors to the operations of the 3 municipalities of Delhi (run by the BJP for a period – a major point of the campaign.

In the elections held in 2020, the AAP retained its total control of the Delhi assembly winning 62 seats (down 5), with 53.57% of the vote. The BJP won the remaining 8 seats (up 5), with 38.51% of the vote share. The INC, after 4 terms as the ruling party polled less than 5% of the popular vote; other parties could not cross even 1%.

Arvind Kejriwal was thus sworn in for his third term as the chief minister of Delhi. During his third term, Kejriwal government has made a great success of the government-run schools of the NCR. However, the principal architect of this success, the deputy chief minister Manish Sisodia, fell foul of the Union government, who has levelled allegations of corruption against him, and he remains under detention as this book goes to press. The next elections in Delhi are due in 2025, if nothing happens out of the ordinary.

Bihar

The state of Bihar, during 2015–20, gained the reputation of baffling the most seasoned observers and undoing all done deals. In the five years since Nitish Kumar led the winning coalition to become the chief minister, everything has been changing except for the person of the chief minister. The assembly elections of 2020 and the years that followed, seem to be running along the same lines.

The NDA alliance, in which the JDU and the BJP made up the 2 principal parties, were faced with the considerable force of anti-incumbency. While the JDU and the BJP agreed to be contesting in a similar number of seats (115 and 110 respectively), smaller parties like Vikashsheel Insaan Party (VIP, 11 seats) and Hindustan Awam Morcha (HAM, 7 seats) were accommodated to prevent voter fragmentation. The only failure in this regard was the breakdown of talks with the LJP (led by Chirag Paswan after the death of Ram Vilas), which decided to contest against the JDU, but not against the BJP. On the other hand, the *mahagathbandhan* of 2020 included the INC, RJD, CPI, CPI(M) and CPI(ML). By October 2020, even the JMM joined the alliance. There were other alliances - such as the Grand Democratic Secular front constituted of the BSP, AIMIM, RLSP, Samajwadi Janata Dal Democratic and Suheldev Bharatiya Samaj Party (led by O.P. Rajbhar); or the United Democratic Alliance of 20 minor parties collectively led by Yashwant Sinha, former BJP cabinet minister.

In the elections that followed, the NDA finished with 125 seats, while the *mahagathbandhan* won 110 seats. Among the NDA allies, the BJP landed up on top of the pile with 74 seats (up

21), and a vote share of 19.46%; the JDU won 43 seats (up 28), with a vote share of 15.39%; the VIP and HAM won 4 seats each. Among the *mahagathbandhan*, the RJD was the single largest party of the assembly with 75 seats (down 5) with a vote share of 23.11%; the INC won 19 seats (down 9) with a vote share of 9.48%; the CPI(ML) won 12 seats (up 9), and the CPI and CPM won 2 seats each. Among other parties, the AIMIM won 5 seats, the LJP and BSP won a seat each.

While Sushil Modi, who had worked with Nitish Kumar for a very long time, was not made the deputy chief minister and sent instead to the Rajya Sabha in place of the late Ram Vilas Paswan, Nitish Kumar was sworn back in as the chief minister in August 2020. Modi's elevation to the Rajya Sabha was followed by a gradual cornering of Nitish Kumar, who finally decided in August 2022 to break with the NDA one more time, and resigned from his office to join, instead, the *mahagathbandhan*. The *Mahagathbandhan* welcomed him back, and then formed a new coalition which had Nitish Kumar being sworn in as the CM once again – the eighth time in 22 years. In that capacity, in 2023, Nitish Kumar started an attempt to forge an all-party alliance – the Indian National Developmental Inclusive Alliance against the BJP. However, early in January 2024, he dumped the *mahagathbandhan* government and the INDIA alliance yet again and went back to the NDA. The new government that was formed had Nitish Kumar sworn in for the ninth time. Bihar waits with bated breath for the tenth of such happy occasions.

2021

Assam

Elections to the Assam assembly held in 2021 marked a landmark of sorts. It elected the first non-Congress government in Assam to be returned to power in 2 elections back to back, beating both anti-incumbency and factional pulls and pressures.

The BJP had been in power since 2016 under Chief Minister Sarbananda Sonowal and the deputy chief minister Himanta Biswa Sarma. The party had worked extensively to deepen its roots not only in Assam but also in the North-East as a whole – a task that was assigned to Sarma. In Assam, the BJP added to its kitty of allies (which already included the AGP) the United People's Party Liberal (UPPL led by Pramod Boro) while going for the elections in 2021.

The INC stitched up its own alliance with the AIUDF (led by Badruddin Ajmal), Bodoland People's Front, CPI, CPI(M), CPI(ML), RJD and the Anchalik Gana Morcha (led by Ajit Kumar Bhuyan).

In the elections to the 126-seat Assam assembly held in 2021, the NDA won a simple majority with 75 seats, of which the BJP by itself won 60 seats, with a vote share of 33.21%; the AGP won 9 seats (down 5), and the UPPL won 6 seats. The INC-led Mahajot won 50 seats, of which the INC won 29, the AIUDF 16, the BPF won 4 seats and the CPI(M) 1.

After the elections, on consultation with the party's top brass, the incumbent CM Sarbananda Sonowal stepped aside, and Himanta Biswa Sarma was sworn in as the chief minister of Assam on 10 May 2021, and remains in that office to date.

Kerala

The elections to the 2021 Kerala assembly were also a landmark election because it for the first time ever in the state returned an incumbent government to power. The revolving door template, which was in a way developed and perfected in Kerala, came to a halt as the LDF remained in power, and the UDF in the Opposition for consecutive terms.

One of the important factors in this was possibly a permutation of political forces in the state. After 2016, KC (Mani) split into two, with one faction remaining with the UDF, while the other left for the LDF. Also after 2016, 4 parties including the Loktantrik Janata Dal and the Indian National League (led by former IUML, Ibrahim Sulaiman Sait) joined the LDF.

In the elections that were held for the Kerala assembly in 2022, the LDF won 99 seats, of which the CPI(M) won 62 seats (up 4) with a vote share of 25.38%; the CPI won 17 seats (down 2); the Kerala Congress Mani won 5 seats (down 1); the JDS and NCP won 2 seats each; the Congress Secular, the LJD and INL won 1 seat each. The UDF won 41 seats, of which the INC won 21 (down 1), with a vote share of 25.12%; the IUML won 15 seats; the Kerala Congress won 2 seats, and the Kerala Congress (J) and RMCI won 1 seat each. The BJP, its ally the AIADMK and Bharath Dharma Jana Sena failed to win any seats between them. Neither did any of the other parties that had been in running.

Pinarayi Vijayan was sworn back in for another term in government in May 2021. He remains in office till date.

Puducherry

The Puducherry assembly elections for 2021 indicate a major shift in the political dynamics of the state. Just 2 months before the end of the assembly term in 2021, CM V. Narayanasamy's government collapsed when 5 INC and 1 DMK MLA resigned from the government and withdrew their support (2 of these later went over to the BJP), necessitating a vote of confidence. The government resigned when the Speaker ruled allowing all the members (who happened to be from the BJP) nominated by Lt. Governor Tamilisai Soundarrajan (who also happened to be from the BJP) to vote in the confidence motion – which is meant to be voted upon only by the elected members.

In the election that was then held in 2021, the INC contested in alliance with the DMK, CVK and CPI. The NDA in the UT constituted of the AINRC, BJP and the AIADMK.

The AINRC emerged as the single largest party in the 30-seat assembly with 10 seats (up 2), with 25.85% of the vote share; its ally, the BJP, won 6 seats (up 6) with 18.51% vote share. The DMK won 6 seats, the INC 2 and independent candidates won 6 seats. The new party of Kamal Hasan, Makkal Needhi Maiam, failed to win any seats at all.

With 16 MLAs, the NDA claimed victory and the BJP announced that N. Rangaswamy was to be the next chief minister of Puducherry. The governor nominated 3 MLAs, whom the Speaker immediately declared co-equal to the elected MLAs. Further, 3 independent MLAs pledged allegiance to the AIRNC and 2 to the BJP. Even the other independent candidate who had won with INC support went and joined the BJP.

While N. Rangaswamy was sworn in again as chief minister in May 2021, the BJP gained the position of the Speaker and 2 ministers; the AINRC was to get 3 ministers. The government continues to hold office as on date.

Tamil Nadu

Between the two elections of 2016 and 2021, Tamil politics lost its 2 pivots with the death of Jayalalithaa in 2016 and then Karunanidhi in 2018. While the AIADMK, after a round of factional struggles, settled in behind the dual leadership of Palanisamy and OPS, neutralizing the Sasikala-Dinakaran faction, the passing away of Karunanidhi did not create much bad blood in the DMK. The party leadership was to go the way of M.K.'s younger son M.K. Stalin, with his daughter Kanimozhi representing the party as an MP in Delhi; the elder son Azhagiri was quietly neutralized, largely because this seemed to be in consonance with the old patriarch's wishes.

The ruling AIADMK, by the time of the 2021 elections, was firmly in the NDA camp. In Tamil Nadu this comprised the 9 parties – AIADMK, BJP, TMC (Moopanar), Perunthalaivar Makkal

Katchi (PTMK), Moovender Munnetra Kazhagam (MMK), All Indian Moovender Munnai Kazhagam (AIMMK), Patrathchi Bharatam Katchi (PBK), Pasumpon Desiya Kazhagam (PDK), and PMK. The DMK put together the Secular Progressive Alliance, consisting of the DMK, MDMK, INC, KMDK, AIFB, CPI, CPI(M), VCK and IUML, Thamizhaga Vazhvurimal Katchi, Makkal Vidhuthali Katchi and Aathi Thamihar Peravai. Two more alliances were formed centering around the Makkal Needhi Maiam of Kamal Hasan and Vijaykanth's DMDK.

In the elections to the assembly held in 2021, the DMK alliance won 159 seats out of 234 seats of the assembly. Of this, the DMK alone secured 133 seats, with 37.70% of the vote share; INC won 18 seats, the VCK got 4 and the CPI and the CPI(M) got 2 each. The NDA won 75 seats, of which the AIADMK alone won 66 seats, the PMK 5 and BJP 4. Neither of the other 2 minor alliances won even a single seat.

Muthuvel Karunanidhi Stalin was sworn in as the chief minister of the state of Tamil Nadu, in which he remains in charge to date.

West Bengal

The elections of 2021 for the legislative assembly in West Bengal came within 2 years of BJP's impressive showing from West Bengal in the Lok Sabha polls of 2019 – when the TMC was reduced from 34 to 22 seats, the INC from 4 to 2 and the CPI(M) to zero, the BJP climbed from 2 to 18 Lok Sabha seats. In the 2 years that followed, the BJP increased its MLA tally from 3 to 53 through defections from the TMC, the INC and occasionally even the CPI(M). There developed a general perception that the opposition space in the state was being appropriated by the BJP, aided by the repeated use of central agencies.

By the time of the assembly elections, the TMC entered into an alliance with the GJM. The INC came to form the Sanjukta

Morcha, of which the other constituents were the CPI, CPI(M), RSP, AIFB, Marxist Forward Bloc and the Indian Secular Front (led by Abbas Siddiqui). The BJP fought in Bengal in alliance with the All Jharkhand Student's Union.

In the elections held in 2021, the TMC had a landslide electoral victory winning 215 seats (up 2) with 48.02% of the vote share, the BJP won 77 seats (up 74) with a vote share of 37.97%. For the first time since 1919, no Congress legislator sat in the assembly; for the first time since 1952, there was no communist legislator either. Only the ISF managed to secure a seat, as did the Gorkha Janmukti Morcha. Such total consolidation of votes between 2 camps happened for the first time ever in the history of Bengal.

Mamata Banerjee was sworn back to power for the third term in a row. Given the pressure on members of her government by central agencies on charges of corruption, Ms Banerjee finds an existential threat in the BJP of the Modi era. This seems to be prompting her to close ranks with the rest of the Opposition, now under the banner of the INDIA alliance. However, Ms Banerjee is unlikely to adjust any seats with INDIA or any other alliance that might compromise her total domination of the political landscape of West Bengal.

2022

Goa

After the death of Manohar Parrikar, Chief Minister Pramod Sawant continued till the end of the assembly term – but several things changed. The Goa Freedom Party, which had set the condition that they wanted Parrikar as the CM, were gradually marginalized and eventually dumped. So by September 2021, the

Goa Freedom Party quit the NDA, and entered into an alliance with the INC – initially for municipal polls, but eventually for assembly elections. Similarly, the MAG also left the NDA to align itself with the TMC, which was trying to make a foray outside West Bengal. The AAP also jumped into the fray in Goa.

In the elections to the 60-seat assembly, the NDA won 20 seats (up 7) with a vote share of 33.31%. The INC remained the second-largest party with 11 (down 6) seats with a vote share of 23.46%; its ally, the Goa Freedom Party, won only 1 seat. The MAG won 2 seats and the AAP won 2 seats each.

Once the picture got a bit clear, the BJP turned back to its old ally, the MAG, and 2 independents looking for support. On the basis of that support, Pramod Sawant was sworn back in for his second term. In 6 months' time, the BJP gave itself a shot in the arm, as 8 of the 11 INC MLAs joined the BJP, pushing its tally up to 28.

Uttarakhand

From the time of its creation, Uttarakhand politics had been experiencing the revolving door template of alternating between the INC and the BJP. In 2017, the BJP had won the assembly elections to come to power. The assembly elections of 2022 became the first when an incumbent government was returned to power in Uttarakhand under CM Pushkar Singh Dhami.

In the elections to the 60-seat Uttarakhand assembly in 2022, the BJP won 47 seats (down 10), with a vote share of 44.33%. The INC won 19 seats (up 8) with a vote share of 37.91%. The BSP won 2 seats, as did independents.

While the BJP won the elections quite easily, Pushkar Singh Dhami lost his seat. But since the party wished him to continue, Dhami had to be elected to the assembly through a bypoll after which he was sworn in as chief minister for a fresh term.

Punjab

When the SAD broke its alliance with the BJP in 2020 over the farm bills, it seemed like the INC would have another term in power. However, the Congress government in Punjab went through a major period of turmoil towards the end of its tenure in 2021, resulting in Amarinder's resignation from the government and the party. In November 2021, Amarinder floated his own party, the Punjab Lok Congress. Between June 2021 and January 2022, MLAs were hopping from all sides, joining parties different from their own. By February, when the elections were due, the AAP's strong showing in the Chandigarh municipal polls indicated that the winds of change were indeed blowing hard.

In the assembly elections of 2022, to everyone's surprise, the AAP won 92 (up 72) of the 117 seats in the assembly, with a vote share of 42.01%, becoming the single largest party. The INC became the second-largest party with 18 seats (down 59) with a vote share of 22.98%. The SAD won 3 seats and its ally, the BSP, 1 seat. The BJP managed to win only 2 seats.

Bhagwant Singh Mann, a one-time comedian and then a member of the People's Party of Punjab, was sworn in as the chief minister of Punjab in March 2022.

Manipur

The Biren Singh government of 2017–22 had laid the foundations of the BJP in the politics of Manipur. The benefits of this spadework were reaped in the 2022 elections.

In the elections to the 60-seat assembly held in 2022, the BJP won 32 seats (up 11) with a vote share of 37.83%. The National People's Party, fighting on its own, won 7 seats, while the INC won 5 seats. The JDU won 6 seats, the Naga People's Front won 5 seats and the Kuki People's Front won 2 seats. After the polls were over, the BJP, NPP and NPF came together to form a coalition government.

N. Biren Singh was sworn in for his second term. Given the breakdown of the social and political fabric in the state in 2023, due to the conflict between the Meiteis and the Kukis, it remains to be seen whether he is able to complete his term.

Himachal Pradesh

Himachal Pradesh remained resolute in its adherence to the revolving door template of political power. The elections of 2021, well into the second Modi government, anti-incumbency continued to operate with a vengeance.

In the 2022 elections to the 70-seat assembly, the INC won 40 seats (up 19) with a vote share of 43.9%. The BJP won 25 seats (down 19) with a vote share of 43%. Independents won 2 seats.

With simple majority to their credit, the INC chose Sukhwinder Singh Sukhu as the chief minister, with Mukesh Agnihotri as his deputy CM.

Gujarat

The elections to the legislative assembly of Gujarat in 2022 went on to show the stronghold the state has become for the BJP. Nearly 3 decades since the beginning of their winning streak, the BJP – far from being dented by any anti-incumbency – actually obtained the biggest ever majority the state has ever furnished any political party with.

In the elections to the assembly in Gujarat that were held in 2022, the BJP won 156 seats (up 57), with 52.50% vote share. The INC won 17 seats (down 60) with a vote share of 27.28%. The AAP made its first inroads into Gujarat winning 5 seats with a vote share of 12.82%, and the SP managed to hold on to just

1 seat. The BSP, AIMIM and others failed to win a seat, while 3 went to independent candidates.

Bhupendra Rajnikant Patel, riding the largest majority ever in the Gujarat assembly, was sworn back in for his second term in office in December 2022.

Uttar Pradesh

Of all the legislative assembly elections held in December 2022, that of Uttar Pradesh was possibly the most significant. Uttar Pradesh in the last 2 decades has gradually moved from unstable to stable governments, from coalitions to one-party governments. Having tried all 3, the people of Uttar Pradesh decided in favour of awarding the BJP the opportunity of remaining in power after the completion of the first term.

Before the elections were announced, the NDA finalized its coalition allies for the UP elections, with seat arrangements for the NISHAD party and Apna Dal (Sonelall). The SP followed suit, aligning with Pragatisheel Samajwadi Party (led by Shivpal Singh Yadav, brother of Mulayam Singh Yadav), Mahan Dal, Janwadi Party, Apna Dal (Kamerawadi), RLD, Suheldev Bharatiya Samaj Party and the NCP. The Left parties – CPI, CPI(M), CPI(ML), AIFB and SUCI – too managed to close ranks. The AIMIM managed to stitch up its arrangement with 6 other small parties of little or no significance. The AAP stitched up its own coalition with the JDU, Shiv Sena, Jansatta Dal (Loktantrik), Vikassheeel Insaan Party, Lok Janshakti Party (Ramvilas) and Azad Samaj Party. The INC and the BJP decided to go alone.

In the assembly elections that were held in 2022, the NDA secured 273 seats out of 403, with the BJP alone winning 255 (down 57), with a vote share of 41.29%; the Apna Dal(S) won 12 seats (up 3) and the NISHAD party won 6 seats (up 6). The SP-led alliance won 125 seats, with the SP alone accounting for 111 (up 64) seats, with a vote share of 32.06%; the RLD won 8 (up 8) and the SBSP won 6 seats (up 2). Among other parties – the INC and the Jansatta Dal (Loktantrik) won 2 seats each, while BSP won only 1 seat – all but snuffed out of existence.

Riding high on the victory, Yogi Adityanath was sworn back in as the chief minister for his second term.

2023

Tripura

While the North-Eastern states of India have come to be totally under the thrall of the BJP from around 2019, Tripura is beginning to show signs that things are stirring. The BJP has successfully broken the most powerful party in the state – the CPI(M) – through all the means at their disposal, and that has released energy that had not been visible on the political landscape in a very long time. In the run-up to the assembly elections, the Tripura Tribal Areas Autonomous District Councils, which had hitherto featured only on the margins – saw the Tipraha Indigenous Progressive Regional Alliance sweep the polls, wipe out the CPI(M) and give even the BJP a drubbing. The central objective of the TIPRA is to create a separate state of Tipraland, where the tribals, not the domiciled Bengali community, dominate. The TIPRA alliance, operating under Tipra Motha party, led by Pradyot Deb Barma, scion of the royal house of Tripura, has begun to raise a voice long-muffled.

In the assembly elections held in February 2023, the BJP won 32 seats (down 4) with a vote share of 38.97%; its ally, the Indigenous People's Front of Tripura (with which the Tipra Motha is in direct conflict), managed to win only 1. The CPI(M) won only 11 seats (with a vote share of 24.62%) and the INC was reduced to only 3 seats (with a vote share of 8.56%). The

Tipra Motha party won 13 seats – nearly as much as the CPI(M) and the INC together – with a vote share of 19.69%.

The incumbent Chief Minister, Manik Saha was sworn back into office in February 2023. In a little over a year, the only proper opposition force in the state, the Tipra Motha party joined the NDA in March 2024 – leaving the treasury benches in Tripura considerably strengthened.

Meghalaya

Historically given towards coalitions, the Meghalaya assembly elections of 2023 were no different than in the past.

In the elections held in February 2023 for the 60-seat assembly, the National People's Party led by Conrad Sangma emerged as the single largest party by a long margin, winning 26 seats (up 6), with a vote share of 31.49%. The UDP remained the second-largest party with 12 seats (up 6), with a vote share of 16.21%. All India Trinamool Congress won 5 seats (up 5) and the INC 5 (down 16). The debutant Voice of the People Party won 4 seats. The BJP, HSPDP and the PDF won 2 seats each.

Conrad Sangma went about forming his post-poll coalition promptly as before, and staked claim to form a government with 26 NPP, BJP, 2 HSPDP and 2 independents. Despite the fact that with the HSPDP wavering for a bit, an alternative non-BJP-NPP government looked likely for a while, Conrad Sangma eventually managed to be sworn in for his second term in office. Of course, given the interesting political history of the state, high drama can be staged any day in the rest of the assembly term.

Nagaland

The Neipjiu Rio-led Nagaland government had a more or less uneventful period at the helm before the assembly elections were announced for the year 2023. The NDPP and the BJP had been gaining in terms of influential politicians over the previous 5 years, which strengthened the hand of the government in the run-up to the elections.

In the elections to the 60-seat assembly, the NDPP (led by CM N. Rio) won 25 seats (up 7) with a vote share of 32.24%; its ally, the BJP, won 12 seats with 18.8%, making up 37 seats in all. The NCP won a surprising 7 seats (up 7); the NPP 5 (up 3); the NPF, Lok Janshakti Party and RPI won 2 seats each; the JDU won 1 seat and the independents won 4.

The NDPP-BJP government was sworn back into power in March 2023, with Chief Minister Neiphiu Rio already being the longest-serving chief minister of Nagaland (2003–08, 2008–14, 2018-to date).

Karnataka

The rumble-and-tumble of Karnataka politics since 2018 – with the BJP allegedly using its money-power to undermine an elected government, and then putting up one of its own – had been entertaining for all observers of politics, but maybe not for the people of Karnataka. Their verdict was delivered late, but delivered well, with the highest recorded turnout in the state's history (73.19%) – a majority so big that the electoral verdict could not be overturned.

In the 2023 elections to the 224-seat Karnataka assembly, the INC obtained a convincing majority on its own, winning 135 seats (up 55) with a vote share of 42.88%. The BJP finished second with 66 seats (down 38) with a vote share of 36%. The JDS won only 19 seats (down 18) with a vote share of 13.3%.

Siddaramaiah was sworn back in as chief minister in May 2023, while the real architect of the victory, D.K. Shivkumar was shunted out to the position of the deputy chief minister – in continuation of the same tradition that has been the bane of the Congress for decades now.

Rajasthan

In Rajasthan, the incumbent chief minister Ashok Gehlot managed to finish his third full term as the chief minister, shaking off challenges from the much younger challenger from within the party, Sachin Pilot. Pilot, who had been initially appointed as the deputy CM complained that he was being steadily marginalized as Gehlot was accused of grooming his own son for the succession. Pilot was sacked as Deputy CM and the president of the state unit in 2020, but was later compensated by being inducted in the Congress Working Committee. However, Gehlot's unbridled populism failed to stop the revolving door that has characterized the political landscape in Rajasthan for the last 3 decades, not simply because Pilot did not play the role he played previously.

In the elections that were held in November 2023 for the 199 seats in the 200-seat assembly, the BJP returned to power with a comfortable majority of 115 seats (up 42), with 41.69% of the vote share. The INC finished with only 69 seats (down 31), with a vote share of 39.53%. Its electoral ally, the Rashtriya Lok Dal, managed to win the only seat it contested. The Bharat Adivasi Party (led by Mohan Lal Roat) won 3 seats (up 3); the BSP finished with 2 seats (down 4); the Rashtriya Loktantrik Party (led by Hanuman Beniwal) won 1 seat, and independents won 8.

From before the elections, signs could be seen that the previous BJP chief minister of the state, Vasundhara Raje, was too independent-minded to defer to the Modi–Shah duo who had established total dominance in the BJP. Hence Raje was not projected as the prospective CM face, and once the elections were over, BJP pushed forth a first-time MLA, Bhajan Lal Sharma (with an unblemished background in the ABVP and RSS for nearly 3 decades). In order to pre-empt any caste backlash over selecting a brahmin chief minister, the BJP also put forward two deputy chief ministers, Rani Diya Kumari (from the royal house of the Kachhawas of Jaipur) and Prem Chand Bhairwa (a second-time Dalit MLA). Sharma was sworn in, largely as a gesture that political satraps could not take their satrapies for granted. It needs to be seen how does this decision impact the party's chances in the 2024 parliamentary elections.

Madhya Pradesh

Despite having lost the elections of 2019, Shivraj Singh Chouhan had ended up as the chief minister of Madhya Pradesh as a result of a split in the ranks of the state unit of the victorious INC. By the time Chouhan's tenure came to an end in 2023, the wind was that years of anti-incumbency might finally catch up with him. The central leadership of the BJP sent union ministers and heavyweight MPs to contest the assembly elections of 2023, which was considered to be an indication that the BJP might replace Chouhan if they were to win.

In the elections that were eventually held in November 2023, to the surprise of everyone (presumably including Chouhan), the BJP finished with its largest ever seats tally in the state – 163 (up 54) out of 230, with a vote share of 48.55%. The Congress, badly beaten, finished with just 66 seats, with a vote share of 40.4%. The Bharatiya Adivasi managed to win 1 seat. The BSP continued to shrink in terms of its presence, failing to win a single seat in the state; the AAP, despite contesting with its usual populist platform, drew a blank.

As an evidence of the current of anti-incumbency, though, despite the party's best ever results, 12 of the ministers from the Chouhan cabinet failed to win their own seats. Hence, as was anticipated by many observers before the elections, Chouhan was axed from the chief minister's office, and was replaced by Mohan Yadav – a 3-time MLA with an impeccable ABVP background before he was inducted into the Shivraj Chouhan cabinet as the minister for Education. Yadav, an OBC politician, was also sought to be balanced with a brahmin Deputy CM, Rajendra Shukla (another former minister from Shivraj Chouhan's earlier cabinets) and Jagdish Devda, from the Scheduled Castes category – all of whom were sworn in during the middle of December 2023.

Chhattisgarh

The Congress went to the polls in Chhattisgarh in November 2023 under the leadership of Bhupesh Baghel, buoyant and confident of victory after 5 years of the kind of populism that makes the INC look like a pale copy of the BJP. All the opinion polls and exit polls were able to concur in taking Baghel's victory for granted, even though with a reduced margin of victory.

In the elections to the 90-seat assembly, however, the BJP successfully toppled the INC government, winning 54 seats (up 39) with a vote share of 46.27%. The INC finished with 35 seats (down 33) with a marginally lower vote share of 42.23%. The Gondwana Ganatantra Parishad led by Kuldip Prajapati managed to win 1 seat (up 1), while its electoral ally, the BSP, failed to win any seat at all.

To the utter surprise of many, the former chief minister Raman Singh was not brought back to the CM's office. Instead, Vishnu Deo Sai, a former union minister and a tribal leader (with an RSS background, and renowned for his leadership in reconversion of Christian tribals to Hinduism – that is, *ghar wapsi*) was sworn in as the chief minister of Chhattisgarh in the middle of December 2023. In order to balance the selection of an ST politician as chief minister, the BJP also appointed 2 deputy CMs, an OBC leader (Arun Sao), and a brahmin leader and first-time MLA (Vijay Sharma). Whether these attempts at galvanizing the cadre base and undermining old established leaders help the BJP or hinder it in the Lok Sabha elections of 2024 need to be seen.

Telangana

Telangana went to the polls in November 2023 after 10 years of rule by the Telangana Rashtra Samithi, later renamed Bharat Rashtriya Samithi, under K. Chandrasekhar Rao, who had occupied the office of the chief minister of the state ever since it came into being in 2013. Since the previous election, as the BJP appeared to be emerging as a party posing a challenge to Rao in the state, Rao decided to fight back. However, the BRS did not agree to join the INDIA alliance since its principal antagonist in the state, the INC, was associated with it. Hence, the 2023 assembly elections turned out to be a triangular contest.

In the elections to the 119 seats of the Telangana assembly, the INC successfully revived itself winning 64 seats (up 45), with a vote share of 39.4%; its electoral ally, the once mighty CPI, contested in only 1 seat, which it managed to win with 0.34% of the vote share. The TRS finished with 39 seats (down 49) with a vote share of 39.74%. The NDA won only 8 seats – all 8 being won by the BJP with a vote share of 13.9%, while its electoral ally, the Jana Sena Party, led by Telugu film star Pawan Kalyan drew a blank. The AIMIM successfully held on to its by-now steady tally of 7 seats (with a vote share of 2.2%).

The INC state unit leader and supposedly the architect of the Congress victory, Anumula Revanth Reddy was swiftly proposed as the chief minister – a man who began his political journey in the ABVP, then made his way through the TDP to finally 'find his place' in the INC as an MP. In a curious turn of events, both the outgoing chief minister K.C.R. and the incoming CM Revanth Reddy were beaten in the contest for the assembly seat of Kamareddy by the BJP candidate there, K. Venkata Raman Reddy. Revanth Reddy had stood from a second constituency from a second seat, Kodangal, which he managed to win; K.C.R. also stood for election from a second seat in Gajwel, which he too managed to win.

Mizoram

In November 2023, 3-time chief minister Zoramthanga led his MNF to the assembly elections, secure in the knowledge that the INC had been effectively snuffed out by the BJP, which in its own turn, was not strong enough to challenge the MNF. The Zoram People's Movement, a 5-party alliance that had suddenly emerged on the political landscape of Mizoram was the nearest Zoramthanga had to consider a functioning opposition.

In the elections that were held to the 40-seat assembly, the Zoram People's Movement scored a surprise victory with a tally of 27 seats (up 19), with a vote share of 37.86%. The outgoing party of power, the MNF, was reduced to 10 seats (down 16) with a marginally lower vote share of 35.96%. The BJP managed to win 2 seats with a vote share of 5.06%, while the INC could manage to win only 1 seat with a considerably larger vote share of 20.82%. The AAP contested 4 seats without winning any.

The ZPM put its leader Lalduhoma – a former IPS who had once headed Prime Minister Mrs Gandhi's security detail, and had later represented the Congress in the Lok Sabha and then in the Mizoram assembly – up for the position of the chief minister. Lalduhoma was duly sworn in as the chief minister of Mizoram in December 2023.

Chapter 17

BEYOND THE BALLOT 1999 AND AFTER

1999

Battleground Bellari: Videshi Bahu vs Swadeshi Beti

The parliamentary poll of 1999, in a sense, marked the rise of Sonia Gandhi. That year, making her electoral debut, Mrs Gandhi contested from 2 seats – the only time she has done so. Mrs Gandhi contested both from Amethi in Uttar Pradesh, a pocket borough of the Nehru–Gandhi family, (won with over 3 lakh votes) and Bellari in Karnataka (won by a margin of only 56,100).

At the preliminary stage, Mrs Gandhi initially decided to stand only from Amethi, which she was confident of winning. Her advisors however suspected that the BJP, to keep her out of the parliament, might place an ailing dummy candidate whose death would postpone the elections. Besides Sanjay Singh who had won the Amethi seat for the BJP in 1998, was thought likely to resort to violent methods to get the poll invalidated in Amethi. Singh was the Nehru–Gandhi family's friend-turned-foe. Third, if Mrs Gandhi contested from only 1 constituency, then the BJP might pitch one heavyweight candidate and concentrate everything in that 1 seat; if she fought from multiple seats, then the saffron party's focus could be dissipated. Hence Bellari was meant as a safety net for Mrs Gandhi because, right from 1952, the Congress had never lost that seat.

On the day Mrs Gandhi went to file her nomination, she went via Hyderabad, ostensibly headed for Cudappah, while party general secretary, Ghulam Nabi Azad was supposed to be going to Bellary. However, APCC Chief Y.S. Rajasekhara Reddy's not waiting for Mrs Gandhi and leaving for Cudappah by himself gave away the clue that he would never have done so if Mrs Gandhi was also headed there; the SPG preparing for security in Bellary confirmed the suspicions that some BJP leaders had had.

With Cudappah in mind, BJP General Secretary, Venkaiah Naidu, had been discussing with Andhra Pradesh chief minister N. Chandrababu Naidu the relative merits of fielding a popular film-star, like Jaya Prada and Vijayashanti (who had lately joined the party), and shortlisted Vijayashanti. However, when V. Naidu was intimated of tightening security at Bellary, he realized Mrs Gandhi was going to file her nomination from Bellary, and after consulting the Union commerce minister Ramakrishna Hegde decided on Sushma Swaraj instead. A Union minister and a former chief minister of Delhi, Swaraj was considered one of the staunchest critics of the Congress president because of her foreign origin. But Swaraj had publicly announced she would not be contesting. In the early hours on the last day of filing the nominations, Swaraj's name was knocked about between BJP President Kushabhau Thakre, Home Minister Advani and the prime minister as well. Swaraj was booked on an early morning commercial flight from Delhi to Bangalore, and then for a helicopter to take her to Bellary, where she arrived with only an hour and a half to spare before nominations closed.

The needless hide-and-seek approach of the Congress came to attach to the contest at Bellary a kind of significance that was otherwise unwarranted. Swaraj's colleague Pramod Mahajan had once said all that hush-hush over Gandhi's nomination made it appear as though Gandhi was fearful of the contest.

Sonia filed her nomination at 2.20 p.m. on 18 August, just 40 minutes before the closing of nominations. Shortly after, the BJP brought in Mrs Swaraj to file her nomination. Despite the huge crowds that turned up for Swaraj, Sonia Gandhi managed to win a convincing victory before she vacated the seat and went to the Lok Sabha representing Amethi.

2004

India Shining, Feel Good, and Yet ...

The majority government of Atal Bihari Vajpayee brought in profound stability at the Centre. This ultimately boosted Indian economy after a long period of time. The majority government provided stability, which gave confidence to the ruling BJP-led NDA alliance. Steady improvement in the some segments of the agriculture sector, with clear improvement in secondary and tertiary sectors of the economy, helped a growth rate for the economy that was the highest since liberalization began.

It was in this backdrop of confidence and positivity that the BJP-led NDA alliance put up two slogans for its parliamentary poll campaign in 2004, 'Feel Good' and 'India Shining'. The BJP or the NDA started campaigning that the people of India are 'feeling good' and, as a whole and 'India is shining' as though they were advertising a commodity.

However, the slogans could be said to have boomeranged. The mood in the villages of India did not mirror the middle-class euphoria of the cities. It was not only the rural poor that were suffering, but the wealthier elements of the rural society as well. The division between India and Bharat was evident. The differences between the rural and the urban in terms of aspirations and achievements had never been this glaring – as became clear in the Andhra assembly elections, when the poster boy of corporate urban India N. Chandrababu Naidu was thrown out of power.

It was probably for the first time in the Indian electoral history that poll slogans were held responsible to a large extent for the defeat of a party. Many critics of the campaign said that the growth story of urban India was not quite matched by the continued agrarian distress and rural backwardness in media portrayal of the NDA growth story. Such critics pointed out that the slogans annoyed the people whose face was not shining and who did not feel good. Those 2 slogans are believed to have stirred and awakened rage, and the outburst was reflected in the poll results, although in a silent manner.

The defenders of the campaign, however, argued that the idea was good, but it was possibly failed by the NDA government. The BJP's Sudhanshu Mittal, a close associate of former Union minister Pramod Mahajan, who was the architect of the India Shining campaign, defended the campaign as a 'popular' one. In Mittal's words, 'The success of a campaign can be evaluated from its recall value.'

Mittal went on to say, he contradiction between the ad and the product is so sharp, people do not believe the ad.'

Two weeks after the result of the 2004 general election was declared, Advani breaking his silence admitted that the twin phrases of 'feel good' and 'India shining' cost the party dearly. He accepted that the catch-phrase of 'India shining' gave the opposition the opportunity to highlight poverty, developmental imbalance, farmers issues and youth unemployment as missing from that India story.

India Worsted by Bharat: N. Chandrababu Naidu

The Andhra Pradesh assembly poll results of 2004 captured well the binary between India and Bharat. Both the polls in the big south Indian state took place simultaneously.

In 1999, Naidu had led the TDP to victory, providing an impetus to his image as a HITECH-friendly, big industry-friendly and foreign investment-friendly dreamer, who had earlier founded Cyberabad (in the west of Hyderabad city) only 2 months after he became the chief minister. By that time, the technology boom had started in India and the Andhra Pradesh chief minister's initiative to establish IT and knowledge hubs elevated Naidu's image in a manner that probably no other chief minister of any Indian state could match. Naidu successfully projected himself as a model chief minister in New India, dominated by the techies.

However, while Cyberabad was winning Naidu plaudits, a series of suicide by farmers on account of rural indebtedness rocked drought-stricken Andhra Pradesh. According to an official estimate, 1,519 cases of farmer suicides were recorded in the state between July 1998 and May 2004. Some unofficial estimates put the figure at 10,000. Moreover, during the period between 1998 and 1999, there was a steep rise in the number of farmer suicides every year.

This took a heavy toll on Chandrababu Naidu both in assembly and parliamentary polls in 2004. Probably for the first time in Indian poll-history, the gloomy scenario in agricultural sector resulting in the suicide of farmers in a state ousted a party from the government, reducing the TDP to its worst tally till then – 47 seats in the assembly and 5 seats in the Parliament; its ally, the BJP, won 2 seats in the assembly and vanished without a trace in the parliamentary constituencies.

The Inner Voice of Sonia Gandhi

Congress-led UPA came to power in 2004, with Sonia Gandhi as the Congress president. She herself won from Raebareli parliamentary constituency of Uttar Pradesh by a margin of 2.5 lakh votes. She was unanimously elected the leader of the

Congress parliamentary party, and was already the leader of the UPA. All the allies and their leaders pledged their trust in her. Not because she was Rajiv Gandhi's widow, nor because she was Indira Gandhi's daughter-in-law. Sonia Gandhi had carved out her own niche in Indian politics. However, with the stage set for her ascent to the office of the prime minister and what could have been the first holder of that office of foreign origin, she let the chance go.

The poll result was declared on 13 May. By 15 May, it was clear that the UPA, to form its government, would get outside support from some other political forces, including the Left parties that emerged as a strong and prominent force and that Sonia Gandhi would head the government. In every nook and cranny of India, the message was clear that India would get its first prime minister of foreign origin. Sonia did not protest, did not deny then. Rather, when a journalist asked her if it was true that the leader of the parliamentary party would be the next prime minister, Sonia replied, 'Normally, that is so.' But on 18 May, it was official that Sonia declined the post, and she chose Manmohan Singh for the post of prime minister despite objections within the party, and from the allies and from those who were supporting from the outside.

From various accounts it would seem that 2 factors prodded such a magnanimous gesture from Sonia. Mrs Gandhi's close confidant Natwar Singh attested that her decision to step away from the high altar of Indian democracy was the outcome of firm resistance from her son, Rahul Gandhi, who was convinced that Mrs Gandhi's elevation to that high office would put her life at risk. He warned Mrs Gandhi against accepting the office. Later, in media interactions, Rahul's sister, Priyanka, seemed to confirm that she shared her brother's apprehension in this regard.

It would, however, also seem that the high-decibel campaign by the BJP playing the foreign origin of the prospective prime minister to the sky was also responsible for Mrs Gandhi's show of prudence and sagacity. Sushma Swaraj, the firebrand lady and orator of the saffron camp, who lost the prestigious fight against Sonia in Bellary in 1999, threatened to don a white saree, shave off her head, sleep on the floor and eat only chickpeas if Sonia Gandhi were to be sworn in as the prime minister of India. Another BJP firebrand, Uma Bharti, argued that having a foreigner at the helm could jeopardize national security. No less significant was the suicide of an ordinary BJP worker in Karnataka, 30-year-old Mahesh Prabhu, in a village near Bangalore, who said in his suicide note that he could not bear the idea of his nation not finding a single Indian to lead the country. Prabhu left behind a widow and a child of 18 months, and people were shocked. Mrs Gandhi recognized that the foreigner issue would never go away.

The day before Prabhu's suicide was reported in the newspapers, in the afternoon on 15 May, Mrs Gandhi had been unanimously elected the leader of the Congress parliamentary party. Addressing her party MPs, she kept quiet on the issue of staking a claim to form the government. Thus, from all the indications available, it would seem that Rahul's apprehensions – voiced on 17 May, was not the cause, but the catalyst that made Mrs Gandhi publicly renounce her prospective claim on the highest political office in the land the next day, 18 May 2004.

She put her decision down to her 'inner voice' – a rarity in Indian politics.

Congress Takes to Coalitions

The Congress had been the dominant force in the Indian political landscape for the first 3 decades from 1947, generally preferring to rule on its own strength in Delhi, even though it often required allies at the regional level (such as in Kerala, Tamil Nadu, Jammu and Kashmir, Meghalaya, etc.). For 2 decades beginning in 1989, however, the landscape became badly fragmented; no single party got absolute majority at the Centre. Post-poll coalitions or pre-poll alliances became the political norm, where governments often survived with outside support.

The Congress's reluctance as much as its inability to accept its reducing strength and electoral support kept the party out of power for nearly a decade from the mid-90s. During the Panchmari session in 1998, the Congress realized the importance of alliances but was reluctant to form any coalition. At the session, Congress President Sonia Gandhi officially acknowledged that India was moving through a phase of coalition politics at the national level, but it was a transitional phase. Coalitions might well be needed, but Mrs Gandhi clearly specified that until such time that the Congress was not in a position to form a single-party government, it would not forge alliances with other political parties (only when that was an absolute necessity).

By 2003, after facing humiliating defeat in 3 state assembly elections – Madhya Pradesh, Rajasthan and Chhattisgarh – the Congress finally changed its tack. When the Shimla Sankalp (Resolution) was passed in July 2003, the party announced a new electoral policy to forge appropriate coalition arrangements with secular political parties based on mutual understanding without compromising the basic ideology of the party. Shimla Sankalp laid the foundations of the United Progressive Alliance (UPA).

Thereafter, senior party leaders were deputed to woo potential allies to the Congress fold. The Congress reinforced old alliances in Tamil Nadu, Andhra Pradesh, Kerala, Maharashtra, and forged new ties in Bihar and Jharkhand with RJD and JMM respectively. Congress, for the first time in its history, recognized that it had to adjust with the aspirations, ambitions and principles of regional parties.

The allies of the Congress added 77 seats to the UPA total, and huge contributions came from the southern and eastern zones, The major partners of the Congress in the UPA, who contributed seats to form the UPA-I government, were Rashtriya Janata Dal (23 MPs), Dravida Munnetra Kazagham (16 MPs), Nationalist Congress Party (10 MPs), Pattali Makkal Katchi (6 MPs), Telangana Rashtra Samithi (5 MPs), Jharkhand Mukti Morcha (5 MPs), Marumalarchi Dravida Munnetra Kazagham (4 MPs), Lok Jan Shakti Party (4 MPs) and Kerala Congress (2 MPs). Each of the other 3 parties in the UPA such as the Indian Union Muslim League got 1 seat. The Left camp with 60 MPs, Samajwadi Party with 39 MPs and the Bahujan Samaj Party with 19 MPs supported the UPA government from outside.

Congress and the Left in the UPA: Long-Lost Friends

The Congress and the Left could always be said to have had a love-hate relationship. The Congress and the CPI had routinely been in political alignment in many parts of India, with the former probably having more socialists than in any other party in India. Thus, once Congress's political strength began to reduce, and it started looking for allies, the Left was always high on the wishlist of a large number of Congress politicians. Hence, when the Congress fell way short of a simple majority, they reached out to the Left.

In 2004, the Left parties recorded their best-ever performance by getting 60-odd seats in which the CPI(M) with 43 seats topped the list. By that time, the CPI(M)-led Left had identified the BJP as its main political enemy, and the first and foremost aim of the CPI(M) and other Left parties was to keep BJP out of power. The Left thus became a sort of anchor for the UPA coalition. As earlier, they kept themselves out of the government and offered support from the outside. But the Left camp was comparatively more active than earlier. Congress strategists, Jairam Ramesh and Salman Khurshid, sat with Sitaram Yechury and Prakash Karat to draft the Common Minimum Programme (CMP) of the UPA government. The advice of two stalwart CPI(M) leaders,

Jyoti Basu and Harkishen Singh Surjeet, was also incorporated in the CMP. Sonia Gandhi made repeated offers and requests to the CPI(M) to join the government. The party was offered cabinet berths, which they declined. Finally, the two sides came to an understanding with veteran CPI(M) leader and MP Somnath Chatterjee who was elected as the Speaker.

Moreover, the UPA-Left Coordination Committee was created as a platform dedicated to coordinate all major policy discussions between the Congress and Left parties. The CPI(M), CPI, RSP (Revolutionary Socialist Party) and the All-India Forward Bloc (AIFB) were the 4 left parties, who had their members in the committee. The UPA was represented by its chairperson Sonia Gandhi and Prime Minister Manmohan Singh.

Office of Profit Controversy and the Raibareli Bypoll

According to Article 102(1) and Article 191(1) of the Indian Constitution, an MP or an MLA is barred from any office of profit under the central or state government.

Sonia Gandhi was accused of holding an office of profit by being an MP as well as the Chairperson of the National Advisory Council, the latter being a post with the rank of a cabinet minister for which no exemption was sought from the Office of Profit Act.

After the Congress had stepped up a campaign against Jaya Bachchan, a Rajya Sabha member of the Samajwadi Party, who also held the post of the Chairperson of the Uttar Pradesh Film Development Corporation. Jaya was disqualified from the Rajya Sabha by President A.P.J. Abdul Kalam.

The BJP used this issue to place a petition before President Kalam seeking Mrs Gandhi's disqualification from the Lok Sabha on the grounds that she also held an office of profit as the Chairperson of NAC. The Telugu Desam Party, a partner of the BJP-led NDA, petitioned the President earlier on the same issue.

Significantly, B.B. Tandon, the then Chief Election Commissioner of India, said on 23 March 2006 that the law would act in the same manner for everyone and the ECI would consider the petition against Mrs Gandhi when it was referred by the President.

Determined to take the wind out of the BJP's sails, Sonia Gandhi resigned in March 2006, even before the EC could rule on the matter. She went on to register a record win for herself in the Raebareli bypoll in May 2006, which she won by a margin of 4.17 lakh votes, more than one-and-a-half lakh votes more than her victory in 2004 over her nearest rival from the Samajwadi party. All her opponents, including BJP General Secretary, Vinay Katiyar, lost their security deposits. By cornering 80.5% of the votes, Sonia had bettered the 22-year-old record of her husband's estranged cousin, Arun Nehru.

2009

Two CECs and One Poll

The parliamentary polls of 2009 are till date the only general election in India that have been held with two Chief Election Commissioners (CECs). The polling schedule for the 2009 general elections was announced on 2 March 2009 by the Election Commission of India headed by Chief Election Commissioner, N. Gopalaswami, who retired as per schedule on 21 April, having conducted only the first phase of the election on 16 April 2009. His successor, Navin Chawla, became CEC on 21 April, and presided over the remaining four phases: 22 and 23 April (phase 2), 30 April (phase 3), 7 May (phase 4) and 13 May (phase 5). On 22 April, the election was held only in a single constituency of Manipur and that was Inner Manipur. The polls in Outer Manipur, the other constituency of the state, took place in the first phase, on 16 April.

This was largely the manifestation of a serious malaise that afflicted the EC. On 31 January 2009, with the general election around the corner, the Chief Election Commissioner N. Gopalaswami recommended to President Pratibha Patil to remove Navin Chawla, who was supposed to be next in line for CEC. This was on account of allegations about Chawla being close to the ruling Congress party. As early as in 2006, the leader of Opposition in the Lok Sabha L.K. Advani and 204 MPs had submitted a petition to the same effect. The BJP had also taken the matter to the Supreme Court, whereupon Gopalaswami claimed, in his affidavit to the apex court, that the CEC had suo moto power to recommend the removal of an Election Commissioner – a claim disputed by the government. Gopalaswami's recommendation for the removal of Chawla was the outcome of persistent differences between the two functionaries in the three years that followed.

Eventually, on 1 March 2009, President Pratibha Patil accepted the government recommendation for rejection of the CEC's report against Chawla and arrived at a 'considered opinion'.

2014

The Anna Hazare Effect

The UPA came to power in 2009 for the second consecutive term. The tally of Congress seats in the Lok Sabha crossed 200 for the first time since the 1991 general elections. However, within 1 year of coming to power, the Congress and UPA-2 were rocked by 3 financial scams – viz. the Commonwealth Games Scam (involving ₹70,000 crores), the 2G Scam (leading to presumptive loss of ₹1,76,000 crores) and the Coal Allotment scam. It was a grim reminder of 1989, when the Bofors scandal led to the defeat of the Congress.

Protests against corruption spread to the streets, with the campaign led by Padma Bhushan Anna Hazare, a Gandhian and social worker, demanding probity in public life. Kisan Baburao 'Anna' Hazare was associated with the promotion of rural development, increasing government transparency and reducing corruption in public life. Hazare's major contribution was the development and structuring of his ancestral village, Ralegan Siddhi. He was awarded the Padma Bhushan in 1992 for his efforts in establishing this village as a model for others. Hazare had till then been associated mostly with his own state, Maharashtra, but when Hazare called for a 'holy war' against corruption during the UPA-II regime, he successfully brought disaffected Indians out to the streets. His movement started in Delhi and it soon took a pan-India texture, impacting many places in the country, demanding that the government's proposed institution of a 'Lokpal' (ombudsman) for fixing probity and accountability in governance be made more stringent and more independence be given to the Lokpal and Lokayuktas (ombudsmen in the states). Anna and his supporters termed it as 'Jan Lokpal Bill'. When the union government rejected Hazare's demand, he began an indefinite fast on 5 April 2011 at Jantar Mantar in Delhi. This galvanized nationwide protests in support of the demand, with social activists like Medha Patkar, Arvind Kejriwal and retired IPS officer, Kiran Bedi, lending their support. The fast ended on 9 April 2011, after the government relented. But once the draft Lokpal Bill turned out to be too weak, the government's sincerity was opened up to doubts yet again.

One thing Hazare declared all along was that he would not allow any politician to sit with him. He projected himself only as a crusader against corruption. But during 2011 anti-corruption movement, it seemed that Anna's one and only target was the Congress-led government in the Centre. In course of time, according to the critics, the Anna movement gradually came out from its so-called apolitical shell. Hazare praised Narendra Modi, then chief minister of Gujarat and Nitish Kumar, then chief minister of Bihar, for their efforts on rural development, saying that other chief ministers should follow their example. While Hazare himself appeared to be an apolitical crusader, the impact of his movement was altogether political. It severely damaged the reputation of the Congress and UPA-II.

The Man Who Would be King

In December 2012, Narendra Damodardas Modi was sworn in as the chief minister of Gujarat for a record fourth consecutive term. By this time, Modi had already projected his Gujarat Model of Development at the national level, in sharp contrast to the 'policy paralysis' that the Manmohan Singh government was being charged with. On the other hand, in the minds of many, Modi's name was still synonymous with the Gujarat carnage of 2002. Despite his 3 consecutive victories in the Gujarat state assembly polls and being in the BJP's most successful vote-catcher, Modi was a risky proposition even to a section of in the BJP's central leadership. But by the time Modi started looking towards the national capital, the Gujarat killings was more than a decade in the past, and a large section of the voters was not even in their teens when the carnage took place.

Given his star-power, on 13 September 2013 – months ahead of the next general elections – the BJP parliamentary board unanimously chose Narendra Modi to be its prime ministerial candidate. The announcement was unprecedented and historic in Indian parliamentary democracy. No anti-Congress party or alliance had ever announced the name of its PM candidate so much ahead of the elections. At the press conference, Modi promised 'nayi soch, nai ummeed (new thinking, new hope)'– a slogan that was catchy to the media and a large section of the electorate alike. After three weeks, Modi was inducted into the BJP's highest decision-making body - the parliamentary board. It was a rare distinction for a chief minister. In BJP's national executive meeting that was held in Panaji in Goa on 8–9 June 2013, the Gujarat chief minister was appointed the chairman of BJP's election campaign committee. This was just one step before making Modi the BJP's prime ministerial candidate. L.K. Advani (aged 85) skipped the Goa meet citing his ill-health.

Over the next 5 months (September 2013 to February 2014), Modi addressed several rallies across the country. Before the parliamentary polls, Modi eyed the assembly polls of four states (Rajasthan, Madhya Pradesh, Chhattisgarh and Delhi) as prelims. He addressed 55 rallies in those 4 states. Though Madhya Pradesh and Chhattisgarh had strong BJP chief ministers, Rajasthan was an acid test for Modi's appeal beyond Gujarat. The genesis of the Aam Aadmi Party (AAP) in November 2012 and its participation in the assembly polls of December 2013 dented BJP's hopes there. Therefore, Modi focused mainly on Rajasthan when BJP wrested the state from the Congress, the credit was attributed to Modi, in order to justify positioning him to be the shadow prime minister.

Modi's Lotus Bloomed, No Official Oppostion

When Narendra Modi was announced as the prime ministerial candidate for the BJP-led NDA, many, even within the safforon party, was apprehensive that the entire Muslim vote-bank would go against the coalition. But a study carried out by Delhi's Centre for the Study of Developing Societies in the immediate aftermath of the 2014 poll results also pointed to a marginal shift in the Muslim vote towards the BJP, which was quite significant.

P.K. FACTOR: THE PROFESSIONAL ELECTION STRATEGIST

For the landslide victory of Narendra Modi in 2014, credit should also go to Prashant Kishor, popularly known as P.K., who is arguably the first ever professional election strategist and tactician in India. Kishor, who hails from Sasaram in Bihar, is a former United Nations health official. For 8 years, he worked with the UN. Then he started working as a political strategist and created the election campaign group 'Citizens for Accountable Governance (CAG)'. P.K. came to the fore in 2012, when his political campaign to re-elect Modi as the chief minister of Gujarat became successful.

In 2014, P.K. designed innovative advertising campaigns for Modi, such as *Chaaye pe Charchaa*, 3D rallies, Run for Unity, *Manthan*, and other programmes on social media platforms. His campaign strategy helped Modi and the BJP win the poll with a thumping majority. The *Economic Times* (publication date: 28 October 2015) wrote, 'For Prashant Kishor, the man who is credited with making Narendra Modi a political brand, the efforts he put in during the 2014 Lok Sabha elections did not just brighten the image of his then subject. He has himself become a brand too, in political strategy consulting.'

P.K. dissolved the CAG a few months after the 2014 general elections and converted it into 'Indian Political Action Committee', popularly known as 'I-PAC'.

Again, immediately after Modi's name was formally announced as the chairman of the BJP's election campaign committee, Nitish Kumar, the chief minister of Bihar, and his Janata Dal (United) party left the NDA raising indirect protest against Modi's candidature. Therefore, many assumed that the BJP would face a debacle in Bihar. But the BJP captured Bihar by winning 22 seats, whereas its allies the Lok Janshakti Party and the Rashtriya Lok Samta Party grabbed 6 and 3 seats respectively. The JD(U) got only 2 seats – 18 seats down in comparison to the 2009 election results. The election results in Bihar showed that the regional factors and caste politics were vanquished before the slogan *Sabka Saath Sabka Vikas,* which was the BJP's war cry. *Vikas* became the keyword for the BJP in that election. Many of Nitish Kumar's supporters even said, '*Is baar hum vikas ke liye vote denge*', This time, we will vote for development and progress' – an allusion to the moniker *Vikas Purush* that Narendra Modi was being referred to as.

Modi led the campaign blitzkrieg for the BJP and addressed a total of 437 big rallies and participated in 5,827 public events. In all, he travelled 3 lakh kilometres across 25 states. In contrast, Rahul Gandhi got down to campaigning at a time when Modi had already taken a sizeable lead in reaching out to the people of the country.

Winning UP, Winning the Poll: The Amit Shah Factor

There is a popular belief among Indian politicians that the party which wins Uttar Pradesh in the general elections rules the country. This was borne out by the BJP in 2014, when it won 71 seats from Uttar Pradesh alone. The BJP's triumph in UP gave Amit Shah, the erstwhile minister of Home Affairs of Gujarat (and the present incumbent in the same ministry at the Centre), the reputation of a master poll strategist with a potential for becoming legendary. It would not be an exaggeration to say that, Modi gained the parliamentary majority courtesy Uttar Pradesh, and it was Amit Shah who ensured that they did.

Since June 2013, Shah asked BJP leaders and workers to work harder and to concentrate on every booth across the state. Even the BJP's then State President Laxmikant Vajpayee had to take charge of a booth to set an example. Though some of Shah's strategies in UP garnered controversy, he eventually made Modi victorious.

2019

Rahul Lost Amethi

Rahul Gandhi is the second person in the Nehru–Gandhi family who lost Amethi, a parliamentary constituency of Uttar Pradesh that was considered an ancestral seat of the first family of the Congress and a bastion of the party. His uncle, Sanjay Gandhi, lost the seat in the 1977 elections. Then the president of the Indian National Congress Rahul Gandhi lost the seat in the 2019 polls to the BJP's Smriti Zubin Irani, a soap opera actress-turned-politician by a margin of more than 50,000 votes. Rahul had won the seat 3 times in a row since 2004.

The general polls in 2014 already indicated that the Congress and Rahul were gradually losing their grip over Amethi. Rahul Gandhi's margin of victory fell to a little over 1,07,000 votes from 3,70,000 votes in 2009. The continuing trend spelled disaster for the Congress in 2017 when it lost all the 5 assembly constituencies in Amethi.

Smelling the opportunity to square the circle, the BJP left no stone unturned to win Amethi back, the seat which they last won in 1998. Therefore, even after losing the elections in 2014 to Rahul Gandhi, Ms Irani visited Amethi repeatedly. Again, once the 2019 election dates were announced, Irani camped there for more than a month-and-a-half, travelling and meeting villagers.

Significantly, in 2019, Rahul contested from the Wayanad seat in Kerala also, where he won by over 4,30,000 votes. By winning Wayanad, Gandhi saved face and was able to enter Parliament, but he lost the prestige fight in Amethi to Smriti.

Nizamabad: Created History With 12 Voting Machines in Each Booth

In the era of electronic voting machines (EVMs), for the first time, the Election Commission decided that it would use ballot papers instead of EVMs in the Nizamabad parliamentary constituency in the state of Telangana in the 2019 parliamentary polls. The EC deemed it necessary as the number of candidates was higher than what an EVM could accommodate. An EVM can accommodate a maximum of 64 names. Whereas Nizamabad, with over 15 lakh voters, had 185 valid candidates, including 178 farmers, who had filed their nominations protesting the alleged failure of the state government to ensure minimum support price for their produces.

The voting took place at Nizamabad parliamentary seat on 11 April. However, at the last moment, the poll panel decided against the use of ballot paper and used EVMs in a strategic way. The ECI conducted the poll with 12 big-sized EVMs in every polling booth. The Electronics Corporation of India Limited (ECIL) was ordered to supply 26,820 EVMs, 2,240 control units and 2,600 Voter-Verified Paper Audit Trails (VVPAT). Those EVMs were arranged in an 'L' shape and each machine was carrying a maximum of 16 names.

Mamata Banerjee: In a League of Her Own

Among the many female politicians in India, very few were able to rise without any family connections or the support of any patron with his own political standing. The one politician who was able to do this to spectacular effect was the firebrand leader from West Bengal, Mamata Banerjee.

Mamata Banerjee began her political career as the general secretary of the women's wing of the Congress party in West Bengal from 1976 to 1980. In the parliamentary polls of 1984,

ARVIND KEJRIWAL: MASCOT OF AN ALTERNATIVE BRAND OF POLITICS

On 26 November, Arvind Kejriwal, a mechanical engineering graduate from IIT Kharagpur, formed the Aam Aadmi Party (Party of the Common People), popularly known as AAP, and thus introduced an alternative brand of politics in India.

Born on 16 August 1968, Arvind Kejriwal worked in Tata Steel for three years and resigned in 1992 to sit for the UPSC examination which he cleared and became an Indian Revenue Service (IRS) officer. Kejriwal was vocal about the implementation of RTI (Right to Information Act that was enacted in 2005). His efforts in the enactment of RTI to empower the citizens who are marginal in terms of monetary power in India won him the Ramon Magsaysay Award for Emergent Leadership in 2006. In February 2006, Kejriwal resigned from the post of joint commissioner in the Income Tax Department and became a full-time activist.

Kejriwal came into prominence in 2011 during the prolonged agitation led by Anna Hazare, a Gandhian social activist, in calling for the *Jan Lokpal Bill.* He was a prominent member of Team Anna and became the civil society representative of the committee constituted to draft the Jan Lokpal Bill. Despite immensely popular and positive public response, the Bill was eventually thwarted by the characteristic machinations of the Indian political establishment. It is said that some politicians even taunted Kejriwal that he should join the system in order to change it from within. Kejriwal accepted the challenge, and the AAP was born, where a section of the representatives of civil society and social activists also joined.

Arvind Kejriwal went on to become the chief minister of Delhi in 2013, following it up with two further landslide victories in 2015 and 2020, virtually eliminating all traces of the Opposition in the assembly. The AAP has since taken power in Punjab, where the party achieved a similar landslide victory in the state assembly elections of 2022.

PAWAN CHAMLING: LONGEST-SERVING CHIEF MINISTER

The distinction of the longest-serving chief minister in the country belongs to Pawan Chamling, who was at the helm in Sikkim between 12 December 1994 and 26 May 2019 – a duration of 24 years and 165 days. As this book went to press, Odisha's Naveen Patnaik is the second longest-serving chief minister in the country, having been in office since 5 March 2000. Patnaik has already beaten Jyoti Basu (who was the chief minister of Bengal from June 1977 to November 2000), and, once he completes his fifth term, he would hold the distinction of the longest-serving chief minister.

A farmer hailing from a remote village, Pawan Chamling started his political career from the grass-root level. The founder of the Sikkim Democratic Front (SDF), Chamling had always given importance to peace and sustainable development. His love for the environment earned him the 'greenest chief minister of India'. Chamling's led leadership, Sikkim to start a green mission the first in India. This increased the state's forest cover and Sikkim became India's first organic state by 2015. Chamling is also an author and a publisher. He has written books in Nepali, English and Hindi. His Nirman Publication has so far 100 books by 55 new as well as well-known writers to its credit. Chamling also brings out *Nirman*, a monthly literary magazine.

In May 2019, the era of Pawan Chamling in Sikkim ended after over 24 years, when his party SDF lost the state assembly elections to Sikkim Krantikari Morcha (SKM), a resurgent political power.

she gained the reputation of a giantkiller by defeating Somnath Chatterjee, the heavyweight candidate of the CPI(M) and 2-time MP from Jadavpur LS constituency by a margin of 19,660 votes.

Indeed she lost the Jadavpur seat in 1989 parliamentary polls but became MP once again in the mid-term poll of 1991 from South Kolkata constituency, where she went on to win the seat 6-times in a row till 2009.

A determined foe of the CPI(M) government in the state, in 1998, Banerjee left the Congress and formed the All India Trinamool Congress (AITC), saying a section of the provincial Congress leaders were hand in glove with the communists. In the 1998 elections (only a month and a half since its inception), the Trinamool astonished everyone by winning 7 seats having little capital but for their leaders' combative spirit, and steadily went on to erode the political space for the Opposition that was occupied by the Congress in the state.

Her opposition to the forces of the Left was credible enough for her to become a part of the NDA government of Vajpayee, holding the portfolio for railways. After serving in the Union cabinet, she broke ties with the BJP on the issue of corruption in the purchase of coffins for Kargil martyrs, demanding the resignation of the defence minister George Fernandes. Mamata's resignation was presumably motivated with an eye on the Muslim voters in the state, forming a pre-poll alliance with the Congress in West Bengal. A couple of months after the poll results, she went back to the BJP and rejoined the NDA, and again became a cabinet minister in the Centre, only to see her party reduced to her own seat in 2004. Even her victory margin (98,438) was the lowest ever after 1991, when she won by 93,663 votes. In the 2006 state assembly elections in West Bengal, Banerjee's party was reduced to only 30 seats – even as her political obituary was beginning to be written.

Banerjee staged a comeback by lending her voice to the agenda of industrialisation pushed by Chief Minister Buddhadeb Bhattacharjee, especially after resistance to the government was met with crackdown in the regions of Singur and Nandigram. In her capacity of the strongest mainstream political opposition force, Banerjee emerged in the forefront of the resistance. In a cause that directly affected Bengal's countryside, Banerjee courted (and received) the support of a large section of the urban intellectuals, who now rallied behind the banner of *Paribarton chaai* (We want change).

The ruling Left Front first felt the jolt in the 2008 panchayat polls – the elections of village-level local governments. Then they received a massive blow in the 2009 general elections, where the Trinamool Congress bagged 19 seats and its allies, the Indian National Congress and SUCI (Socialist Unity Centre of India), won 6 seats and 1 seat respectively. The election left the Left Front red-faced, as CPI(M) finished the race securing only 9 seats and its allies collected 6 more seats in total.

Finally came the assembly elections of 2011, which put an end to the 34-year long Leftist rule in the state. Banerjee was sworn in as chief minister in May 2011, and has continued to occupy that office through 2 consecutive elections in 2016 and 2021.

ACKNOWLEDGEMENTS

This book could not have been written without the help and support of many other people, who often contributed unwittingly.

The authors would like in particular to thank Sri Hirak Bandyopadhyay, Editor, *Ei Samay*; Rajat Roy, Senior Journalist and Political Commentator; Sukalpa Chattopadhyay, Publisher, Poet and Writer.

A huge amount of discussion, data sets, analysis and resources were tapped in to collate the information that have gone into the making of this book. Discussions before and during the research for this book sharpened the understanding of the authors regarding the political landscape of the country; resources were also made available without which this book would not have seen the light of the day. The authors would like to thank in this regard Professors Subhas Ranjan Chakrabarti, Bhaskar Chakraborty, Shouvik Mukhopadhyay, Shantanu Chakrabarti, Ritwika Biswas, and in particular Rajsekhar Basu for the long hours they had to endure discussing politics – never a very healthy idea. The authors would also like to acknowledge the value added by discussions with Hirak Shubhra Roy, Binoda Kumar Mishra, Sanjay Pulipaka, Anindya Sengupta, Atoorva Sinha, Anshuman Tiwari, Madhumita and Girish Buddhiraja, Ayman Haque and Aditya Phatak, Professors R.C. Thakran, Dipankar Gupta, Shubhashish Gangopadhyay, Syed Akhtar Hussain, Ajay Dandekar, Shashidhar M., Ved Pal

Rana and Kishor Gaikwad long before even the idea of the book came into being.

A special word of appreciation for Shireen Maswood for being a pillar of strength and support; and for the late H.S. Vasudevan, without training from whom in the study of politics this book may have looked altogether different.

The authors would further like to express their gratitude to Professor Pulak Narayan Dhar, Late Professor Amal Kumar Mukhopadhyay, Professor Prashanta Roy, Professor Kritya Priyo Ghosh and Late Professor Dipak Dasgupta – all of whom taught politics and helped in forming a political mindset without becoming partisan. A special word of gratitude is due also to Suman Chattopadhyay, whose political pieces inspired and taught many of us to write on politics right from our school days.

The authors would also like to acknowledge late Jitendra Nath Biswas and Sri Chittaranjan Biswas, as well as late Manoj Kumar Chatterjee, Ardhendu Sekhar Mukherjee, Santosh Chatterjee and Sri Ajit Chatterjee who made us conscious about politics long before we developed sufficient interest to study it. Both of us are also indebted to late Professor Gautam Chattopadhyay, who instilled a sense of the political as we finished school.

Safoora R. Haque and Qazi Benzarul Haque are valued for innumerable things, not least for allowing work on the book during what was meant to be an exclusive period of relaxation.

Malika Sen is valued for her capacity of endurance faced with the insufferable. Abeda Razeq is valued for the same (not least by way of suffering being inflicted with thousands of political trivia as this book was being written), and also for her determination to keep the authors from straying onto the domain of the libellous.

Finally, a word of appreciation for Anirban Sarkar of Hachette, whose capacity of handling the lethal combination of a journalist and a historian is a lesson in professionalism.

IMAGE COPYRIGHT INFORMATION

NOTE: CCA-SA refers to the Creative Commons Attribution-Share Alike Wikimedia Commons/ International Wikimedia Commons licences; Public Domain/PD: All public domain photographs have been sourced from: Wikimedia Commons/ Public Domain; PIB: Press Information Bureau; GODL: Government Open Data Licence – India; GoI: Government of India

Page 10: Sukumar Sen: Open Government Licence version 1.0/The National Archives UK/https://commons.wikimedia.org/wiki/File:Sukumar_Sen_1953_cropped.jpg
Page 20: Jayaprakash Narayan: GODL–India/India Post
Page 27: C. Rajagopalachari: GODL–India/India Post
Page 188–189: *from left to right*, Jawahar Lal Nehru: PD–India
Gulzarilal Nanda: GODL–India/India Post
Lal Bahadur Shastri: GODL–India/India Post
Indira Gandhi: CC0 1.0 Universal Public Domain Dedication/Anefo/Nationaal archief
Morarji Desai: PD–India
Charan Singh: GODL–India/India Post
Rajiv Gandhi: GODL–India/India Post
Vishwanath Pratap Singh: CC0 1.0 Universal Public Domain Dedication/ Rsamy2008
Chandra Shekhar: GODL–India/India Post
P. V. Narasimha Rao: CCA 3.0 Unported/ Biswarup Ganguly/ https://commons.wikimedia.org/wiki/File:P._V._Narasimha_Rao.JPG
Atal Bihari Vajpayee: GODL–India/Government of India
H. D. Deve Gowda: GODL–India/Prime Minister's Office
Inder Kumar Gujral: GODL–India/India Post

Manmohan Singh: GODL–India/Prime Minister's Office
Narendra Modi: GODL–India/Prime Minister's Office
Page 220: Jyoti Basu: CCA 3.0 Unported/ Biswarup Ganguly/https://commons.wikimedia.org/wiki/File:Jyoti_Basu_-_Convention_Centre_Inaugural_Ceremony_-_Science_City_-_Calcutta_1996-12-21_086.tif
Page 230: Karpoori Thakur: GODL–India/India Post
Page 237: M. Karunanidhi: CCA–SA 4.0 International/ Government of Tamil Nadu/ https://commons.wikimedia.org/wiki/File:M._Karunanidhi_.jpg
Page 265: Farooq Abdullah: GODL–India/Ministry of New and Renewable Energy
Page 273: N.T. Rama Rao: GODL–India/India Post
Page 297: M. Veerappa Moily: GODL–India/Ministry of Petroleum and Natural Gas
Page 300: Sivaji Ganesan: GODL–India/India Post
Page 312: Jayaram Jayalalithaa: GODL–India/Prime Minister's Office
Page 320: Asaduddin Owaisi: CCA–SA 4.0 International/ Batthini Vinay Kumar Goud/ https://commons.wikimedia.org/wiki/File:Asaduddin.jpg
Page 324: Nitish Kumar: GODL–India/Planning Commission
Page 335: Sheila Dikshit: GODL–India/Election Commission
Page 372: Sonia Gandhi: GODL–India/Ministry of Parliamentary Affairs
Page 373: Somnath Chatterjee: GODL–India/Ministry of Parliamentary Affairs
Page 387: Chandrababu Naidu: CCA–SA 4.0 International/Hemshah171095/ https://commons.wikimedia.org/wiki/File:Chandrababu_Naidu_2017.jpg
Page 390: B.S. Yeddyurappa: GODL–India/Prime Minister's Office
Page 402: Captain Amrinder Singh: by courtesy of PIB
Page 406: Uma Bharati: GODL–India/Ministry of Water Resources
Page 409: Vasundhara Raje Scindia: CCA–SA 4.0 International/newsofrajasthan/ https://commons.wikimedia.org/wiki/File:Rajasthan_CM_-_Vasundhara_Raje_(cropped).jpg
Page 410: Manik Sarkar: CCA 3.0 Unported/Adv.tksujith/https://commons.wikimedia.org/wiki/File:Manik_Sarkar_in_a_Rally_at_Alappuzha_in_2013_2.JPG
Page 414: Vilasrao Deshmukh: GODL–India/Ministry of Rural Development
Page 419: Tarun Gogoi: GODL–India/Prime Minister's Office
Page 465: Arvind Kejriwal: GODL–India/Ministry of Home Affairs

INDEX

A Few More Quick Facts...

Longest tenure as chief election commissioner

K.V.K. Sundaram (1904–92) served as chief election commissioner for 8 years, 9 months and 11 days, from 20 December 1958 to 30 September 1967. He was the second chief election commissioner of India.

Shortest tenure as chief election commissioner

V.S. Ramadevi (1934–2013) held the post of chief election commissioner for only 17 days, from 26 November 1990 to 12 December 1990. She was the first woman chief election commissioner of the country. It was an acting position. She was succeeded by T. N. Seshan.

First transgender election ambassador

Gauri Sawant, a transgender activist from Mumbai, Maharashtra, was appointed as the first transgender election ambassador in the country in 2019.

Highest polling station

The polling station at Tashigang in Spiti Valley, Himachal Pradesh, is not only India's but the world's highest polling station. It is situated at an altitude of 4,650 m (15,256 ft).

First 'others' category of voters

A third gender category of voters, called 'others', was introduced in the electoral rolls in 2014. As many as 28,314 voters enrolled in this category in 2014 and 38,970 voters in 2019.

When age is not just a number

The year 1999 was the 115th year of Indian National Congress. It was founded in 1885. First time ever the age (115 years) of the Congress

Party exceeded the number of its members (114) in the Lok Sabha – the lower house of the Indian Parliament.

Highest margin

In 2014, Pritam Gopinath Munde (BJP) won a parliamentary by-election from Beed in Maharashtra with a staggering margin of 6,96,321 votes – highest ever in India's electoral history.

Some memorable election slogans that changed the political landscape of India

1. *Sansopa ne bandhi Gaanth, Pichhde pave Sau mein Saath*: mid-1960s by Samyukta Socialist Party
2. *Ek sherni, sau langur/Chikmagalur, Chikmagalur*: for the 1978 by-election at Chikmagalur by the Congress
3. *Gali gali mein shor hai, Rajiv Gandhi chor hai*: for the 1989 Lok Sabha election by the Opposition led by the Janata Dal
4. *Tilak, Tarazu Aur Talwar Inko Maro Jute Char*: reportedly in the mid-1990s by the Bahujan Samaj Party (also reportedly later disowned by the party chief Mayawati)
5. *Maa, Maati, Manush*: for the 2009 Lok Sabha election in West Bengal by the All India Trinamool Congress
6. *Abki Baar Modi Sarkar*: for the 2014 Lok Sabha election by the BJP
7. *Ache beete 5 saal, lage raho Kejriwal*: for the 2014 Delhi legislative assembly election by the Aam Aadmi Party